In August 1994, Alfredo Jaar went to Rwanda to see with his own eyes what had happened there. There he was faced with an absolute genocide: millions of people killed, wounded or disappeared. Two ethnic groups, Hutus and Tutsis, locked in a battle to the death, in a society ravaged by poverty, disease and hunger.

That trip culminated, in the year 2000, in one of his most important and meaningful works, a piece that today forms part of the MUSAC collection: *Emergencia*. A black pool, out of which, at regular intervals, the African continent heaves itself up like a Leviathan. If his work has always explored and denounced limit situations of exploitation, immigration, exile and illegality, the brutality of the Rwandan genocide led Alfredo Jaar to undertake a more scientific work, setting out to understand the vision the world forms of realities through the images available to it.

In the light of the importance of this work, the Government of the Autonomous Region of Castille and Leon is inaugurating the Museum of Contemporary Art of Castille and Leon (MUSAC) with an exhibition entitled *Emergencias*. This exhibition, in which the work of Alfredo Jaar has a special importance, sets out to highlight the role played by artists and their work in interpreting the events that accompany our daily lives.

Approximately five years ago, the BildMuseet in Sweden published, to accompany the exhibiting of this piece, a book with the same name, *Emergency*. In this publication, 18 African writers, whose roots lie in this forgotten continent, narrated their dreams, their desires and their hopes for the land that produced them.

Today MUSAC adds its weight to this project by publishing an extended version of this book, which includes 7 new essays, thereby offering an overall vision of what is going on around us. Whilst marking the inauguration of this new artistic space, the project also sets out to illustrate the commitment of contemporary art to our society.

Silvia Clemente Municio
COUNCILLOR FOR CULTURE AND TOURISM

Small orphans

Rafael Doctor Roncero
Director of MUSAC

(...)
y sobre todo, cuando
la guerra ha comenzado,
lejos –nos dicen- y pequeña
-no hay porqué preocuparse-, cubriendo
de cadáveres mínimos distantes territorios
de crímenes lejanos, de huérfanos pequeños...

Ángel González. "Primera Evocación"

With these lines, Ángel González closes a poem in which he remembers his mother. Through different images he tries to draw near the feeling of hard times of war and a harsher post-war, a time when 'neither did the wind bring back what was snatched away/ nor could the rain/ erase the traces of blood'. For the poet, the Spanish Civil War is compressed into the fear and the pain that rescue the living memory of his mother; the anguish, the horror and the injustice of such a devastating event through the feelings of another person, who although close, the closest, is an other. The poem ends with a greater distancing and, in an exercise of sincerity, the successive wars for him, an inhabitant of a territory that has been peaceful ever since, begin far away and their narration makes them small; there is no alarm, for they are not here, and anyway they produce 'slight cadavers', 'orphans' that are 'small' because they are never too close.

These lines speak of the difficulty of attaining understanding and feelings of the injustices that we do not assume to be our own. The remoteness of the events and, above all, the narration of them, turn us into spectators of occurrences where the cadavers are slight and the orphans small. (Faraway, they tell us). At the very moment that I am writing this text, there are reams of reports arriving of a devastating tsunami that has razed the coasts of Southeast Asia. I hear and read the same thing over and over again and the number of thousands of victims multiplies from one news broadcast to the other. As on so many other occasions, and through the catastrophes that occur sporadically in the world every year, I feel a cold distance that allows me to contemplate the horrors from the living room and watch the hecatombs live, while at the same time getting the creepy feeling that the milk I have bought is skim rather than whole, or whether there will still be any tickets left for next week's concert. And the thing is, however much I would like to be interested in the event, the cadavers I see in the papers and on the screen are slight and the orphans are still small. In this sense, I try to recognize in a personal way my real cowardice at being just another well-off Westerner, and by the same token I would like to make manifest my anguish for having made of my understanding a place suitable for unabashedly directing small deaths. Yes, I declare this contradiction that makes me a part of a world that always seems to be on my side, for I belong to a highly-developed society where one does not see but glimpses, where one does not participate but help, where reality's sense of representation is much more powerful than the very evidence of the data and the figures that at the same time represent individual people.

The project "Emergencies" that we are now presenting is not meant to be categorical. As MUSAC's general project, it is born as a jumble of living questions and approaches I believe have to do with the world to which we belong. "Emergencies" aims to analyse, starting from the first phase of the MUSAC collection, the contemporary art-ist's commitment to the world to which he belongs. It is by no means meant as a catalogue of situations of injustices in the world. How-ever, through the works collected in this first stage, we have dared to recapitulate diverse forms of artistic commitment with sometimes close and most times faraway problems. The project does not aim to sustain any thesis but rather to pose some questions: Is social and political commitment possible from contemporary art? If it is possible, how will it really affect the society for which it has been engendered? What is the function and the situation of the contemporary artist in relation to the resolution of current problems? What strategies does today's artist adopt to express his troubles with the current situation of the world? Does it make any sense to carry on with a weapon we call contemporary art?

Emergency(ies)
In 1998 I was invited to attend the "Primavera Fotográfica de Barce-lona". At the Santa Monica Art Centre, right on Ramblas avenue and as a part of the event, an Alfredo Jaar exhibition was presented. Upon my arrival, I expected to find those black boxes with texts narrating the image they were hiding, or the light boxes ironically making a spectacle of the situation attracting attention. This is how it was, but in the centre of the exhibition, in semi-darkness, there was a huge metallic tank filled with ink or black water. There was silence. But it was broken by a sound that signalled change. Something started to loom up from the dark liquid. At first I thought it was excrement. Then I thought it was some abandoned clothes that to me were sug-gestive of drowned people. Soon afterward, when the emersion was concluded, an immense topographic map of the African continent ap-

peared plainly before my eyes. I stood still carefully observing what I had in front of me. A little later the immersion began and again the wet clothes, the excrement and the black void. I thought that if that continent really did sink it wouldn't matter at all. It also occurred to me that the whole continent was a nuisance and the Western world actually wished it would sink so as to rid itself of the problems it did not care to resolve. After that Africa 'emerged' again but I had already left that exhibition hurt, as never before, by an artwork. The experience not only provoked a reconsideration of my role as a citizen of a country that is highly developed in comparison to the African continent; thanks to this piece I definitively understood how a work of art can radically communicate a clear and well-founded stance with regard to the world's problems.

The work was shown again a few years later in Sweden and since then, possibly due to its being technically difficult to set up, it has been in storage. When we began to put together what is the first phase of the MUSAC collection, "Emergency" appeared by accident, though I always wanted to think that it seemed to be waiting to become a part of the project we were working on. Right away, we committed ourselves to acquiring it, thus converting it into one of the focal points of the incipient collection. "Emergency" is one of the most radical and most forceful works produced in the West to confront the problematic of others. With just a map, a title and the silence of the black water, the artist manages to generate an endless number of questions capable of flooding whoever has a few moments available to contemplate the piece directly.

From the start "Emergency" has been the core capable of radiating the presence in the collection of other 'emergencies'. The duality at the root of the title (emergence / emergency) is befitting of the overall project approach. What social or political urgencies pervade contemporary art? What is now emerging as a solution to current issues? We should consider each and every one of the works comprising this exhibition as micro policies of action with regard to some of the world's current issues reflected in contemporary art.

On the other hand, our intention has been to depart from something specific, therefore venturing to suggest the evolution from one work to the generality of a collection. Within the project "Emergencies", Alfredo Jaar's installation possesses its own individual entity that keeps it simultaneously isolated and joined and participant with respect to the rest of the pieces. We thus aim to attract attention to the individual piece within the collective. Possibly, each work of this collection could likewise centre the focus of another exhibition or collection.

The exhibition

The exhibition project is outlined though an itinerary through the different parts of the building where something more than contemplation is going to be required of visitors. They will neither find a stream of masterpieces of contemporary art, nor a succession of famous names alongside their great icons. First and foremost, we hope that visitors perceive that the reading of the work is what builds the essence of what the work presents and, above all, that the true nature of contemporary creation lies in the discourse, in the posture adopted by the artist and later reinterpreted by the viewer.

Before entering the exhibition, in a side patio, a large luminous sign announces "Vivo sin trabajar"; in an ironic and humorous tone, with this piece Fernando Sánchez Castillo questions the very concept of the situation of art and artists of our day. We don't know whether it's a joke, a provocation or simply effrontery. The fact is that through it and in this precise spot there is a desire to affect the viewer by leading him to ask: Who are today's artists? What do they do? What do they devote themselves to? What is their purpose in an absolutely materialist world? Are they at all advantageous to society? Do they really work or not? We enter the exhibition and Rogelio López Cuenca's piece announces the various issues we will encounter throughout the itinerary we have begun. In the same space the work *Trilogy* ("Consuming Pleasures", "Crash Course" and "Sprawville") by Sven Påhlsson introduces us into the world of simulation through images built and manipulated with the aid of technology and featuring the society of speed, security and consumption as now dissected main protagonist.

This introduction is the beginning of a journey whose first stop is the micro-cosmos housing the works that sketch, from different angles, the urban misfortunes and, in general, the spatial occupation of individuals: Alexander Apóstol and Marjetica Potr with a counterpoised vision originating in the urban reality of the city of Caracas; Olafur Eliasson dissecting the buildings of Reykiavik underlining their social or individual functions; Andreas Gursky and the image of an unfathomable rubbish dump of Mexico City; Anri Sala with a report in which the mayor of Tirana conceives a new vision of the city by changing the colours of the façades; Francesco Jodice and the architectural absurd and consequent inequality inherent in the habitability in big cities; Ángel Marcos confronting images of buildings with that of faces of workers sustaining them; Sergio Belinchón and his crude description of the environmental offences committed by urban development generated by tourism; and Corina Schnitt and the definitive loss of paradise.

The itinerary continues with works that specifically address the diverse 'others': women hidden under religious-cultural burkhas by Joana Vasconcelos, blacks in Western culture by Yinka Shonibare, children working in third-world countries by Jorge Pineda, the inner drama of the Western Judeo-Christian family structure by Eija-Liisa Athila, and the excluded, beggar, crazy or outcast by Paul Graham, Pierre Gonnord and Boris Mikhailov.

We now enter a large space where several forms of representation of current direct human conflicts appear: the anti-globalization movement as seen by Immo Klink, violence in the Basque Country through Pepo Salazar's eyes, the recent war in the Balkans by Simeón Saiz Ruiz, the war in Afghanistan by Luc Delahaye and the vision of ongoing armed conflicts in the world of Thomas Hirschhorn.

Here we could make another stop in an adjoining space that works as an exhibition within an exhibition, where the conflicts inherent in Western women are portrayed through Tracey Moffat's works as representations of battering and domestic violence; Pilar Albarracín, Ruth Gómez and Kristen Geisler and the permanent dissatisfaction with the body; Marina Núñez and the metaphor of madness as exclusion of difference; Gilda Mantilla, Julia Montilla – on this occasion with collaboration of Juan de Jarillo – and Carmela García with the stereotypes of accepted representations; Daniele Buetti and Cristina García Rodero and the dictatorship of fashion; Trine Søndergaard and prostitution; and Shoja Azari with his filmic vision of gender violence.

The exhibition continues with works related to the "emergencies" intrinsic in the very concept of the social individual, whether as alienated individual being (Tony Oursler) or as reconsideration of the Western concept of family (Enrique Marty and Mira Bernabeu). And then again we find another appendix space, this time a museum within a museum. We are before the LiMac, the Contemporary Art Museum of Lima, a utopian project by Sandra Gamarra in which she outlines the contradictions of globalization in an absolutely unequal world. After that, Julien's work "Paradise Omeros" continues relating other cultural emergencies, as does Martín Sastre's work. Next to these two works are "Climate" by Iñigo Manglano Ovalle and "Solid Sea 03: The road map" by the group Multiplicity, two different sides of the concept of security.

Emigration in Spain with El Perro, Valeriano López and Chus Gutierrez, the situation of gender inequality in societies such as that of Bolivia in Mujeres Creando ('Women Creating'), the dignified use of resources and the representation of work in Africa with Superflex and Zwelethu Mthetwua respectively, bring us to the end of our itinerary with two black stains confronting each other: Allan Sekula's images of the ecological disaster caused by the oil tanker Prestige, and "Emergency", the work by Alfedo Jaar whence the entire project departs and which gives rise to the title of our voyage.

The exhibition begins and ends in the reception of the building with the work "Reason to Believe" by the artist Marc Bijl, in which the whispering voices of different 20th century political leaders are blended, thus creating a sensation of intense confusion, a perfect allegory of the time represented.

It is necessary to insist that this is not meant as an overview of the world's problems, but merely one of the works of the collection that represent them plastically. Likewise, it is important to emphasize that several of the world's urgencies are missing here, as they are not represented explicitly. In this light, we could mention AIDS, hunger and racism. However, all of these do converge in Alfredo Jaar's work, the beginning and the end of the exhibition project. I would also like to point out that this first part of the MUSAC collection includes additional works that relate other conflicts prevalent in the world, but the objective of the show is to present a specific vision carried out by the current museum staff, which can be complementary to those others may carry out in the future, based on the first Catalogue Raissoné of the collection.

The publication

This publication does not aim to be an exhibition catalogue but rather an additional integral part of the exhibition, serving to broaden it. We have attempted to convert it into yet another space where the differing voices resound together in one central theme, utopia, along with other cruder voices: the data and the statistics interpreting the state of the world at the dawn of the 21st century. Our intention is none other than to compare the realm of criticism and dreams with the objective space of figures that translate everything we wish to discuss. Once again our objective is to provoke a swelling stream of questions, in this case by contrasting two apparently opposite poles: statistics of injustice and artist's dreams.

In the artistic realm, we have requested of some of the participants concurring written contributions on the reflection of utopia in the programme of their works, especially regarding the specific subject matter they address. The value of utopia has always been essential; throughout history, it has acted as a depository of ideas and solutions for seeking ways out of every prevailing conflict. Now more than ever, utopia should be taken care of and valued as objective and projection of contemporary man's dreams of justice. The prevailing mindset of capitalist absolutism enables us to forget the transcendence of all that does not bring immediate results, and which is posited from the realm of yearning or dreams. And this is why discovering other solutions is more urgent than ever before. Today it is necessary that artistic production become a place in which to question from parameters unlike those governing the behaviour of the efficient and materialistic societies to which we belong. Utopia has to challenge the barriers of rationality and establish itself as the future to thus push man forward. Each of the texts composing this book are at the same time statements of intentions for a solid world that must face the challenge of forging ahead far beyond the dictates of economic precepts and tend toward building, day by day, a society where the values are not limited to those of pragmatic capitalism.

Alongside the dreams put forth in the artist's texts, we wished to counterpoise the crude objectivity captured in the material that analyses the distinct forms with which injustice and inequality are disguised. To this end, we have counted on the collaboration of the Institute of Studies on Conflicts and Humanitarian Action, which has divided the issues into poverty and hunger, migratory movements, natural disasters and environmental degradation, pandemics, culture and education, media, gender and other forms of discrimination, human rights, armed conflicts and Africa.

Parallel to this publication, the work "Emergency" by Alfredo Jaar is presented with its own publication consisting of twenty-five texts by young African writers who, from different points of view, reflect on the current situation of the African continent.

The birth of a 21ˢᵗ century museum.
With the project we initiate the endeavour of a museum that is born at the dawn of the new millennium with the mission of broadening the scope inherent in the very institution. MUSAC wishes to establish itself in a framework of activity befitting a contemporary art centre where the collection is active, participatory and exemplary of current creative production. We realize that a centre of these characteristics does not necessarily have to be a mere receptor or legitimizer of ready-made history; it can also be a place for reflection and creation itself. An active centre does not need to corroborate what is sent down from major centres with institutional weight within what might be considered the art world, but rather its very peripheral role obligates it to adopt new working strategies that allow for a broadening of the field of what is already acknowledged.

As we take up our task at MUSAC we ask ourselves several questions:

What is the present? What should a 21ˢᵗ century art museum be? How should a contemporary art collection be approached? Where are the frontiers demarcating the artistic spaces of contemporariness? What activities should be generated by a museum institution focusing on the present time? What is the role of the peripheral museums in a civilization increasingly governed by large urban centres? What role does the artist fulfil in the museum setting? Is it possible to establish a museum while obviating the historical perspective? What is a museum other than a collection? Can a public museum institution constantly reconsider its theoretical presuppositions? Can something be projected without knowing exactly what the end result will be? Can a museum be a risky project? For whom are contemporary art museums designed? What disciplines shape the spectrum of art today? How to react to globalization from a city removed from the large commercial and critical centres? What strategies should be followed to involve a public not accustomed to contemporary art?

All these questions are the basis of our work. Without categorical answers to them, we now begin our journey establishing ourselves along certain guidelines:

First of all is understanding that artistic creation is necessary in a world with particularities such as ours. At a time when it is difficult to judge art's purpose and its influence on society, we believe that creative activity itself should become one of the solid structures where individual liberty, and therefore its projection in the society in which it is generated, should rule. Far from the bewildering figures of the auctions, the trivialization of the names and icons of the acclaimed 20th century artists, artistic creation proclaims a space of its own in which to play a role far more profound than that of generator of recognizable and acceptable iconographies for a world where visual consumption and decoration occupy prime space. Nowadays, art seeks its own space where, without detaching itself definitively from the achievements accomplished, it will become an essential and constructive element of contemporary man's unfolding. The artist becomes an inconvenient but necessary personality in a society that is oversaturated, where the productive means have been multiplied and where the worthiness of art objects is tirelessly reconsidered. The dispersion of the spheres of creation has definitively undermined the very concept of art and more so that of the artist. The realm in which MUSAC is to lay its foundations as a 21st century art museum is that of the evolution of fine art, this being that which generates works rooted in the historical perspective of Art History, leaving out other autonomous disciplines such as architecture, dance, design, fashion, theatre or film, which by themselves have shaped their own autonomous language and history. Nevertheless, the relations of the contemporary artist with all these areas are those defining, to a large extent, the meaning of his function.

Secondly, we think it is possible to eliminate the communication barrier that for decades has been erected stalwartly between the public and the artwork. In this light, we believe it is crucial to determine the causes of the awkward divorce that maintains this essential communicative space hanging by a tiny elitist thread not sustainable beyond the strange and doubtful ecosystem of 'the artistic'. This is doubtless one of the yet to be resolved problems with which the century is born, and it can be solved only from a change in perspective originating in an education that does not mutilate people's creative and interpretative sense. Why isn't contemporary art understood? Or still graver, why is there not even the least effort made to understand it? This question is contradictory if we consider the maxim that art is the manifestation of the feelings of a specific time. It is necessary to regain the confidence in the search for effective communication with society, and not with the absurd idea of producing a large number of visitors for the statistics, but with the intention of producing a real dialogue between the work and the beholder, in addition to this becoming as fruitful for the receiver as for the producer. As the intermediaries of this process we have a decisive role to play, for the policies defining the field of action where this work must develop are in our hands. At MUSAC we aim to experiment with different strategies of communication and seduction that will make this dialogue possible. After all, this is the ultimate purpose of the work of art. The minority and classicist context sustaining what is considered the "art world" should make way for proposals capable of expanding the channels of communication and which thus facilitate real repercussions in contemporary society.

Thirdly, we set out with the understanding that the activity of a museum goes far beyond what is related to the art works and their exhibition. An institution of these characteristics should never establish itself under the parameters of exhibition-reception. This being the base, other elements capable of improving communication should intervene. It is necessary to generate a whole series of specific activities for each of the exhibitions, for the exhibition should not be considered the ultimate end. A commitment to the art of our time should imply an intention that goes far beyond accumulating and showing. The wall and the storeroom are not the only places in which to act. A 21st century museum is obligated to experiment and generate other forms of production. Similarly, a museum can be a centre of action where generating is not incompatible with contemplating.

Finally, it is our understanding that belonging to an era means accepting its contradictions and at the same time being a part of its dreams. We are increasingly established in the entertainment society and our only way of protesting about this seems to require the acknowledgement of its parameters and contradictions so that through that knowledge we can find spaces that are conducive to liberty. Entertainment embodies elements of speed and consumption capable of bewildering us and putting us in a situation of bafflement where our alienation is irremediable. We are before the stage: 'slight cadavers, small orphans'. It is here where art should act from its primordial uselessness and stand up to resolve problems that can be redirected toward the construction of a freer, more just world.

With this first project, Emergencies, we broaden the scope of our foundational questions and we ask ourselves: Where does social commitment belong today in contemporary art? For some the answer is in the irony, for others it is in the glass tower, for still others it is in the very insistence on persisting in parallel or in directly denouncing specific facts. We are not capable of offering a categorical answer, though we do dare to make individual statements about works and authors who base their intentions on the analysis of or approach to diverse issues of the times in which they live.

MUSAC is born at the dawn of the new millennium and right from the start we have opted to understand the conflicts of this world as the only place from which to develop a possible path from the present to the future. With a whole set of questions and another set of dreams we begin a venture toward the coming times in which we believe that the artistic act itself must fulfil a fundamental constructive role.

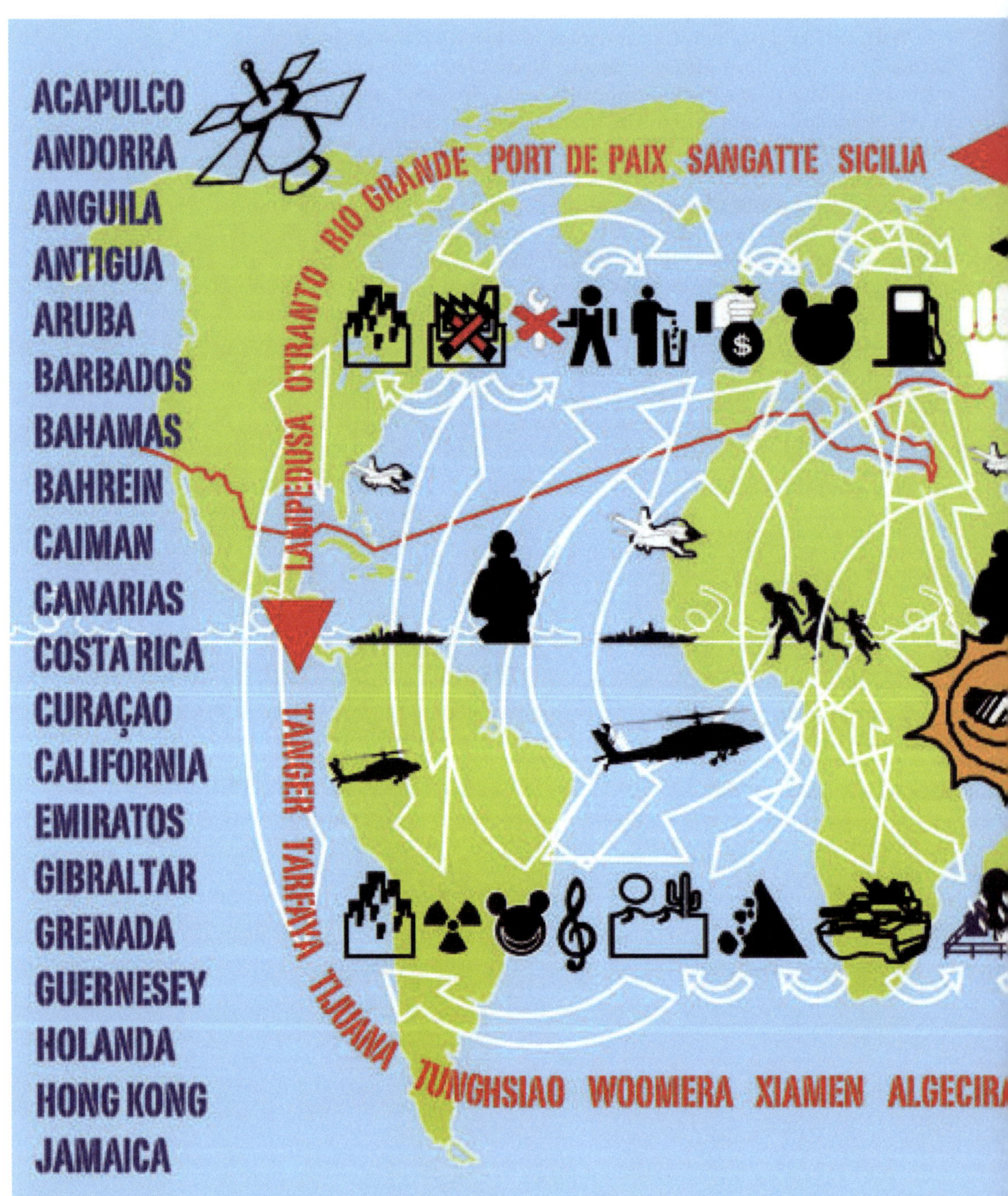

Rogelio López Cuénca
TEIXH, 2005

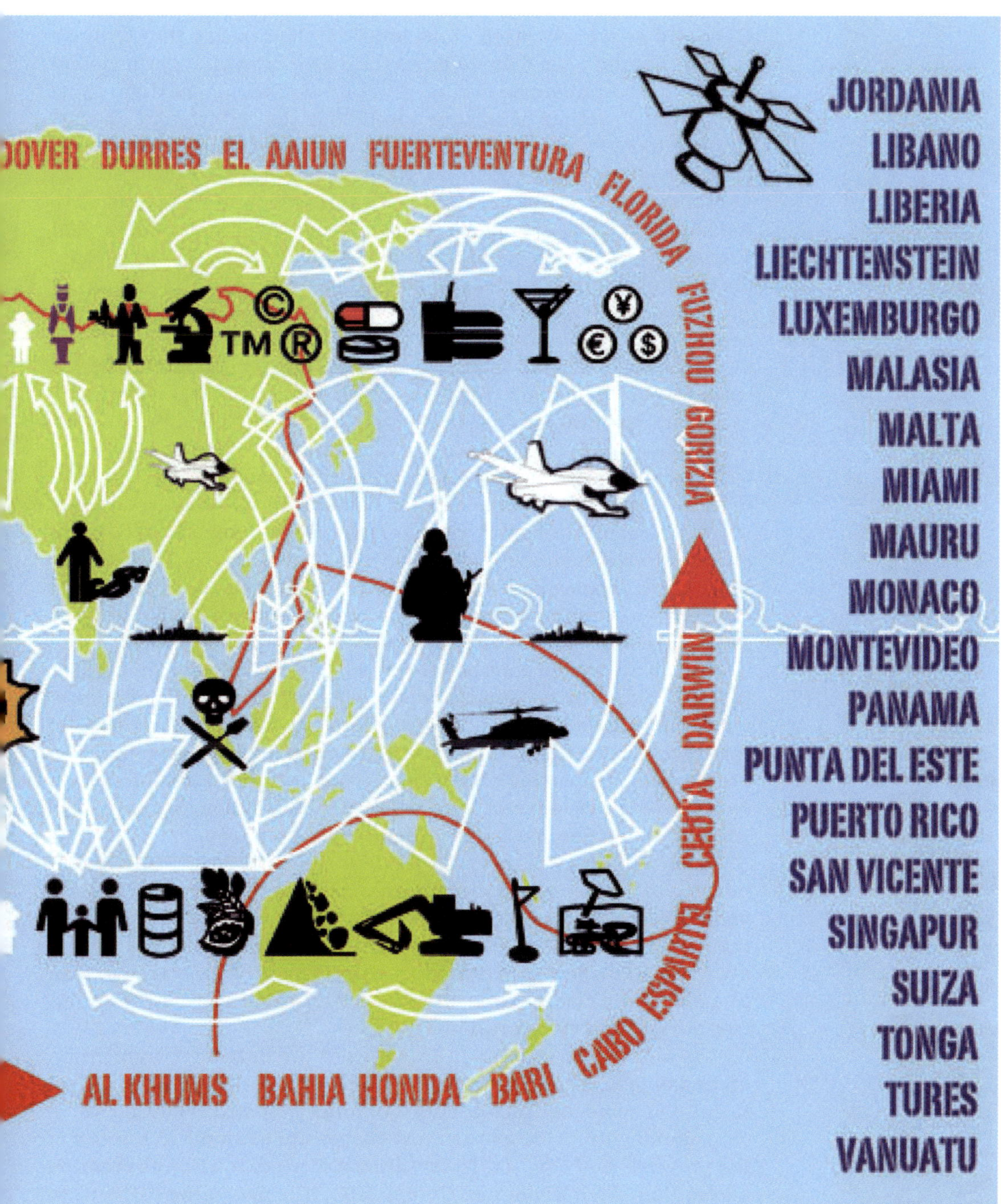

DOVER DURRES EL AAIUN FUERTEVENTURA
FLORIDA
FUZHOU GORIZIA
DARWIN CEUTA ESPARTA CABO
AL KHUMS BAHIA HONDA BARI
TM R
JORDANIA
LIBANO
LIBERIA
LIECHTENSTEIN
LUXEMBURGO
MALASIA
MALTA
MIAMI
MAURU
MONACO
MONTEVIDEO
PANAMA
PUNTA DEL ESTE
PUERTO RICO
SAN VICENTE
SINGAPUR
SUIZA
TONGA
TURES
VANUATU

Over and above any other consideration, the century that we have just left behind us is defined more than anything else by its violent nature. The numbers do not lie. Compared to the approximately 17 million fatal victims of various conflicts in the 19th century, the 20th century has left a sad record of more than 200 million human lives lost in about 300 armed conflicts. No corner of the planet has been left untouched by the lethal capacity of a technology that, as applied to the battlefield, has extended its reach from conventional warfare, at a level never before seen, to the most sophisticated weapons of mass destruction, be they nuclear, biological or chemical.

The end of the Cold War momentarily gave rise to not only a sensation of relief, insofar as it seemed that we had left the threat of nuclear terror behind, but even to a feeling of hope that an end to wars was close at hand. Today, however, within the framework of a 'war on terror' that is as self-interested as it is pernicious, we find ourselves once again immersed in a cycle of violence that has ended up with a world-wide annual average of 40 armed conflicts, just like the most difficult days of confrontation between the two superpowers.

Armed conflict, or call it war, has long been and seems to go on being an undesirable, but also inseparable, travelling companion of humanity. With stones, in times gone by, and nowadays with supposedly 'intelligent weapons' – a contradiction in terms if ever there was one, the human race still does not seem to have found a better way to defend its interests. There is so much work to be done before we get to the stage of understanding that our own security cannot be achieved through the accumulation of more weapons, and that dialogue and negotiation are the most powerful of tools for solving the controversies that we face. In the final analysis, we are not talking about the elimination of conflict from the human agenda so much as the creation of channels of communication that will allow peaceful solutions to be found when differences emerge.

Conflict as such forms part of human nature and plays an important positive role in devising formulas for coexistence and compromise between communities with differing perceptions and views of themselves as groups. War, on the other hand, must not be passively accepted, like a sentence of expulsion from paradise, but rather, seen as a mistake, a colossal and oft-repeated mistake, from which we can free ourselves if we act rationally.

As a first sign of hope in this regard, we only have to mention an example that is close to home, the European Union (EU), which, in spite of some significant shortcomings that still remain, can be considered with pride as the most successful example in history of the prevention of conflict. Today, almost fifty years after its creation as the European Economic Community, it is becoming difficult to remember that for a long time the history of the continent was being written to the drumbeat of wars that today we would regard as civil wars. This example, even with many features yet to be defined, already serves today as a model for other countries that understand the advantages that the processes of regional integration can have for development and stability, both economically and politically.

By way of defining concepts
The idea of conflict is very broad and covers so much ground that there is a risk of it becoming unmanageable. For the purposes of what interests us here, we must put to one side that image of conflict which is taken to be any kind of divergence or incompatibility between two or more objectives, each one defended by a different protagonist, whether an individual or a group. It is not individual conflicts that deserve our attention here, however painful they may turn out to be. Rather we are concerned with those that involve groups – whether the principal players be nation states or, as is happening more and more frequently, non-state actors – who resort to armed violence in the belief that this is the best means of securing their objectives.

Following this line of thought, and with the understanding that not all conflict implies either direct violence between the parties or the impossibility of co-operation or negotiation between them, there is a growing consensus concerning a classification, already well-established, that defines for us:

— Minor conflicts: those that cause at least 25 battle-related deaths in a year, but fewer than 1000 overall.
— Intermediate conflicts: those that cause at least 25 casualties in a given year, but in which there are over 1000 fatalities during the course of the conflict.
— Wars: armed conflicts in which there are over 1000 battle-related deaths in a single year.

Although in other times there was an understanding of the distinction between organised crime and armed conflict – in the sense that the former referred to conflicting interests of individuals or groups, whereas the latter referred to state interests – the character of organised violence nowadays no longer conforms to this view of things. On the one hand, most of today's armed conflicts take place within the borders of a state, with clashes between state actors, normally in the name of the national government, and others who are frequently difficult to characterise – rebels, guerrillas, insurgents, terrorists, etc. On the other hand, we are witnessing a proliferation of violent non-state actors, in whose case it is impossible to determine whether they are acting in the name of private interests or on behalf of a community. The dimensions of the drug trafficking trade, of organised crime, and of illicit commerce pave the way for the emergence of groups with the capacity to engage in violence on a planetary scale, which makes any kind of attempt to catalogue them even more complicated.

A basic background description

Be that as it may, today's conflicts have been taking on a profile that marks them out as different from those that took place not too many decades ago. In short, the following characteristics should be stressed:

- Unlike what happened during the Cold War, when most armed conflicts were in essence **inter**state, the scene is now dominated by the **intra**state variety, which tend to arise in so-called fragile states. Although a major conflict involving the most powerful countries on the planet can never be ruled out, this is not currently seen as a probability, unlike during the era of confrontation between the two super-

---

African child soldiers: childhood lost

The case of boys, and girls, used as combatants is particularly dramatic, because of their vulnerability and the mark it leaves on them. Used indiscriminately as nothing more than killing machines – their age makes them particularly fearless, as sex objects or for doing menial work, their presence is a phenomenon found in every kind of war anywhere on the planet. Although it is extremely difficult to quantify the problem, various estimates lead to the assumption that there are currently no less than 300,000 minors who have become combatants; of these, according to an Amnesty International report, approximately 120,000, mostly under the age of eight, take part in the various conflicts being fought on the African continent.

In general, those involved are children who have been kidnapped, dragged from their homes at gunpoint, and subjected to violent abuse in training camps, as a result of which, according to Amnesty International, it is not unusual for them to die in these camps, given the terrible conditions they have to suffer.

Once the training period is over, they are sent to the front line, although they also serve as cooks and porters of ammunition, water or food. They are also used as sex slaves, especially the girls. One example of this is the case of E.B., a 14-year-old, who was kidnapped together with four friends in an unofficial camp for internal refugees in Monrovia (Liberia). Along with the other girls, she was raped, and they were then forced to work on the front line as cooks and porters under threat of death if they did not obey.

It should come as no surprise that, if they do manage to get out of this situation alive, these children suffer severe psychological trauma and end up traumatised for the rest of their lives. Just as bad for some girls is that, on top of the physical and psychological brutality of the treatment they receive, in many cases there is the additional impact of rape and sexual assault, not to mention the transmission of HIV/AIDS or other diseases of a sexual nature.

Is it really necessary to have to stress that the recruitment of minors of less than 15 years of age is a flagrant violation of human rights and is a war crime? It does not appear to be a matter of major concern to a good number of African governments who still have not ratified the Optional Protocols to the Convention on the Rights of the Child – which deals with such cases – and the African Charter on the Rights and Welfare of the Child.

Signatory countries to the African Charter on the Rights and Welfare of the Child	Signatory countries to the Optional Protocols to the Convention on the Rights of the Child in Armed Conflict
Algeria, Angola, Benin, Botswana, Burkina Faso, Burundi, Cameroon, Cape Verde, Chad, Comoro Islands, Egypt, Equatorial Guinea, Eritrea, Ethiopia, Gambia, Guinea, Libya, Lesotho, Mali, Malawi, Mozambique, Tanzania, Togo, Uganda, Zimbabwe, Mauritius, Namibia, Nigeria, Niger, Rwanda, South Africa, Senegal, Seychelles, Sierra Leone.	Botswana, Cape Verde, Democratic Republic of Congo, Lesotho, Madagascar, Libya, Morocco, Namibia, Rwanda, Senegal, Tunisia, Uganda and Tanzania.

Source: African Union 2004

powers. On the contrary, the scene is dominated by minor conflicts, not that these are any less destructive – the death toll in the first half of the last decade, when nothing out of the ordinary seemed to be happening, reached 5.5 million. In addition, there is a highly worrying increase in the number of so-called asymmetric wars involving actors that, at first sight, are extremely unequal in strength, but, as can be seen from the sobering example of Al Qaeda, can limit the freedom of action of a superpower.

• An ever-increasing fragmentation of the combatants involved has been taking place. As opposed to the traditional image of two armies coming face to face, each one representing a state, what is happening now with ever-increasing frequency are confrontations in which regular armed forces are supplemented by paramilitary groups, self-defence groups and, of growing importance, mercenaries employed by private companies that provide 'security services'. This panorama adds enormous complications to the task of negotiation aimed at achieving peace accords that can satisfy all the conflicting parties in an equitable manner.

• Behaviour patterns have altered substantially, to the point that the civilian population has become a clear objective of the violence. It has become untenable to go on perpetuating the myth that considers civilian deaths in armed conflicts to be unwanted collateral damage arising from unrestrained violence. The elimination of the sector of the population that does not agree with the stated aims of the dominant fighting forces in a given territory has become an explicit objective of the perpetrators of violence, whose interest is served by the creation of a climate of terror that makes life unbearable for those who are not willing to support their plans. If, at the beginning of the last century only 15% of victims killed in conflicts were civilian, by the time it was coming to a close, the percentage had risen to 85%. Only from a standpoint of utter cynicism could it be considered that this is the result of errors arising from the very uncertainty that accompanies every war.

• In spite of the tremendous potential for devastation represented by weapons of mass destruction and even the more sophisticated conventional ones, neither of them are the ones that end up causing most victims in armed conflicts. On the contrary, it is small arms, that can be carried by a person or in a light vehicle, that play the most prominent role in this sorry state of affairs. It is estimated that there are approximately 600 million of these weapons spread around the world (250 million of them within the territory of the United States) and control over them is an enormously complicated matter, given the multiplicity of countries with the capacity to produce them.

A special case in this category of weapons concerns antipersonnel mines. There was a stock of some 200 million units in 1999, quite apart from those already scattered around conflict zones. These are deadly devices that can remain active for decades, condemning the affected populations to a constant loss of human life, and large swathes of land, where violence has taken place, to be turned into areas unsuitable for use as possible agricultural land or simply for traffic. To the ease of manufacture can be added the difficulty of detection and elimination, so that it is actually more expensive to dispose of them than to make them. Consequently, and still now, six years after the signing of the Ottawa Treaty, which decreed their elimination from the arsenals of armed forces by the end of the present decade, 15,000 people continue to die every year and governments like those of the United States, China and Russia are still refusing to sign the treaty, unlike the more than 150 countries that have already done so.

• Economic factors acquire increasing importance in originating conflicts as well as in fuelling them. The illicit trade in drugs, arms, people, diamonds, etc. estimated to be worth €1.5 billion a year, finds the perfect setting in which to flourish in conditions of instability and, at the same time, provides the means to finance the violence. In this way it is becoming ever more obvious that the old scheme of things, in which violence was seen as an instrument that served political objectives, is rapidly becoming outdated, to be replaced by another where violence becomes an end in itself.

For many of those who become personally involved in conflict, violence becomes an ideal way of life, since it provides them with what no formal type of activity could ever offer. This is especially so in those fragile states where the state apparatus has never really managed to consolidate itself in the face of other actors, nor been able to satisfy even the most basic needs of a population largely excluded from the benefits of the system.

No country can be considered immune to, or safe from, organised violence, but we can outline a basic profile of those that are most exposed to this danger. They are the countries that have endured a conflict in the last twenty years, that are at the tail end of income levels by international standards, and that show marked horizontal inequalities between the different groups that make up their population. As has already been stated, fragile states generally conform to this profile, considering that their weak economic and political structures derive from the fact that the theoretical central power does not even succeed in controlling all parts of the national territory. In addition, they are entities that do not exercise a real monopoly in the use of force, the distinguishing sign of a real nation state, and thus they become challenged, in many cases successfully, by non-state actors – the so-called 'warlords', who defy their authority and are equipped with the means to control parts of the national territory by force.

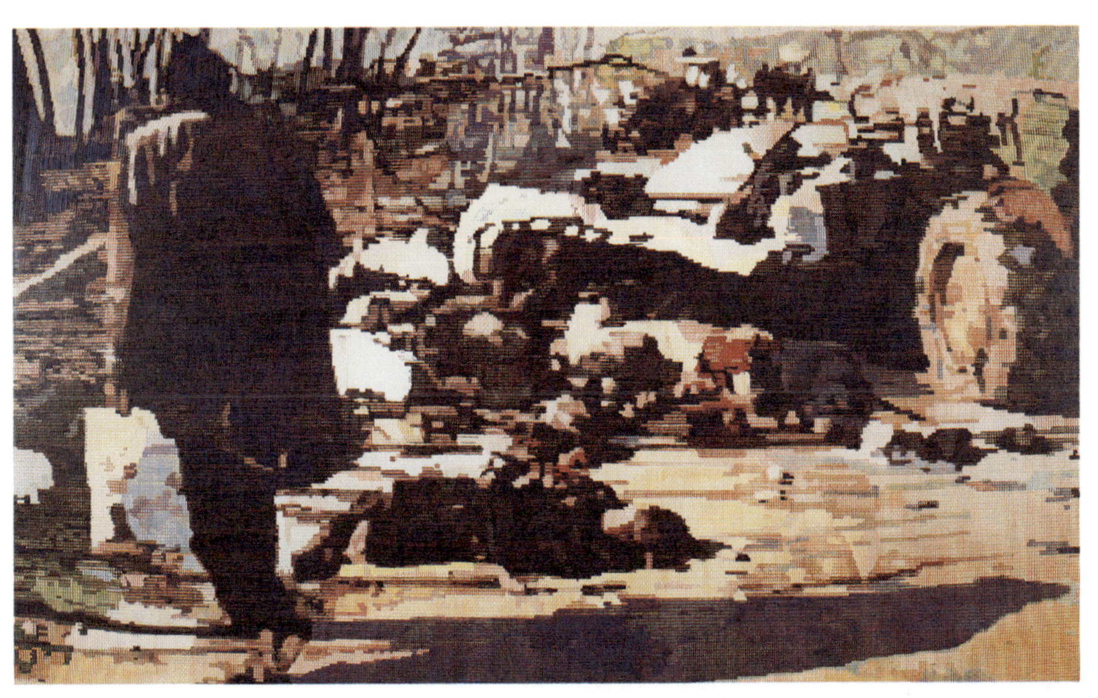

Simeón Sáiz Ruiz
Carretera entre Prizren y Djakovica cerca de Meja, el 14 de abril de 1999, 2003
Oil on canvas
240 x 390 cm

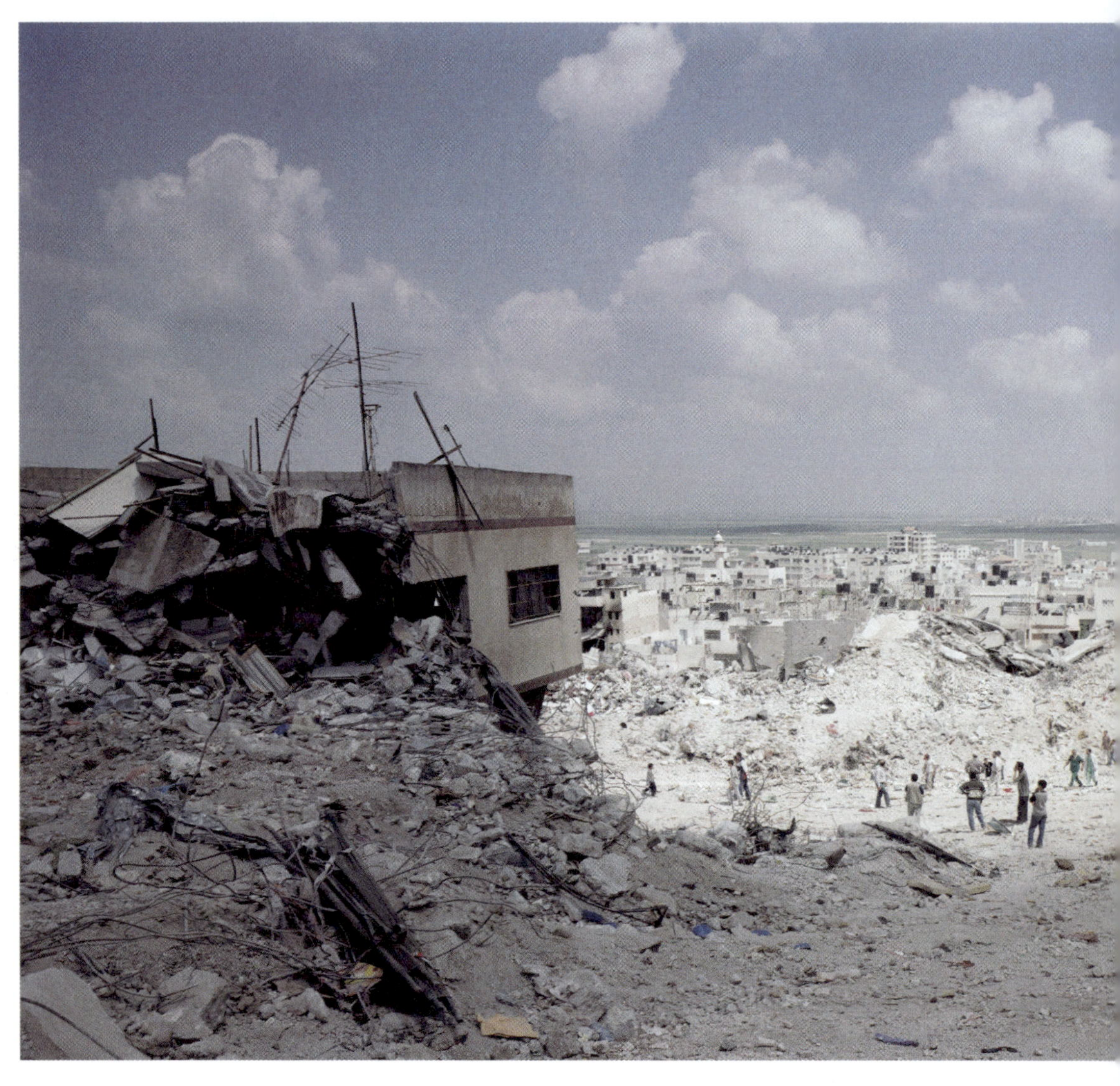

Luc Delahaye
"Jenin Refugee Camp", from the series
History, 2002
Colour photograph
111 x 241 cm

24

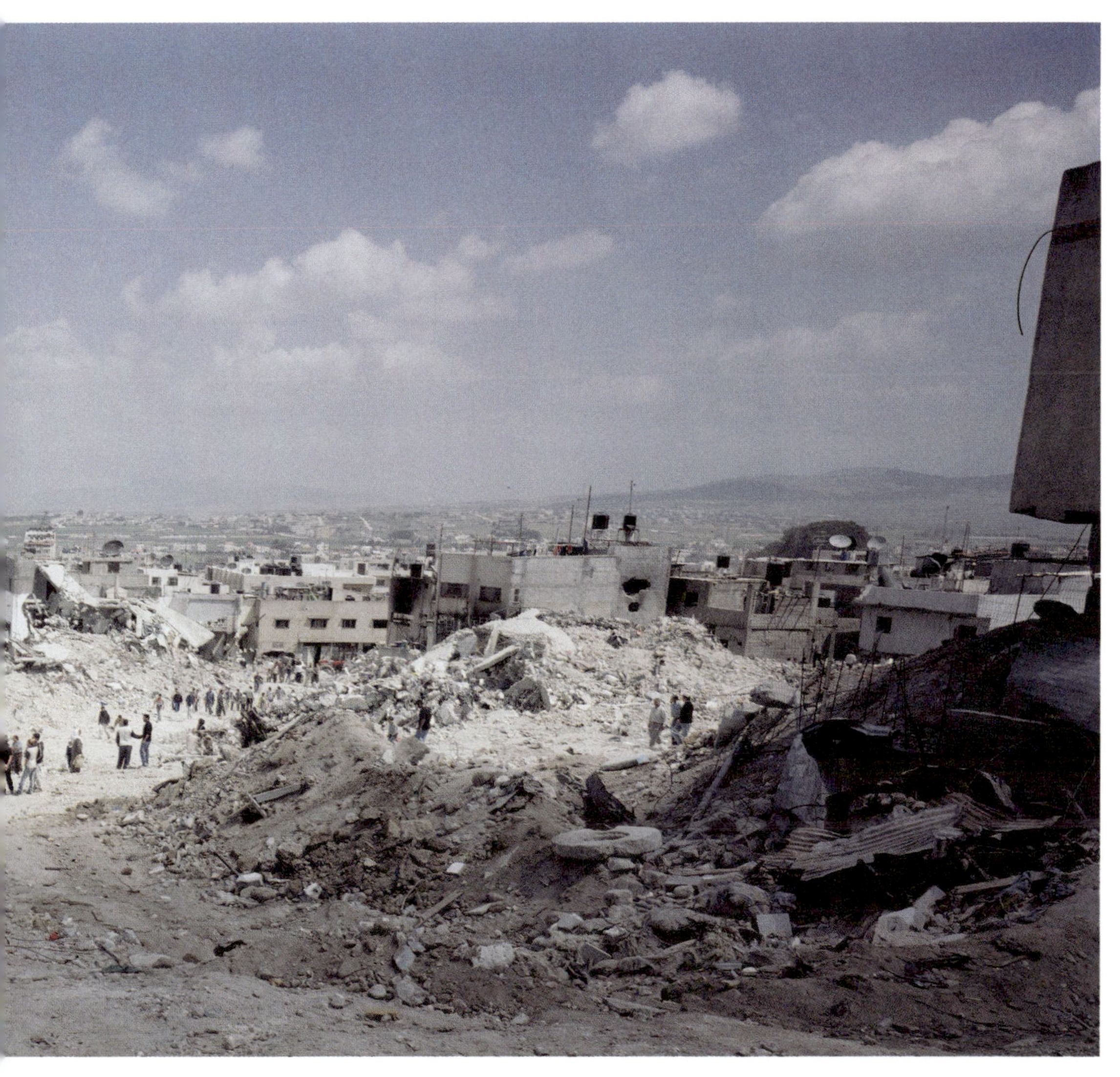

Some possible solutions

Within the broad context of international security, the tragic attacks of September 11, 2001 have brought about change, the consequences of which still cannot be totally predicted. During recent years, the agenda of the 'war on terror', badly defined and ill-focused as it is, seems to be dragging the world back to times that it seemed to have already got over, while also continuing to obscure other real conflicts that appear unworthy of either the attention of the media or the efforts of the international community. Within the framework of the aforementioned asymmetric wars, in which apparently weak non-state actors no longer feel restrained by the apparatus of dissuasion that was effective against states, we are left without an effective road map to interpret and respond to present risks and threats.

Colombia in search of peace

For more than forty years neither the political authorities nor the insurgent movements have been able to find a solution to the Colombian conflict, either by military means or through negotiation. In this context it is important to analyse the role that the civil society can play when faced with the prospect that, once again, the current strategy of Alvaro Uribe's government may come to grief much as others have done in the past.

In the seventies the unions had already introduced initiatives supporting social demands related to the conflict. During the following decade, the first Colombian NGOs for the defence of human rights came into being, though it would take until the nineties before the first peace initiatives emerged during the all-out struggle against the social movements.

In 1997, to be precise, the Mandate for Peace was issued, and one year before that the Children's Mandate for Peace was declared, in which 2.7 million children voted in favour of the right to life and the right to peace, within the framework of a project promoted by REDEPAZ (Network of Citizen Initiatives against the War and in favour of Peace), UNICEF, and the National Registry of Marital Status. After that came the Citizens' Mandate for Peace, in which 10 million Colombians symbolically registered their vote for peace.

Of a more permanent nature, mention should also be made of the Permanent Assembly of the Civil Society for Peace, which brings together a broad cross-section of social activists, and which holds plenary sessions every two years. Its first declaration was to stress the fundamental role of the civil society in building peace. Although it is true to say that the conflict is still going on right up to the present time, and it cannot therefore be said that the proposals and direct involvement of social activists have secured any better results than the official plans - either President Pastrana's, with his proposal for a 'table of dialogue and negotiation' between the Government, the FARC and the ELN, or Uribe's current 'Plan Colombia' – it has become obvious that they want to be reckoned with in an area that affects them very directly. It was precisely on the occasion of the launch of this latest plan that Colombian civil society as a whole set in motion the Peace Colombia initiative, in which it was decided to analyse the causes of the conflict, rather than its consequences, as a basic idea that would allow a real peace proposal to be put forward. One of the most significant successes of this initiative has been the holding of an international conference on peace, human rights and international humanitarian law (San José de Costa Rica, 2000). The lack of direct results in terms of immediate peace has not slowed the momentum in Colombian civil society, as demonstrated by the renewed efforts of women's movements in favour of peace, and the acts of civil resistance led by indigenous movements.

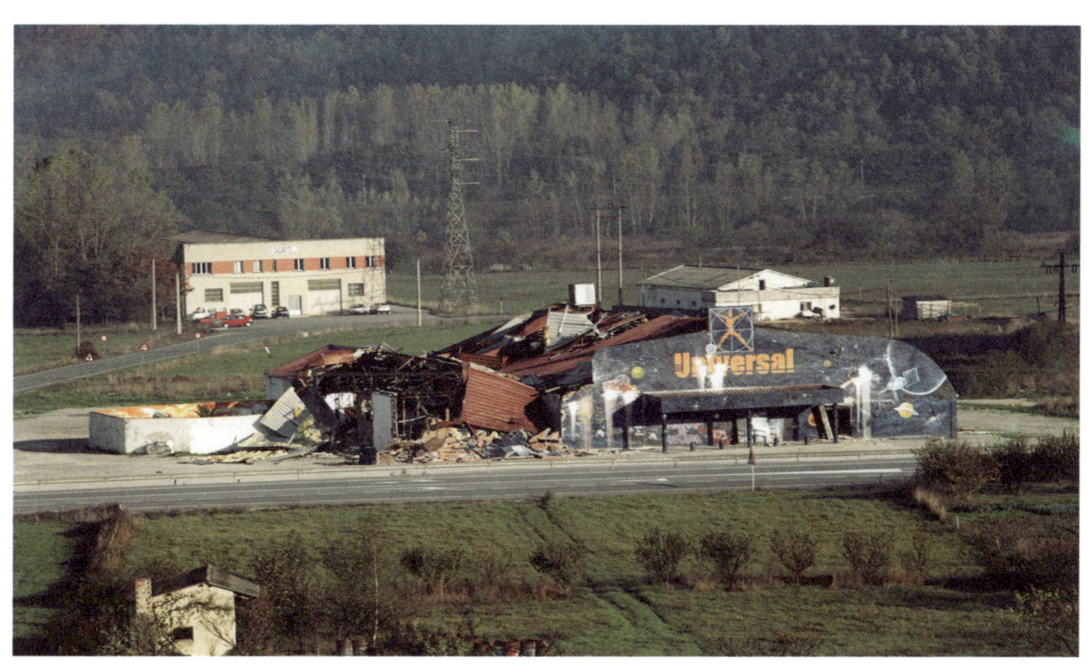

Pepo Salazar
Sarabande, 2002
Colour photograph
180 x 360 cm

With George W. Bush's administration in charge, the overriding response is to insist on heading down the wrong track, with military means as the preferred solution to tackling problems that are directly rooted in social, political and economic questions. This reactionary and militaristic approach not only contributes to an intensification of the clash of civilisations as an inevitable medium-term scenario but, in addition, is leading to an erosion of the very rights and liberties that have come to define democratic and open societies as something very different from those that are hostile to dialogue.

In any case, and parallel to this temporarily predominant dynamic, one has to remember that other initiatives exist that are attempting to find new ways of resolving current conflicts as well as, in an ideal world, preventing them. Among these, and in summary form, it is important to mention the following:

•   The Responsibility to Protect: In September 2001, the International Commission on Intervention and State Sovereignty was set up as a result of an initiative by the Canadian government, with the aim of finding possible solutions to massive and systematic human rights violations. The most visible result was a report – 'The Responsibility to Protect', which proposes a re-interpretation of the traditional notion of national sovereignty by imposing internal limits on state power and removing the barriers to the right of interference in domestic affairs, and urges nation states and the international community as a whole to assume the responsibility of protecting victims and preventing abuses of this nature.

This path, based on continuing confidence in the power of the UN Security Council, the principal organ for the guaranteeing of peace and security, has been progressively leading to a culture that has moved on from the original concept of the sovereign impunity of states to another view of how national and international accounts should be rendered.

•   In connection with this approach, mention should also be made of the establishment of the International Criminal Court which, in spite of not yet having been able to exercise all its powers, has already become a most important forum for the prosecution and punishment of the authors, instigators or accomplices of crimes of genocide, of crimes against humanity, and of acts of war and aggression.

•   Human Security: As opposed to the traditional approach centred on concern for the security of states, in whose name so many barbarities have been perpetrated, a new paradigm is emerging, based on security for human beings, to which any other consideration must be subordinated. This novel approach sets out to address human needs, not only in terms of meeting their demands for physical security,

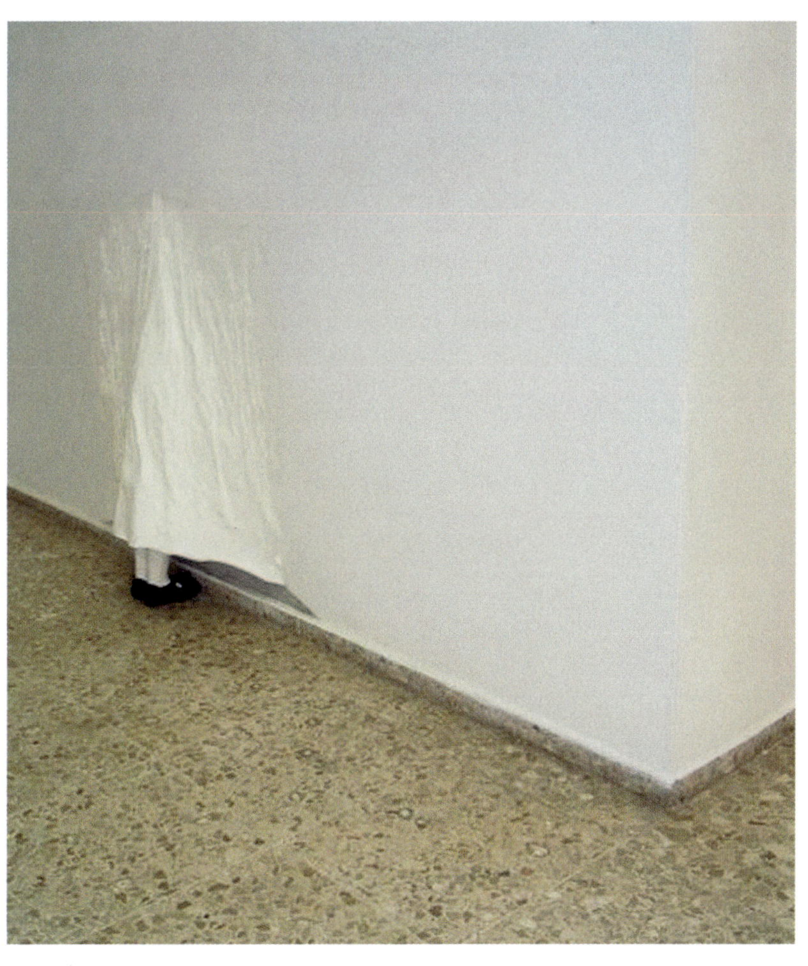

Jorge Pineda
Santos Inocentes, 2003
Installation consisting of a sculpture
made from plastic, plaster and white
acrylic, and silicone- coated cloth
Variable dimensions

but also taking account of other aspects such as economic, social and emotional considerations, as well as respect for dignity, protection of human rights and the ability to exercise fundamental freedoms.

•   Reform of the UN: In spite of the criticisms of its lack of effectiveness in carrying out the missions it is charged with in its own founding Charter, and of the marginalisation to which it is being subjected, the United Nations has been careful in recent years to adopt resolutions that emphasise its role in preventative actions. First came the previous Secretary General's 'Agenda for Peace' in 1992, and now, in December of 2004, the Report of the High-Level Panel 'A more secure world: our shared responsibility', not to mention the earlier report in the year 2000 on peace-keeping operations, and another in 2001 by the Secretary General himself on the subject of prevention of armed conflict. What can be demanded for the UN, which is to say for its member states, is that it be given the tools and the decision-making capability to fully exercise its potential in this sphere. The process of reform today continues to progress slowly, and it is still not possible in the short term to predict when a successful conclusion will be reached.

Other examples of this same preventative approach should be mentioned, such as those espoused by the European Union, which defines itself as a civilian power with military capabilities, and as being oriented towards conflict prevention and resolution; it also understands that, for the sake of its own security, it must take a direct interest in contributing towards the emergence of a better world. Finally, and of no less importance, emphasis should be placed on the work undertaken by non-governmental organisations, especially as regards their efforts to mobilise public opinion and issue early warnings.

•   The Culture of Peace: The combination of efforts devoted to prevention aspire to reverse the classic principle that has ruled the sphere of security for so long that 'if you wish for peace, prepare for war' (*si vis pacem, para bellum*); instead, we should start out with the idea that, if we really wish for peace, emphasis must cease to be placed on preparation for war. Seeking peace means preparing for it, by bringing into play the numerous and varied potential resources that the international community can deploy. It also means anticipating the outbreak of violence, by mobilising the massive economic and political resources that have now been built up for the purposes of preventative diplomacy, political dialogue and the application of formulas to the peaceful resolution of conflicts.

Unlike the concept of peace in the negative, as being that which is 'not war', peace should be perceived in positive terms, along with its elements of social justice, satisfaction of basic needs, respect for human rights, etc. In short, it implies seeking peaceful means of reconciliation, a task that is not the exclusive responsibility of nation states and international organisations, but rather, one that must involve individuals with their respective capabilities, aspirations and demands.

It also depends on you

The enormous task of modifying prevailing thinking, which is entrenched in an attitude that sees security only in military terms and which prefers reaction as a response, affects us all. Through public awareness we need to recognise our own strengths, both as individuals and within the framework of the social movements that have emerged as new actors on the international scene, in order to take collective responsibility for reforming prevailing ways of thinking. The failure brought about by the culture of war – the outcome of which can be seen in an ever more insecure world – must lead us to make an absolute commitment to the culture of peace; after all, we should realise that if human beings are good at making war, they are also capable of finding the paths to peace.

It is possible to bring about a revolution without violence by fostering fundamental changes in the social, political and economic order, and in such a way, reduce or eliminate the present-day inequalities that, above all else, sow the seeds of insecurity and instability.

Document prepared by researchers from the
Institute of Studies on Conflicts and Humanitarian Action (IECAH)
Madrid, January 2005

Marc Bijl
Reason to Believe

In a New York subway tunnel there was the beginning of a poem on the wall (a commissioned art piece) starting with 'I am so tired.' Somebody had illegally written 'of Bush' next to it.

Another person had added 'haters' next to that first added opinion.

And this is pretty much the situation in a democracy like the US; you are either in favour of or against your government and you will give each other a hard time for a few years until another party takes over.

For those strong believers in democracy there are two lifestyles (including music/bars/brands) that you can choose from. There is the leftwing 'freedom for all mankind and save the trees' utopian and there is the proud patriot and hard-working family man. With all their talk lately about democracy and freedom (and how to live with it) I just can't listen to them anymore; worse, I don't believe in it anymore. Or to be completely honest with you, I never have believed in democracy and freedom as such.

'Power goes to two poles', said Saul Alinsky, the pioneer of Community Organisation, 'to those who have got the money and to those who have got the people.'

In my opinion both these poles are brainwashed to the core by their beliefs in politics; it has become like a religion or, as some unemployed voter in the US said, 'I am a born Republican'. He is not the only one who considers himself some kind of honest 'purist'. Again, socialism is considered to be a working-class party; to me it's all the same.

All of a sudden I knew that President Bush would win the election in the US just like the Christian Democrats have won in the Netherlands; they have the money AND the (religious) people. In times like these, a combination that's hard to beat. They don't need to have an enlightened point of view based on equality and all that social nonsense because they know and accept that there is no such thing as equality. It is always war. It was war against the Nazis, war against the Communists, war on drugs, war on terror.

Their voters are (re)born Christians and/or (re)born Conservatives, afraid of a changing world (because it would only create a different enemy). They believe in universal moral values. If there was ever a horrible moment of equal rights and no class system, then it must have been that horrible period of the sixties and seventies (actually the eighties) when the 'mistakes' that brought about the loophole for misuse of the social system (by anarchists like myself and by immigrants) were made, and when the image was created that the 'West' was a godless, lawless, sex orgy and money-spending machine while a big part of the (Muslim) world was dying of hunger.

It came as no surprise to me that anarchist punks and (Muslim) terrorists use the same slogans against Western civilisation, and that Bin Laden's rhetoric after 9-11 was not much different from that of the left-wing socialist groups of the eighties criticising capitalism, or even of some intellectuals today.

And it comes as no surprise either that American soldiers have to give their lives (again) to keep the world from falling into the hands of (self-created) enemies. It's their belief (as in religion) and I support them in that because they are our democratically chosen leaders.

I also believe that fundamentalist enemies of the western world want to destroy the image that they think they know about, by destroying its symbols and public life(style). Basically this small group, which doesn't represent either a country or company, doesn't want to negotiate to restore something that was lost, no, they want to kill. Let's not beat about the bush; according to their Koran we (in the West) are a waste of space. According to the 'war on terror' coalition forces, they can only be stopped by invading Iraq. In contrast to most people, I think 'oil' was a good reason for war against Bin Laden, simply because this enemy is not a nation but coalition forces are still needed for him as well. Iraq was the only (semi)legal option that the US-led coalition forces could find to get their troops into the region. Thank God there was an economic reason for US to free Europe, and thanks to Hitler for declaring war against US in the first place. Anyway, as an almost logical outcome of events, before you know it, war is the only option left. Like in the former Yugoslavia, or the Palestine/Israel conflict, or the story of the chicken and the egg – which came first? The victims will never forget and will find a new leader who will give them hope, which is easier than finding a solution. It's easier to find an opinion against the politics of Israel than to understand the absurdity of the

Palestinian martyrdom that is being fuelled by ancient hate-songs straight out of the Koran. I cannot believe how fathers and mothers let their children throw stones at military tanks and let them be killed and dragged to the nearest TV camera; neither did I understand this self-same scene in Belfast in the eighties; children against an army; it's never worth it. Just don't go there. Don't have blind faith in your leaders; distrust them because they consolidate their power through chaos and war. And fathers and mothers don't know what to do, so they put their trust in religion; a mindfuck by definition.
I am not a democrat in the strict sense of the word; I will not die for my country; I do understand that leaders should be like 'technocrats' leading a company or country to prosperity. Populists do not therefore make good leaders but can easily get elected because of the democratic system. In Algeria the outcome of the election was a victory for Muslim fundamentalists. Did former colonizer France, the World and Algerian intellectuals accept this? No. Did they have a point? Yes. But do countries like Iraq or Afghanistan or Israel or Palestine need democracy? No. They all need

a pragmatic 'technocrat' who, at the same time, will help them out of this mess; but unfortunately they have chosen this ancient democracy model again.
Do we need democracy in the Netherlands? Technically speaking, no. I would suggest a company board type of structure where the manager is busy selling people good ideas rather than ideology. Do we need countries? No. But they come in handy to get things organised. Do we need culture? Yes, it's the stuff that surrounds us. Do we need structures? Yes, so that anarchists can be connected, and the art world and the music scene can be structured; I play in a Gothband and it's known all over the world within a particular cult. Do we need a family? Yes, but not necessarily blood-related. Do we need friends? Just a few. Do we need ourselves? Unfortunately, yeah. We have to act from this starting point and evolve into other situations. We cannot go back in time. The piece "Reason to Believe" that I produced, and is now in this opening show at MUSAC, comes out of these kinds of thoughts that I had, and how much I would have liked to be part of a movement. Anti-Globalist, Anti-Fascist, a Communist maybe,

but I never liked the idea of one ideology where rules and behaviourism is part of your life (style). I read the ideology of various organisations for my own interest and for my work, but I have never found my 'club'. Sometimes I feel like a Conservative, a Republican almost, a Fascist; next day I am as weak and soft as hippie ice-cream on a sunny day, with flowers in my hair.

I was collecting ideologies on my computer from various Internet sources, and I was thinking of a way to present them in a sort of Tower of Babel. I did not want to leave out any of the rhetoric that did actually change some personal points of view. The message is – they are telling you what to think; sometimes that's good, sometimes that's bad; but in this case it's all unbearable.

The title is from a Bruce Springsteen song. In my case I think I got more ideas from listening to song lyrics than to art theories or philosophy; anyway, I wanted to give the Tower a Rock and Roll kind of material use; old speakers, like at a club, piled up to the ceiling. Sometimes you actually see speakers of this kind of during political speeches improvised on a stage before a protest singer starts his acous-

tic songs. At the previous installation at the Stedelijk Museum, Amsterdam, there was a motorcycle in the corner. This 'suicide-machine' was aimed at the Tower and it wanted to silence the rhetorical speeches.

I would like to burn books sometimes, or kill politicians I don't like, but the thing is that such actions are so counter-productive. What can an artist do about society but make art about its contradictions in political visions? Can I do more? Maybe I can, but I don't want to. I don't want to be part of a movement.

This is my message in my work, in the art world. The people' are being fooled by the politicians who want to stay in power and so stay popular. In these times politicians can stay popular by telling fearsome stories about Bush or about terrorist groups. There are so many other storytellers you can hear if you listen closely to my Tower. They are all interested in you; 'The people'.

Kalle Lasn (editor Adbusters), Subcommedante Marcos, Naomi Klein (political writer), Charles De Gaulle, Pope John Paul II, Jimmy Swaggart (american Tv Preacher), Noam Chomsky (linguist/ political writer), Jello Biafra (singer of Punk band 'Dead Kennedy's), Abu Hamza (Muslim Leader in London), ETA (anonymous declaration), Michael Moore (Filmmaker), George W Bush, John F. Kennedy, Malcolm X, Mao, Martin Luther King, Fidel Castro, Salvador Allende, Che Guevara, Ronald Reagan, Adolf Hitler, Baader Meinhoff group / R.A.F., Vladimir I. Lenin, Joseph Stalin, Leon Trotsky, Neville Chamberlain, Abba Eban, Yasser Arafat

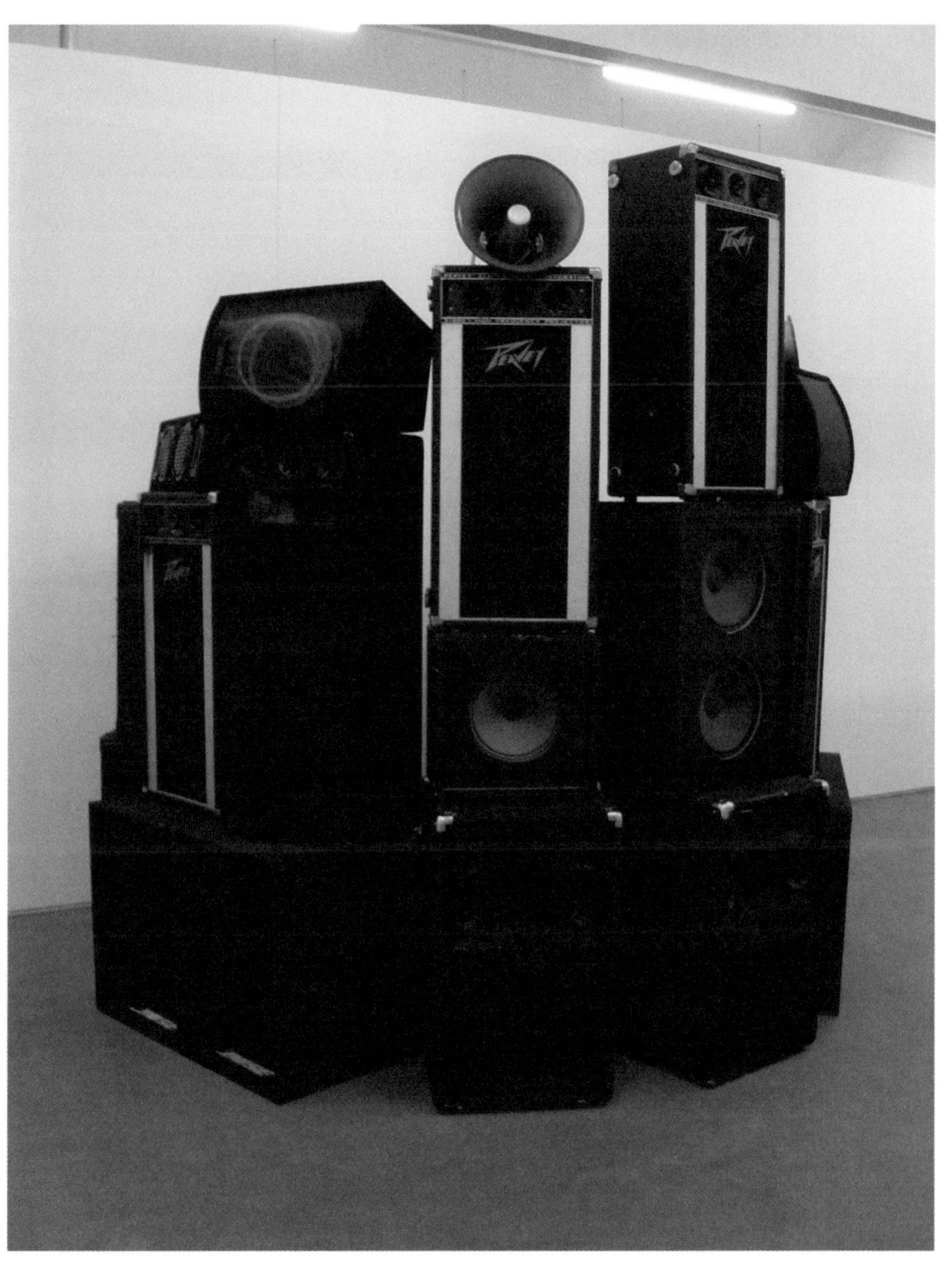

Marc Bijl
Reason to Believe, 2004
Installation composed of twenty-two
speakers and twenty-two CD players
Variable dimensions

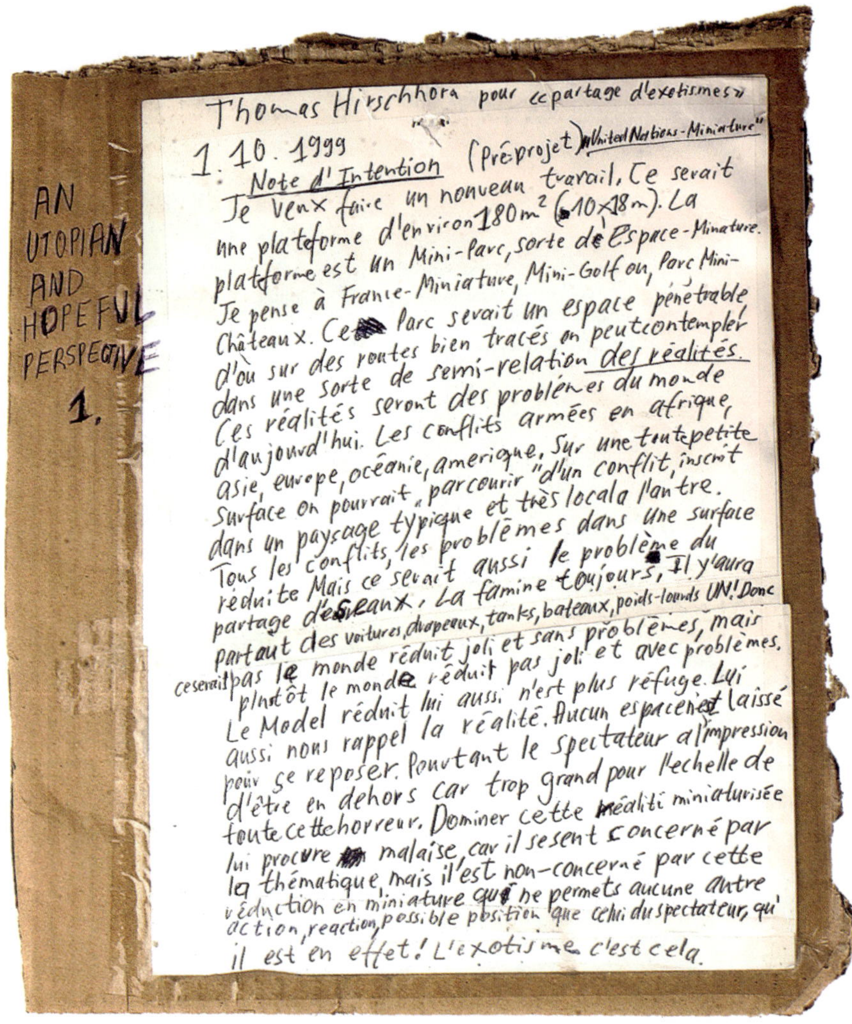

Thomas Hirschhorn for "partage d'exotismes"

1.10.1999
Intention notes (Preliminary) *"United Nations-Miniature"*
I want to carry out a new work. It would be a platform of around 180 m² (10 x 18 m), a miniature park, a kind of miniature space. I am thinking of France-Miniature, Mini-Golf or Parc Mini-Châteaux. This park would be an impenetrable space where on well-traced routes we can contemplate *realities* in a kind of semi-relationship. These realities will be problems of today's world: the armed conflicts in Africa, Asia, Europe, Oceania, America. On a very small area it would be possible to pass 'through' a conflict recorded in a typical scene, very local to the cave. All the conflicts, all the problems in a small area. But it would also be the problem of sharing water. Always famine; there will be cars everywhere, flags, tanks, ships, UN trailers! Then the world would not cease small, pretty and without problems, but rather the reduced world is not a refuge either. This also reminds us of reality. No space is left to rest. Spectators have the impression of being outside and too large for the scale of all this horror. Dominating this miniaturised reality causes them unease, as they are concerned with the subject but not concerned with this miniature reduction that does not allow any other action, reaction, possible position than that of the spectator, which it is in effect! Exoticism is that.

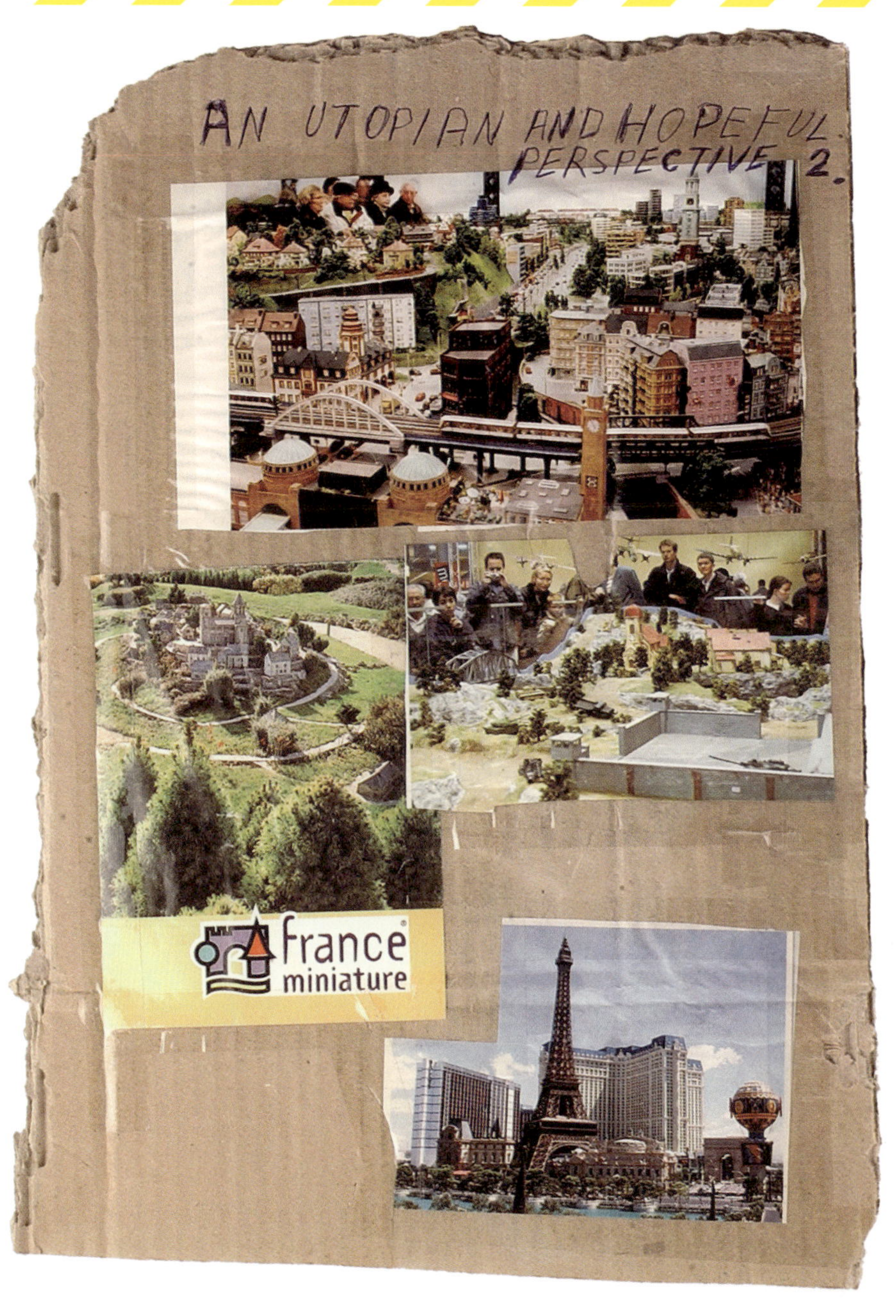
AN UTOPIAN AND HOPEFUL PERSPECTIVE 2.
france
miniature

Book of the week

21.06.03

Michael Meacher is convinced by a radical argument to reform trade and finance systems

What the world needs now

The Age of Consent
by George Monbiot
288pp, Flamingo, £15.99

This is an extremely important book. The biggest single geopolitical issue today is the overweening power of the US in a unipolar world and the problem of how it should be handled by all other nations. No political leader can be said to have satisfactorily resolved this problem.

George Monbiot offers a searchingly rigorous analysis of the sources of American power and presents a package of proposals that would radically redraw the present world order. It is breathtaking in its radicalism, but for anyone who is serious about tackling the current US hegemony, it is difficult to fault the logic.

His basic thesis is that the institutions set up in the past 50 years to run the world in a democratic fashion are in fact deeply undemocratic. The UN General Assembly is dominated by the Security Council's five permanent members, who can veto whatever they don't like. If any attempt is made to remove their dominance, they can veto any attempt to remove their veto.

The International Monetary Fund and World Bank are dominated by the G8 nations, which hold 45% of the votes, though that suggests that if all the other 176 nations voted together, they could still overturn the richest nations. However, all major decisions require an 85% majority, so the US, which alone possesses 17% of the votes, can veto any significant resolution it wishes, even if the resolution is supported by every other single country.

The World Trade Organisation has an aura of democracy in that every nation belonging to it has one vote. However, before a new round of trade talks begins, the agenda is fixed by the "Quad" — the US, EU, Canada and Japan. Together with a small and variable number of poorer countries, they decide all the main business of the new trade round in a series of "Green Room" meetings. The WTO is therefore as exclusive as the UN, with the Green Room acting as the WTO's Security Council and the Quad its permanent membership.

The consequences of this system are clear for all to see. The US goes to war with Iraq without a second resolution in the Security Council, defying three of its permanent members and most of its temporary members.

The World Bank and IMF have become the bailiffs of the world economy, putting the whole burden of maintaining the balance of international trade on the poorest debtor nations. Sub-Saharan Africa paid twice the sum of its total debt in the form of interest between 1980 and 1996, yet still ended up owing three times more in 1996 than it did in 1980.

Equally, the WTO enforces free trade on weaker nations according to rules with which the richer countries, especially the US, do not comply. Debtor nations are required to remove barriers to trade and capital flows, to liberalise their banking systems, reduce government spending on everything except debt repayments, and privatise assets for sale to foreign investors. By contrast, the US, after the so-called Doha development round in 2001 aimed to liberalise trade and increase access to western markets, raised farm subsidies to its own farmers by 80%, thus massively cutting world prices and bankrupting tens of millions of farmers in the poor world.

Monbiot's solution to this behemoth of growing world inequality in wealth and power is not tinkering with the existing institutions but replacing them wholesale. The key to his proposals is a return to the brilliant innovative insight of John Maynard Keynes in 1943 in preparation for the Bretton Woods conference, which determined the postwar international economic architecture that has prevailed ever since.

Keynes's idea was a new global bank called the International Clearing Union (ICU) with its own currency, the bancor. Every country would have an overdraft facility in its bancor account no more than half the average value of its trade over the previous five years. The system he devised gave a strong incentive to both deficit and surplus countries to clear their bancor accounts annually, ending up with neither a trade deficit nor a surplus.

Deficit countries would be charged interest on the overdraft, rising as the overdraft rose; they would have to reduce the value of their currency by up to 5% to promote exports and would have to prevent the export of capital. Keynes's innovation was to apply similar pressures to surplus countries too. Any such country with a bancor credit balance more than half its overdraft facility would be charged interest (or demurrage) at 10%. It would also have to raise the value of its currency and permit the export of capital. But if this was not enough and its credit balance at the end of the year exceeded its permitted overdraft, the surplus would be confiscated.

Keynes's system would, quite simply, maximise worldwide prosperity and level the power of nations. The ICU would entail no forced liberalisation, no penal conditions on the poorest countries, no engineered opportunities for predatory banks and multinational corporations, no squashing of democratic consent. But the obvious question remains: how can the rich nations, especially the US, be made to accept it?

Monbiot's answer is to turn the instruments of rich nations' power against themselves. The poor world's debt to the commercial banks and IMF and World Bank, at some $2.5 trillion, is nearly twice the combined reserves of all the world's central banks. In effect, as Monbiot himself puts it, "the poor world owns the rich world's banks". But he is not recommending a mass default. Rather, he proposes that the indebted nations, which can never repay their debt, should demand a conditionality for their compliance — exactly as the rich nations do — namely the replacement of the institutions causing the problem (IMF and World Bank) by arrangements that automatically achieve a balancing of trade (the ICU). Blackmail, of course, but if well orchestrated it might just conceivably work.

He rounds off this central theme with two other radical proposals. One is that a Fair Trade Organisation (FTO) is needed to govern the rules of trade very differently from the market fundamentalists of the WTO. Following the precedent of the rich countries, which in nearly all cases (certainly in the case of the US) got rich initially through protectionism, the FTO would permit the poorest countries to defend infant industries with tariffs, other import restrictions and export subsidies. Foreign investors would be required to leave behind more wealth than they extract and to reimburse for any destruction, environmental or otherwise, that their trading produces. Rich nations would be required to remove all barriers to trade — tariffs, import restraints and perverse subsidies that keep out imports from poorer nations.

Again, what hope in hell is there of such a radical (and utopian) system being accepted? Monbiot's reply is unequivocal: a fair trading system should be added to an ICU as a condition of refraining from a mass coordinated default.

Linked to this is Monbiot's final major proposal — a democratised UN General Assembly where votes are weighted by size of population and in accordance with a global democracy index, to incentivise high standards of governance. This restructured assembly would also take over the functions of the UN Security Council which, as Monbiot says, has already largely been sidelined by US actions over Iraq.

Again, there is a breathtakingly radical sweep to all this. But before it is dismissed as the rabid fantasising of the Global Justice Movement, certain caveats are in order. This is not a whinge, but a very well argued statement of a positive alternative agenda. And if it is far too radical for some tastes, can they suggest any lesser options that will produce the same vast improvement in world justice and prosperity? The floor is theirs.

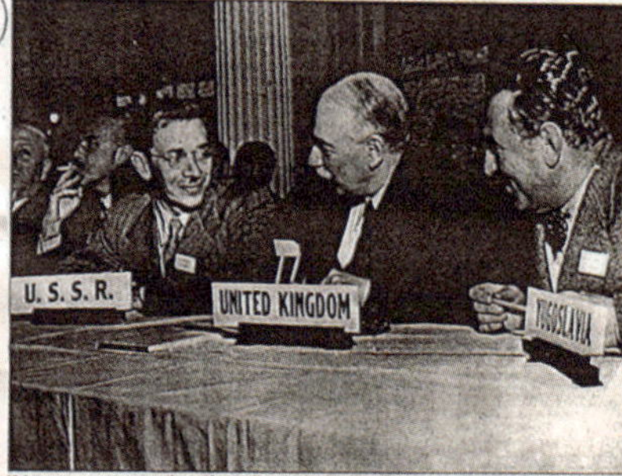

Visionary... John Maynard Keynes at a UN International Monetary Conference in 1946

Michael Meacher was environment minister from 1997–2003, and is MP for Oldham. To order a copy of The Age of Consent please see details of the Guardian book service on page 20.

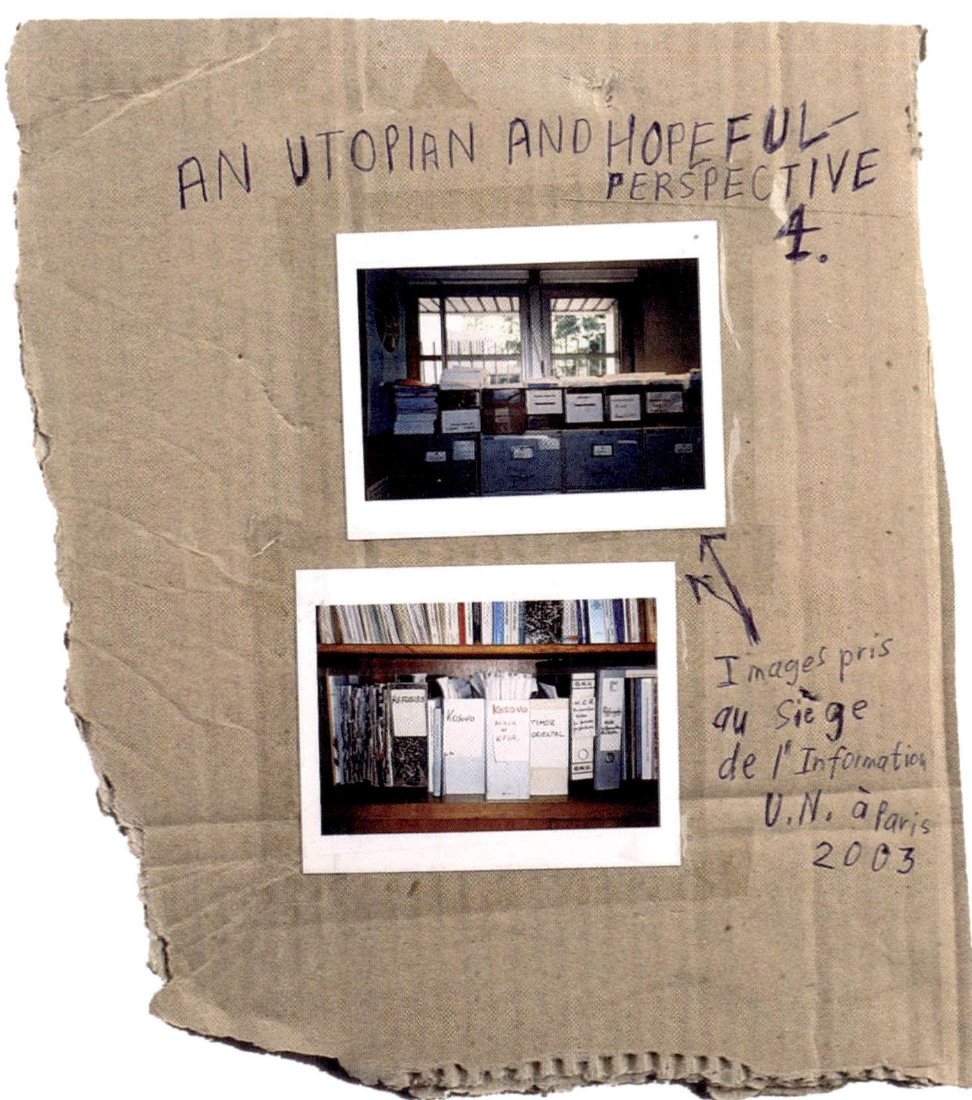
AN UTOPIAN AND HOPEFUL-
PERSPECTIVE
4.
Images pris
au siège
de l'Information
U.N. à Paris
2003

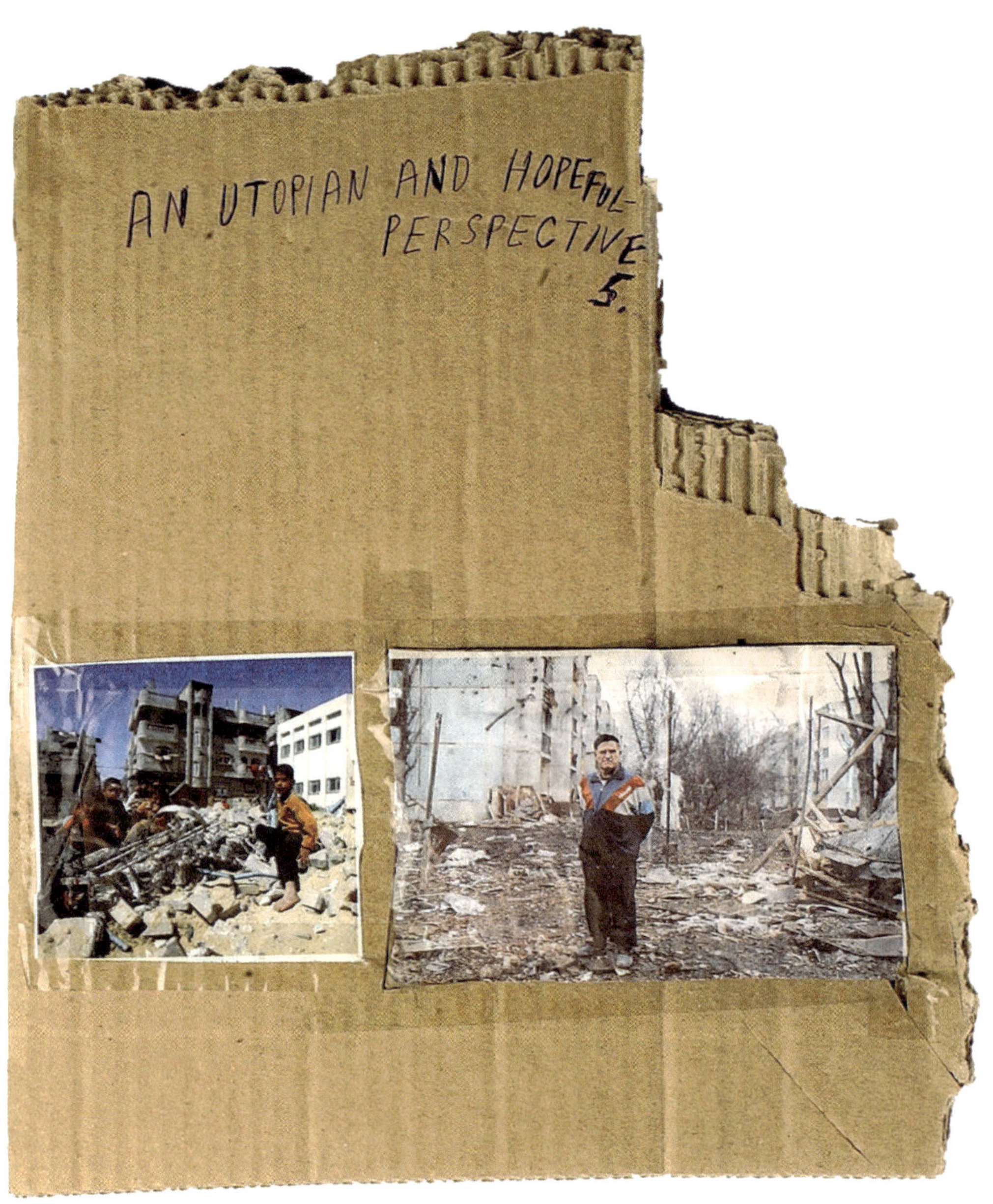
AN UTOPIAN AND HOPEFUL
PERSPECTIVE
5.

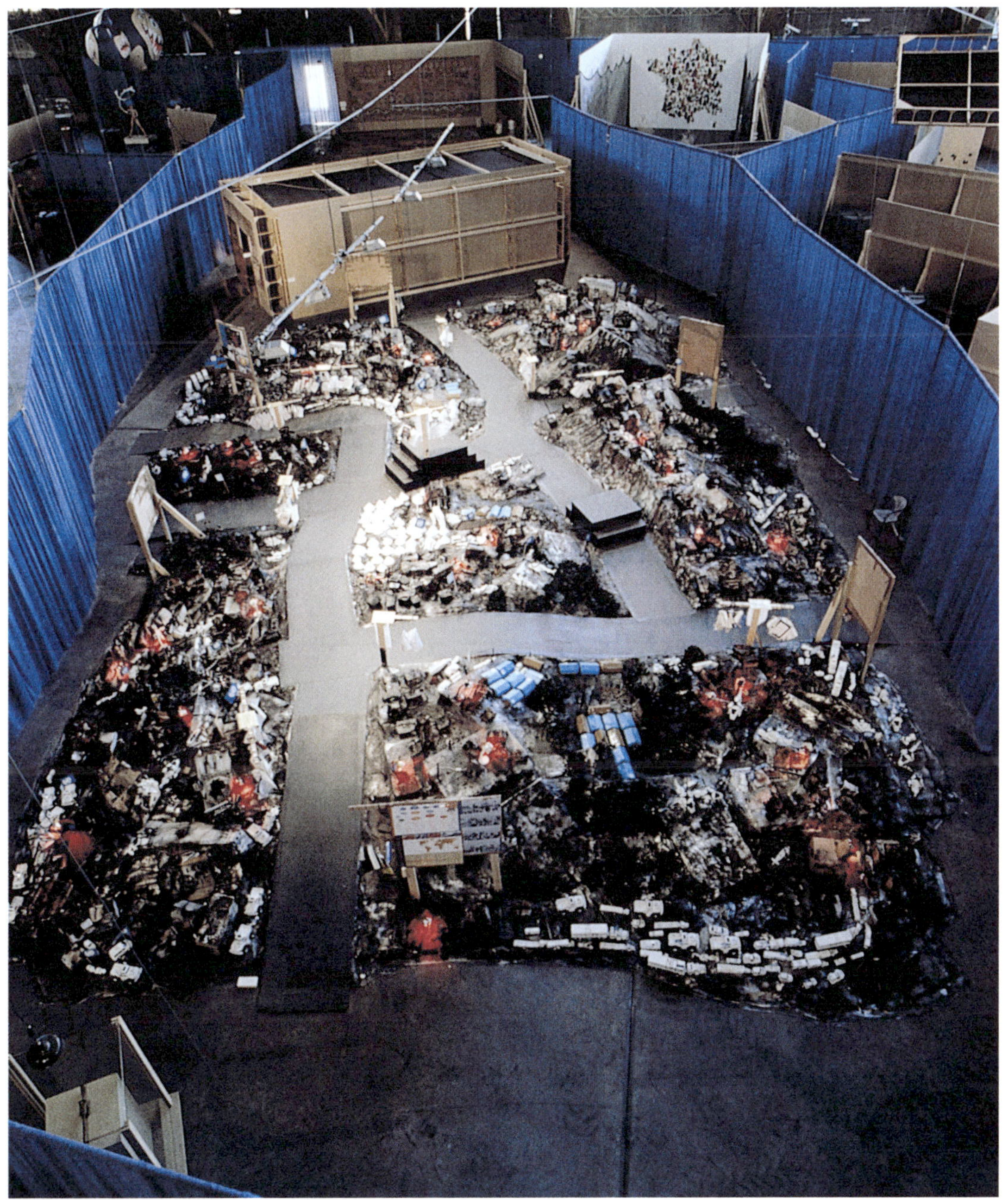

Thomas Hirschhorn
United Nations-Miniature, 2000
Installation consisting of aluminium,
wood, models and other materials
Variable dimensions

Further reading

ARCHIBUGI, D. (1992): *Models of International Organization in perpetual peace projects*, in Review of International Studies.
ARON, R. (1985): *Paz y guerra entre las Naciones*, Madrid, Alianza Editorial, Vol. I.
BOUTROS-BOUTROS, G. (1992): *An Agenda for Peace: Preventive Diplomacy, Peacemaking and Peace-keeping*, New York, Department of Public Information, United Nations).
BULL, H. (1977): *The Anarchical Society*, London, MacMillan.
FISHER, R. (1997): *Coping with International conflict: a systematic approach to influence in international negotiation*, Upper Saddle River, NJ, Prentice Hall.
GALTUNG, J. (1996): *Peace by peaceful means. Peace and Conflict Development and Civilization*, London, Sage/International Peace Research Institute, Oslo. Part IV, *'Cultural Violence'*, 196-210 and *'Conclusion: Peace and Conflict, Development and Civilization'*.
GLEDITSCH, NILS P., WALLENSTEEN, P., ERIKSSON, M., et al. (2002): *Armed Conflict 1946-2001: A New Dataset*, Journal of Peace Research.
HELD, D. (2002): *Governing Globalization*, United Kingdom, Polity Press.
KALDOR, M. (1997): *Reconceptualizing Organized Violence* in Governing Globalization, United Kingdom, Polity Press.
RAPOPORT, A. (1992): *Peace. An Idea whose Time has Come*, Ann Arbor, The University of Michigan Press. Chapter 10 *Conceptions of Peace*.
REPORT OF THE INTERNATIONAL COMMISSION ON INTERVENTION AND STATE SOVEREIGNTY (2001): International Development Research Centre, Canada.
REY, F. and DE CURREA, V. (2002): *El debate humanitario*, Barcelona, Icaria.
SUHRKE, A. (1999): *Human Security and the interest of States*, in Security Dialogue, 30, N° 3, Sept.

Websites of interest

- USA Patriot Act (2002):
  http://www.lifeandliberty.gov
- A secure Europe in a Better World (2003):
  http://ue.eu.int/ueDocs/cms_Data/docs/pressdata/EN/reports/78367.pdf
- A more secure World: Our shared responsibility (2004):
  http://www.un.org/secureworld
- The Campaign for Innocent Victims in Conflict:
  http://www.civicworldwide.org
- UN Charter (1945):
  http://www.un.org/aboutun/charter/contents.htm
- Escola de Cultura de Pau:
  http://www.pangea.org/unescopau
- International Committee of the Red Cross:
  http://www.icrc.org
- International Crisis Group: http://www.icg.org
- Observatorio de conflictos:
  http://www.nodo50.org/observatorio
- Human Security: http://www.humansecuritynetwork.org
- Oneworldnet: http://www.oneworld.net

Region	List of Conflict Zones
Asia	Afghanistan, Kashmir, Korea, Philippines, Indonesia, Iraq, Solomon Islands, Laos, Nepal, Middle East, Sri Lanka, Turkey, Yemen.
Africa	Angola, Algeria, Egypt, Ethiopia-Eritrea, Guinea Conakry, Namibia, Central African Republic, Democratic Republic of Congo, Sahara, Senegal, Sierra Leone, Somalia, Sudan.
Europe and Caucasia	Azerbaijan-Armenia, Kosovo-Serbia, Macedonia, Chechnya, Tajikistan-Kyrgyzstan-Uzbekistan.
Latin America	Colombia, Mexico.

Source: oneworld.net

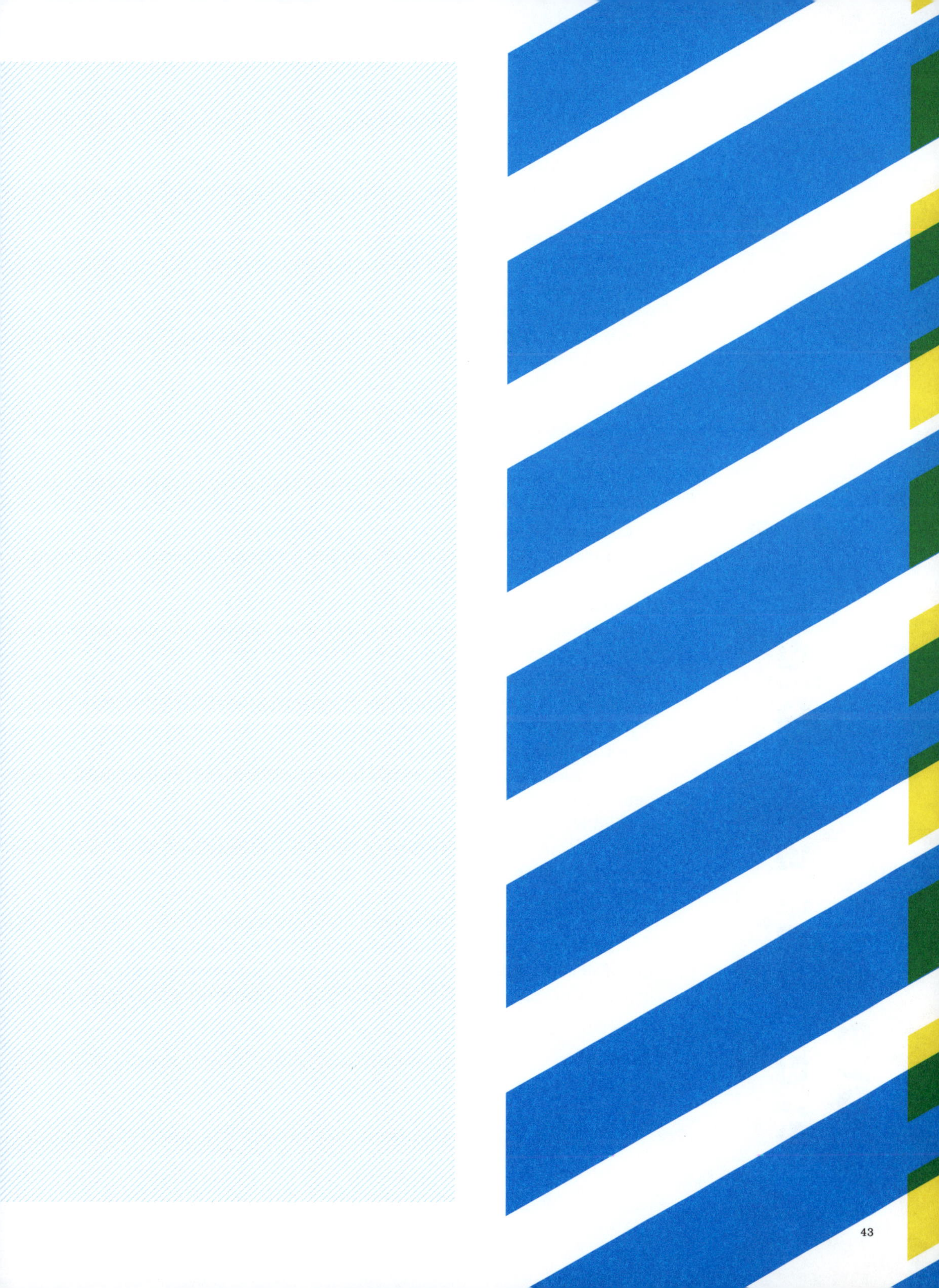

Even though the prevailing idea of poverty is that of living with a daily income below a certain level – one or two dollars, for example, the great Amartya Sen (winner of the Nobel Prize for Economics, to boot) has taught us to look further. If we only consider the economic aspect, and the problem should be viewed from a much broader perspective, to be poor means having a level of income which is insufficient to be able to develop certain basic functions, taking into account the circumstances and social requirements of the individual's environment. Following this line of thought, Sen recommends that we calculate how far a person can develop with this income, bearing in mind that social, political, and cultural aims and those related to security should be included with economic goals. It should also be understood that the result varies enormously from one individual to another and from one place to another.

In other words, even though poverty has a large and undeniable economic component, in order to give it its full dimensions, many other variables must be taken into account, such as state education, hospital services and even the actions that individuals themselves or communities may undertake to improve their living environment. We must escape, in some way, from the powerful influence of classical economics, which has taught us to interpret the world according to quantifiable economic variables without taking into account the fact that our capacity for doing so is still very limited - we have only just managed to evaluate the level of income per capita, which has become the yardstick par excellence – and that, even more importantly, many other factors are excluded from this accountancy. In short, if income is not the sum total of human life, neither can lack of income be the sum total of human privation.

Thanks, once again, to the beneficial influence of Sen, a significant step forward, however small it may yet be, has been taken by the United Nations Development Program (UNDP) with the drawing up, since 1990, of Annual Reports on Human Development. These provide us with a valuable tool to study the individual situation of 177 countries by means of a clearer image, that of the Human Development Index, and their evolution in time.

The conclusion we can draw is that it is necessary to avoid speaking of poverty exclusively as an abstract phenomenon which we subject to analysis, and to remember that what really exist are poor people, that is to say, human beings who lack basic necessities and who are denied the possibility of integral development. Consequently, the priority of the fight against poverty should be seen not only as an effort to increase the material wealth of a society, but also as a way of channelling greater resources into investment in people. The aim of this strategy can only be to place economic growth at the service of human development, thus improving the citizens' capacity to participate, their productivity and their access to productive resources. It is not, therefore, merely a question of increasing the monetary wealth of society but rather of enriching the life of its members.

Child slaves

It is estimated that a total of 246 million children throughout the world are subjected to the slavery of the 21st century: child labour. One in every six children in the world works, many of them exposed to health risks, through the use of toxic substances, through ill-treatment from their 'owners' and, in many cases, through prostitution. In New Delhi, some of these children are kidnapped and obliged to work from five in the morning till nine at night. Others are obliged by their own parents to work for long hours every day making carpets. In these cases there is obviously no question of wages or contracts. An example of this situation appears in an article by the El País journalist, Alexia Torres (9-5-2004) in which she describes the conditions in which fifteen people work, eat, sleep and relieve themselves, crowded into the 20 square metres which also house two large looms. The calculation is that the fingers of 7-year-old girls are ideal for making knots on tensed threads, and worth, in the best of cases, two plates of rice and lentils a day and €20 a month for their parents. Even though the law prohibits harmful work for children of under 14 years of age, it is obvious that the combination of the lack of political effort in enforcing it and the interests created around these activities means that the situation is highly unlikely to improve in the short term. Whether it is a question of paying the debts that they have accumulated themselves or that have been accumulated by members of their families, or of pure exploitation of a defenceless worker, both employers and authorities, or their families, lie about the family relationships, the working conditions or the duration of the working day of the children. They justify their attitude by asserting that they are only helping those in need and blame poverty for the necessity to act in this way. In spite of their reluctance to recognise the problem, the state authorities estimate that there are some 11 million children working in India (the NGOs, on the other hand, calculate some 60 million).

As the ILO and other international bodies state, in reality poverty is not only the cause but also the consequence of these situations, because it is well-known that child labour produces generations of illiterate individuals who perpetuate poverty. Once again, to sever the vicious circle of poverty, the solution lies – as the UNICEF is demonstrating in its principal field of study – in the schooling of these children. This would not only enable them to enjoy a decent standard of living, but would also benefit the economy of their country in that it would result in improvements in health, in professional conditions, in production... However, this way of thinking does not seem to have caused any reaction amongst those who, in the State of Andhra Pradesh, employ 84,000 children, who work in the worst possible conditions in the cultivation of cotton seeds, at the service of multinationals such as Monsanto, Bayer, Advanta and Emergent Genetics.

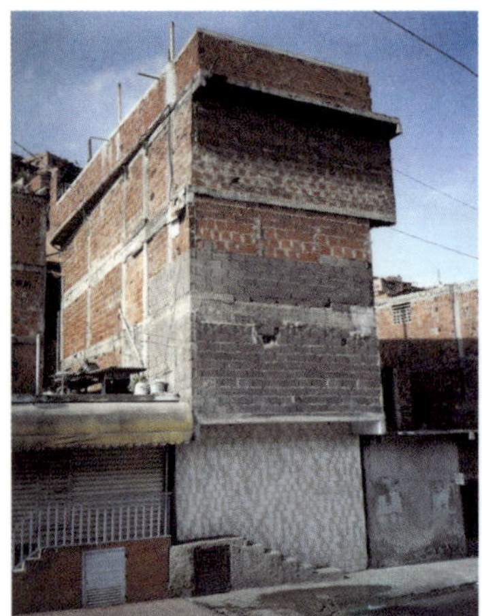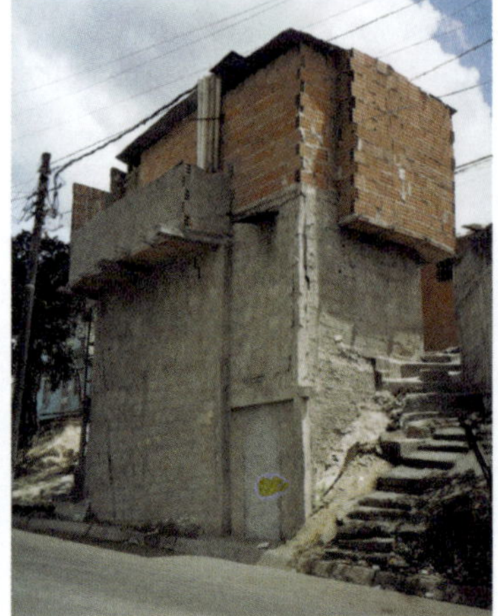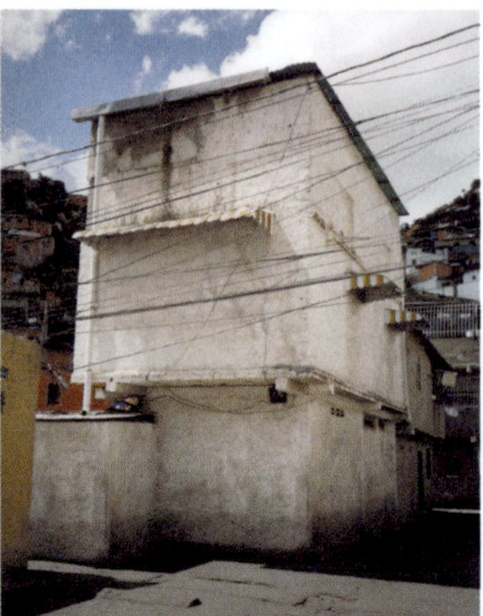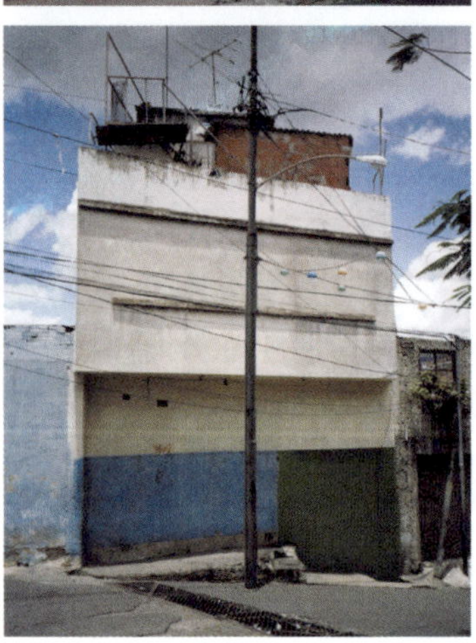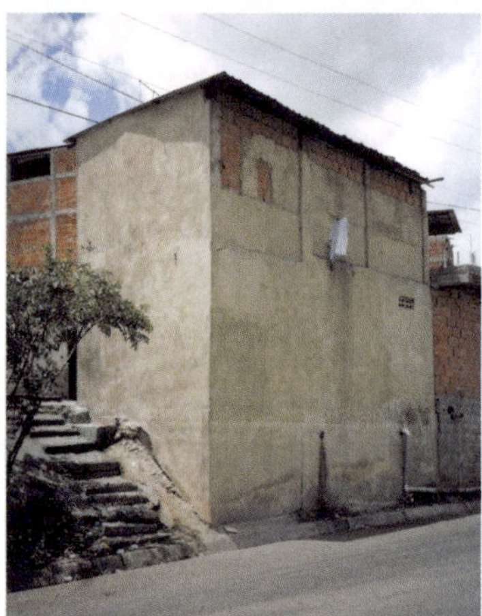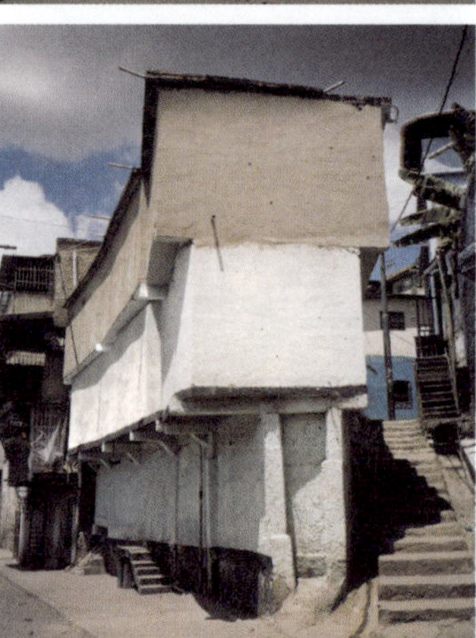

Alexander Apóstol
Residente Pulido. Ranchos (serie), 2003
6 colour photographs
195 x 150 cm each

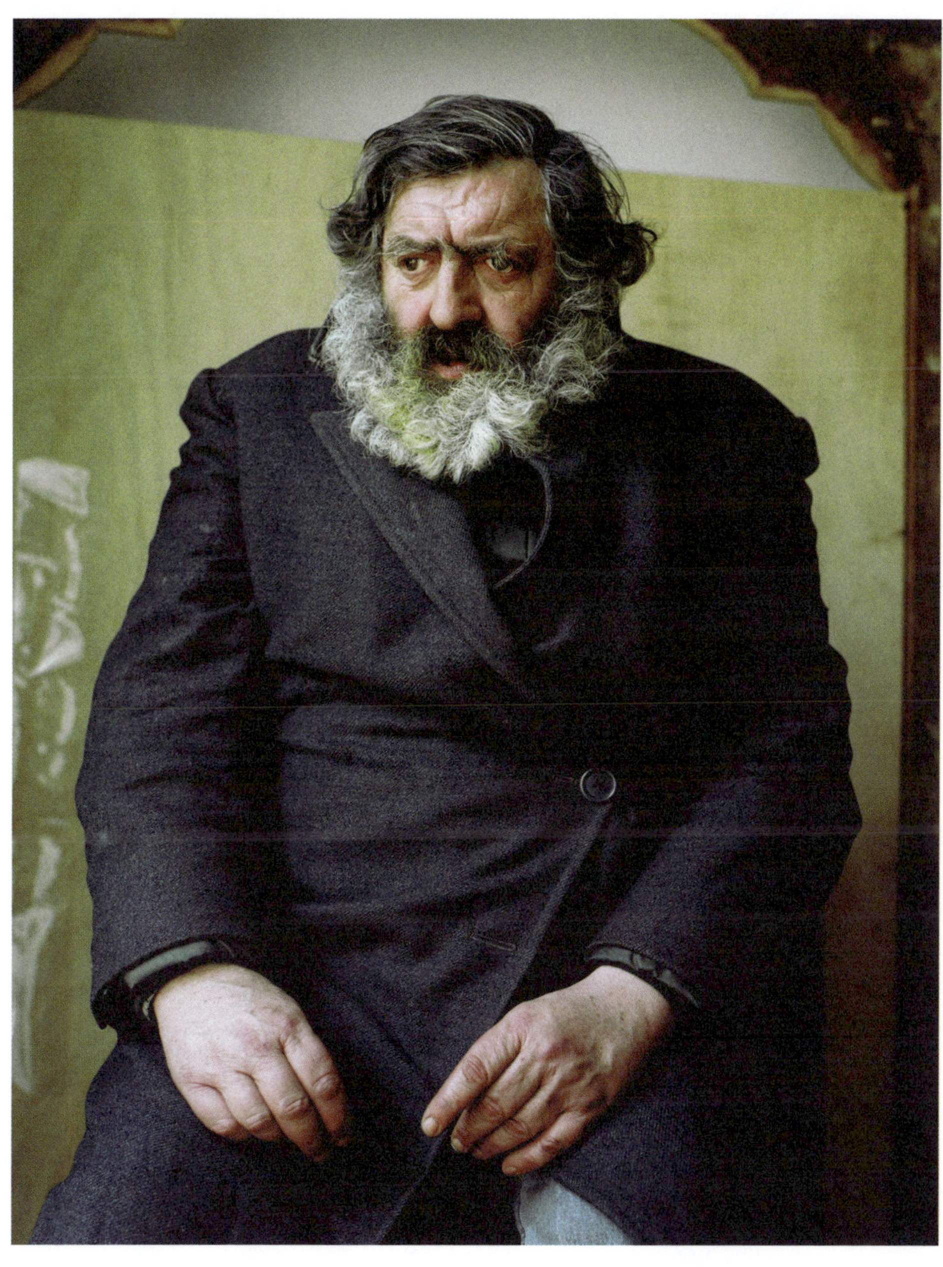

Pierre Gonnord
"Antonio", from the series *Utópicos*, 2004
Colour photograph
165 x 125 cm

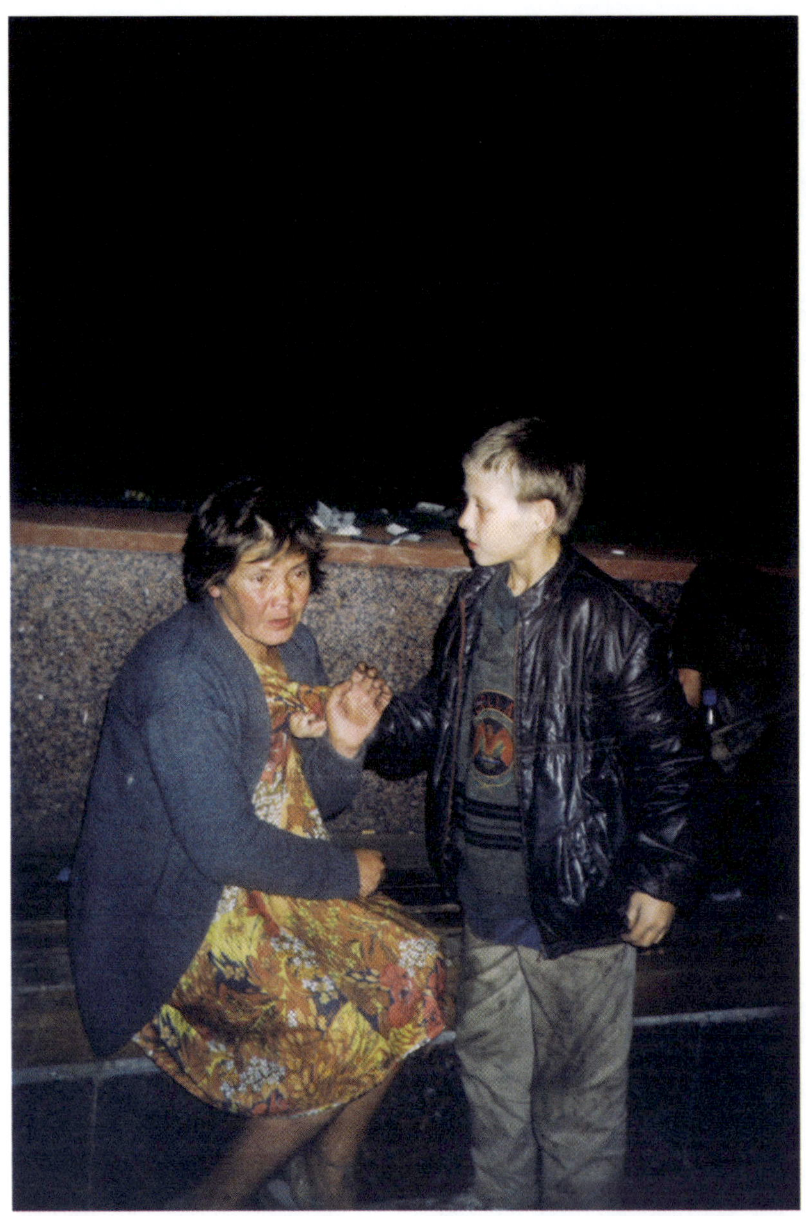

Boris Mikhailov
"Untitled", from the series *Case History*,
1998-1999
Colour photograph
150 x 100 cm

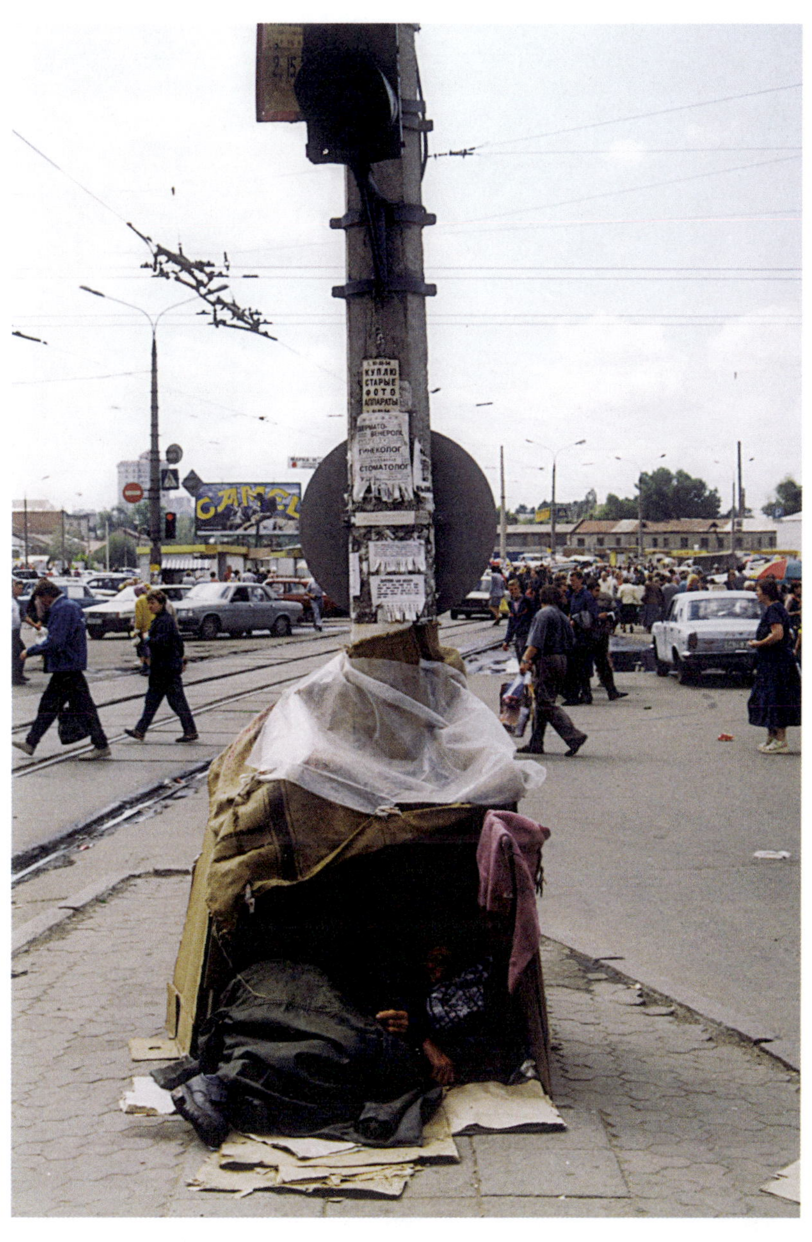

"Untitled", from the series *Case History*,
1998-1999
Colour photograph
150 x 100 cm

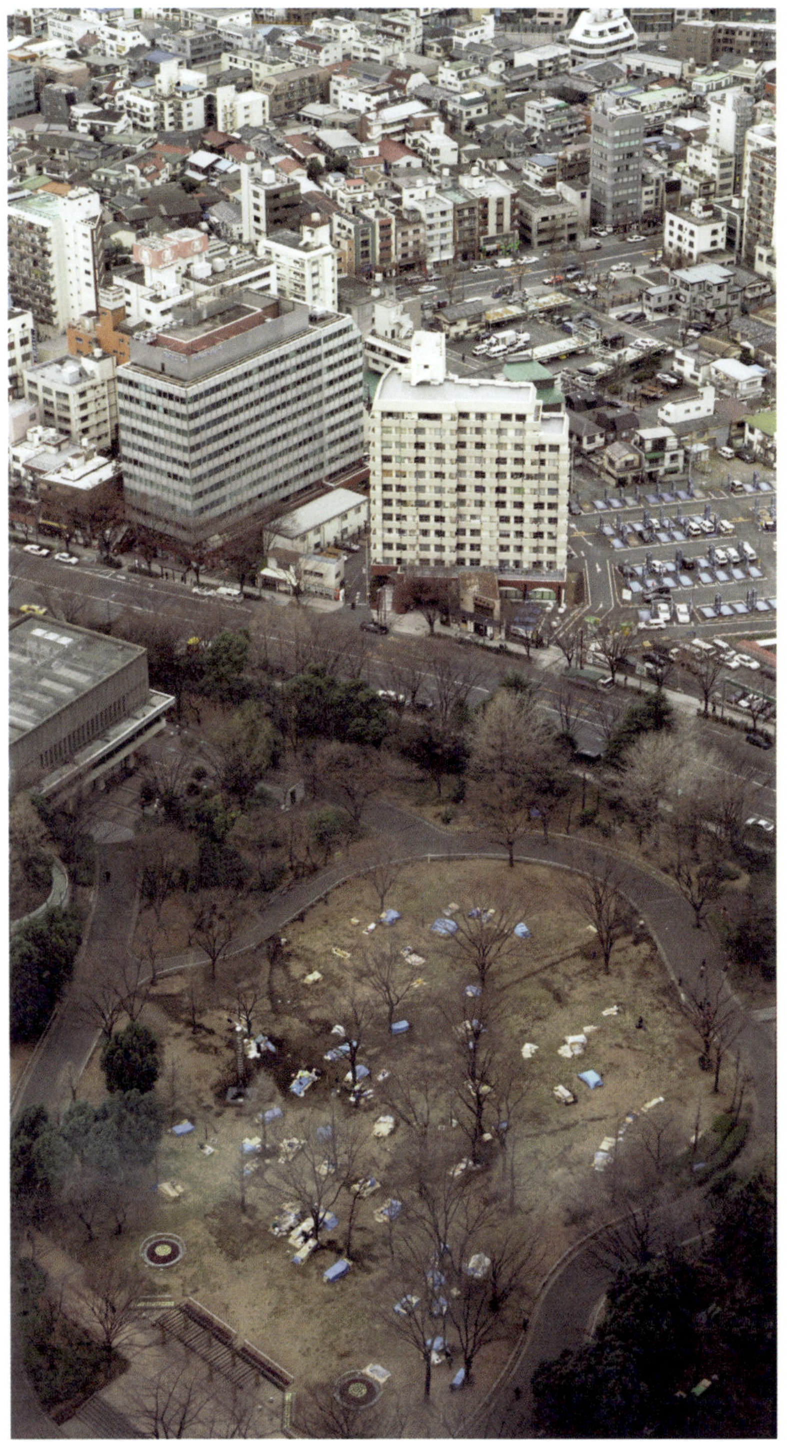

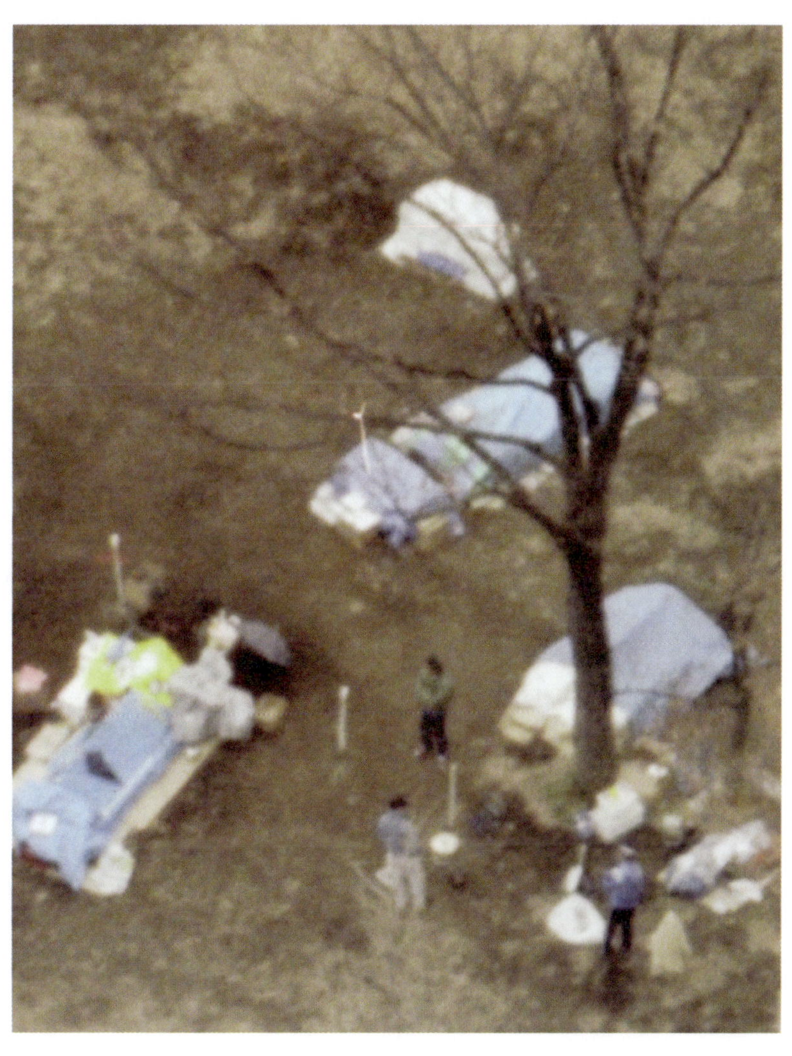

Francesco Jodice
What We Want-TOKYO-D01AB-1999,
1999
Colour photographic diptych
188 x 98 cm / 32 x 24 cm

Basic features of the problem

If we look at the progress made since the middle of last century, it might seem absolutely impossible to us today that mainstream economic thought of that period considered that development was an objective that could be achieved by every country and every individual. The illusion existed that, in spite of different historical situations, with the vast gap that was evident between the central countries and those which had just gained their independence, everyone would finally reach a similar level of welfare. Reality has persistently demonstrated that the so-called developed countries have been able to build up their privileged position precisely thanks to the underdevelopment of many others, condemned to becoming mere sources of supplies – of raw materials for energy, of labour, of natural resources and agricultural products with constantly lowering prices on the international market, all to the greater glory of the former. As the defenders of theories of dependence and those known as 'structuralists' were careful to explain at the end of the 60s, on the international stage there are a series of countries which dominate the new technologies, trade relations and financial flux and decide their own rate of expansion, with the result that they dictate the conditions of development of the rest of the world economies. A closer look at today's world from the viewpoint of poverty discloses a panorama of which the principal characteristics are the following:

- Market control: Since the mid-1980s, a neo-classic counter-revolution in economic thought has dominated – and continues to do so. This presents the market as the solution for all ills and at the same time condemns the State to a minimum field of action as it is faced with the uncontrollable advance of the leaders of a supposedly necessary general process of privatisation of the economy.

On the one hand, it has become evident over this period there is no sincere commitment to free trade, since the powerful countries continue to hide behind their own protectionist barriers while they exert pressure to break down those that the weakest economies have been trying to create. To do this, they have worked to instrumentalise international bodies for their own purposes, coming to occupy an obvious position of control (the World Trade Organisation, the World Bank and the International Monetary Fund are the most paradigmatic examples).

On the other hand, what is needed in many cases, and particularly in fragile States, is not a slimming down of the State system, but rather quite the contrary. State administrative structures must be set up, which are really capable of exercising their authority throughout the country, assuming the responsibility of carrying out tasks aimed at satisfying basic needs, and creating sufficient public services to respond adequately to the demands of the population as a whole.

As a general rule, the private sector does not have a reputation for assuming commitments to basic health, primary education, decent housing, or, to put it bluntly, to solving the problem of hunger, unless it sees the possibility of profits. Basic social services are, by definition, matters for the State administration.

- Continuous deterioration: Despite evidence of the negative effects of this neo-liberal model and of the existence of certain alternative initiatives, mainstream economics still identify with the idea of the market as the outstanding point of reference. We know where this leads - more inequality, more poverty, more exclusion - but there does not seem to be any political will to divert this tendency which results in the scandalous paradox of the more apparent wealth it creates, the more poverty it produces. Today, there are already more than 1,200 million people living with less than one euro a day, while the figure reaches 2,800 million people with no more than two euros. The gulfs created by inequality, the principal breeding ground of conflict and violence, continue to grow, with the result that the rich become richer and the poor irremediably poorer.

- Absence of political will: If it were not tragic, it might even be entertaining to look back over the many international initiatives and commitments made to solve this problem. Without going further back into the past, in 1993 the United Nations passed a resolution which determined, with no trace of irony, the eradication of poverty from the face of the earth. Along the same lines, they approved the dedication of one particular day (17 October) to favour this end. Later, they launched the 'Decade for the eradication of poverty' (1996-2006). In 1998, they also agreed that the year 2005 should be the "International year of the Micro-Credit", aimed at increasing public sensitivity to the importance of this activity as an instrument in the fight against poverty since it increases the capacity of people who are normally non-existent for the traditional financial system. Finally, in September 2000, world leaders met to sign the Millennium Declaration with which they assumed the commitment to achieve eight basic goals, amongst them the halving of the number of poor people in the world before the deadline of 2005.

This need to repeat the same commitment in different formats gives some idea of the lack of results obtained during more than a decade. Today, when it is time to review the path outlined in the Millennium Summit, the UN Secretary General himself is obliged to announce the bad news that it is already clear that, at the present rate, it will be impossible to achieve the goal. Is it perhaps due to a lack of financial means or of knowledge of the mechanisms that could solve the problem? Rather than this, it seems to be the result of an unjustifiable abdication of responsibility on the part of the principal economies of the world, fully occupied in other more immediately profitable matters – it should be remembered that the UN is only the spokesman of the community of nation states.

• The scandal of hunger But what are we really talking about? Can anyone really accept without flinching that in our world today 35,000 people die of hunger every day? The FAO reiterates every year in its report on the state of nutritional insecurity in the world that the repeatedly announced reduction in the number of people suffering severe malnutrition is not being achieved, either. The figures show 852 million people suffering malnutrition in 2004, to which must be added 2,000 million more who are lacking the micro-nutrients essential for a healthy diet. In order to achieve the goal of halving this number by 2015, every year the figure would have to be reduced by 24 million but the fact is that the reduction is only 2.5 million. Surely it is not necessary to point out that, as the FAO itself states, the goal is obtainable and even – if we have to use this type of argument – profitable, for each euro spent to this end "could represent profits of five times, or even more than twenty times, as much".

• Poverty knows no boundaries: Although it is dramatically obvious that the scourge of poverty is particularly cruel in the less developed countries, it cannot be ignored that there are people living in great poverty in the richer countries. In Spain, to quote just one example, it is estimated that some eight million people live below the poverty line. This figure could be alarming if we consider it in the context of the criteria applied on an international level, but it is somewhat different if we consider that it includes those who are living on less than half the national income per capita. In other words, there are also poor people in the developed countries and their number is gradually increasing, but there is no comparison between this situation and that of the less developed countries. It should also be remembered that the population of the industrialised countries represents barely 15% of the world population yet it accounts for 76% of global consumption.

There is a way out
Poverty and hunger are not insoluble problems. Nowadays we have the means to put an end to them, without altering in any way the bases of the present-day economic model. It is not, in essence, a question of the availability of means, but rather of activating a political attitude which will establish an order of priorities different from that which considers that a person is only poor if he wishes to be so - the favourite viewpoint of the market fundamentalists, or that the responsibility lies only with the governments of the countries that suffer this scourge – a popular opinion with those who take the Washington Consensus as an immovable reference, or that the most intelligent course is to defend oneself tooth and nail against the threat of those outside the privileged circle – taking up arms to do so and sheltering behind supposedly impregnable walls.

Surveying the future, we are obliged to accept that it is possible, whether our motivations be moral, ethical or purely rational calculation, to eliminate a scourge that, if it were not for the passiveness and lack of sensitivity that, like a virus, seem to have infected large social, political and economic circles, should be figuring as one of the most urgent problems on the world agenda. Some of the factors to be considered in the fight against poverty may be summarised as follows:

• The problem to be solved is not only that of poverty, but of exclusion. The goal to be achieved must be formulated in terms of welfare and security as the principal aspirations of human beings. Integrated individuals are synonymous with reasonably satisfied and stable people. On the other hand, people who are excluded, whether for race, ethnic group, religion, economic situation or any other motive, are the perfect breeding ground for instability, insecurity, and, in extreme cases, for violence. The way ahead seems clear: a determined policy of integration, by means of a combination of the enormous social, political and economic possibilities that exist on every level, individual, community, national and international.

• Hunger must also be eradicated from the planet. We know how to do it and we can carry it out. It is not only a question of activating technical resources, though this is fundamental, but also of undertaking thorough reforms of economic and political systems in order to facilitate the emergence of leaders who are sensitive to the needs of their citizens. 'In democracies, there is no starvation,' Amartya Sen reminds us. There is not only a need for seeds and tractors but also for good government and responsibility. The initiative of the Alliance against Hunger, initially launched by the President of Brazil, Lula da Silva, and backed by the UN and by 55 Heads of State and governments, must not be allowed to fail. This would be an unacceptable abdication of responsibility.

• The efforts made must be sustainable, both in economic terms (prolonged in time) and in terms of the environment. Firstly, we must recall the disgraceful non-fulfilment of the commitment made by the most developed countries in the 70s to contribute 0.7% of their GNP to aid for the poorest peoples. With a few notable exceptions, these countries have never contributed more than an average of 0.35%, and at present the figure is 0.25%. Though we might mention that even with the promised 0.7% it would be impossible to solve the main problems of poverty, it is necessary to insist that this commitment be fulfilled as soon as possible. At the same time, the concept of co-operation for development should be broadened to include aspects such as the adoption of fair trade regulations, which would give the products of the lesser developed countries access to international markets, a far-reaching reform of the present structure of international finances, which would allow the poorer economies to explore channels other than those permitted by the financial bodies controlled by the leading world powers, the solution of the problem of overwhelming external debt, which lies like a dead weight on the future of these countries, and the sharing of technology in order to prevent a widening of the digital gap that is clearly discernible today. Unless these components are included in policies of co-operation for development, it will never be possible to achieve the desired goals.

• Co-operation for development must concentrate all its efforts on the fight against poverty leaving aside, without hesitation, other goals (commercial, political, or of security) which may be equally legitimate but which may not only clash with the fundamental aim but too often push it into the background. We must understand that poverty is at the same time, along with other factors, the cause and consequence of violence and therefore its eradication contributes very directly to a greater state of stability.

• The voice of the poor must form an integral part of this process. In those countries where decentralisation has been carried out, where the potential beneficiaries have been incorporated into the processes of the identification of necessities, the formulation and follow-up of projects, better results have been achieved. The direct and collective action of these peoples not only involves them personally in the various programmes to be carried out, but also results in qualitative advances in their capabilities, which are important for their futures. Perhaps the best example we can quote is that of Participative Budget, launched in Porto Alegre. This began in 1988 as an alternative practice set up by the Workers' Party of Brazil and followed at present by a growing number of municipal, regional, and even national authorities in other parts of the world.

• Increasing the capabilities of individuals is a vital element in this fight against hunger. But it is also essential to insist on the central role of the State and consolidate its social functions so that it can assist those who are in need in areas where the private sector shows no interest in intervening.

• Focusing attention on women as the protagonists and motors of development is the best way to succeed. They should, in any case, be a priority for attention since they are always the poorest amongst the poor. But the many tasks they carry out in the family and the community make them multiple agents of development, both in the purely economic sphere and in basic health care, education and social change.

• A universal basic income should not be considered a utopian dream but rather a realistic aspiration for the not-too-distant future. It is not only a human right but also a goal which can be achieved with the resources available today, and it is a formula which is effective in encouraging the development of human capabilities.

• If we had to single out a field for priority action, even though there will always be matters requiring more urgent attention, this would be education. Education, education and education: this should be the constant priority in order to achieve the development of human capabilities. Individuals who are better educated, better prepared and more capable are not the only ones to benefit: their family, community, country and the world in general advance.

• Both the economic and political models that dominate today need to be thoroughly reformed in order to eliminate their characteristic features of inequality. Nevertheless, without losing sight of this objective, we should initially aspire to seeing that commitments already acquired are fulfilled, even though this may seem to some to smack of excessive optimism in today's world. To others, however, this goal may seem insufficient, but we should remember the enormous potential, if they were fully applied, of documents and commitments such as the Universal Declaration of Human Rights or the Millennium Goals.

• The purpose of development is to improve people's lives, by giving them more freedom, more opportunities for self-realisation and greater dignity. The Millennium Goals, in spite of their limitations and the fact that they cover only a minimum of the items of an agenda that should embrace far more areas, are still valid world-wide and cannot be abandoned.

It also depends on you
Extreme poverty and social exclusion are a violation of human dignity and of human rights. The lack of resources essential to cover the most elemental necessities constitutes a drastic limitation of the capacity of a human being to exercise his rights. The redress of this situation is, as we have already pointed out, possible, necessary and urgent. Up till the present, the balance has not inspired much hope, showing a constant reneging on the agreements already reached, both on the part of national States and international bodies – which all too often tend to be mere instruments for the transmission of the wishes of those same States.

On an individual level, it is not sufficient to stand up and demand that political leaders really fulfil their promises in these matters. Obviously social pressure is necessary to create a world in which there is greater equality, greater solidarity and greater sustainability, a pressure based on the knowledge that in order to achieve this, success in the fight against poverty is the crucial question. Equally important is giving support to non-governmental organisations involved in development through their permanent work solving the specific problems within their scope. The same must be said of spontaneous solidarity in response to catastrophes; we need only recall the extraordinary reaction of the citizens of the world after the recent seaquake that terminated last year so traumatically.

Perhaps particular emphasis should be placed on this last point. Nobody can now hide behind the excuse of ignorance of the injustices in the world, nobody can look the other way in an attempt to make others responsible. We must, at least, recognise that these are problems that are crying out to each of us, individually. In other words, in addition to overcoming the passiveness that may cripple us (the necessary initial drive), in addition to expressing a critical attitude to make the authorities, according to their respective levels of responsibility, carry out a mandate to help those in need, it is also our responsibility to ask ourselves individually if, for example, the goal of 0.7% of GNP, that every developed country should be contributing to aid development, should not also be an imperative for us, an aim on a personal level. Should we not be contributing a minimum of 0.7% of our time, our energies, our capabilities and our income to these causes?

Document drawn up by researchers from the
Institute of Studies on Conflicts and Humanitarian Action (IECAH)
Madrid, January 2005

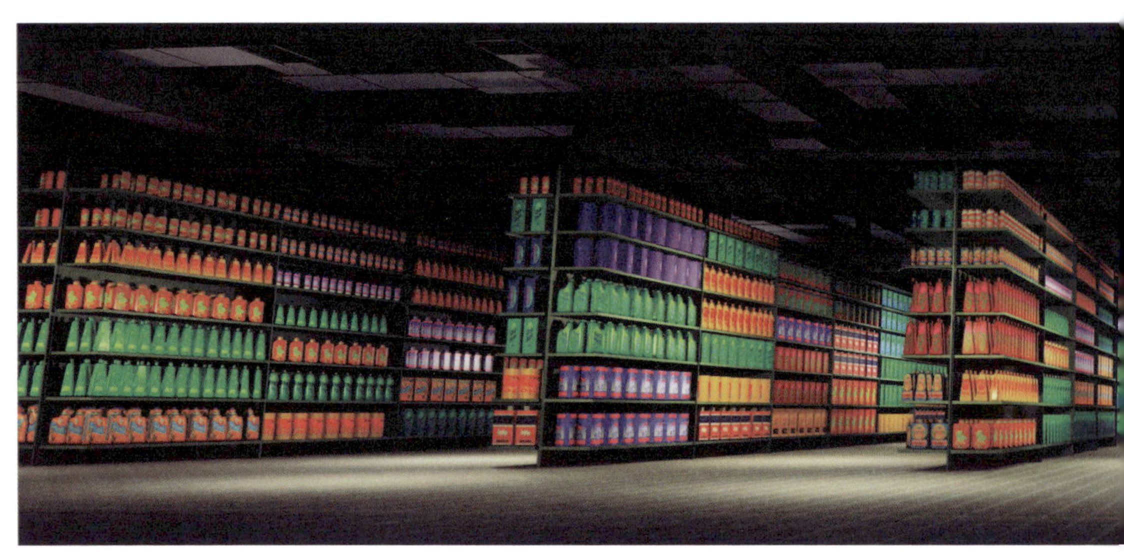

Sven Påhlsson
Consuming Pleasures, 2003
3D animation. DVD colour video with
sound
11'

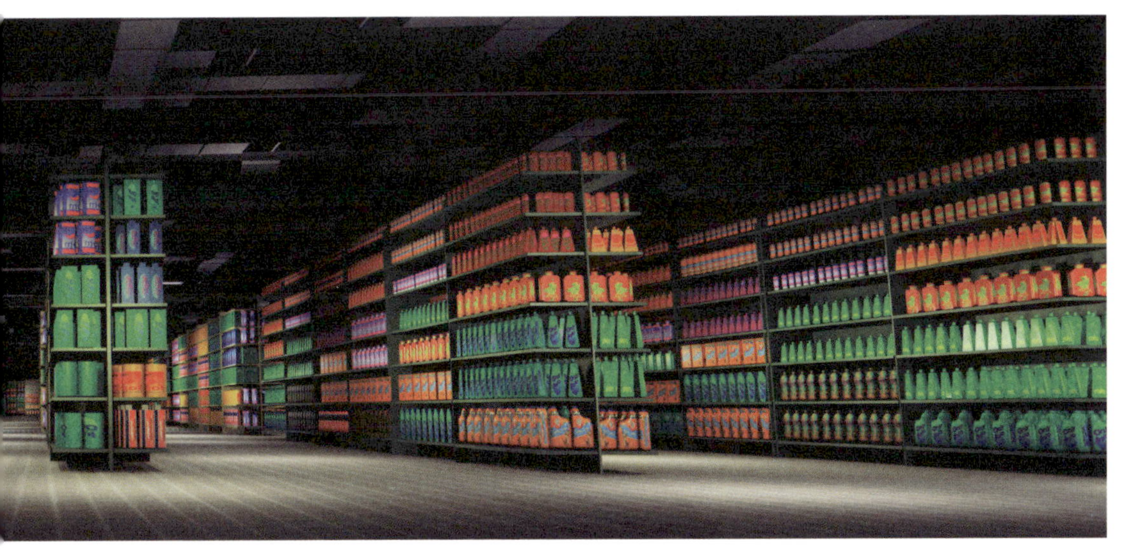

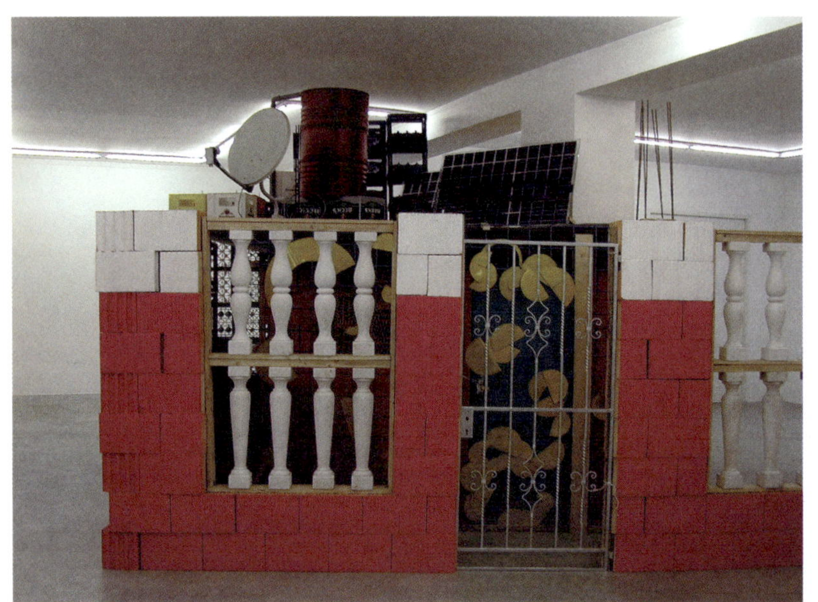

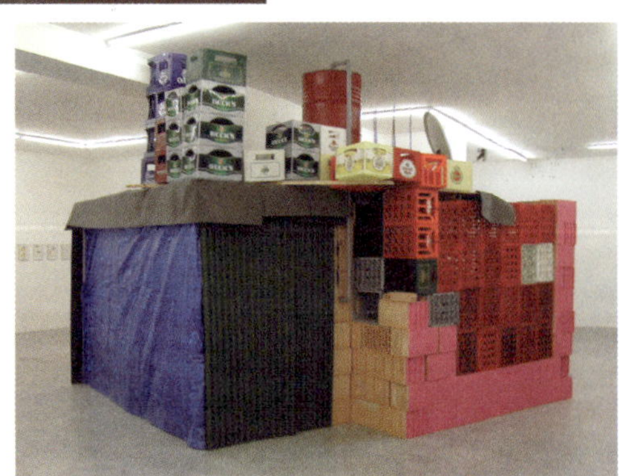

Marjetica Potrč
Caracas: House with Extended Territory,
2003
Installation consisting of building
materials and energy and communication
infrastructures
Variable dimensions

Marjetica Potrč
Temporary Territories

At the Kunst-Werke Café

Two weeks ago, on a rainy afternoon, I was sitting in the Kunst-Werke Café in Berlin with Kyong Park. We were talking about cities in the Balkans. Should we make a research trip there? The autumn rain was pouring against a glass wall and transforming the pavilion where we sat into a kind of island, a Berlin island. I thought, what is it that draws me away from islands – to walk through cities no one else seems to care about and some might be afraid to visit? I still remember the e-mails I received, back in the spring of 2003, cautioning me not to go to Caracas. At the time, I wondered whether I would be able to tell the stories of a city in crisis – I mean the stories embedded in its architecture? Would people back home understand narratives that did at first glance not appear to concern them? Now, looking back at my Caracas experience, I feel that the opportunity to study the city was an extraordinary gift, one that has helped me better understand the cities I love. A number of my recent projects had their start in Caracas. I am most proud of the Istanbul and Liverpool projects, which were realised recently. I consider the "Dry Toilet", constructed on site in a Caracas barrio, and the "Urgent Architecture" exhibition, which I dreamed up with Michael Rush, then director of the Palm Beach Institute of Contemporary Art in Florida, to be the best work I have ever done. The PBICA exhibition gave body to recent trends in contemporary architecture, such as the emphasis on private space and personal security – remember, it is individuals who make a city and it is their concerns that matter. For me, the most important thing about this exhibition was the attempt to construct an understandable language out of the apparent madness of cities in crisis. After all, the architecture of such cities tells vivid stories, since reality seems somehow enhanced there. Caracas has served as a case study for my cities. Look at Berlin, of all places; here I sit and all is well – today.

The City of Caracas

The city's underground passages were full of people pressing onwards, and always too close to my body. Above ground, the city weighed heavy. It was noisy and loud, and never slept. It was smelly and dirty. The tropical rains, which unleashed a pure natural energy, seemed to be the only thing able to calm the city down and give me a chance to catch my breath. Caracas is a pagan city. I felt its raw energy smelling of survival in the midst of individuals who stake their claims to happiness in an apparently collapsing city. Never walk through the narrow alleys of La Vega barrio alone. In the formal city, always take a taxi after dark. Push down on the gas pedal when the light turns red. Never stop at a traffic light at night, especially when you are driving alone. You must always be present in both mind and body, but above all listen to your instincts. Never plan anything. Events impose themselves on you easily in Caracas, whether crimes, floods or celebrations. I found that, once I had arrived, this dangerous and divided city would not let me go. I came to Caracas in order to research the informal city, which is one way of referring to the barrios of Venezuela. In Caracas, this informal city, climbing up the hills, encircles and presses in on the formal city, which occupies the valley below. The communities that inhabit the two cities are alien to each other, with different value systems that breed a mutual mistrust. They co-exist in close proximity, however, and must constantly accommodate each another. The divisions in Caracas are unmistakable. I had no problem accepting this fact, the permanence of this division. When you think about it, the finality of the division is, more or less, the only thing that is really permanent in Caracas. Everything else exists in a flux of decay and expansion in the midst of permanent crisis.

The formal city, once a proud modernist town, was now in decline and fast becoming a modern ruin. It seemed to me that it was losing its body as well as its mind, wildly and without regret. Oversized billboards, sometimes bigger than the houses they were built on, were left empty. The Parque Central building complex, once the pride of Caracas modernism, was deteriorating and being overtaken by nature. Built-on additions and vegetation sprouted from its monumental façades. The ground-floor shopping mall was deserted, with barred windows barricading the shops. The elevators were not working.

Parque Central seemed consumed by its own malaise and had apparently abandoned modernism's quest to display the values of functionalism and consumer society. Parque Central's demise felt almost biblical. Or did it? A block away, the Urban Agriculture Co-operative occupied a former public park. Red peppers and lettuce were growing in green fields and were being sold to passers-by. Those who lived in the vicinity viewed the urban farm as an invasion of the rural into their urban landscape; the barrios, too, were considered a form of rural architecture, an alien growth in the modernist city. Though the barrios were not as nearby as the urban farm in the park, they were constantly present. From virtually anywhere in the formal city, you could see the outlying hills populated by barrio communities. Who were those people and why did they persist in invading the modern city with their urban farms and informal marketplaces? They had arrived in Caracas from the rural hinterland and had stayed, becoming the construction workers who built the formal city by day and their own city by night. The barrios are not planned settlements; they were created by individuals who built their homes on public land without obtaining any permit or title. These homes are self-initiated structures that have been upgraded and expanded as need arose. In Caracas, the barrios are growing, not decaying, and they exude a confidence in their own body. This is a rural architecture made of tightly interwoven buildings and alleys. The people who live in the barrios had prevailed against all odds, growing their houses as their families grew, shamelessly showing off this growth with construction wires that sprouted from every rooftop. This ephemeral city was clearly here to stay.

Urgent Architecture
Hybrid House: Caracas, West Bank, West Palm Beach
2003, building materials, energy and communication infrastructure
Marjetica Potrč: Urgent Architecture
Palm Beach Institute of Contemporary Art, Lake Worth, Florida, 2003
Massachusetts Institute of Technology, List Visual Arts Centre, Cambridge, Massachusetts, 2004
Hybrid House juxtaposes structures borrowed from the temporary architecture of Caracas, the West Bank, and West Palm Beach, Florida, and shows how they negotiate space among themselves. Each of these community-initiated structures formulates its own language, which, in all three cases, has much in common with archetypal (and not modernist) architecture. Emphasis is placed on private space, security and energy and communication infrastructures.
Near the end of my six-month stay in Caracas, I had the seemingly wild idea to compare Caracas with the West Bank Territory in the Middle East. My intuition told me that there might be similar strategies of contemporary architecture in both places, and this eventually proved true. I knew that Eyal Weizman, an Israeli architect based in Tel Aviv and London, had done a map-making project that examined international law violations and human rights abuses committed in the West Bank by architects and planners.

These two case studies – Caracas and Middle East – created a language that put in perspective the recent architecture of both places. The terms we came up with were useful in explaining the facts on the ground, though I must admit they sounded like a dictionary of architecture from either the distant past or some sci-fi future: dynamic mapping, vertical geometry, colonisation and the claiming of land, the appropriation of public space, invasions, temporary territories, and so on. These were strategies and direct actions that grew out of extreme urban environments. In both Caracas and the West Bank, public space was eroding and private space expanding. The modernism that Tel Aviv and Caracas are so proud of, and which in my view attempted to visualise democracy by creating shared public spaces, was being obliterated. In its place, sharp divisions between public and private space had emerged. Mutually alien communities co-existed in close proximity and had to constantly accommodate each another, whether we were talking about Palestinians and Jewish settlers, or the inhabitants of the formal city of Caracas and the barrio dwellers. These are dynamic and hostile territories. Defence architecture takes hold, illustrating an obsessive personal control of territory. In an apparent absence of democratic values, there is a seemingly regressive return to archetypes, such as gated communities on the level of the city, and fortress-like houses on the level of the family: My home is my castle. My conversations with Eyal confirmed my feeling that both Caracas and the West Bank – on the face of it, very different and unconnected places – had developed similar strategies while shaping their environments. Were these strategies just Babylonian murmuring? We demonstrated that this was not the case; this was articulate speech. Is it important to look at cities in crises? I think so, for we are all in this together. The first floor of the Caracas house was made with heavy concrete building blocks, a common building material in Caracas barrios. All doors and windows were barred, reflecting the enhanced security found throughout the city. The second floor was built with milk crates – these would be beer crates in Caracas – indicating the kind of recyclable material that is used in barrio structures. A watchtower was placed in the corner of the house to suggest the need for personal surveillance of territory. Most importantly, the house had an extension on the ground. I called this extended territory, and it is a common strategy for enlarging a barrio home. A false façade would be built in front of the house, complete with windows and doors, as a way of declaring one's intention to occupy land.

As for the temporary building material that barrio structures use, such as corrugated metal sheets, these soon become permanent features. Here again are parallels between Caracas and the West Bank. In the West Bank, a strategic position on top of a hill allows for personal surveillance of the territory below, while containers – a form of temporary architecture – soon transform themselves into a fortress-like architecture. So, perhaps as an afterthought, it seemed a natural idea to install a Jewish-settlement container on the second floor of the Caracas house. In both the Jewish settlements of the West Bank and the barrios of Caracas, territory is continually being negotiated, often in unusual ways. Consider the notion of vertical geometry, a term Eyal uses to describe contemporary spatial strategies in the West Bank, such as ring roads: two separate road systems are imposed on one another, and this, in fact, separates forever the two West Bank communities, the Jewish settlers and the Palestinians, rather than connecting them. "Hybrid House" consisted of five structures: a Caracas barrio house, the "Dry Toilet" Liyat Esakov and I initiated in La Vega barrio, a Jewish-settlement container, a Palestinian house, and a West Palm Beach trailer. These were family-size houses that attempted to portray the determination and the aspirations of settlers who claim a place in the contemporary urban setting.

Caracas: Dry Toilet
Dry Toilet
2003, building materials and sanitation infrastructure
A collaborative project by Liyat Esakov and Marjetica Potrč, Supported by La Vega community, Caracas; the Caracas Case Project and Federal Cultural Foundation of Germany; and the Ministry of Environment, Venezuela
The Dry Toilet project was the result of a six-month stay in Caracas, during which time Liyat Esakov and I researched the informal city under the auspices of the Caracas Case Project. A dry, ecologically safe toilet was built on the upper part of La Vega barrio, a district in the city without access to the municipal water grid. The project attempts to rethink the relationship between infrastructure and architecture in real-life urban practice in a city where about half the population receives water from municipal authorities no more than two days a week.
As it often is with the best things that happen in life, I never expected that I would one day be building a dry toilet in a Caracas barrio. In our collaboration for the Caracas Case Project, the Israeli architect Liyat Esakov and I knew only that we wanted to work inside the informal city and not merely analyse it from a safe distance. It was some time before we could actually walk through the alleys of the barrio. You always had to have an escort when you went there; it was too dangerous to visit alone. With the aid

of Raul Zelik, another participant in the Caracas Case Project, we made contact with community leaders and were eventually shown around. Most importantly, we were able to discuss living conditions with barrio residents. What was most obvious, and most shocking, was the breakdown of the energy infrastructure and the lack of public utilities in the informal city. This was not what we had anticipated, since we were all focused on the fascinating and seemingly precarious architecture of the barrios. But we soon realised that the failure of the municipal infrastructure in the barrios was a logical outcome of the houses' construction process. In a planned city, the various forms of public infrastructure are set in place before construction starts. In the barrios, the houses are built first with infrastructure problems being dealt with later.

Liyat and I asked a group of barrio residents what they thought about self-sustainable energy solutions such as solar panels for bringing additional electricity to their homes. They could not care less. They were happy to steal electricity from the municipal power grid. They saw self-sustainable alternative energy technologies as something only rich people would be interested in. But drinking water was another matter, since it was provided by the city for only a few hours twice a week – if you were lucky. The upper part of La Vega barrio, where we eventually built the "Dry Toilet", had no access at all to running water. This was a place ruled by

necessity. Could barrio residents perhaps apply their survival strategies to utility infrastructures in a more focused way? Instead of shooting bullets into the municipal water pipes in order to get more water through an illegal water connection, they could take a different approach. Perhaps, they could reduce their consumption of water. They would use less water if they had a toilet that did not need it. In this way, they would solve the infrastructure problem themselves, independent of municipal authorities. Our idea caught the attention of the community. The "Dry Toilet" made sense, after all. And so it was built by a team of construction workers from the community in La Fila, the upper section of La Vega barrio, on Raquel's property (if you can speak in this way about occupied public land); her house had never had a toilet before. Barrio buildings are self-initiated and self-upgrading structures that function on a small scale. I still wonder why no one had previously thought to apply their strategies – their tropicalism, their non-linear logic – on a city-wide scale. For Liyat and me, it was extremely important that Hidrocapital, the municipal water company, supported our "Dry Toilet" project. It made sense in a city where reservoirs were quickly losing water. For the La Vega community, the project provided a long-term sustainable solution for the problem of wastewater, radically reducing the community's water consumption. Houses collapse in the barrios not only because of the torrential tropical rains, but also because of leaking

sewage. At one point Hidrocapital envisioned building full-scale models of the dry toilet in every municipality as an educational endeavour. Remember the urban farm in the middle of the formal city? This same co-operative considered erecting a dry toilet on its premises, but eventually decided against it out of a fear of controversy; the dry toilet might be seen as another invasion in the formal city simply because it can function on its own, without any connection to the municipal utility grid of the modernist city.

Looking back, I remember that Liyat and I both felt at home in La Vega barrio. Liyat eventually rented a room there and had to learn to bathe with only one cup of water. In a way, the "Dry Toilet" happened to us because we could see potential in an informal solution. I cannot speak for Liyat, but my heart is instinctually drawn to individually initiated small-scale strategies, perhaps because I was raised in a socialist society. I have learned to have particular respect for the voices of individuals. Have Liyat and I romanticised the informal city? I do not think so. I am proud that we were able to draw attention to the shift from the power of institutions to the empowerment of individuals. In the context of Caracas, where the social state never really materialised, individual initiative is a natural route to take.

Raquel to standing on the ground between the *Dry Toilet* and the house she had built with her own hands – first collecting wood, then using mud to fill in the cracks in the wooden structure – she was in fact standing right in the middle of an additional room she had planned. Raquel's house was a growing house in the midst of a growing city.

Istanbul: Rooftop Room
Istanbul: Rooftop Room
2003, building materials, energy and communication infrastructure
Poetic Justice: The 8th International Istanbul Biennial, Istanbul
Rooftop Room is a site-specific project realised for the 8th Istanbul Biennial. It consists of a tin roof constructed on top of a privately owned flat-roof house in the Kustepe suburb of Istanbul. After the exhibition closed, the family who lives in the house replaced the temporary curtain walls with permanent walls.

I was asked by curator Dan Cameron to create a project for the 8th International Istanbul Biennial, which had the title *Poetic Justice.* It became a matter of ethics for me that whatever project I made for Istanbul should be as meaningful as I thought the "Dry Toilet" was. I knew from the start that I did not want to make this project in a public space. I am aware of the fact that Europeans are unconditionally committed to public space, but this is something I have never really understood. Such dedication to the concept of public space has little to do with what these spaces actually became, that is, territories controlled by special interests. In my view, the European commitment to public space is largely symbolic and is most probably due to the reliance on the social state.

One could get sentimental and look for reasons as far back as the Renaissance, when public space became a significant issue along with the democracy. A public square was intended to be egalitarian, free for everyone – consider the fact that the Swiss still vote in town squares. The notion of public space is linked with democracy and is, therefore, untouchable.

What I see in contemporary cities is not only a privatisation of public space, but also its erosion. In Caracas, where what little there is of the social state has been dissolving, public space is either lacking or abused. In the informal city, there is no real public space. All public space is privately negotiated, and vice versa – private space becomes public when such is needed. In the formal city, public squares have been invaded by hostile groups of people on a temporary basis, for instance, by Chavista demonstrators. Sometimes public squares end up being permanently occupied by street-sellers. Temporariness, not stability, characterises contemporary Caracas. While the Venezuelan capital might be an extreme example, the West Bank presents an even harsher scenario, in my view. There, the temporary condition is sealed behind walls while security measures are pushed to the limit. Both places are telling in the way they put an emphasis on private space and personal security. Could they become case studies for European cities, which have been experiencing the gradual decline of public space and

are consumed by private concerns? Let me give you an example from Liverpool in regard to the imposition of private security in public spaces. In the Paradise Street development in the city centre, the developer plans to implement a private security program; if successful, the city may follow its example and, possibly, use private security throughout the city.

For "Poetic Justice", then, I decided to create a project in private space. I focused on a family. By making a project in private space, I pointed to the ongoing process of the privatisation of public space, but did not waste any energy criticising it. At the same time, I pointed to individuals – the people who make up a city. If public space thinks of citizens as a group, my project attempts to think of citizens as individuals.

My proposal was to build a temporary roof on top of a privately owned flat-roof house. I asked the Istanbul team to find a flat roof where a family planned to build another floor. I presumed that my project, though conceived as temporary, would most likely stay in place, and this eventually proved to be the case. Orton Akinci got back to me, saying that they had found a family in Kustepe, a suburb of Istanbul, who would be glad to get a temporary roof. I flew from Caracas to Istanbul. A construction worker showed us around. The roof was quite large. We decided to build a seventy-square-meter tin roof using metal construction. No plans were drawn up, and the construction was agreed on orally. The temporary intervention was approved by the city. During the Biennial, blue plastic curtains were chosen to encircle the space, and it all looked quite beautiful. A plastic table and chairs – a popular style that has seemingly been around forever, were placed there. I never saw the completed "Rooftop Room" in person, but Orton sent me pictures showing how the family had subsequently upgraded the area under the constructed roof earlier this year. And so the project did turn into something permanent. I was happy to see that the plastic table and chairs were still being used.

"Rooftop Room" touches on several issues. This was a public project in a private space. In creating it, I diverted money from art to life. The project was not centrally located – Kustepe is an outlying suburb of Istanbul. Surprisingly, Biennial organisers raised no questions either about the dislocation of the project or about the fact that a public project was being implemented in private space – visitors to the Biennial could not enter the site. By making a temporary project that became permanent, I pointed to the legitimacy of so-called temporary architecture, which is, I believe, the most permanent aspect of contemporary cities. There are a few details that I especially love about this work, such as the temporary curtain walls being replaced with permanent ones, and the fact that a private household was taking care of a public project.

Liverpool: Balcony with Wind Turbine

Balcony with Wind Turbine
2004, building materials and energy infrastructure
The 3rd Liverpool Biennial, Liverpool, Great Britain
In collaboration with Nova Stran, Studio for Architecture, Ljubljana
Balcony with Wind Turbine was installed on the fourteenth floor of the Bispham House towerblock. Originally part of the movement for social housing, towerblocks are today increasingly being pulled down. Of the seventy-two social-housing high-rises once in Liverpool, only twelve remain. With the dissolution of the social state, these remaining towerblocks are being privatised. While underscoring private space and wind-generated energy, the project improves living conditions for two families.

My Liverpool project developed at the same time as the Istanbul project; the difference was that I first made a research visit to Liverpool before making the proposal. The Biennial crew showed me around. Then, unexpectedly, I learned something that reminded me of the work I had done with the Caracas Case Project: Liverpool is a shrinking city. Both the Caracas Case Project and the Shrinking Cities Project examined the informal city, and although I knew that such towns as Detroit, Michigan, and cities in the former East Germany had declining populations, I was not aware that Liverpool and Manchester did, too. Caracas is a special case, since it comprises two forms,

once considered anomalies: a growing informal city and a shrinking formal city. But from my first-hand experience I could see that Liverpool and Caracas had many things in common, though in differing intensities, such as the privatisation of space, an almost absurd amount of personal security measures, the irrational treatment of space, and the collapse of large-scale systems (whether large industry or the public utilities) – the usual list of calamities that one cannot really talk about comfortably with socially hypersensitive people. Of course, Liverpool appeared to be a more balanced city than Caracas, but it was not necessarily less wild, in my view: next to London, Liverpool has the greatest number of security cameras per inhabitant in the world. But what I remember most from my Liverpool visit is this. Although widely considered to be mismanaged, Liverpool's misguided investments and radical formal attempts to solve its problems (including the continual resettlement of residents from low-rises to high-rises and back to low-rises and, my favourite, the transformation of a slum – the city's most densely populated area – into a park) have left the city with its eyes open and its body flexible to change. Social politics is another issue. I find it strange for people to be resettled three times simply for the sake of new approaches to housing issues and yet not to really have a say about it.

As late as the 1960s, Liverpool had a slum that could have been straight out of a Charles Dickens novel. There was even open sewage there. The slum was eventually razed and the area transformed into a park. The population was resettled into towerblocks in socially subsidised housing. I was told that residents used to throw garbage out of the windows – this was something I had seen first-hand in Caracas, too, in the social housing complex of Ventitres de Enero. Of Liverpool's seventy-two towerblocks, sixty were recently torn down, with the population being resettled in bungalows. Not that residents really appreciated the change. They had formed tightly knit communities in the towerblocks and felt uneasy about the security problems they faced in the new environment.

For my project, I focused on the Bispham House towerblock and its residents. My original proposal was to attach a bay window to an apartment in the high-rise and upgrade the architectural addition with a wind mill, which would provide energy for the apartment. I made my decisions based on the facts on the ground. In Liverpool, modernist architecture is generally disliked and has been abandoned without regret. I thought that an addition to the flat surface of the towerblock would not be an eyesore. As for the extension of the private space, I felt it was appropriate in a city that was preparing to transform a public park into a residential gated community with big gardens. One of most important points I wanted to make was that tenants do not have

to be resettled in order to improve their living conditions. The project hinted at what a small customised addition could do. The wind-mill was loaned by Windsave, the Glasgow-based company that developed the domestic wind unit. I imagined it would be inspiring for tenants to be independent of the municipal power grid, to be able to generate their own energy.

In the process of implementing the project, which lasted a year and a half, the bay window was transformed into a balcony. The change mirrored a new trend: balconies have suddenly become a desirable feature on residential buildings in Liverpool. As for bay windows, with which Liverpool abounds, I was reminded of the transformations they went through in contemporary Caracas. In this once-proud modernist city, bay windows used to display the interior of a home; now, they hide it. They serve to survey the outside territory from inside the house, just as in Liverpool and Manchester. I heard the tenants where we installed the "Balcony with Wind Turbine" are happy with the enlargement of their private space, as well as with the wind-generated energy, and want to keep the balcony, which offers a fantastic view of Liverpool.

Alan, the caretaker, has been volunteering to show people around who visit the towerblock.

Further reading

COHEN, Daniel (1998): *Riqueza del mundo, pobreza de las naciones,* Fondo de Cultura Económica, México D. F.
FAO (2004): *The State of Food Insecurity in the World.*
LEISERING, L.; WALKER, R. (1998): *The dynamics of modern society poverty, policy and welfare,* Bristol, Policy Press.
NGANGUÉ, E. (2003): *L'OCDE et la faim dans le monde,* Le Courrier ACP-UE.
UNDP (2004): *Human Development Report,* UNDP.
REISEN, M. van (2002): *Tackling poverty: a proposal for European Union aid reform,* Bond, London.
ROSS, E. (1998): *The Malthus factor population, poverty and politics in capitalist development,* London, Zed Books.
SACHS, Jeffrey (2005): Investing in Development: A Practical Plan to Achieve the Millennium Development Goals, UN Millennium Project, (Director), Earthscan: New York.
SEN, Amartya (1999): *Development as freedom,* Anchor Books, New York.
SEN, A. (1982): *Poverty and famines: an essay on entitlement and deprivation,* Oxford, New York, Clarendon Press.
WORLD BANK (2003): *Poverty Reduction Strategies,* World Bank, Washington.

Websites of interest

- ACP-EU Civil Society Information Network: http://acp-eu.euforic.org
- Poverty Reduction Strategies: http://www.ilo.org/public/english/comp/poverty/index.htm
- Poverty Erradication: http://www.undp.org/idep
- Millennium Development Programme: http://www.undp.org/mdg
- World Bank and Development Goals: http://www.developmentgoals.org
- UN and Millennium Goals: http://www.un.org/millenniumgoals
- Human Development Report 2004: http://hdr.undp.org/reports/global/2004

Human Development Index (HDI)

The HDI measures the average advance of a country, taking into account three basic dimensions of human development: a long and healthy life, the level of knowledge and a decent standard of living. As this is a compound index, the HDI is based on three variables: life expectancy at birth, educational advances (advance in the literacy of adults, the gross rate of the combined registration in primary, secondary and tertiary education) and the real GNP per capita in dollars.

Country (2003)	HDI average
Underdeveloped countries	0'663
Less advanced countries	0'446
Arab States	0'651
Western Asia and the Pacific	0'740
Southern Asia	0'584
Sub-Saharan Africa	0'465
Central and Eastern Europe and CIS	0'796
OECD	0'911

Human Poverty Index (HPI)

The HPI measures privation in relation to human development. While the HDI measures the general progress of a country towards human development, the HPI reflects the distribution of progress and measures the privation that still exists. The HPI deals with the developing countries (HPI-1) and the industrialised countries (HPI-2). There are 95 developing countries classified in the HPI-1: amongst these, Guinea-Bissau, Mauritania, Chad, Mozambique, Zambia, Zimbabwe, Ethiopia, Mali, Niger and Burkina Faso occupy the last ten positions. In the HPI-2, Belgium, Australia, the United Kingdom, Ireland and the United States appear at the bottom of the table.

Country (2003)	HDI
Norway	0'956
Sweden	0'946
Australia	0'946
Burkina Faso	0'302
Niger	0'292
Sierra Leone	0'273

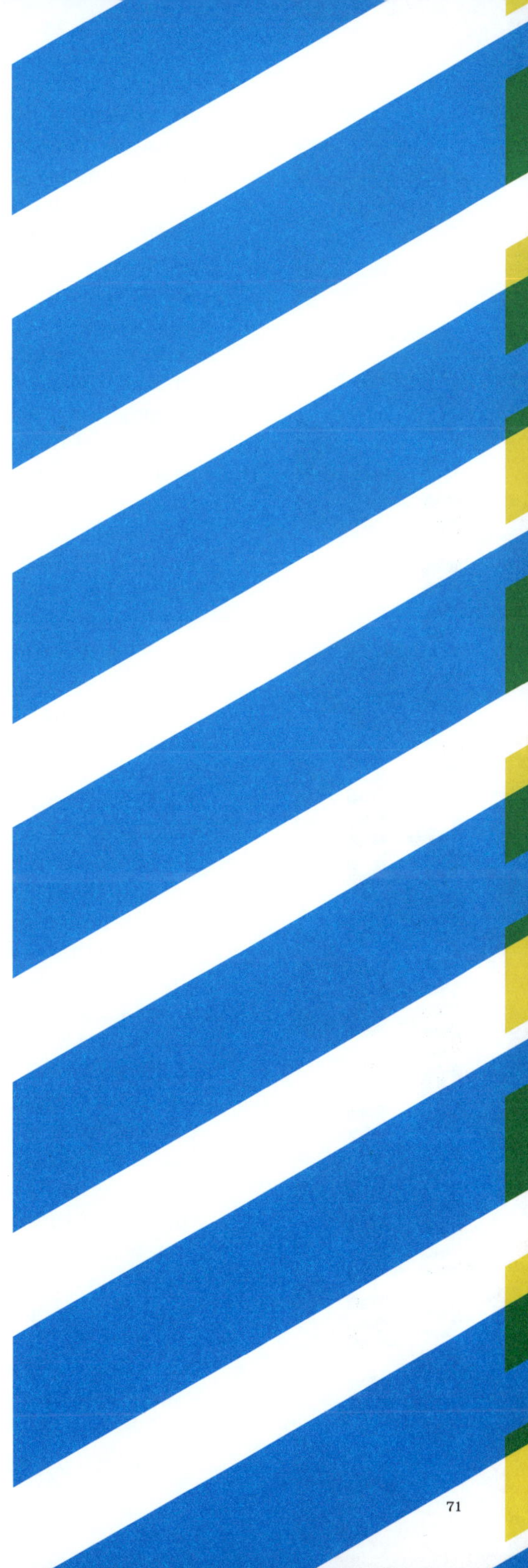

According to the overall public opinion, it seems to be taken for granted that demographics and population flow are synonymous with problems and conflicts. The reality, however, does not always coincide with this vision. It is enough to look at Japan, an overpopulated country if there ever was one, in order to observe that there is no particular immediate preoccupation in that country about the untenability of its model or the well-being of its habitants. The problems, in any case, could come from a population structure that shows evident symptoms of ageing (something that is occurring in Japan, but also in Spain and, in general, in Western Europe) given that in such a supposition, the replenishment of the population by new generations, which is a fundamental component in the maintenance of the welfare system that characterises developed countries, would not be guaranteed. In other situations, such as those facing the least advanced countries, the problem is not so much the number of inhabitants and the quantitative evolution, but instead the weakness of their economic structures or production, which translates into an economic growth that is inferior to population growth.

The situation, in general terms, is defined by the existence of countries which need new brainpower to maintain their systems, admitting that in the medium term, they will not be able to sustain the situation by counting only on their own citizens. Other countries, regardless if they are more or less populated, are not able to offer a dignified life to their habitants. This imbalance, insofar as human resources are still vital to the healthy development of current economic models, results in a permanent migratory flow. This reality responds not only to the never ending search for a more hopeful future for those who do not accept misery and exclusion as God-given destinies, but also, and that is something which is frequently forgotten, to the necessities of the more advanced countries to maintain their current living standards. In summary, they come not only because they aspire for something better, which has been denied to them in their countries of origin, but also because we need them.

To this dynamic of migratory flow – which is fundamentally explained by economic reasons, connected in any case to others of a social or cultural nature – it is necessary to add, in order to briefly complete the picture, other population movements which are forced, though for different circumstances. Natural catastrophes, armed conflict, organised violence, persecution for ethnic, religious, or cultural reasons are all factors that are behind the waves of refugees and displaced people which are increasingly formed in different parts of the world.

We are talking about, in terms of these three basic components, some 200 million people that, for one reason or another, live outside of their countries of origin. We are not, it should be stressed from the outset, living through the historical period of the most intense migration, not even in absolute terms. What should still resonate in our memory is the impressive displacement of 40 million European citizens towards the American continent between 1815 and 1914. In successive waves, they tried to flee from their miseries and the violence unleashed during different wars. Thinking more specifically about Spain, perhaps it would also be interesting, now that we have become a country that receives immigrants, to remember the solidarity that others demonstrated towards older generations of Spaniards when they were forced to leave the country as a consequence of the civil war or underdevelopment.

Concentration camps in the 21ˢᵗ century

In the Mediterranean area, there is a migratory pressure provoked by the enormous gulf of inequality which separates both shores and by the failure of some governments that, after more than 40 years of independence, have not been able to adequately provide for the basic needs of their growing populations. Already forgotten is the period in which it was the very politicians and economists of the EU who were worried about attracting these people. Today the prevailing attitude is to close the doors and only let in those who fit our economic necessities.

The reality demonstrates, tragically in many cases, the impossibility of erecting a fortress that can immunise us from the negative effects of underdevelopment and the instability that surrounds us. Although it is obvious that much of the responsibility for this situation lies with the governments of that region, on a level much closer to home, it can be verified that, for its part, the EU is designing its immigration policy in very restrictive terms to deal with a situation that foresees the arrival of one million immigrants and about 300,000 asylum seekers. One of the latest ideas to reinforce this line of thought is the proposal to set up, with community financing and the approval of the UNHCR, transit camps for migrants and those applying for asylum, that would be installed on the southern shore of the Mediterranean. Although it is true that this idea has created a very clear divergence of opinion between some member states, it is also necessary to say that in October 2004, the European Commission took on the responsibility of studying this idea, indicating that in no case can the issue be considered closed. With precedents of a similar kind, which set out to win the collaboration of our southern neighbours and convert them into the first and the most important obstacle to slow those trying to reach Europe (technical and financial assistance, training of their police forces, equipment...), this new proposal aims to take a definitive step forward, and one which cannot be ignored. With the eternal argument of its supposed effectiveness, a measure of this type involves many shady areas that are difficult to ignore. If these installations are put into place one day, they are destined to become prison camps, no matter how provisional this situation is supposed to be, and will be located in countries that are not precisely known for their scrupulous respect for human rights and democratic values.

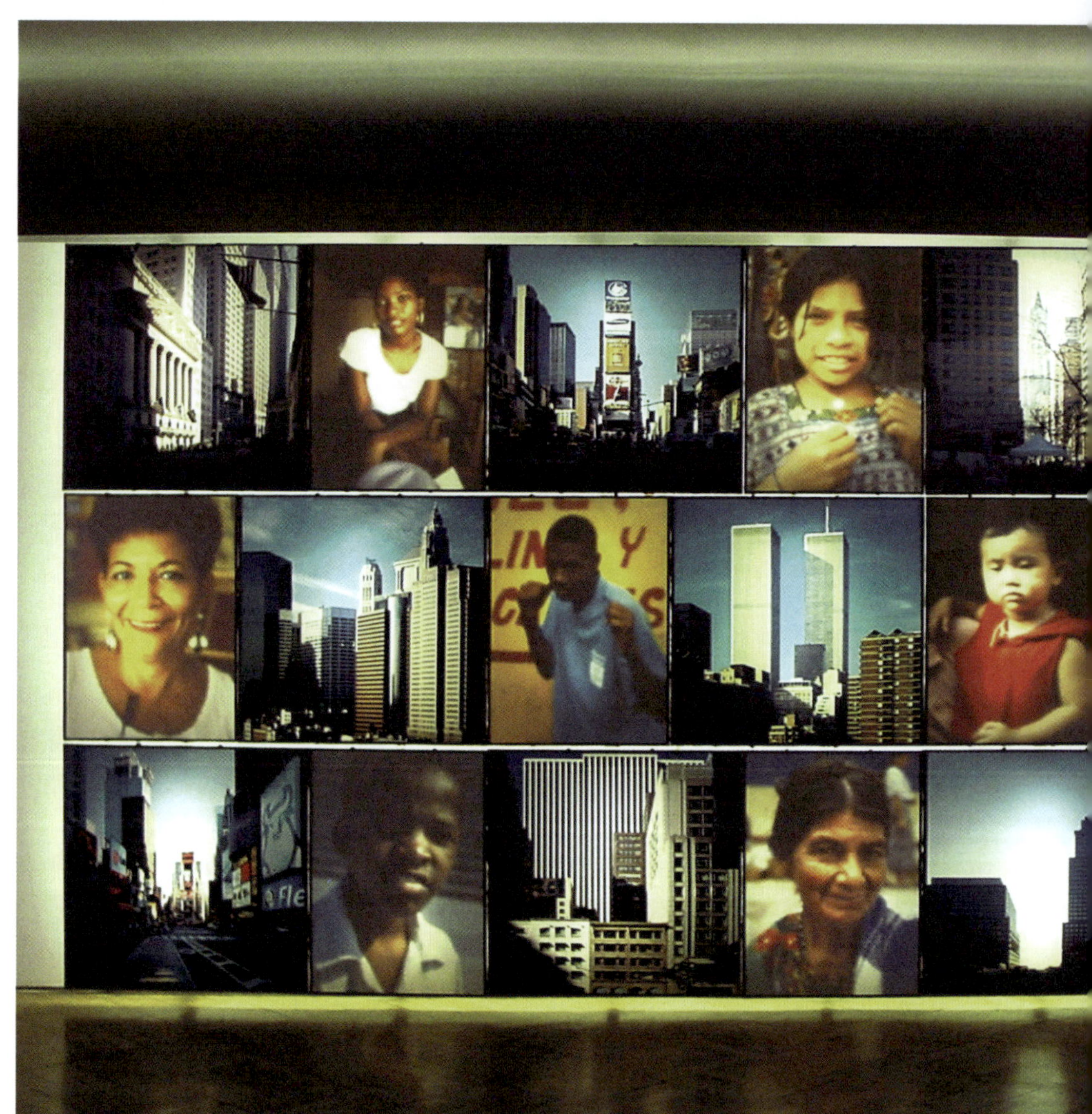

Ángel Marcos
Alrededor del sueño 15, 2001
Photographic installation consisting of
thirty light boxes (15 measuring 70 x 50 cm
each and 15 measuring 70 x 70 cm each)
Variable dimensions

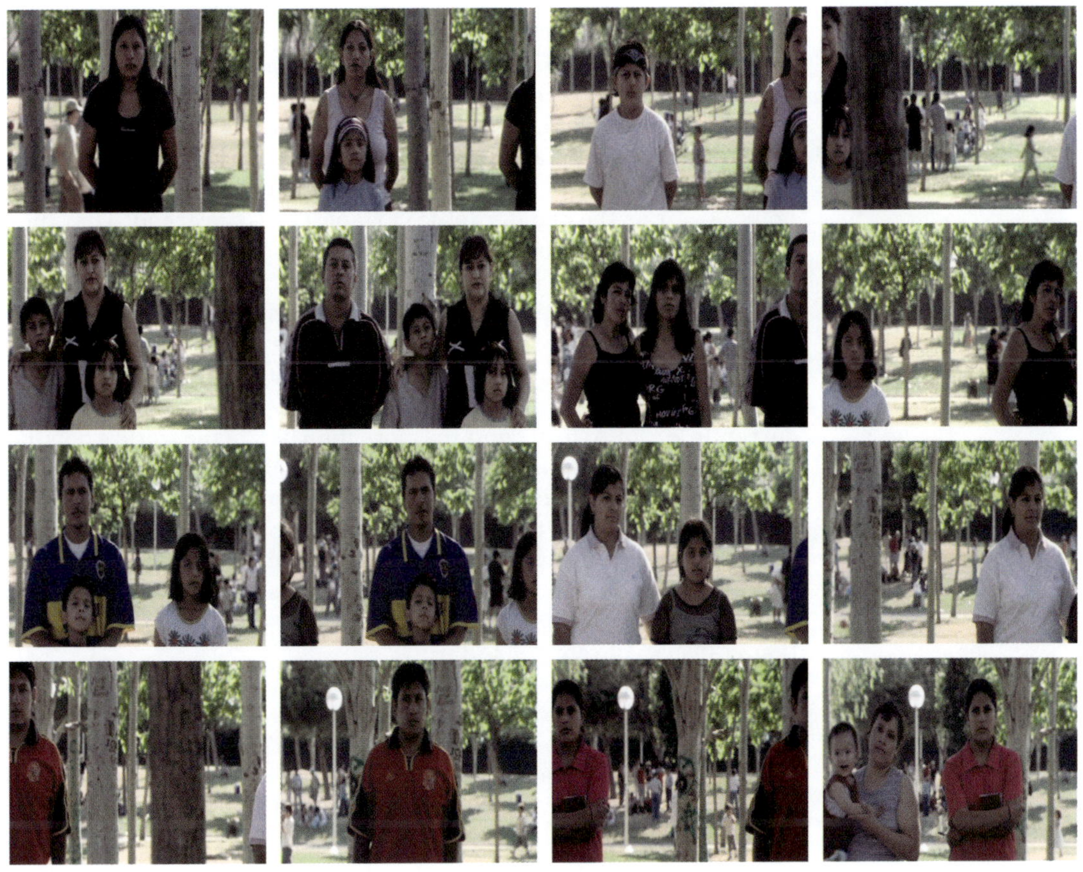

What we have before our eyes

In order to analyse the key aspects of this theme, there is no point resorting to wishful thinking that has no connection to harsh reality, but neither should we be alarmist, an attitude that only serves a xenophobic or exculpatory way of thinking. The reality shows data and forecasts that we should take into consideration as a starting point. As far as the demographic variables are concerned, what they indicate to us in essence is that:

• The world population has already surpassed 6.4 billion people, as a result of a rhythm of growth incomparable to any past era, being double that of 1950. Africa is the continent that has registered the biggest increase, growing from 220 million people in 1950 to 810 million currently. As for Asia, it contains more than half of the world's population, with China and India as authentic world demographic powers. Latin America is maintaining, also in this area, its characteristic dualism, considering that its spectacular growth is the result of the combination of a high fertility rate with a not much lower mortality rate. In general terms, the developed countries have suffered a strong decrease in population, from containing 31.6% of the world's population in 1950 to barely 17% today.

• Western Europe, to be exact, is the most glaring example of this process of reduction, considering that if in 1900, it contained 25% of the world's population, the current situation seems likely to lead to its having only 7% in 2050. At present, European fertility rates barely exceed 1% while the natural replacement rate, which would ensure the maintenance of the population, is set at 2.1 children per fertile woman. There are countries, such as Germany, Italy, or Spain, whose current population would already be less than five years ago, if it had not been for the continuing arrival of immigrants over the last few years. With these figures, to which can be added a strong decrease in the mortality rate, it should not surprise anyone that the image of Europe is that of a rapidly ageing continent.

• If we abide by the moderate scenario prefigured by the UN, it is predicted that the world population will reach 9.3 billion habitants by 2050, after first passing the 7.15 billion mark in 2015. The absolute average growth rate of the world's population is currently at 75 million people per year. These figures, quite different from what were used to at the end of the last decade, insinuate, despite appearances, that the demographic explosion has slowed down.

• The population distribution is not equitable all over the world. In truth, of the 150 million square kilometres of the planet's total surface area, only 0.8% is really inhabited, although it should be remembered that 60% of the total is, by definition, uninhabitable. A quick glance at the current world shows us that it is impossible to establish a direct relation of cause and effect between overpopulation and poverty.

There are very large countries which are barely populated, such as Australia, that are developed, together with others, such as Central Africa, where a low population density coincides with a high level of poverty. On the other hand, we can compare Holland, which is a small country with a high population density that enjoys a notable level of economic development, to Bangladesh, which is also very densely populated but very poor.

• The process of concentration into urban centres appears to be unstoppable, as indicated by the fact that 50% of the world's population already live in cities. Although the cities located in developed countries are not without problems, those in countries that are in the process of development are putting to the test the human capacity to create sustainable environments that are able to satisfy at least the basic needs of those who cannot find solutions in their places of origin.

As far as migratory flow is concerned, the basic characteristics of the phenomena indicate that:

• The history of humanity is also one of massive population movements. Without having to go back to our ancestors, and recognising that we live in a globalised world in which the unstoppable development of transportation and telecommunications systems enormously facilitates movement on any level, we should remember that the current picture of the planetary demographic structure is the result of the incessant flow of people. This is not so much in the South-North sense, as we tend to imagine, for even stronger is the movement in the South-South sense.

• What has varied, in any case, are the causes which provoke these movements. In the first place, one can talk about environmental causes, the result of ecological disasters or as a result of a very pronounced deterioration of the conditions that guarantee survival in the place of origin. Although initially it may seem that these factors should have been overcome by this stage in the history of mankind, they have returned to centre-stage in our days, as can be seen in the examples of diverse communities in Sub-Saharan Africa, the old Soviet Union, and the Amazon.

• Economic causes, for their part, are associated with the search for more and better opportunities to improve the level of personal well being. Included here are internal displacements – from the country to the city or from less sophisticated areas to others that are more developed, as well as external – in which the adventure implies trying to reach another country. During colonial times, these movements were normally in one direction only, carried out by citizens of each of the world powers, essentially Europeans who migrated from their country of origin to the colony in question. What was also very characteristic of those times was the permanent flow of European citizens, though also Chinese and people from other areas, attracted by the emergence of a centre of development as powerful as that of the United States. Later on, after the emergence of a good number of new independent countries, the direction of those same movements was reversed, with the old colonising countries needing workers from their ex-colonies to cover their production needs. In the current situation, both the United States and the European Union continue to be magnets for those seeking work, although the attitude of both is basically restrictive, very far from those days where they did their utmost to attract workers.

• Finally, political causes have traditionally been considered to be temporary or related to a certain historical time, resulting from specific situations, such as armed conflicts or political persecutions carried out by dictatorial regimes. After World War II and the re-settlement of millions of people displaced by the conflict, instruments specifically designed for these situations were developed, such as the right to asylum or the creation in 1950 of the United Nations High Commission for Refugees (UNHCR). These served as identity symbols for the most democratic governments and also as a demonstration of commitment from the international community towards those persecuted by totalitarian systems.

According to UNHCR's own figures – which situate Iran, Pakistan, and Germany as the countries which absorb the greatest number of refugees – we have gone from 17 million in the world in 1990 to 17.1 in 2003, having reached 27 million in 1995. What is detected is not a real decrease of conflicts or reasons that cause people to abandon their places of origin, but rather an increasing pressure on the part of the international community to prevent refugees from being transferred to other countries, which might in turn be destabilised in an undesirable domino effect. Apart from what the UNHCR tries to do with its limited resources - an annual budget of $1 billion, it is well known that the international community is loath to assume many of the responsibilities assigned to it under the International Agreement on the Status of Refugees (1951).

The displaced people are no less of a problem. They are obliged, just like refugees, to abandon their places of residence, but unlike them, do not have to leave their countries of residence. As a result, they are not even able to count on the same level of assistance and protection theoretically provided to refugees. The added difficulty in counting them only allows for a rough estimate of their numbers, with a total of 20-25 million people, with Sudan, the Democratic Republic of the Congo, and Colombia as the three countries with the largest displaced populations.

• Although the majority of refugees tend to return to their countries when the reasons that caused them to flee have disappeared, one can detect a growing current of asylum seekers in the host countries as a clear sign of their choice to prolong their stay. The principal receivers of these requests are Pakistan, Germany, Tanzania, and the United States. At the same time, the European Union is maintaining the tendency to more restrictive policies, which are inexorably pushing it further away from its traditional humanistic and hospitable attitude towards those suffering any kind of persecution. In 2003, there were 350,000 registered requests for asylum (only 5,770 in Spain, a country which is always reticent to admit them) in EU territory, the lowest number in these last ten years.

What keeps us occupied

If we look at the European Union (EU), what really seems to fundamentally occupy the attention of the authorities in modern times is very contaminated by their focusing on the 'war against terror'. We are witnessing a constant process of the curtailing of basic rights and liberties that affect the European Union's own citizens, especially those people that originally come from other countries. One can detect an increasing tendency to move away from the goal of integration in order to obsessively concentrate on security, which causes us to perceive all foreigners as suspects. With about 60 million immigrants residing in the territory of its 25 members, the European Union is determined to set up common border control systems, which involve not only the police but also the military, to fortify its frontiers. In this sense, a plan has already been approved to create the Border Management Agency, as have recent directives concerning asylum and family regrouping of immigrants as well as agreements with the immigrants' countries of origin to readmit their citizens, or other people who illegally entered the EU from their territories.

From a social point of view, what can also be seen is the habitual application of a reductive logic that tends to view those who arrive simply in terms of their role as workers. To quote the Swiss playwright Max Frisch 'we want workers, but what comes to us are people'. What is sought are mere instruments to be fitted into productive mechanisms, without any attention being paid to their needs as citizens or as simple human beings.

The discourse of a 'clash of civilisations', which presents Islam as a whole as an enemy to be defeated, casts a long shadow over the territory of the Union. From this perspective, which turns its back on a social reality that has already become multicultural, the temptation seems to have loomed up once again to rid ourselves of those that are different, to expel the 'others' from the European scene. In this line of thought, the biased confusion between immigrants and delinquents – and here we are not even talking about 'terrorists' – cannot augur well if, finally, it ends up being part of the collective discourse of European public opinion.

The model that is being applied to deal with the migratory theme treats the question as one of policing, with a very narrow point of view. Evidently, it is necessary to act decisively in the persecution of delinquents, both citizens and foreigners, especially those who traffic in people. However, these measures by themselves cannot cover the wide spectrum of actions that have to be part of a common EU policy on immigration. Any plan that is developed, in order to be effective, should also contemplate an effective integration policy covering all those who are already residing in the European Union. A common policy of migration management is also required, and one that includes a strong commitment to aid the governments of the countries from which immigrants come – in the form of action and not just words, as usually happens – to help accelerate the process of political and economic reforms that are so badly needed.

Immigrants in Belize

In the year 200, the United Nations Centre for Human Settlement and the Arias Foundation for Peace and Human Progress, with the collaboration of the International Research Centre for Development, promoted the project 'Support for the local processes of integration of the displaced migrant population in Central America and Colombia'.

One of its focal points was the analysis of the integration of Central American immigrants in Belize, the country in the region that, from 1983 onwards, had received the largest number of foreigners. By 1994 these people represented 20% of the national population. The impact of this process on the access to land or the sharing of resources ended up becoming a source of internal conflict between the native population and some immigrants who did not want to return to their countries of origin, claiming that Belize had more opportunities for development.

The deterioration of the situation – in a country that despite having accepted successive waves of immigration cannot be considered a model of multicultural tolerance – brought about the adoption of strategic plans and laws aimed at facilitating coexistence.

In 1996, the government approved a specific law for the immigrant population in Belize, 'aliens' as they are colloquially known, that granted residence permits to the wives of native Belize men (after being married for at least one year), to professionals who were specifically needed by the national economy, and to retired people who received pensions, dividends, etc., from other countries and wanted to live in Belize.

This new approach helped to substantially change the panorama. If until then, 50 to 60 irregular immigrants were expelled or deported every week, now the authorities are open to helping these people, granting them temporary or permanent residence permits and even work permits and nationality certificates. One of the most important initiatives to improve the situation was the 1999 amnesty that, with the help of financing from the UNHCR, allowed 20-25,000 people to regularise their situation.

In reality, it is not only the government of Belize that was involved in this successful process, with other international groups and agencies also providing backup and resources. The UNHCR, in addition to the support already mentioned, supplied legal assistance and protection during the entire process and promoted seminars and publicity campaigns that facilitated both the social acceptance on the part of the native population and the involvement of international organisations in the process.

In addition, the International Conference on Central American Refugees (a UN sponsored conference) contributed to bringing the immigrant population closer to the native society so they could be integrated more easily into Belize. The Rescue Committee and PRODERE (Development Programme for Displaced Persons, Refugees, and Returnees in Central America) also led projects dealing with the construction of infrastructures - drinking water supplies, bridges, hospitals – and support programmes for primary schools.

Local groups and agencies were also active. Aid for Progress, created to address the unsatisfied needs of the rural areas, served as support for the amnesty beneficiaries to help them receive either their temporary or permanent residence permits or else their nationality certificates. BIB (Breast is Best League), which helped women and children in the areas of nutrition, gave support to the immigrant population, as they had already been doing with the native population, through projects related to improving postnatal feeding, vegetable gardening, maternal nutrition, and childcare.

Finally, but without going through the entire list of all the local organisations involved in the project, the Cayo Centre of Development and Co-operation organised social integration programmes for the immigrant population and supported international projects.

What should worry us

Without renouncing the ultimate objective of the arrival of getting back to the time, not so long ago, in which the borders of countries did not limit the necessity or anxiety to seek out new worlds, the current situation demands thinking that is more pragmatic, but no less ambitious. It is worth mentioning, though only in an outline form, some of the basic points of this desirable orientation:

- As was commented on previously, we have to go after those who, for their own profit, take advantage of others' dire necessities in order to traffic with people. This is a task that requires international co-operation and this community framework offers a good opportunity to develop common lines of work among the distinct national authorities in co-ordination with their security forces and police.
- The full integration of those that already reside in EU territory has to be a central objective of any community policy on immigration worthy of its name. Following the practice spelled out in the own-initiative opinion adopted in 2002 by the EU Economic and Social Committee, on 'Immigration, integration, and the role of organised civil society', the greatest possible efforts should be made with the idea of turning into reality its maxim of 'equal rights, equal obligations'. If, as the UN asserts, when talking about demographic themes, the European Union needs to double its current number of immigrants in order to at least maintain its population level in 2050, this cannot be done with the discriminatory practices that are in place today.
- Full and real integration implies substantial reforms in the way that we do things. Services in education, health, housing, and citizens' participation cannot be excluded from this; on the contrary, specific steps have to be taken to accelerate the process of integrating the immigrant population.
- Integration is something very different from assimilation. It obliges one from the very start to abandon any trace of superiority, understanding that the 'other' contributes values and advantages to the host society. A common future cannot be constructed on the basis of acculturation and the systematic erasing of the identity symbols of those who arrive. It is important, therefore, to formulate a new concept of citizenship that implies both parties moving from their initial position in order to build something in common.
- The 'other' is not, by definition, a threat to the well being, the security, and the cultural identity of the host society. On the contrary, and looking only at this complex question from an economic viewpoint, that 'others' contribute directly to the enrichment of those who have admitted them.
- Neither can the answer be, under any circumstances, permissiveness with behaviour that goes against the legal framework that corresponds to a lawful State. In any case, it is important to under-

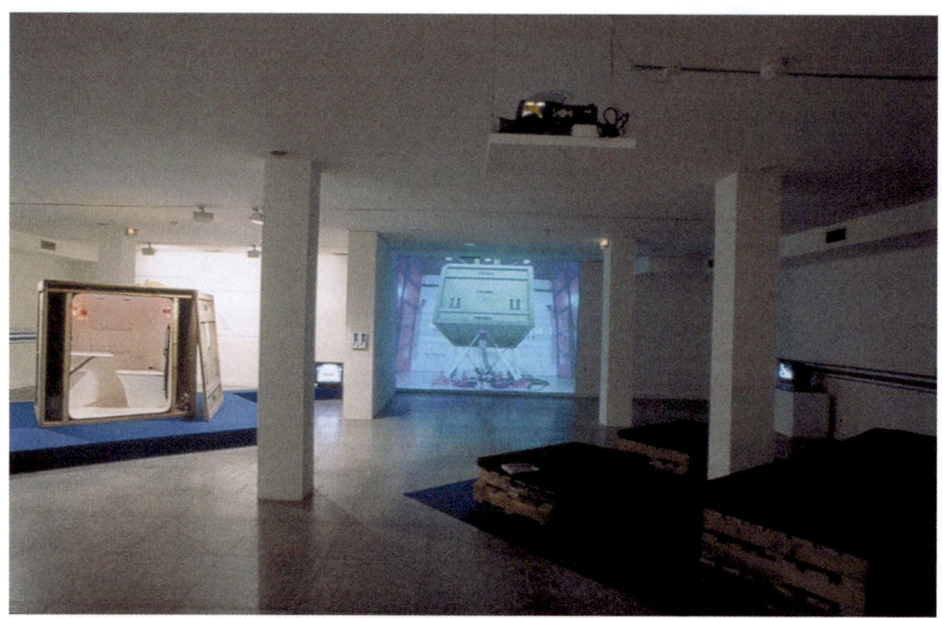

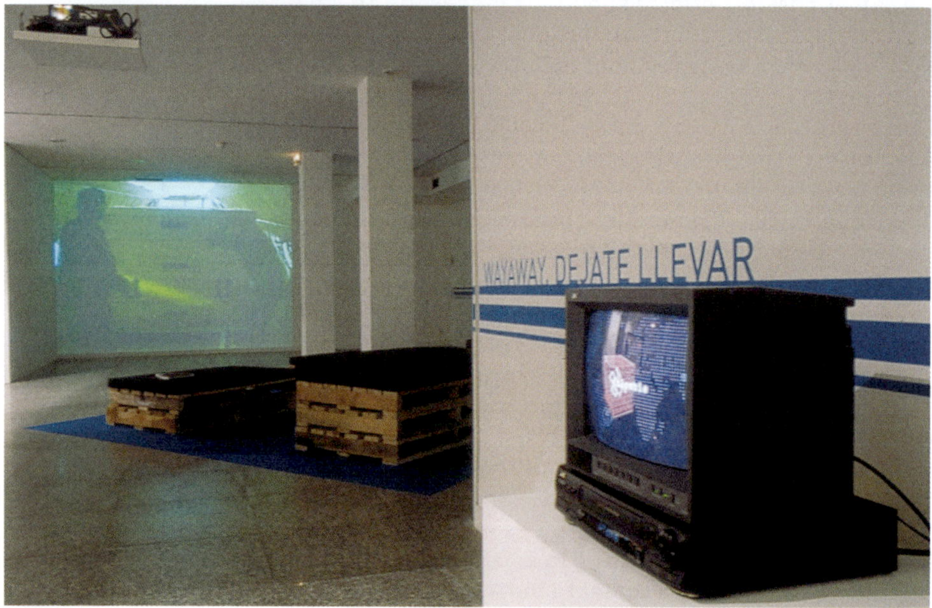

El Perro
Travelbox (Wayaway), 2000
Installation consisting of a wooden and
polyester cubicle (158 x 156 x 108 cm),
a video projection (DVD colour video with
sound, 4') and a monitor (DVD colour
video with sound, 4')
Variable dimensions

84

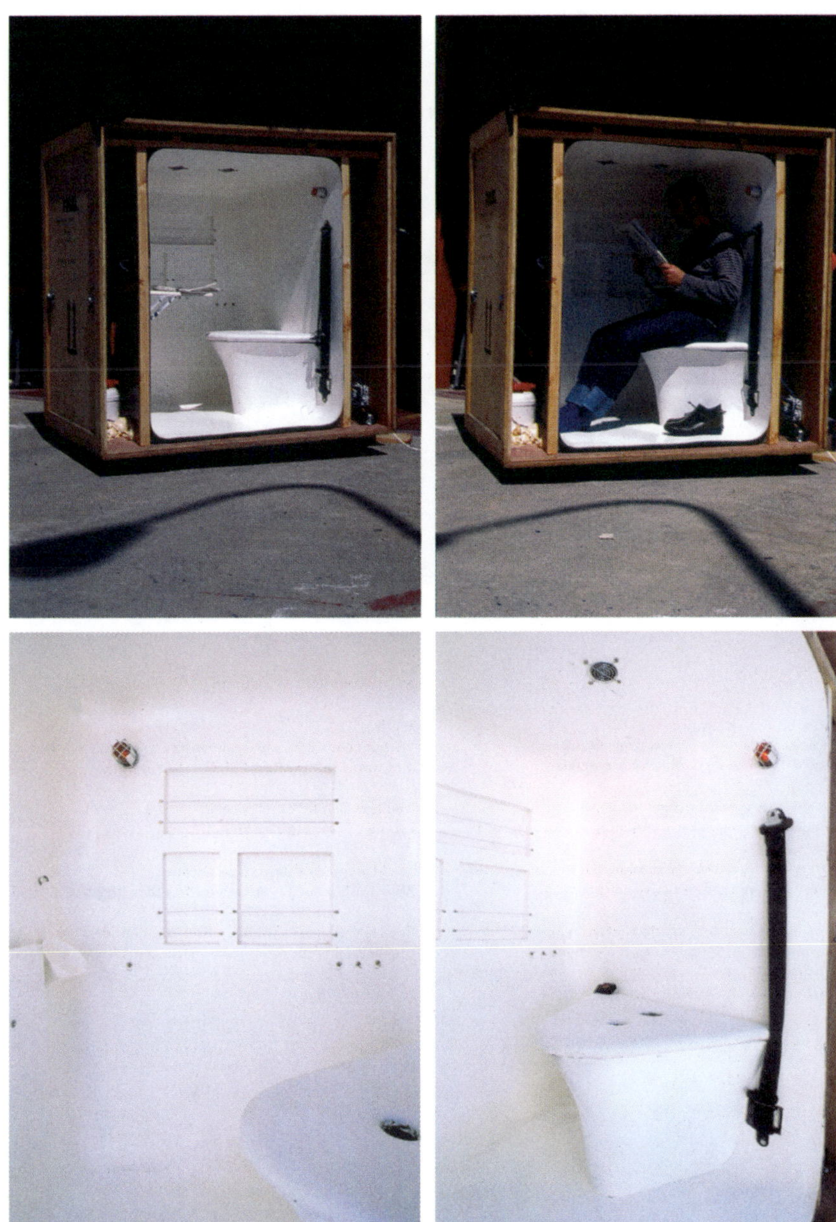

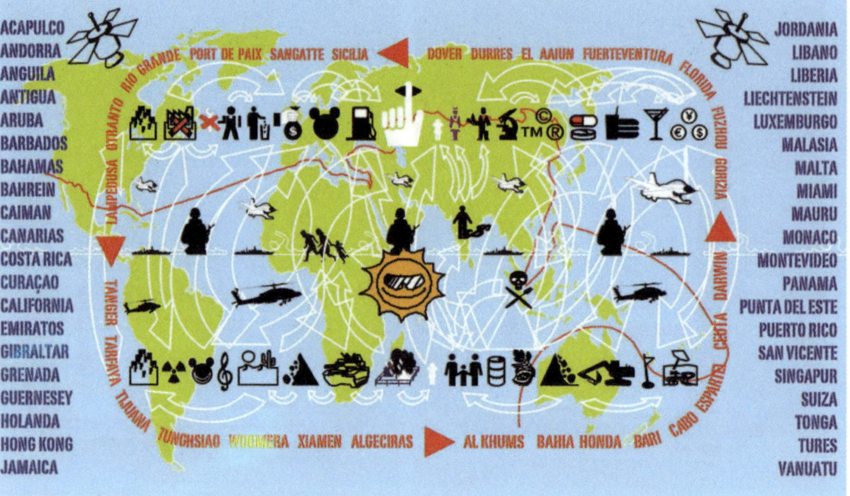

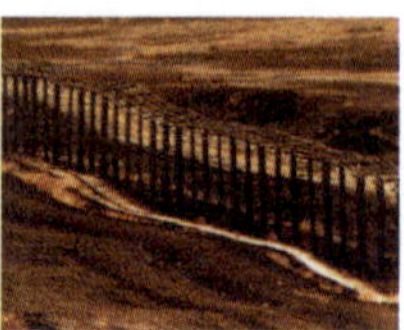

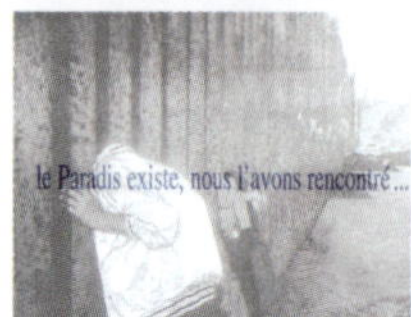

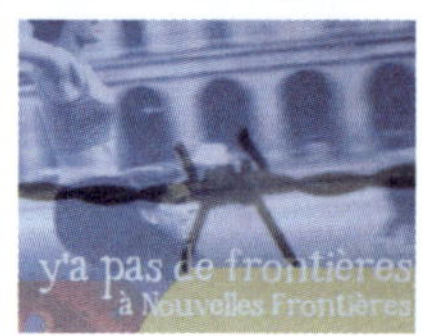

Τείχη

Χωρίς περίσκεψιν, χωρίς λύπην, χωρίς αιδώ
μεγάλα κ' υψηλά τριγύρω μου έκτισαν τείχη.

Και κάθομαι και απελπίζομαι τώρα εδώ.
Άλλο δεν σκέπτομαι: τον νουν μου τρώγει αυτή η τύχη·

διότι πράγματα πολλά έξω να κάμω είχον.
Α όταν έκτιζαν τα τείχη πώς να μην προσέξω.

Αλλά δεν άκουσα ποτέ κρότον κτιστών ή ήχον.
Ανεπαισθήτως μ' έκλεισαν από τον κόσμον έξω.

Κωνσταντίνος Π. Καβάφης (1896)

Walls

Without consideration, without pity, without shame
they have built great and high walls around me.

And now I sit here and despair.
I think of nothing else: this fate gnaws at my mind;

For I had many things to do outside.
Ah why did I not pay attention when they were building the walls.

But I never heard any noise or sound of builders.
Imperceptibly they shut me from the outside world.

K. Kavafis (1896)

Rogelio López Cuenca
ΤΕΙΧΗ, 2005
Installation consisting of injet print on
back-light canvas (300 x 500 cm) and
DVD colour video with sound (6' looped)
Variable dimensions

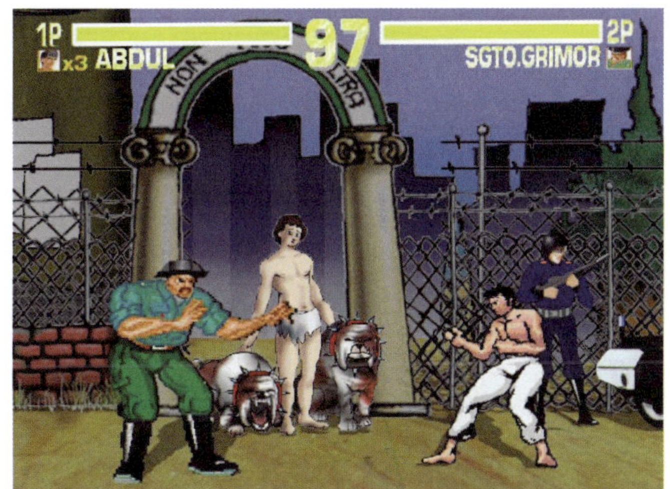

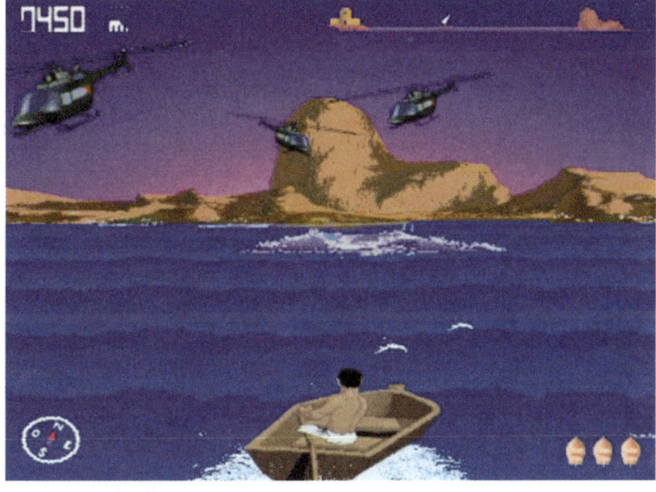

Valeriano López
Estrecho Adventure, 1996
Animation. DVD colour video with sound
6' 22"

stand that diversity and intercultural exchange can fit perfectly within this framework. As Mahatma Gandhi once said, 'I don't want my house to be closed off from all sides or the windows sealed. I would like all the cultures in the world to be able to come in contact with my house as freely as possible, but I refuse to be swept aside by any of them'.

• The United Nations Development Programme, in its 2004 reports about human development, largely dedicated to the issue of cultural freedom, indicates four principles that should guide the multiculturalism strategy in the context of globalisation: a) Do not confuse tradition with the personal liberty to choose. Promote the freedom of choice without tying it to patterns imposed from the outside. b) Understand diversity not as end in itself, but rather only as a means of offering distinct alternatives. c) Live as both a local and world citizen, with the possibility of developing multiple and complementary identities based on being citizens of a State, a community, a cultural group, or of the world. d) Deal with the asymmetries of power, and prevent some cultures dominating others because of their relative economic strength.

• The common management of migration is something else to consider. In the short term, some governments encourage their emigrants to leave because they are more interested in ridding themselves of the corresponding social obligation and benefiting from the remittances of money which are sent back. They do this without considering, perhaps, that these migrations can end up being harmful in the medium or long term. From that perspective, it seems that the control of those migrations is only worrisome for the host countries. In practice, and as has already been demonstrated – Spain could be a good example in this sense, it is possible and desirable to formulate common migration management mechanisms among governments that would prevent the influence of the mafias who end up taking advantage of the emigrants' needs.

• Finally, but probably most importantly from a strategic perspective, the policies concerning support for and development of those countries should be reviewed. If the gulfs separating us from our neighbours are only becoming wider, regardless of the responsibilities of their own governments, it is not difficult to imagine that there is something we are not doing well. The current situation obliges us to think about approaching those governments in a different way, understanding that their countries' development is our development as well. If it were true, something that does not appear to have been proven in practice, that we do not need the immigrants and that we do not want them to come, the best way for us to ensure that they stay in their countries of origin would be to help create the conditions of development which would permit them to live their lives without having to face the unknown. In theory, beyond the adventurous spirit of a few, most human beings prefer to stay close to their origins, if, in fact, they are able to construct a dignified life there.

It also depends on you

Population flow is a phenomenon, not a problem, which forms an inseparable part of our life on this planet. All of us are of mixed blood, products of the permanent interchange between different groups of people, until the point that we should be talking, in reality, about only one race: the human race. Instead of seeing this as an undesirable consequence or a curse, we should look at it as a permanent enrichment that allows us to become more adaptable and to continuously learn from others.

Instead of taking refuge in our privileged ivory towers, convinced that we represent the maximum expression of human development, we should admit that more and more, a big part of our well being depends on others. In a world of permanent communication, we cannot consider our models to be the definitive ones, nor that history will only evolve in the sense of increasing the number of countries that end up copying us. Evolution is the result of interaction, which obliges us to be open to new ideas and theories. The model we have understood as that of the nation-state is no longer relevant, as neither is the political representation of the idea of only one language, only one nation, and only one culture. It is up to us to be open to the development of a new model of social coexistence, established on the recognition of the legitimacy of all the groups that make up our society and based on the common respect for a framework constructed by all of us.

This process should also make us be careful with the language we are accustomed to employing on different occasions. To give some examples: How much time must pass before a person is no longer identified as an immigrant? How can it be explained that the denomination of 'illegal immigrants' is so widespread for people who should only be known as 'irregular' because that is their real situation? What is the nature of their supposed illegality?

While we are trying to answer these questions, perhaps it would be convenient to stop for a moment in order to consider that perhaps the problem is not that they come; the real problem would be if they did not come.

A document produced by researchers from the
Institute of Studies on Conflicts and Humanitarian Action (IECAH)
Madrid, January 2005

Multiplicity
Currents and Confines in City Europe: the Multiplicity research

1. Multitude

Urban Europe has grown enormously in the last few decades. Whilst immense untidy masses have grown up around the fringes of large cities, within their boundaries closely interwoven conurbations have developed replicating the industrial areas and the most dynamic zones. Unstable configurations, of uncertain profile, for just as with telluric phenomena, Europe is being reshaped by alterations made up of a myriad of small displacements, rather than great, homogenous currents.

The 'multitude', the exponential growth of the urban fabric and its progenitors, is the form that the *new* assumes in our everyday experience. We catch a faint glimpse of it when we pass through that dusting of small isolated or clustered buildings that make up the DNA of a city that is growing bigger and bigger, and sprawling over ever more territory.

But the 'new' does not only appear where the space dilates, on the outskirts, in the ever encroached on countryside. It flows and penetrates as well in the central areas and the quieter parts of the 19th century city.

It lays waste to the old mono-functional fortresses (the slaughterhouses, the fruit and vegetable markets, the large factories), it sub-divides the public space inundating it with a molecular and mobile commerce, it exaggerates the role of the interior spaces of the city (housing, exhibition halls, leisure centres) mixing them up and transforming them into television *sets*. The multitude rewrites and subdivides the closely punctuated European urban space, while simultaneously tracing a highly dense network of relations; relations at a distance, woven by the journeys of its citizens, increasingly mobile and yet always firmly rooted in the private space of the family. The multitude divides and unites at the same time, subdivides and extends, evincing a society in which the number of its subjects in a position to invest in space and create a refuge of their own has increased enormously. However, the multitude is not chaos. A glance downwards from a moderate altitude, from a small light aeroplane for example, would show us an archipelago of enclosed precincts, islands, straight lines, circles and rhizomes. Organisms that often function perfectly internally, but that are blithely unconcerned when it comes to conversing with their neighbours. A small number of spatial figures, inward looking and replicated *ad* 'infinitum', specialised as well as being hybrids: the super highway and its spurs, the manufacturing area and its enclosed precinct, the residential area with its detached houses and the sports centre, the market street with its shops and stalls, the shopping centre and its car park. The alterations that are rocking the European space are the sum of these sectorial rationalisations, which in turn condense the multitude of private stirrings that move the European city. An archipelago of decisive subsystems, with the players engaging in a *horizontal* competition that only a distracted observer could continue to view as hierarchical and pyramidal. In fact, ports, airports, stations, industrial areas, leisure zones, protected residential areas and theme parks are the key players in a single game; each with its own reasons and its idiosyncrasies, each with its own dreams of privatising its territory. A 'polyarchic' society has finally constructed a territory in its own image and likeness, a territory from which emerges, after an initial appearance of chaos, an excess of equivalent norms. But the European urban archipelago is not simply a sum of enclosed precincts. The fragmentation of the built-up area, the compression of the activities and the speed of displacements combined with the persistence of people's strong sense of belonging to their places of residence, have transformed Europe into the cradle of new experiences of urban life. Fluid spaces and 'self-organised' places are continually being created, growing out of the pragmatic imagination of the users – created to facilitate the experiencing of new and surprising associations. To the extent that today the most innovative European architecture is perhaps no longer that based on the work that appears in the journals. It does not arise out of public policy decisions with respect to the territory or the grand urban projects, but rather from the twists and turns of everyday life. It is an architecture born in the moveable shacks in Belgrade; in the subversive idea of a Parisian billiards player being of Asian origin; in the domestic-productive capsules in Elche; in the mobile phone-calls of a collective life lit up by the 'rave-parties': in the hi-tech 'gardens' that are scattered throughout the Alpine regions; in that divided and yet shared landscape reflected in the Tunisian community of Mazara del Vallo and the Sicilian community in Tunis, to cite just a few examples that the investigation USE ('Uncertain States of Europe'), promoted by Multiplicity, has begun to select. Europe, rather than being a continent, is a cultural entity; an entity that has constituted its own specific space, independently of its changing geo-political limits, characterised by the sedimentation of density and the metabolising of exogenous ways of living. This same urban Europe that, in other times, invented and exported new spatial concepts (in turn imitated by other worlds) such as the patio, the block and the neighbourhood, today finds itself taking stock of an explosion of self-organised local arrangements, which are not merely 'spontaneous', throughout its territory. Innovative, but not always virtuous. Invisible, since they are not promoted by architects nor discussed by critics. If we truly wish to restore a social utility to our professions, we will have to turn our gaze more often towards these places that are rich in energy and difficult to govern, instead of focusing on those projects lauded by 'high' architecture.

2. Currents and Confines

The space, the physical space that we tread, that we inhabit, that we traverse when we move, seems to have become something 'flat' for many of those who interpret the contemporary world. A flat, horizontal support across which glide the warm currents that globalise the economy and information, where extensive virtual networks of communication are freely available to all, a space traversed by the increasingly intense dominant currents of goods, people and ideas.

For many thinkers, starting with the Spaniard Manuel Castells, author of an important essay on the diffusion of the Network, the contemporary world can be interpreted and understood above all from this angle. The same perspective as that found in the idea – expressed by the Dutch sociologist Saskia Sassen – that few 'global cities' have the weight to alter the direction of the currents in a planet that is almost completely interconnected. Or those who read in the fluidity of trans-national relations and the weakness of the 'vertical' institutions (that is, those that are rooted in a single place, in a single history and in a single community), the incessant emergence of a 'liquid' modernity, as in the writings of the Polish sociologist Zygmunt Bauman. However, an important aspect of the physiognomy of that which is contemporary seems to defy these suggestive interpretations. In truth, it seems that the space that surrounds us, not only the geopolitical space of international relations, but also that circumscribed in everyday life, is increasingly grooved, corrugated by confines. Reduced by walls, enclosed precincts, thresholds, obstacles, limits, control and surveillance systems, virtual borders, specialist areas, protected zones, surveillance corridors. Nowadays moving, taking yourself from one airport to another or from one street to another, means facing and defying a growing number of systems of control, passing though a proliferation of confines.

Rather than being flat, space – at least in this part of the world – seems to have become a dense agglomerate of subsystems that corrugate the territory, reasserting local identities (those of the dominant social,

cultural, ethnic and religious groupings). Instead of flowing freely,
our movements increasingly come to
resemble a series of pulses and pauses,
a 'stop and go' sequence, a ballet of
'passwords' and identification documents. And though the proliferation
of confines might be interpreted as
a reaction to the fluid movement of
bodies and images, as a response to
the multiplying of the possibilities of
relating, as a defence of old identities,
we should surely ask ourselves if this
is not precisely the key, as yet almost
completely ignored, to understanding
the contemporary world. As if it were
the confines, and not the currents,
that were its true 'hallmark'.
However, as the investigation "Bor-
der-device(s)" has observed, the confines are not only walls; they are not
only lines.
Along the whole of the Mediterranean
coastline there are confines that act as
'funnels': facing the sea they direct,
order and channel towards the coast
disorganised currents of people, goods
and memories. Elsewhere there are
confines that resemble 'tubes'; cylindri-
cal and impenetrable like the elevated
roads that connect, passing above the
rooftops of the Palestinian villages,
the Israeli settlements in the 'Occupied
Territories' of the West Bank.
But there are also confines that arise
out of abandoned spaces – the 'no
man's land' of the film by Danis
Tanovic, or the deserted strip that
separates the two sides of the wall that
divides Nicosia where the space is an
'inlet', a pleat between two protected
territories. On the other hand, there
are confines that resemble 'sponges',
that unexpectedly absorb both populations waiting for change and stable
settlements of 'commuters'; parasitic
passers-by who, as between the Ben-
elux countries or along the borders
with the countries of Eastern Europe,
shuttle incessantly across the frontiers
in search of advantages (financial,
commercial or in terms of leisure).
And often these singular linear cities,
where the confine becomes longer
and 'charged', are nothing more than
a memory of old militarised confines
that continue in operation even after
losing the dignity of being marked by
Walls – just like when the brain insists
on perceiving a 'phantom limb' even
though it no longer exists. Europe,
starting precisely with Germany,
is today divided into fractions by
many of these limits which are invisible yet still discriminating.
But above all, above everything
else, there are confines that delimit
'precincts': precincts of cement or
barbed wire, like the camps that hold
those seeking to flee; immaterial
precincts controlled by closed circuit
TV cameras and light sensitive cells
like those that watch over the offices
of the banks; stable long-established
precincts and mobile precincts,
unpredictable like the areas under
military control that the Colombian
guerrilla groups shift around the
country on a daily basis.
In short, then, we should stop thinking, once and for all, of today's confines, more controversial and conflictive than ever, as being simply long
walls peppered by control towers and
'check points'. If we looked around us
and began to observe closely the varie-
gated multitude of confines that divide
and enfold our everyday life, that
fragment and destroy entire areas of
our planet, perhaps we would come to
understand that confines, apart from
being magnificent detectors of indices,
are extraordinarily responsive sen-
sors capturing the movements of the
contemporary world, the dynamic and
three-dimensional forces that palpitate
and strengthen the energy and resistance that accompany – for good and
naturally for ill – present day history.

3. Multiplicity

3.1
Multiplicity is a research agency that
investigates the nature of the urban
condition. An interdisciplinary approach, the *a priori* choice, that takes
the form of investigating the visions of
diverse observers, sociologists, artists,
architects, filmmakers, photographers
and geographers, all focused on the

same phenomenological field: the urban space.

3.2.

The starting point of Multiplicity is the idea that local urban space is today an authentic and appropriate metaphor for the society as a whole – a rich rag-bag of indicators of contemporary life that deserves to be carefully observed, even by those who are not interested in architecture, town planning or geography.

That which the Multiplicity researchers observe and investigate, like 'detectives' hunting out innovation, is in fact the local 'space' understood in an anthropological rather than an architectural sense: space as a mesh of various levels of reality.

3.3.

Multiplicity is interested above all in those areas of reality where innovative phenomena are produced. In reality, it is in the innovation, in the creation of new urban landscapes where we most clearly note the existence of this mesh – though we might also talk of continual tension – of aspirations, interests, inherited spaces, traditional forms of living, that we call urban 'space'. And that which is 'new', the innovation that, although virtual, immaterial, will inevitably have to pass through the 'eye of the needle' that is the local physical space.

3.4

It is often the run-of-the-mill stories in the newspapers or on the TV news, rather than in the specialist journals, that alert us to the places where something new is happening. Multiplicity searches out that which is new where it is actually taking place; in those portions of inhabited space – in areas of interaction and in isolated areas, in the domestic realm, in work and leisure places, in those spaces dedicated to the looking after of the self and in the channels of currents – there where the anthropological space is spawning a fertile resistance, criss-crossed by social energies and throwing up new configurations. In fact, that which is 'new' often arises where we are least expecting it, for these are places that we are not used to observing.

3.5.

But in order to do this, to gather and work with the spatial indicators of new social relations, which constitute the raw material of Multiplicity's research, it is necessary to use analytical techniques and forms of representation that are, in part, completely new, and in every case very heterogeneous. It is necessary to turn the local space upside down and use other 'ways of looking', creating in this way 'eclectic' atlases that are capable of mapping the new relations, of distinguishing them from the things, words and symbolic images we project onto them. It is precisely thanks to the sum of these ways of looking at a single phenomenological field and the eclectic nature of the observations that derive from them, that Multiplicity is able to carry out its investigation into the field of the urban condition.

3.6.

Multiplicity is thus an indicative project, one which argues for a radically different way of looking, a way that recognises that the physical world and the local space are the principal area in which economic, social and cultural phenomena are made manifest. Not because these phenomena occur in the physical territory sooner than in the other spheres of that which is real, just the opposite: the energies that determine them are essentially slow-acting. The difficulty is not so much the local physical space, but rather the place where these processes become decipherable and comparable.

In reality, space changes more slowly than living habits and therefore a divergence is produced. And it is in this divergence where the signs and indications of new life-styles are to be found. It is this divergence that we have to learn to decipher. Like 'detectives' of space.

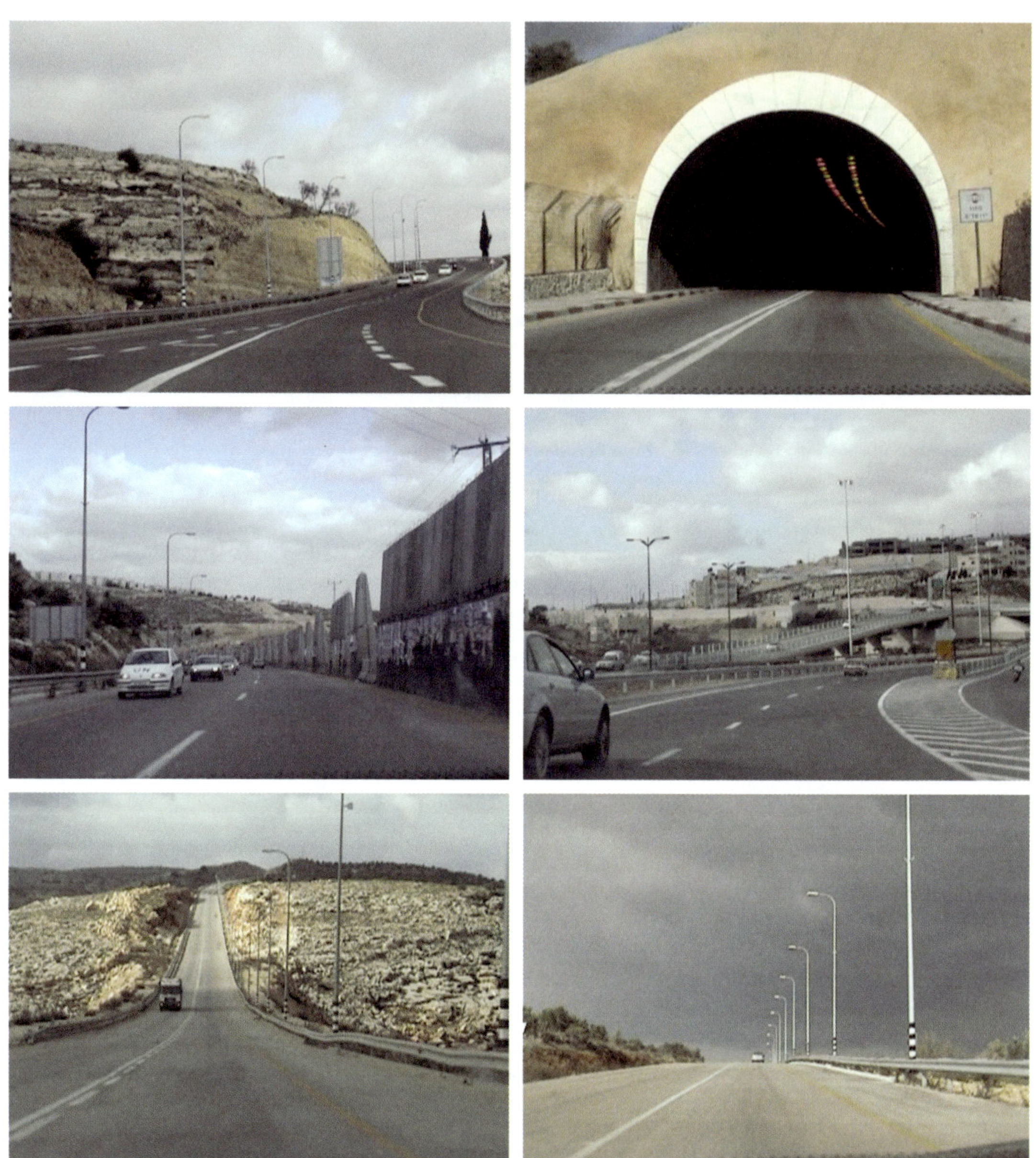

Multiplicity
The Road Map, 2003
Video installation consisting of two
projections (DVD colour video with
sound, 29' looped) and four monitors
Variable dimensions

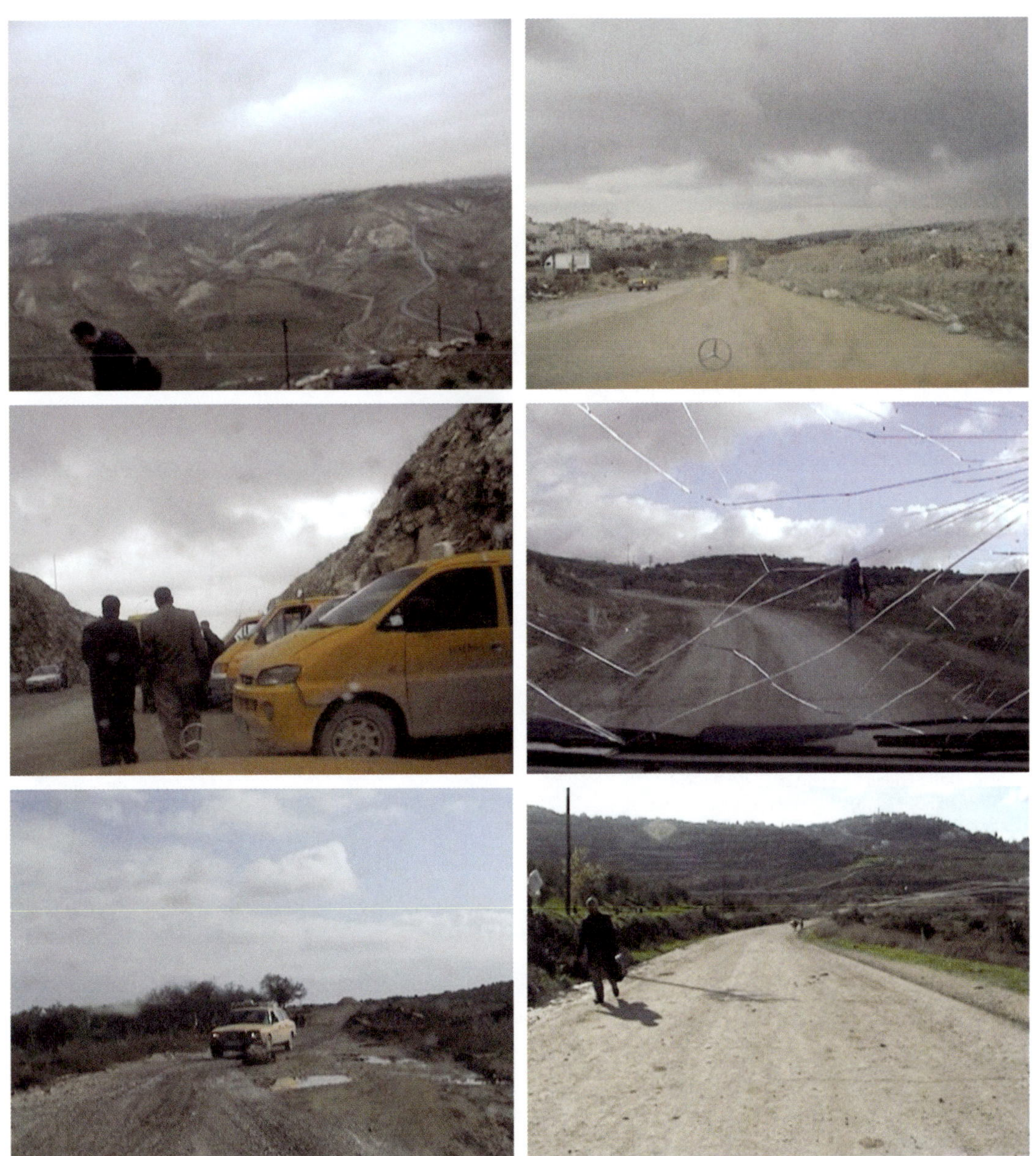

Further reading

UNHCR (2004): *The State of the World's Refugees. Fifty years of Humanitarian Action,* UNHCR, Oxford University Press.
ARANGO, J., SANDELL, R. (2004): *Inmigración: prioridades para una nueva política española,* Real Instituto Elcano/I. U. Ortega y Gasset, Madrid.
BUSTAMANTE J.A. (2002): *Soberanía, Migración Internacional y Derechos Humanos: Migración internacional y Derechos Humanos,* Mexico, Universidad Nacional Autónoma de México.
COHEN, R., DENG, F. (1998): *Masses in Flight: The Global Crisis in Internal Displacement,* Washington, D.C., Brookings Institution Press.
FISAS, V. (1994): *Las migraciones: El olvido de nuestra historia,* Zaragoza, Seminario de investigación para la paz.
UNFPA (2004): *The State of the World Population 2004,* UNFPA.
GEORGE, Susan (2002): *The Lugano Report,* Pluto.
GIL, S.; DAHIRI, M. (eds.) (2003): *Movimientos migratorios en el Mediterráneo Occidental, ¿un fenómeno o un problema?,* Ayuntamiento de Córdoba.
IZQUIERDO, Antonio (2003): *Inmigración: mercado de trabajo y protección social en España,* Consejo Económico y Social, Madrid.
LUCAS, Javier de (2002): *Blade Runner. El derecho, guardián de la diferencia,* Tirant lo Blanch.
MARTINELLO, M. (2003): *La Europa de las migraciones. Por una política preactiva de la inmigración,* Bellaterra, Barcelona.
SIPRI-UNESCO Handbook, (1998): *Peace, Security and Conflict Prevention,* New York, Oxford University Press.
VVAA (1992): *Migración, racismo, Xenofobia. El otro yo,* Madrid, Universidad Complutense de Madrid.
WOODHAMS, S. (2003): *Migrants and Minorities,* London, Rivers Oram.

Websites of interest

- European Research Centre on Migration and Ethic Relations: http://www.uu.nl/uupublish/onderzoek/onderzoekcentra/ercomer/24638main.html
- United Nations Population Fund: http://www.unfpa.org/index.htm
- International Organization for Migration: http://www.iom.int
- Center for Migration Studies: http://cmsny.org
- Instituto Univ. de Estudios sobre Migraciones (U. Pontificia Comillas, Madrid): http://www3.upco.es/pagnew/iem
- CIDOB: http://www.cidob.es
- IMSERSO: http://www.imsersomigracion.upco.es/

	Population (millions of inhabitants)	Area (km²)	Density (hab./km²)
Africa	812,6	30.500.000	26
Anglo-Saxon America	317,1	19.500.000	15,6
Latin America	526,5	22.500.000	22,2
Asia	3720,7	44.000.000	81,5
Europe	726,4	10.000.000	73
Oceanía	30,9	9.000.000	3,3

Countries which have more than 500,000 refugees
Iran (1.8 million), Pakistan (1.2 million), Germany
(975,500), Tanzania (622,200), United States (513,000),
Guinea (501,500), ex Yugoslavia (500,700).

Origins of the top ten refugee populations*
Afghanistan (2.6 million), Iraq (572,100), Burundi
(524,400), Sierra Leone (487,200), Sudan (467,700),
Somalia (451,500), Bosnia and Herzegovina (382,900),
Angola (350,700), Eritrea (345,600), Croatia (340,300).
*In addition, around 3.5 million Palestinian refugees
arrived in the Middle East under the mandate of the UN
Agency responsible for Palestinian refugees. (UNRWA)

Sample of countries according to the percentage of their immigrant population (2000)	Percentage
United Arab Emirates	68
Kuwait	49
Jordan	39
Israel	37
Luxembourg	37
Singapore	34
Oman	26
Switzerland	25
Australia	25
Saudi Arabia	24
New Zealand	22

Source: UN, 2003

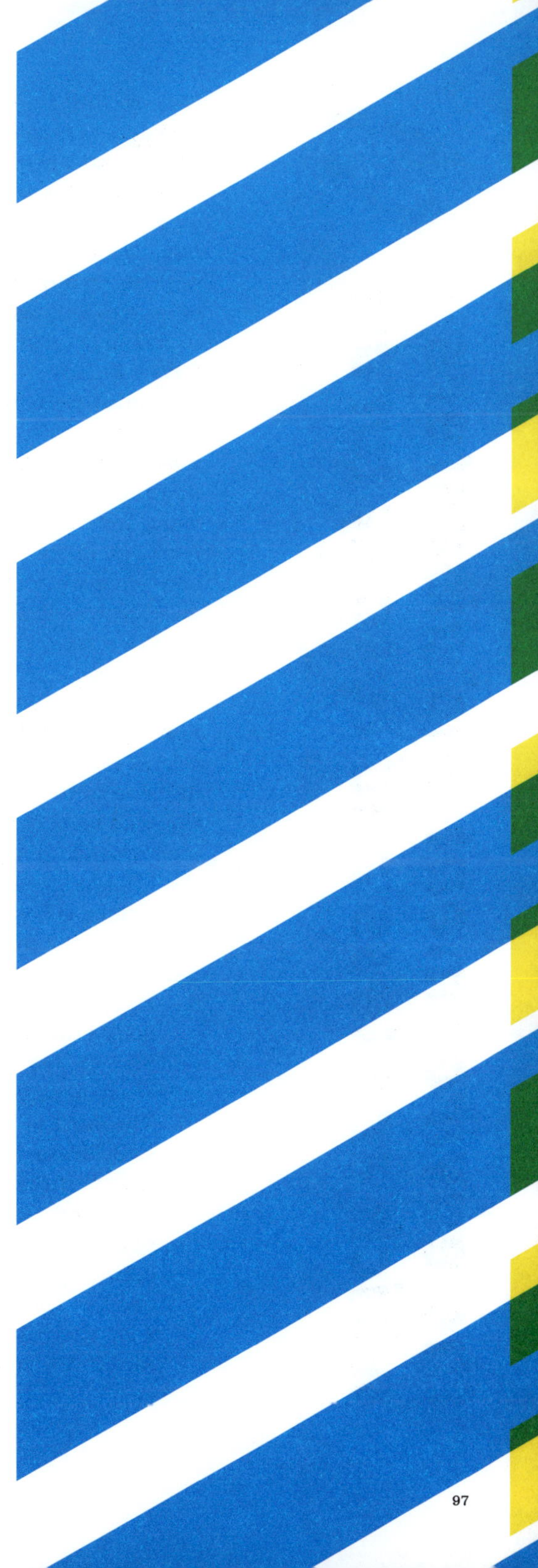

Nature and human society interact constantly and dynamically. The constant manipulating of nature by us humans is an attempt to satisfy our needs and, in the opposite direction, nature responds to those acts. For too long, we have convinced ourselves that we are the owners of the planet (using arguments whose roots can even be found in religion) and, therefore, we have the right to exploit its assets according to our own, and only our own, desires. In addition, we have chosen to believe that those assets are, by definition, inexhaustible or, in the very least, renewable in such a way that nature would always have the capacity to absorb the impact of our actions and re-establish an equilibrium, which could then be upset on occasions.

It must be this complacent vision of the environment that we have absorbed over the last few millennia, together our tendency to look no further than the short term, which allows us to accept, without worrying too much, the news that we receive about the serious deterioration of the environment, climatic change included, and about the consequences of 'natural' disasters, which are not in fact, as natural as we would like to believe. Behaving in this way means closing our eyes to a self-evident reality:

• Between 1980 and 2000, those disasters caused more than 1.5 billion deaths. Without taking into account the tragic outcome of the recent tsunami in Southeast Asia, on average 184 people die every day due to these causes. To give an example, the UNDP emphasises the high level of vulnerability and human loss associated with three phenomena: tropical cyclones, earthquakes and floods:

– Tropical Cyclones: 119 million people are exposed to them. It is estimated that 251,384 people died as a result of cyclones between 1980 and 2000. 60% of the victims during this time have been in Bangladesh, while Honduras and Nicaragua are also particularly vulnerable.
– Floods: 196 million people are exposed to this natural phenomenon. Around 170,010 died as a result of floods in the same period. The most vulnerable countries are Pakistan, India, Bangladesh, and China.
– Earthquakes: The macabre death toll reached 158,551 between 1980 and 2000 and that around 130 million people are directly exposed to their effects. Iran heads the list of most vulnerable countries as confirmed once again by the tragedy of Bam in December 2003, followed by Japan, Indonesia, and the Philippines. Also the USA, Chile, and Mexico, in America, as well as Turkey and India, in Asia, are high up on the list.

• If these are the most graphic and noteworthy statistics because of the human lives involved, no less important is the hidden effect of the notable loss of biodiversity. The recent Biodiversity Conference (Paris, January 2005), sponsored by the French president and organised by UNESCO, sounded the alarm once again about the processes leading to the extinction of live species, comparable to, they tell us, the disappearance of the dinosaurs 60 million years ago. Given this, it does not seem as if the 188 countries that signed the Biodiversity Agreement in 1992 have mobilised efficiently to react the situation. Not even has a determined attempt been made to find out more about what actually exists, for it is estimated that we only have 1.8 million species catalogued out of a total thought to be between 10 and 30 million.

• Although some officials, as powerful as the current United States administration, persist in denying its very existence, sufficient evidence has been accumulated to indicate that the planet is experiencing a climatic change. The full consequences of this remain unknown, though some of the results can already be seen. The frequent climatic alterations, which are significantly affecting normal rainfall patterns in many parts of the Earth, the gradual rise in temperatures with the consequent melting of the polar icecaps, the increase in levels of atmospheric pollution are all clear indicators that things are not going very well.

• In quite a few cases, the task of identifying the cause of the tragedy produced is resolved rather quickly by taking a simple look around. We are not talking here about either Divine Providence seeking to make humanity see its irrelevancy, nor an act of revenge on the part of the gods. Plainly and simply, what we are dealing with here are the results of rational(?) deeds by men and women who constantly demonstrate their foolishness by putting in motion processes which they either do not know how to, or simply can not control. The most elementary principles of precaution get pushed aside on too many occasions under the pressure of commercial interests or because of just plain selfishness.

• Natural disasters and underdevelopment are very directly connected. To confirm this, it is enough to analyse the effects, on both human beings and infrastructures, of the earthquakes in Turkey and Iran, on the one hand, with those in Japan and the United States, on the other. Corruption and poor urban planning combine with important levels of exclusion and rejection that leave the very poorest to confront these problems alone.

• However, the effects of natural disasters are no respecters of the frontiers between more developed countries and less developed ones. Recent well-known examples might include the dramatic consequences of the floods in 2002 in various countries in Central Europe, or the heat-wave which affected France and other countries, leaving more than 20,000 people dead and economic losses, basically in agriculture, estimated to be more than €8.2 billion. At the same time, the flooding of the Yangtse and Huai rivers in China and the tornadoes and forest fires in the United States and Canada are only a few more examples, from that same year, of the indiscriminate nature of those 'natural' disasters. At the same time, and although they rarely receive the same amount of publicity, various chronic and seasonal disasters in many parts of the Third World were carrying out their quiet but highly efficient work of destruction.

• In the UN Conference on Climate Change (Milan, December 2003) it was reiterated once again that the climatic change, together with the bad management of natural resources, is leading to an increase in both the frequency of disasters and in the number of registered victims. The World Health Organisation (WHO) talked about 150,000 deaths in 2003 as a result of global warming, while associated economic losses were estimated at €50 billion in the same year, an increase of €5 billion on the preceding year.

• As so often happens, it was this last factor, the economic cost, which served to highlight the other two. According to the UNDP, with data supplied by the Swiss insurance company 'Munich Re', the most reliable international source for the quantification of the costs of disasters, "the most important economic losses form part of an alarming tendency related to climatic change". It seems that this argument was not weighty enough to convince some countries, such as the United States – responsible for 25% of all the emissions of greenhouse gases – to ratify the Kyoto Protocol. However, fortunately, after the agreement on the part of Russia, it appears that the Protocol will soon come into effect.

To analyse the consequences of these destructive processes, we can count on a basic instrument to measure the vulnerability of countries facing three types of very specific threats: earthquakes, tropical cyclones, and floods. The Disaster Risk Index (DRI), developed by, amongst others, the UNDP, identifies developmental factors which increase risk and it also allows for the taking of political decisions to reduce the possible consequences of future disasters and, in the best of cases, to prevent them. It is, in reality, a basic tool for the fostering of a culture of sustainable development and prevention.

GLIDE (GLobal unique disaster IDEntifier number) is another basic instrument developed in this area. It functions as a single identifier of world disasters, the product of joint work carried out by international agencies, universities, and humanitarian organisations, based on an idea which came out of the Asian Disaster Reduction Centre. Its existence and application constitute an important step in avoiding earlier difficulties in disaster identification. In the past, no common system existed to identify disasters and accelerate the process of creating an effective and useable international database of national and international disasters. This identification system allows efficient responses to be made more quickly when a disaster occurs in any part of the world, as long as the political will exists to do so.

The ignorance of local realities has caused a disaster in Pakistan

The drainage project "Left Bank Outfall Drain" (LBOD), in the Pakistani province of Sindh, forms part of a programme financed by the International Development Association (IDA) of the World Bank at a cost of $285 million. The LBOD was designed to drain saline ground and surface water in three districts of Sindh – Nawabshah, Sanghar and Mirpurkhas – with the objective of alleviating the flooding and the salinity.

However, the LBOD contains important technical defects. The flow of drainage water goes against the direction of the wind, which often causes breaches. Poor usage and maintenance of the system, together with the build-up of sediment and seepage have made the whole system inefficient. In 1999, a cyclone made the problems even worse, causing substantial damage to the marine outfall. The structure has deteriorated with various breaches forming and consequent floods that have made much of the local land unfit for cultivation because of increased levels of salinity. Due to constant dumping of residues, the ecosystem of the wetlands, which served as a natural barrier against the intrusion of the sea, has also been adversely affected.

The area, which was already classified by the UN as one of the most impoverished in Pakistan, provides a living to the local inhabitants through agriculture, cattle rearing, and fishing. However, the reduction in the flow of fresh water has caused devastation in those three sectors. Far from improving the situation, these enormous projects have caused many people to be more vulnerable and exposed to new dangers and risks. During the rains of July 2003, more than 30 people died in just one of the districts and people lost cattle, harvests, and fishing – their principal means of sustenance.

In September 2004, a petition with more than 2,000 signatures was presented to the IDA inspection panel, who then declared that "the local communities, especially the coastal people affected, had been kept absolutely in the dark about the plans and the environmental evaluation". They also mentioned that the project had caused significant changes to their lives, which made them vulnerable to both the cyclone of 1999 and the floods of 2003.

(Extract from a text by 'Ayuda en Acción' (Aid in Action) presented to United Nations Conference on Reducing Disaster Risk (Kobe, 18/22-1-05).

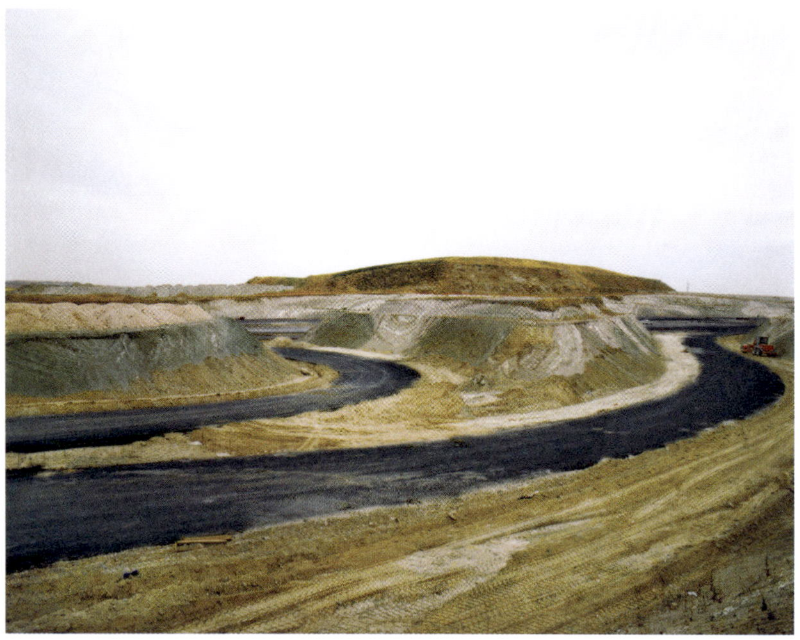

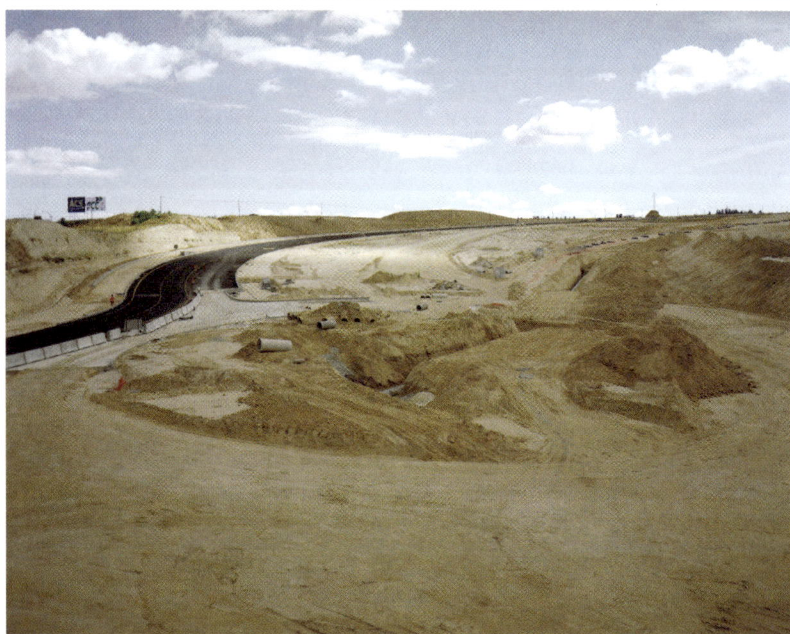

Sergio Belinchón
"Untitled", from the series *Suburbia*, 2002   "Untitled", from the series *Suburbia*, 2002
Colour photograph   Colour photograph
100 x 124 cm   100 x 124 cm

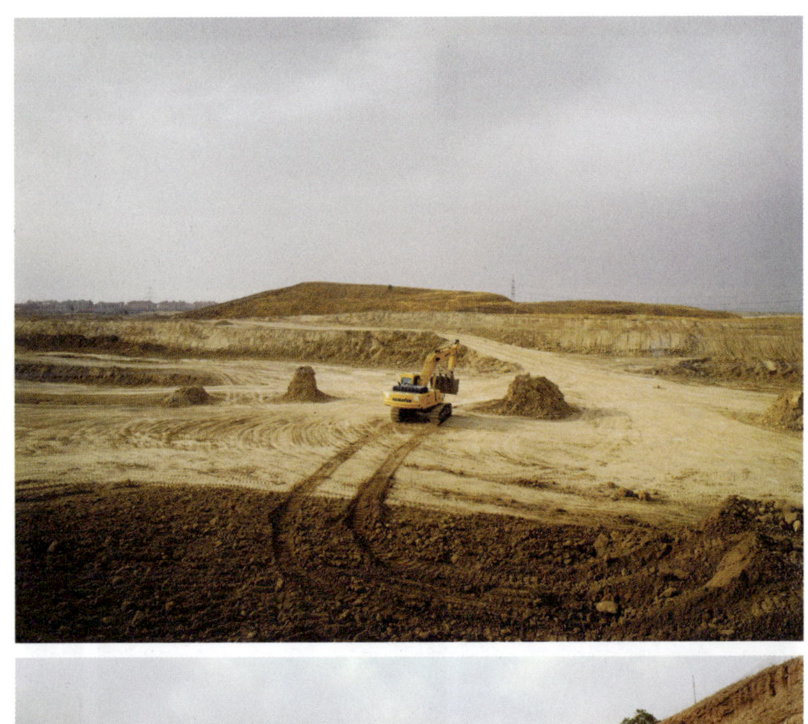

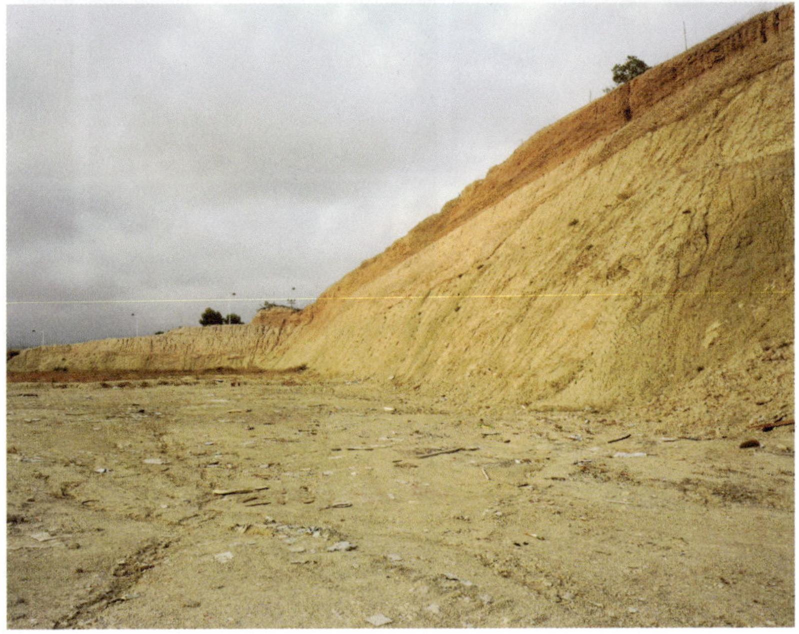

"Untitled", from the series *Suburbia*, 2002
Colour photograph
100 x 124 cm

"Untitled", from the series *Suburbia*, 2002
Colour photograph
100 x 124 cm

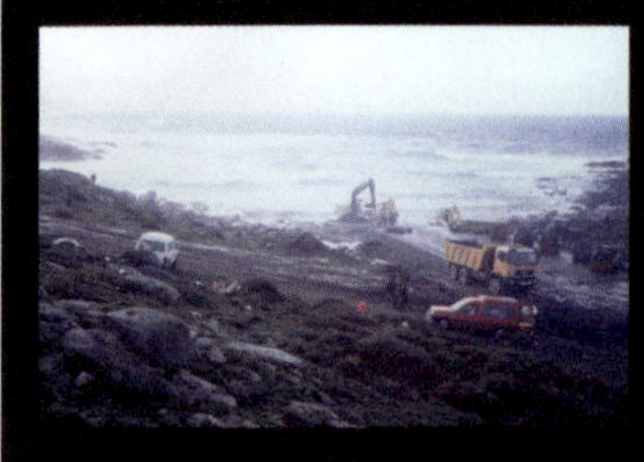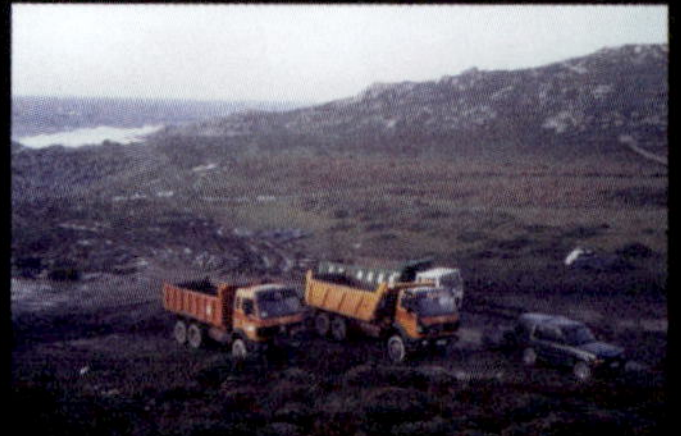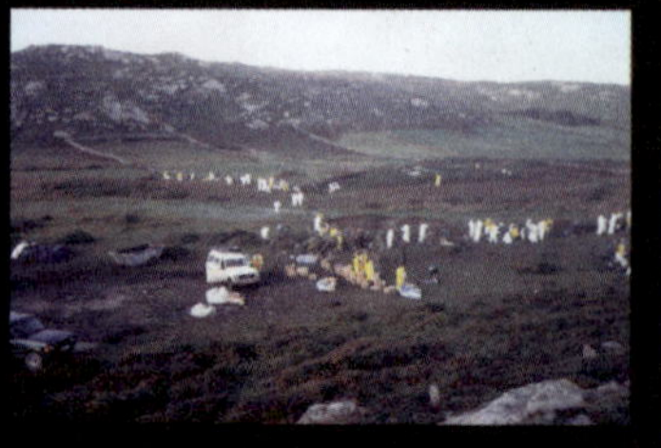

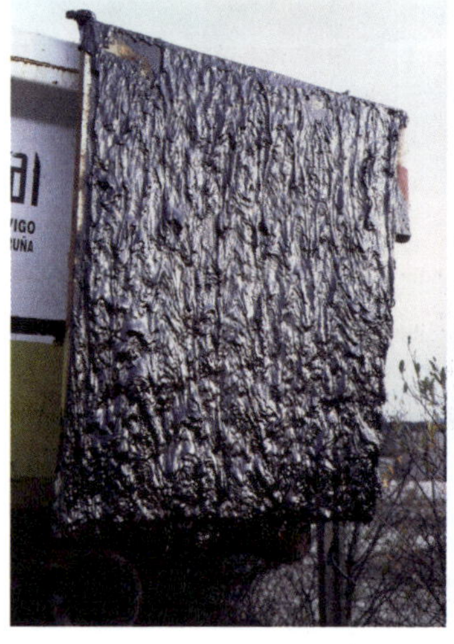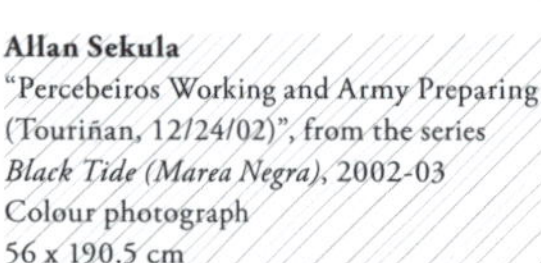

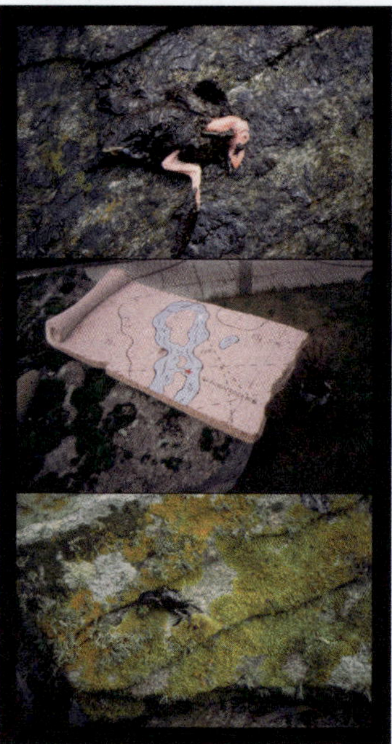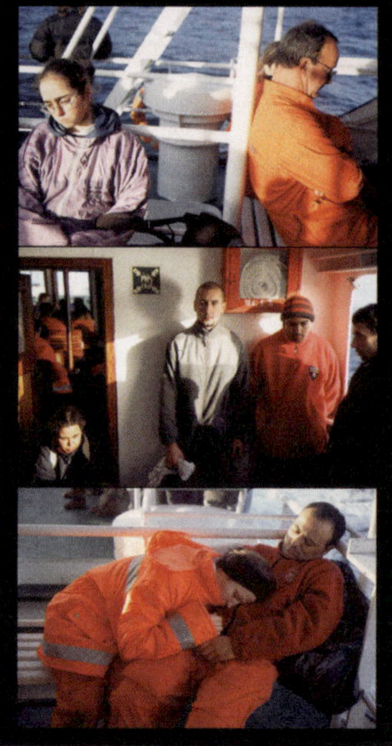

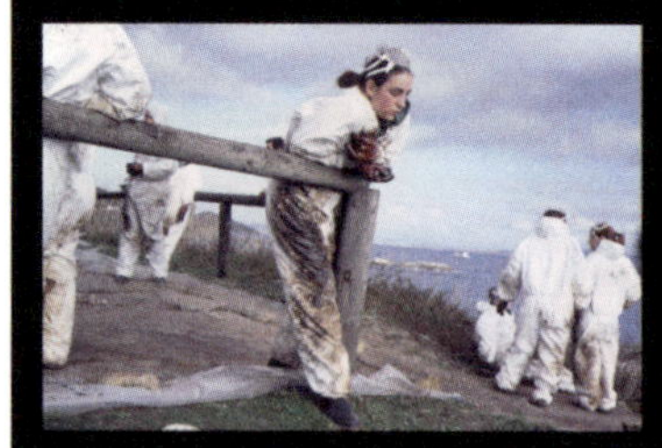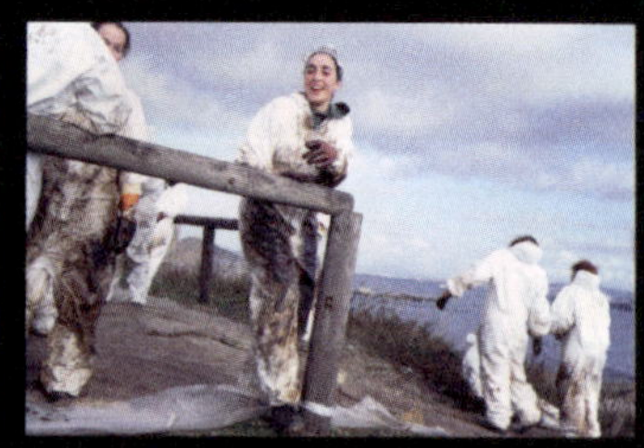

Allan Sekula
"Percebeiros Working and Army Preparing
(Touriñan, 12/24/02)", from the series
Black Tide (Marea Negra), 2002-03
Colour photograph
56 x 190.5 cm

"Dripping Black Trapezoid (Lendo,
12/22/02)", from the series *Black Tide
(Marea Negra)*, 2002-03
Colour photograph
102 x 74 cm

"Large and Small Disasters (Illas Cies and
Bueu, 12/20/02)", from the series *Black
Tide (Marea Negra)*, 2002-03
Colour photograph triptych
127 x 68.5 cm

"Exhausted Volunteers (En Route from Illa
de Oms, 12/19/02)", from the series *Black
Tide (Marea Negra)*, 2002-03
Colour photograph triptych
185.5 x 122 cm

"Volunteer Watching, Volunteer Smiling
(Illa de Oms, 12/19/02)", from the series
Black Tide (Marea Negra), 2002-03
Colour photograph diptych
63.5 x 172.5 cm

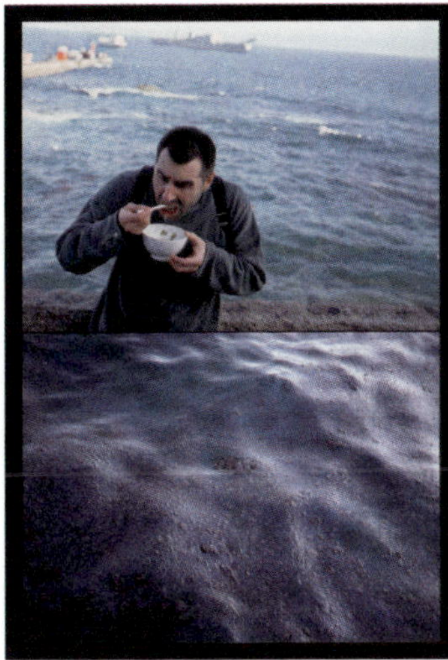
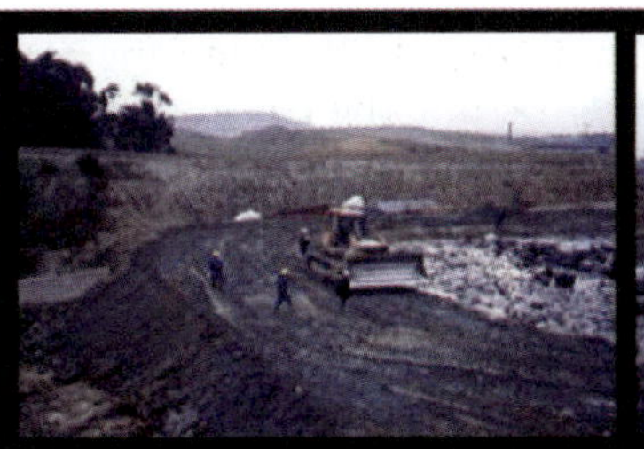
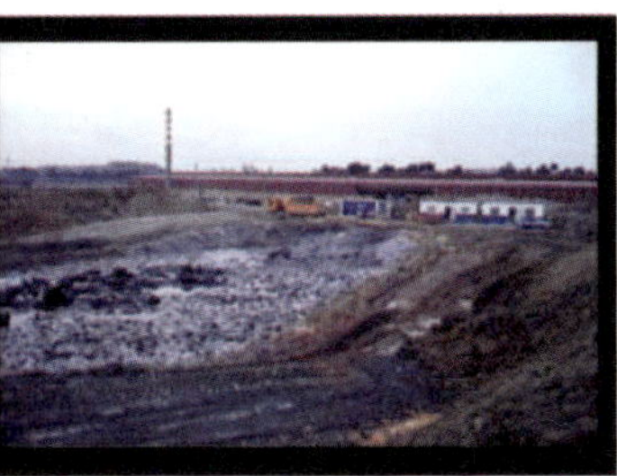
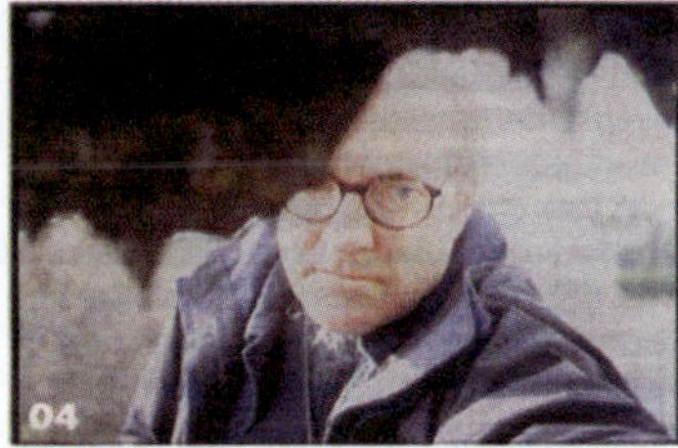
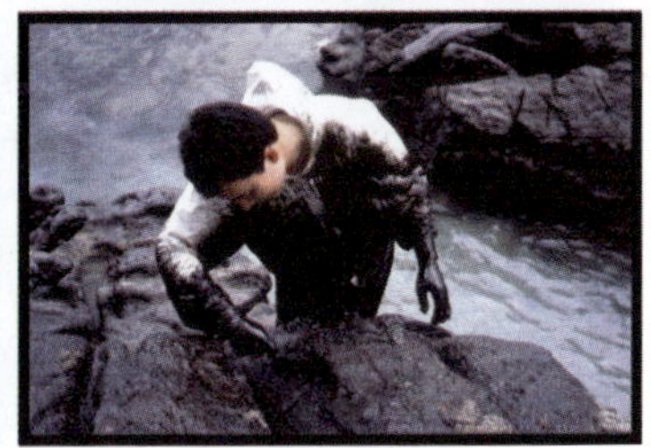
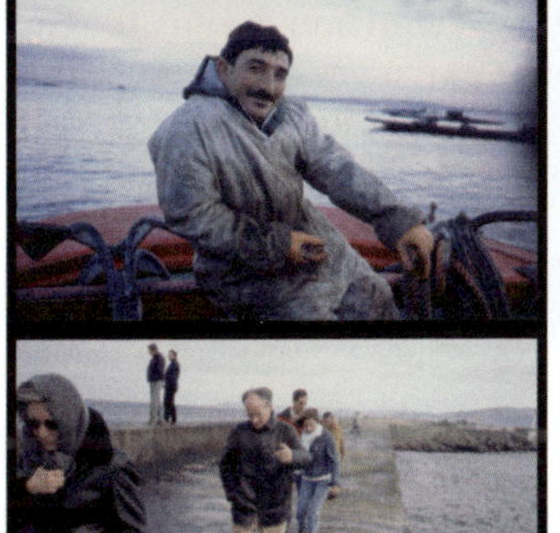

"Volunteer's Soup (Illa de Oms, 12/19/02)", from the series *Black Tide (Marea Negra)*, 2002-03
Colour photograph diptych
203 x 127 cm

"Disposal Pit (Lendo, 12/23/02)", from the series *Black Tide (Marea Negra)*, 2002-03
Colour photograph diptych
48.5 x 127 cm

"Selfportrait (Lendo, 12/22/02)", from the series *Black Tide (Marea Negra)*, 2002-03
Colour photograph
41 x 51 cm

"Fishing for Fuel, Surveying the Damage (Ría de Pontevedra, 12/19/92; Museu do Alemán, Camelle, 12/22/02)", from the series *Black Tide (Marea Negra)*, 2002-03
Colour photograph diptych
124.5 x 99 cm

"Volunteer on the Edge (Illas Cíes, 12/20/02)", from the series *Black Tide (Marea Negra)*, 2002-03
Colour photograph
73.5 x 101.5 cm

Constantly challenging the planet

Some years ago, the German sociologist Ulrich Beck proposed the term 'risk taking society' to define our world. It is true that we are facing new threats to which we are very vulnerable and for which we are not prepared, threats that represent a new type of risk for the citizens and the ecosystems. But it is also true that most of these threats have been created by human activity and they can hardly be classified as natural. Nevertheless, we continue to behave with an unprecedented level of irresponsibility, both towards ourselves, but even more so towards those who come after us. This behaviour is the fruit of models of economic exploitation and social uses that squander our limited assets, without being restrained by any effective judicial framework, or at least, this legal and judicial structure has still to be created.

As a result of what we are discovering in different fields, it would seem as if we define our relationship with the small planet we inhabit in terms of a constant and unlimited betting against the bank, without understanding that this irresponsible behaviour means that everybody loses. More oil consumed every year, more gas, more water, more air, more forests more.... Until when? In whose name?

The State and risk prevention: Cuba

Cuba has demonstrated a low vulnerability to natural disasters despite its exposure to them, being situated as it is in a zone punished by frequent hurricanes and cyclones. This positive reality is even more surprising if we consider the problems of the country in many sectors of its economy. Recurrently, the reports dealing with the these types of disasters tell us, on the one hand, of important losses and all types of damage to the infrastructure, but, on the other hand, there are practically no deaths, if any at all. On quite a few occasions, the outcome is much more favourable for Cuba than it is for its American neighbour – which usually also suffers the effects of the same meteorological phenomena, considering the obvious difference in economic recourses that both countries can count on. This was demonstrated in 2002 when hurricanes *Lily* and *Isidore*, barely two weeks apart, brought devastation to Cuba. The damage was very great. 57,000 homes were destroyed, the majority of them in rural areas and 600,000 people had to be evacuated. However, it was not necessary to mourn the loss of any human life. The government, with the support of the UNDP, immediately initiated a programme to rebuild the affected housing and put into effect policies designed to reduce future risks, which turned out to be very useful in facing, for example, the new tropical storms in the summer of 2004. What the Cuban case demonstrates to us, among other things, is that economic capability is not everything when confronting these catastrophes. Cuba, with its limited resources, and despite the notable and generalised precariousness of its rural areas, has shown itself to be very capable of dealing with dangerous situations. Organisation, urban planning appropriate for the circumstances, strong citizen consciousness, appropriate evacuation plans for the endangered population, constant perfecting of the vigilance and warning system, and other factors, all make Cuba an exemplary country in this area.

•   With respect to energy production, our economies continue to be fundamentally based on the consumption of fossil fuels – petrol, gas, and coal. So much is this so that all the forecasts for the next two decades indicate that, despite the initiatives which have begun to take root in the area of renewable sources of energy, our dependence on fossil fuels will increase even more – particularly oil and natural gas. As if we were unaware of the fact that we are dealing with highly polluting and non-renewable resources, we consume more and more every year, with the current of 77 million barrels per day set to rise to an estimated daily consumption of 112 million barrels by the year 2020.

•   What all analysts agree on is that demand for oil and gas in the Western economies will continue to grow while their own reserves are running out. The North Sea is probably the best example of this, in a European Union which is hardly over-endowed with these resources. Thus, the structural energy deficits of the Western economies will increase – with Canada being the exception to this rule. In addition, an overwhelming proportion of the known oil and gas reserves is concentrated in the Persian Gulf, and, increasingly, in the area of the Caspian Sea. The simple fact that two-thirds of all known oil reserves are located in this region sends a clear message to us about the importance for the principal world consumers of who controls those strategic resources. Saudi Arabia and Iraq are the stars of the sector – without belittling in any way other producers such as Russia.

•   As far as natural gas in concerned, everything indicates a notable increase in its use on a world-wide basis, including even replacing oil, because of its lower, though hardly insignificant, level of pollution. However, the situation is similar in both cases: a small number of developed countries without much in the way of this resource, facing a few natural gas producing countries which, with the exception of Russia, are also located in the Persian Gulf – Iran, Qatar, Saudi Arabia, and the United Arab Emirates.

•   In this situation and even recognising the fact that in practice the limitations established by the Kyoto Protocol do not seem enough to oblige a change of this model, the reticence displayed by the principal consumer nations in the exploration of alternative sources of energies is still rather shocking. While the possibility of a hydrogen era can be glimpsed on the horizon, the current powers in the field of renewable energies do not inspire hope in the medium term. This is particularly so as they take up once again, with increasing fervour, the arguments in favour of nuclear energy as the only possibility of reconciling us to the Kyoto restrictions.

•   On another front, the exploitation of the forests, which cover a quarter of the Earth's surface, continues unabated. According to a Greenpeace report, 80% of the planet's primary forests have already disappeared and the other 20% are in serious danger. Is it necessary to repeat over and over again that these forest masses are vital for an ecological equilibrium, for despite occupying only 7% of the land surface, they support half of the world's known plant and animal species? If that in itself is not sufficient, is it not also known that our forests play a fundamental role in local and planetary equilibrium by contributing to the conservation of those same species, to the water cycle, and to the protection of the soil against erosion, at the same time as being home to various indigenous communities? Clearly, the problem is not one of ignorance, but rather the result of the domination of short term economic interests in their exploitation over any other consideration. In Africa and Southern Asia simple energy self-sufficiency forces the inhabitants of many of these areas to cut down the trees for use as firewood. In Latin America, on the other hand, the deforestation is basically caused by agricultural and cattle-raising colonisation as well as the imposition of corporate interests on the part of big multinational companies and governments who look to become rich quickly. Finally, the timber and rubber industries are the important causes of the destruction of the forests in Eastern Asia.

•   In the case of water resources, it is even more necessary to sound the alarm due to the scarcity that is already very dramatically demonstrated in many places on the planet, to the extent that water is a clear cause of conflict between countries. Perhaps the most evident example of this is the Arab-Israeli conflict, which cannot be understood without taking this variable into consideration. The scarcity of water resources in the region explains the movements of the parties involved to achieve control of the few aquifers. It is on this 'blue planet' that, as the UNDP is constantly reminding us, more than 1 billion people lack access to uncontaminated drinking water and more than 2.4 billion people do not have access to basic sanitary services. This means, among other things, that more people are hospitalised for water transmitted diseases than for any other cause.

Necessary (and sufficient?) responses

Already part of our everyday language – although in many cases we are unaware of the exact technical meaning – are concepts such as greenhouse effect, acid rain, atmospheric pollution, radioactivity, climatic change, deforestation, water pollution... We first became familiar with them in the seventies, with an initial reference in the Club of Rome reports. In 1972, that institution published its first reports, (World-2, by Jay W. Forrester, and World-3, by Dennis L. Meadows), that set out to call attention to the unsustainable nature of infinite growth since the resources in question had always been, and would continue to be, finite. The only possible solution was to slow down economic growth to make it compatible with environmental quality and the sustainability of the planet.

In fact, this sounding of the alarm did not lead to a very strong reaction, except in academic circles and the even more limited ones of the ecologists, and did not become a regular item on the international agenda. In 1973, the United Nations organised its first Conference on the Environment. Later, in 1987, the Brundtland Report appeared, produced by the WCED, the World Commission on Environment and Development. This report declared that any model of economic development should be accompanied by good practices in questions affecting the environment to enhance the possibility of 'sustainable development'.

We would have to wait until 1992, with the celebration of the Earth Summit (Rio de Janeiro, Brazil), for a significant majority of the world's Heads of States and Governments, 178 in all, to vote in favour of making commitments on environmental issues. They also adopted the principle that those who pollute should pay the costs of their pollution. At this summit meeting, called under the slogan "Solidarity to save the planet", it was finally recognised that the then current crisis represented the final gasps of a style of development that had shown itself to be ecologically depredatory, socially perverse, and politically unjust. The most important results were the adopting of "Agenda 21", a detailed plan of action about the programmes that governments and international organisations should apply in order to deal with environmental and developmental problems, the "Framework Convention on Climate Change", which committed industrialised countries to put a stop to global warming, and the "Convention on Biodiversity", which aimed to guarantee the survival of global diversity and ecosystems.

The Kyoto Protocol continues along the same line, with the agreement to reduce emissions of greenhouse gases by 5.2% from 1990 levels by 2008-10. Although its signing by Russia means that the Protocol will finally be implemented, there are serious doubts about its effectiveness, given that some countries appear set to remain outside the process and, above all, the deterioration appears to be much faster than first believed. This was confirmed at the second Earth Summit in Johannesburg in 2002 and means that the limited measures taken by the compliant countries seem unlikely to have any significant impact in reversing the process.

If this is the type of reaction we are used to in questions of the environment, it cannot be said that, in relation to disasters, things are going much better. To centre our attention on one of the many aspects of disasters, while recognising the enormous complexity of these phenomena which cannot be fully explored here, one of the most glaring examples is that of the unceasing process of urban agglomeration on a world level that is creating a number of supersaturated macrocities. In those chaotic environments, not only are the public services incapable of satisfying the needs of the population, but it is also practically impossible to put a stop to the spontaneous appearance of all types of illegal shantytowns, the 'bidonvilles' and 'favelas' being two of the best-known examples of this phenomenon. In Bogota, Bombay, New Delhi, Lagos, or Lusaka, between 50 and 60% of the population live in these types of improvised shantytowns. However in cities such as Cairo, Casablanca, or Luanda, that figure is in excess of 70%.

In this regard, we should refer once again to the UNDP reports. In 'Reducing Disaster Risk: A Challenge for Development', it stated that between 1980 and 2000, 75% of the world population was living in areas that had been punished by earthquakes, tropical cyclones, droughts, or flooding. The magnitude of the problem often greatly exceeds the capacity of the humanitarian organisations that act, after the fact, to alleviate the effects of a natural disaster. Efficient as their work is, it is necessary to reiterate that the key factor in this area is prevention. The occurrence of the catastrophe must be anticipated, with measures designed, planned, and applied with the direct and sincere co-operation of the public administrations, without forgetting the essential involvement of the local organisations and population in this process.

In this sense, and taking into account that the gravity of the problem requires solutions on an international level, the United Nations has been trying to develop initiatives that help to prevent risk, that reduce vulnerability, and therefore, significantly reduce the exposure to danger of many countries with a medium or low Human Development Index (HDI). It was not until 1971 with the creation of UNDRO (United Nations Disaster Relief Organisation), that an organisation specialising in this area was first set up by the international community. Later on, in 1991, the Department for Humanitarian Affairs (DHA) was created to promote and implement the mandate of the UNDRO. In 1997, with the objective of emphasising even more the importance of co-ordination in emergencies and crises, it was decided to change its name to the Office for the Co-ordination of Humanitarian Affairs (OCHA), currently in operation and responsible to a Vice Secretary General of the UN.

In parallel, large international meetings have taken place. The first of these was the first World Conference on Disaster Reduction, held in 1994 in the Japanese city of Yokohama, under the theme "For a safer world in the 21st century". This led to the drawing up of a strategy for the International Decade for Disaster Reduction (1994-20004). This work has continued, the most recent conference being in Kobe (18-22 January 2005), which produced a far from optimistic evaluation of the work done to date, as well as working under the tremendous pressure of the tsunami disaster which brought the year to an end. One of the common threads in this effort is that of trying to identify and apply instruments which permit much more accuracy in the detection of threats before natural disasters occur. In addition, the conclusion has been reached that solutions to the problems of natural disasters must form an integral part of a sustainable development agenda.

Finally, and to add an initiative linked to the management of water resources, the CAP-NET (Capacity Building for Integrated Water Resources Management) should also be mentioned. It is a network that sets out to foster the capacity for integrated management of water resources. It is a joint initiative involving the UNDP, the World Association for Water, and the UNESCO Institute for Water Education, with financial support from the Dutch foreign ministry. Its objective is to create an operative framework on a local, regional, national, and international level for the interchange of information and for improved training in this field.

The fact that there are still two million children dying annually because of infections derived from the consumption of contaminated water speaks volumes of the need to improve the ability to respond to this problem, as well as those others already mentioned. It is in this light that it must be stated that no matter how positive some of the measures adopted up to now might be, in the end it is all insufficient to modify the negative tendencies detected so far. In no way can we state that structural changes leading to more hopeful situations have taken place.

It also depends on you

It seems obvious to accept that the global nature of the problems caused by the deterioration of the environment and natural disasters inevitably means that responses also have to be global, involving national governments and international organisations in co-operative efforts. That assumption, however, does not free us, the people, from our responsibility. One reason is because what we are dealing with here are problems that directly affect all of us. We cannot simply wait around hopefully for the day when the political will of those aforementioned groups allows for more efficient preventive treatment and a more decisive response to what all the reports about these issues consistently indicate. What is emphasised, over and over again, in all the communiqués and reports from the specialists in this area is that local capabilities and behaviour are what most decisively contribute to modifying ways of doing things, and also to a more efficient response to the unwanted occurrence of any kind of disaster.

Another reason is that all of us interact with our environment. Depending on how we do so, we can contribute positively or negatively to this process. Therefore, it is in our hands to contribute to a substantial improvement of what we hold nearest and dearest to us, knowing that our sensitivity and our mobilisation will be felt in the centres of power. The old principle that requires us to 'think globally and act locally' is, now more than ever, especially relevant.

Document produced by researchers from the
Institute of Studies on Conflicts and Humanitarian Action (IECAH)
Madrid, January 2005

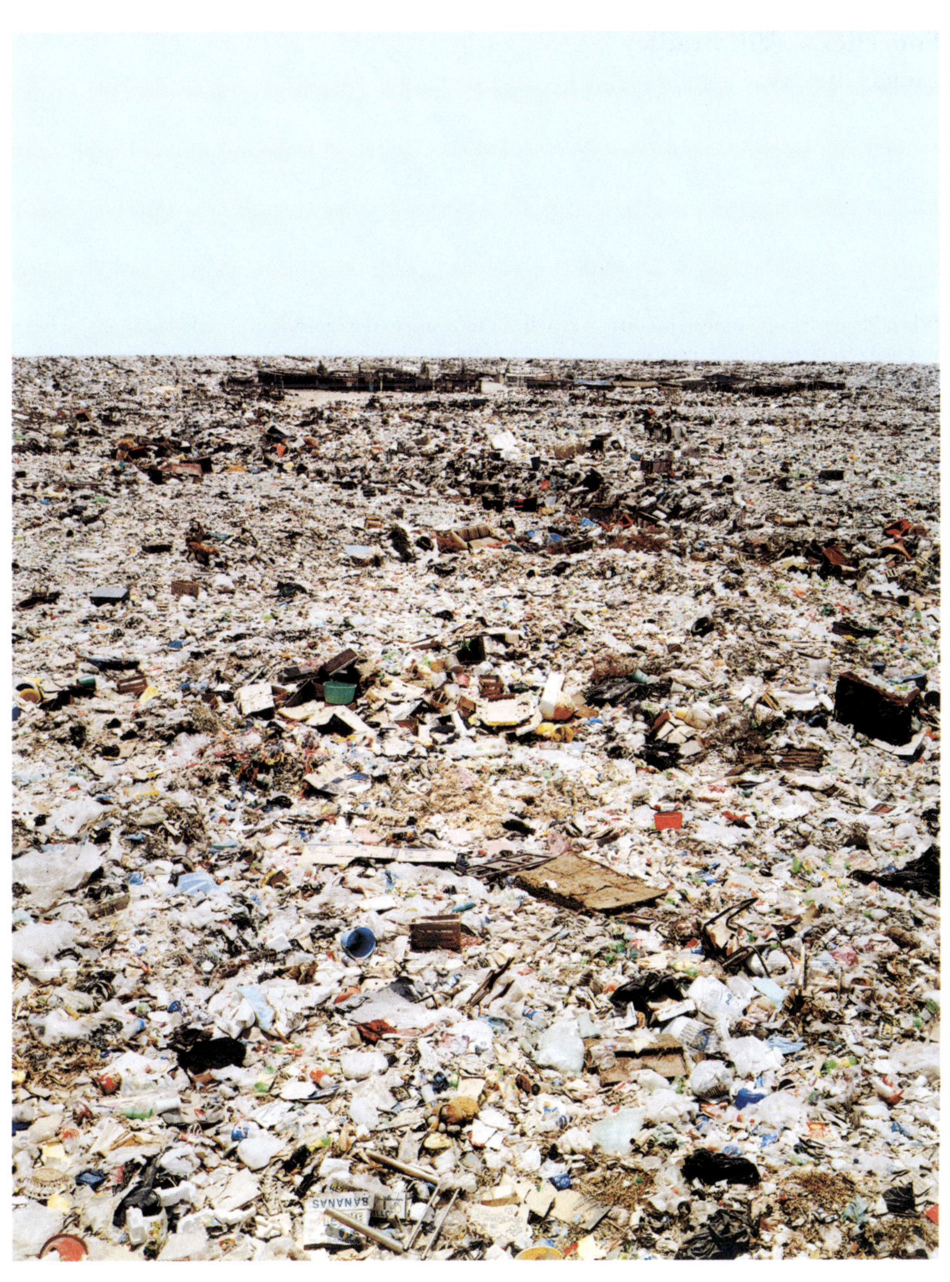

Andreas Gursky
Ohne Titel XIII (Mexico), 2002
Colour photograph
277 x 206 cm

Superflex + Will Bradley
Biogas in Africa

When Piero Manzoni canned his own shit in 1961, he was simultaneously asserting and satirising the recently-won freedom of the avant-garde artist to claim anything as art. Fascinated by the power of his own signature to apparently transform anything into a valuable and desirable artwork – the Tate, the Pompidou and the New York MOMA, among many other museums, have examples of the Merda d'artista – Manzoni remained too caught up in the endgame of Modernist authenticity to see the real possibilities that this strategy of negation opened up, but within a decade the entire art-making paradigm had shifted. Waste disposal, along with a thousand other areas of human life, had become not only a legitimate art process but a whole field of art action with a host of social, political, ecological and economic implications.

In 1969 Mierle Laderman Ukeles wrote the 'Manifesto for Maintenance Art', proposing an exhibition, entitled 'CARE', that would involve polluted earth, air and water being treated, purified and recycled within the art museum itself, and her idea of maintenance art was formulated as a direct response to the ego-driven practice of the previous generation: '[Jackson] Pollock appeared autonomous, didn't need anybody, hardly needed gravity itself. It wasn't living in the world, on a planet that has finite resources, where we need to stay alive, in connection with other people. It was a total phoney thing. It had an evil underside of autonomy, only the "I"; not acknowledging who holds you up, and who supports you, and who's providing the food, and the raw materials, and who the people taking them out of the earth are, and what their working conditions are, and what the pollution costs of moving materials all around the world are, who's paying for what, and any fact of human life.' (Mierle Laderman Ukeles on Maintenance and Sanitation Art in Tom Finkelpearl's book *Dialogues in Public Art*, MIT Press, Cambridge, MA, London, 2001)

In parallel with Ukeles other artists began working with similar processes and relationships, employing methods that were less concerned with authentication or validation in an art context and more with processes and relationships that began and ended outside the gallery. In particular, Hans Haacke's Rhinewater Purification Plant (1972) – piping the poorly-treated, filthy outfall of the Krefeld Sewage Plant into the exhibition space of the Museum Haus Lange to publicly undergo additional filtration – founded an entire genre of artists' water-purification projects, though while many of these are vast in scope they have had relatively little profile in the formal artworld. All of these projects can be seen as the artworld ancestors of Biogas in Africa, but Superflex have moved their practice about as far beyond the modernist conception of the artwork as it is currently possible to go without leaving the field entirely. Biogas in Africa involves the development of a better biogas plant for farmers in small rural communities without a highly developed infrastructure, and the presentation here documents the installation of a prototype unit on a small farm in Tanzania in 1997, in partnership with the SURUDE Foundation for Sustainable Rural Development. The biogas principle is simple. Shit, human or animal (buffalo, apparently, is best of all), is mixed 50-50 with water and fermented for several days in a warm, airtight container called a 'digester'. The action of bacteria (the active strains found in cattle dung include Ruminococcus flavefaciens, Eubacterium cellulosolvens, Clostridium cellulosolvens, Clostridium cellulovorans, Clostridium thermocellum, Bacteroides cellulosolvens and Acetivibrio cellulolyticus) breaks down the waste and, in these anaerobic conditions, produces biogas which is around 65% methane. After fermentation, almost all of the pathogenic bacteria and viruses in the waste have been killed, along with most of the harmful parasites, and the resulting slurry makes a good, nitrogen-rich fertiliser. The Superflex prototype uses a flexible plastic balloon as the digester, the African sun keeps the temperature favourable, partial burial makes for excellent insulation, and the balloon inflates as gas is produced.

The fact is that the biogas plant was a shiny, brightly coloured and modern-looking prototype – even the sound of the words 'prototype' and 'biogas' themselves seem to imply that the technology is at the heart of the matter – but this is misleading. Small-scale, relatively low-cost biogas generation apparatus has been in use in rural Africa for years (there was, predictably, a 1970s fad for biogas among Western development agencies and Jan Mallan, one of the principal engineers who worked with Superflex on the system, has been developing the technology for nearly two decades) and, although the Superflex implementation represents a useful refinement and has even led to a patent application for a two-chamber system that uses the pressure of the biogas itself to stir the fermenting slurry, it is still primarily the result of tuning and retro-application of well-known procedures.

So, although the technology is more innovative than that employed in, for example, Haacke's filtration unit, it is neither the motivation for Superflex's experiments nor the justification for the project overall. But if Superflex are not technologists, though they work with technology, and if they reject the model of the artist-as-auteur, though they often exhibit aspects of their work in galleries and museums, then what exactly are they trying to achieve? Superflex often describe their projects, including this one, as 'tools'. Against the Modernist conception of the artwork as an intellectually or aesthetically rewarding exercise that is otherwise emphatically useless, and also in contrast to the 1970s idea of the eco-artwork that is functional but ultimately constitutes a closed situation directed and controlled by the artist's vision, Superflex aim to produce tools that can be taken up and used in ways that are independent of the circumstances of their creation. If art has traditionally aimed to reach an audience, Superflex's projects hope to find users. A tool, in this sense, can be an idea, a method, or a technology, combined with a framework within which it can be made available for general use. Forming the idea of the artwork as a tool involves rethinking, or setting aside, much of the twentieth century debate around aesthetics. The role of the artist becomes more complex, collaborative and social, while at the same time control of the final outcome is surrendered. Artists can never control the reception of their work; there will be as many interpretations and responses as there are viewers. Here, however, every aspect of the production process becomes collaborative and harder to clearly define, until finally the tool is placed in the hands of the user and escapes entirely from the art context. Of course the artworld has never been a magic realm set apart from society at large. It is a constituent part of our culture and its products have always been descriptive of that culture, embedded in social situations, and subject to the same power relations and economic pressures as the rest. Superflex's method changes the usual emphasis, making these aspects central, and rather than being a scene laid out for aesthetic contemplation, the installation Biogas in Africa is a little like something you might see on a stand at a trade fair, a 3D marketing display extolling the benefits of the biogas unit. Here, the artworld itself is being used as a tool: as a space and a support structure for the development of new ideas, as a platform for public discussion and the dissemination of information, and as a machine for turning public interest in the development process into what is

effectively a kind of cultural venture capital.

At this point new questions and problems arise. Though the financial support of the vestigial state mechanisms in European cultural funding makes it possible (though not easy) to develop an idea this way, practical implementation can be more problematic. Outside the publicly-funded world of the state institution, market forces have the final word, and even with the kudos of artworld success and the backing of cultural institutions, it's often difficult to make the economics work. This is when the few artists who explore this field of action usually retreat, happy to have created an image, a metaphorical effect, but Superflex push their projects further, into the heart of the contradictions of ethical capitalism.

Of course, the majority of successful artists are developing products for the international marketplace, and using the support of the institutions of art to do so. Those products are mostly high-priced, one-off artefacts that compete for the attention of a relatively small number of specialised art buyers. A tool, in the Superflex

sense, is something different. If a product is anything that can be made and sold, the tool brings with it an idea of empowerment. A product gets consumed, but a tool can itself be used to produce. With the right tools, it might be possible to move from a position of dependency to one of independence, to claim ownership of a small part of the means of production. The importance of Superflex's approach lies in the creation of new, real-world models for this kind of activity. Rather than producing, or re-producing, rhetoric about the admittedly massive and manifold problems that attend our current mode of political and economic organisation, they are actively searching out possibilities and contradictions, gaps in the system where an alternative approach might still take root.

The ultimate aim of the biogas project itself is a production model that is cheaper to produce and easier to maintain than previous systems and genuinely viable for small farmers in developing countries even outside the aid economy. To this end, a company has been formed, Supergas Ltd., which includes the

engineers who have worked on the prototype as well as outside investors, and further biogas tests have since taken place in Cambodia (in collaboration with the University of Tropical Agriculture there), and in Thailand (in collaboration with CMS Engineering).

Another project, the Superchannel, offers software and server space for independent groups to produce easy, cheap web TV, and their latest venture, GuaranaPower, is a collaboration with a Brazilian farmers' cooperative, COAIMA. The condition for Western aid – even for access to loans at market rates – to developing countries is inevitably that of opening their domestic market and resources to exploitation by international capital, and Brazil with its massive debt to the IMF is a sitting target. The COAIMA farmers grow guarana, a caffeine-rich berry used mostly as an ingredient in soft drinks, and the corporations that dominate the market for the crop have forced the price down to subsistence levels. GuaranaPower is an experiment in using a different kind of tool, what Superflex describe as a 'counter-economic strategy': the farmers are working with Superflex and a Danish soft drink producer to make and distribute a product that not only bypasses the corporations' predatory cartel but also uses their own actions and their own brand identity against them.

The prototype biogas installation in Tanzania is still functioning and, though its efficiency has declined over the last seven years, it's still useful and still being used. That's seven years of heat and light in return for a little maintenance and a large amount of what is probably the world's cheapest raw material. It's a long way from Manzoni's showmanship, and it's a small victory on a very big planet, but it offers an opportunity to consider the interconnected social, political and economic facts of human life – along with their relationship to an artworld that still mostly prefers shit that can be canned, signed, and sold.

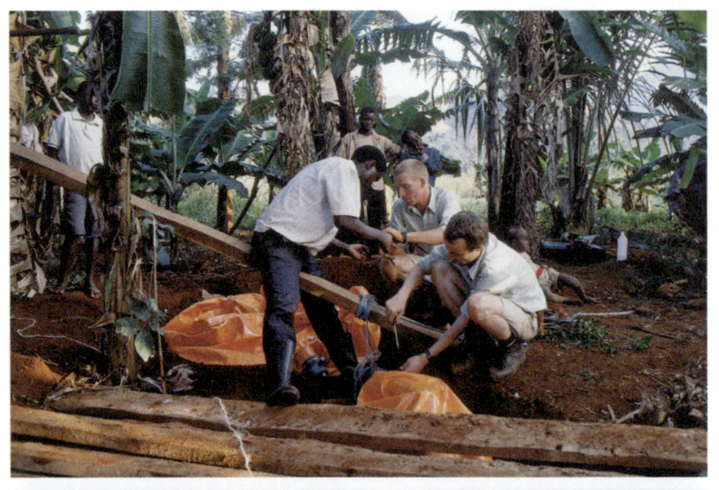

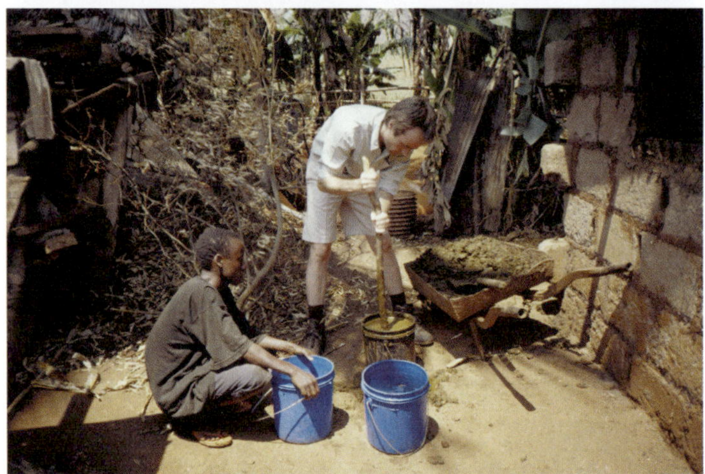

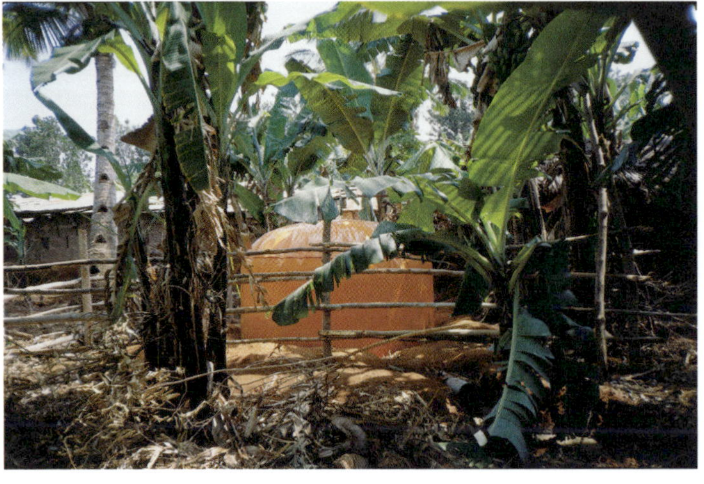

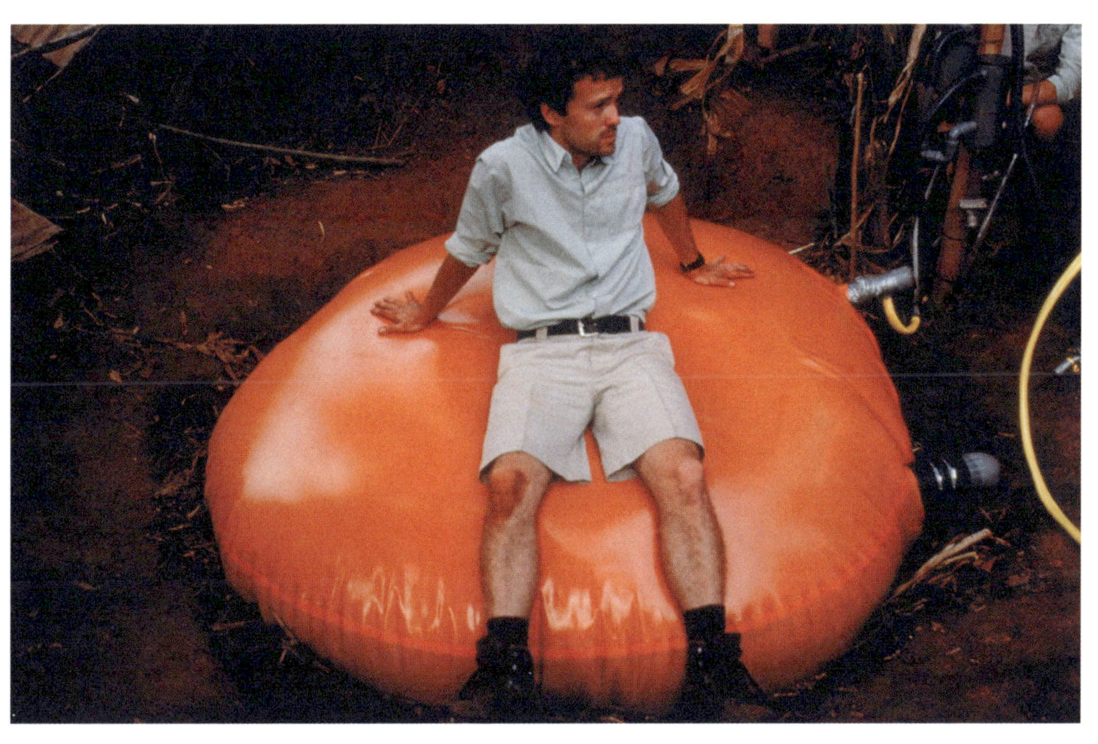

Superflex
Superflex/Supergas/Massawe Family,
Tanzania, 1997, 1997
Installation consisting of an orange
balloon (Ø 200 cm), video projection
(DVD colour video with sound, 6'),
photograph (133.5 x 120 cm) and vinyl
Variable dimensions

Further reading

ABBOTT, P. (2003): *Natural disasters*, McGraw-Hill College, UK.
AZAPAGIG, A.; EMSLEY, A.; HMAERTON, I. (2003): *Polymers: The Environment and Sustainable Development,* John Wiley & Sons Ltd, UK.
BIFANI, P. (1999): *Medio ambiente y desarrollo sostenible*, IEPALA, Madrid.
CARON, D. (2001): *Les aspects internationaux des catastrophes naturelles e industrielles,* Martinus Nijhoff, The Hague.
WORLD COMMISSION ON ENVIRONMENT AND DEVELOPMENT (1987): *Our common future*, Oxford U. Press, UK.
COOPER, P., VARGAS, C. (2004): *Implementing Sustainable Development: From Global Policy to Local Action,* Rowman & Littlefield Pub Inc, UK.
GARZÓN, Ernesto (2004): *Calamidades*, Gedisa, Barcelona.
GOODLAND, R. (1997): *Medio ambiente y desarrollo sostenible más allá del informe Brundtland,* Trotta, Madrid.
INTER-AGENCY SECRETARIAT OF THE INTERNATIONAL STRATEGY FOR DISASTER REDUCTION (2004): *Disaster risk reduction 1994-2004*, ISDR.
UNITED NATIONS DEVELOPMENT PROGRAMME (2004): *Reducing Disaster Risk: A Challenge for Development*, UNDP.
TOULMIN, S. (1992): *Cosmopolis: the hidden agenda of modernity*, University of Chicago Press, Chicago.

Websites of interest

- Greenpeace: http://www.greenpeace.org
- The Ecologist: http://www.theecologist.org
- Asociación Española de Ecología Terrestre: http://www.aeet.org/ecosistemas/portada.htm
- International Strategy for Disaster Reduction: http://www.unisdr.org
- Global Unique Identifier Number: http://www.glidenumber.net
- ReliefWeb: http://www.reliefweb.int/rw/dbc.nsf/doc100
- World Conference on Disaster Reduction: http://www.unisdr.org/wcdr/
- The World Conservation Union: http://iucn.org/

Primary Forests 8000 years ago

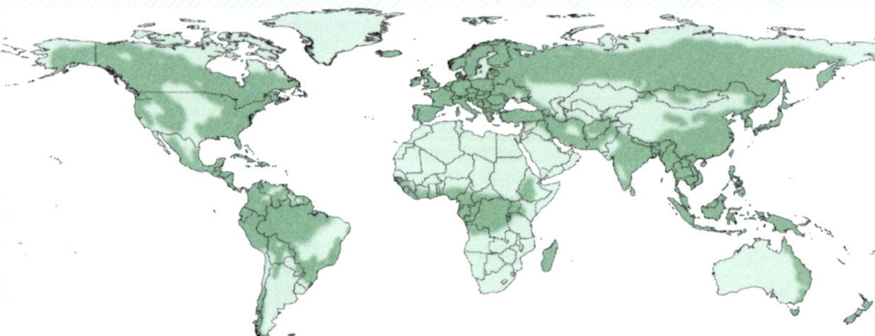

Source: Greenpeace.

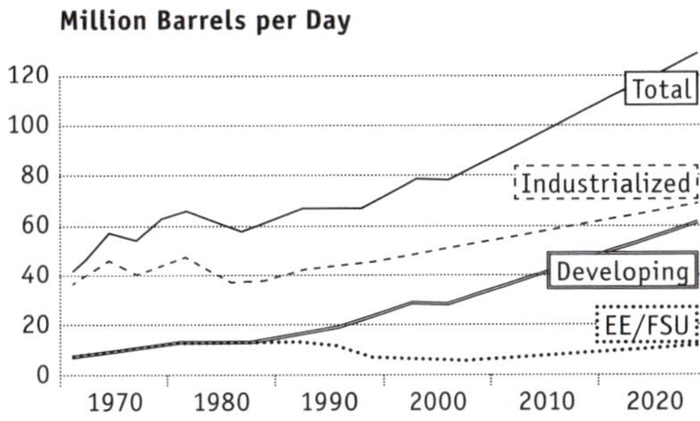

Daily consumption (in millions of barrels) historically and its projection for:
- Developing countries.
- Eastern Europe and ex Soviet Union.
- Industrialised countries.
- Total: world consumption

Sources: Energy Information Administration (EIA),
International Oil Monthly),
EIA, World Energy Projection System (2000)

Great catastrophes, such as that which has recently struck South East Asia, become the focal point of attention for the media, non-governmental organisations and, equally, for the public. Human resources and enormous amounts of financial aid are mobilised in response to the disaster but, on many occasions, this aid never reaches its destination, while the concern aroused soon fades away as the situation is no longer front-page news. This compulsive solidarity is understandable and all resources are valuable in order to alleviate emergencies; but meanwhile, many diseases which have been eradicated in the developed countries still exist and are causing the death of many people in underdeveloped areas. These are the forgotten pandemics, the 'silent emergencies' which are affecting millions of human beings.

Today, malaria, tuberculosis, leishmaniasis and trypanosomiasis are still killing millions of people. These diseases, which are things of the past in developed countries, only affect poor countries that disappeared from the world political agenda a long time ago. It is intolerable, and even obscene, that people continue to die from diseases which are now banal, rare or even non-existent in the 'first world'. This widespread indifference leads to a lack of investment in research aimed at reducing these epidemics. It is not only a question of AIDS, which of course appears in the media since it affects the developed countries, but also of other curable diseases which do not receive sufficient attention.

Africa represents 1% of the pharmaceutical market and Latin America, 4%. It is not profitable for the large pharmaceutical conglomerates to invest in the countries affected by these diseases, with the result that they have gradually abandoned the production of appropriate drugs, or else those that are still produced are obsolete. The drugs that are distributed date from the 60s and 70s and the pathogenic agents have developed a resistance.

In order to deal with this situation, it is necessary to activate research programmes in these areas and boost the distribution of generic drugs which are more accessible for the countries that need them. For example, in the case of leishmaniasis, the conventional drug, 'Pentostam', (manufactured by GlaxoSmithKline), costs roughly €60 whereas the Indian generic SAG costs only €10. What is preventing an advance in the treatment of these pandemics? Which diseases are the most important?

Malaria

This affects 40% of the world's population, concentrated in 91 countries. It is caused by a parasite called 'plasmodium' and is transmitted by the anopheles mosquito. It is difficult to detect since it produces high temperatures and this symptom is also associated with other infectious diseases. Laboratory tests with microscopes are necessary to arrive at an exact diagnosis and these are expensive.

Diagnosis is the first difficulty encountered in the treatment of malaria. 50% of diagnoses are erroneous and at times drugs are administered to people who do not have the disease and consequently develop a resistance to the medication. In addition, some drugs which are distributed, such as 'Cloroquine', have side-effects and their poor quality means they have little effect as a treatment. The use of other more adequate drugs, such as 'Malarone', comes up against the prohibitive price of €50. Investigation into new drugs is slow and preventive measures are also costly. Vaccine research is almost at a standstill and is not supported by the industry.

Tuberculosis

In developed countries, this disease was considered practically eradicated. However, it is still killing two million people a year. It is caused by Koch's bacillus and is transmitted through the air. In Africa there is a preoccupying re-emergence that has already affected 70% of those who are seropositive and it is appearing as a multi-resistant tuberculosis (MR-TB). There is a drug, 'Thioacetazone', which is contraindicated for AIDS patients but nevertheless, is used in developing countries where the majority of those suffering from tuberculosis are seropositive. It costs €1,300 and the World Health Organisation (WHO) and Médecins Sans Frontières (MSF) are negotiating with the pharmaceutical industry to reduce the price to €300, even though this would still be high for the economies of these countries.

Leishmaniasis

Every year leishmaniasis infects 500,000 people. This pandemic is caused by 15 types of protozoa of the leishmania genus, which weaken the immunological system and thus facilitate the spread of other illnesses such as pneumonia or diarrhoea. It may be cutaneous, mucocutaneous or visceral and may be fatal if it is not treated. 12 million people in 88 countries are affected, 90% of whom are in Sudan, India, Bangladesh, Nepal and Brazil, and it was also present in southern Europe in 1998 when the 'kala-azar' infected 1,400 people who were seropositive.

One of the most dangerous aspects of this disease is the diagnosis, since it is necessary to carry out a puncture of the spleen. Besides, this costs 6, a price that many of those affected cannot pay. The treatment is toxic and costs some 180. The multinational *GlaxoSmithKline* owns the patent and commercialises the drug under the name of 'Pentostam', but does not guarantee sufficient production.

Trypanosomiasis

There are various types: it causes sleeping sickness in Africa, and Chagas' disease in Latin America. Sleeping sickness, caused by the tsetse fly, threatens some 60 million people, especially those living near rivers. There may be about 500,000 people infected. The pharmaceutical company, Bayer, has reached an agreement with the WHO and MSF to continue supplying 'Sodium suramine' free of charge for five years and has committed itself to commercialising it cheaply from then on. Aventis has a similar commitment to supplying 'Pentamidine' free for five years. Two other drugs are promising: 'Nifurtimox', used in the treatment of Chagas' disease and produced by Bayer who are supplying it free for five years, and 'Eflorentine', used in hospitals – Aventis supplied the last ampules and handed the patent over to the WHO since production of this drug was not profitable.

HIV-AIDS is no longer a synonym for death, but only in the developed countries

To understand present-day pandemics and epidemics it is necessary to have knowledge of the causes of propagation. Human migration and the structures of social integration help to spread these diseases and, at the same time, hinder attempts at control. The outbreak of SARS (Severe Acute Respiratory Syndrome) is an example, where a rapid reaction was crucial in limiting the epidemic. The speed with which these diseases spread is greater, possibly, in the case of AIDS since the contaminating agent can travel extremely easily. The best medicine is prevention amongst the population at risk – in this case, amongst the population as a whole.

AIDS can affect any part of the population and does not respect social classes; however, it is obvious that there is greater risk in the developing countries, especially in Africa – although statistics in China and India are already worrying – where there are fewer possibilities for prevention and treatment. Apart from regional conflicts, a shifting population and extreme hunger are also factors which facilitate propagation.

Over the last few years, there have been advances in the treatment of AIDS, with what has been called the drug 'cocktail', which is a lifelong treatment since the disease reappears if the drugs are not taken. As it is, the application of these drugs has meant that AIDS has become a chronic rather than a fatal disease. The problem again resides in access to this medication, since 90% of those suffering AIDS in the developing countries cannot pay for such costly treatment.

AIDS has been the topic of the 2004 annual report of the WHO "World Health Report 2004: Changing History". In this report, special attention is paid to prevention, treatment, attention and support as basic tools for the eradication of the disease. Certain facts give us a rough idea of how serious the challenge is:

The world panorama:
— AIDS is the main cause of death in adults between 19 and 49 years of age.
— More than 20 million people have died from this disease since the pandemic began in 1985.
— It is estimated that between 34 and 46 million people are currently infected.
— Heterosexual relations without protection are the principal cause of transmission of the disease.

Africa:
— One in twelve African adults is seropositive.
— In 2003, two thirds of those affected were in Africa.
— In the area of Africa south of the Sahara, prevalence among adults has remained stable over the last few years since the total adult population is growing.

Other regions.
— It is estimated that in 2003, 840,000 people were infected in China and 3.8 to 4.6 million in India.
— In Eastern Europe and Central Asia the disease is already present.
— In Western Europe, thanks to antiretroviral treatment the number of those infected is higher than the number of deaths.
— In the eastern area of the Mediterranean, there are 750,000 people infected.
— In America, the region most affected is the Caribbean. In Latin America there are 1.6 million people infected
— In the United States, there are 30,000-40,000 new cases of infection every year.

In spite of the unreliability of the figures relating to those affected by the disease – some governments even refuse to recognise its existence amongst their peoples and sometimes local customs help to hide it from the eyes of others – it is obvious that the number of people who live with AIDS is on the increase. Available data show that, despite the positive impact that preventive strategies may have, the number of people living with HIV has increased in all the regions of the world, as is also the case amongst the population aged 15 to 49.

An analysis of the data from the point of view of the different sexes shows that women are more vulnerable to AIDS than men. The main cause is, obviously, that women are more likely to be infected through sexual relations and that is why, today, 58% of those infected with AIDS in Africa are women. This reality is even more dramatic when we see that every year 2.2 million seropositive women give birth. The tragic possibility of the mother transmitting the virus to her child during pregnancy is confirmed by the fact that 4 million have been infected in this way in the last two decades. It is estimated that there are 14 million children infected with AIDS in the world, the majority of whom are in Africa, and it is expected that by 2010 this figure will have risen to 25 million.

In the UN Declaration of Commitment on HIV/AIDS (2001), it was recognised that the situation of inequality of women was reinforcing the epidemic. In this Declaration, the participating governments committed themselves to putting into action strategies aimed at reducing the vulnerability of women and girls. Their objectives for 2003-2005 are:

— To tackle the aspects of the epidemic related to gender.
— To foster a full application of human rights for women in order that they have the possibility of taking effective precautions against HIV.
— To eliminate situations of discrimination against women, such as violence, sexual trading and exploitation.
— To reduce mother-child transmission of HIV by improving the access of women to preventive, prenatal and information services.
— To study the economic and social impact of the epidemic, especially amongst the women who act as carers.

In addition, the United Nations Development Fund for Women has launched a programme to increase activities related to women and human rights in 10 countries widely affected by HIV — Barbados, Brazil, Cambodia, India, Kenya, Nigeria, Rwanda, Senegal, Thailand and Zimbabwe.

As is to be expected, women's movements are beginning to react. As a representative example, we can cite the Global Coalition on Women and AIDS, set up in 2003. This is made up of representatives of many non-governmental organisations, with seropositive members and personnel of the UN, united in their aim to promote policies which may have a positive impact on the life of women and girls likely to be affected by the disease. From a wider perspective, involving all the sectors of civil society that are aware of this problem, we must mention the Civil Society Initiative (CSI) set up by the WHO in June 2001 with the aim of encouraging collaboration, exchange and dialogue with the non-governmental organisations and others present in civil society. In addition, the WHO plans to strengthen its support of Member States in their work with the non-governmental sector in questions related to health, and to increase contacts with all the civil entities that are working towards the goals of the organisation. The WHO proposes the following, as specific activities of the CSI:

— The creation of a data base with information on the NGOs that have contacts with the WHO.
— The collection of information related to the protagonists of civil society and to the analysis of policies which could be useful for the WHO, the Member States and public opinion in general.
— The improvement of communication and dialogue between the WHO and civil society.
— The strengthening of the WHO's capacity for facilitating the relationship between the Member States and civil society.

Cholera: a preoccupying case

The starting point for the study of this disease is the identification of the bacteria which causes it: the vibrio cholerae. The main symptom is severe diarrhoea which can lead to serious dehydration and death, if it is not treated correctly. It is transmitted through water or contaminated foodstuffs and mainly affects Africa, South America and South and South East Asia.

The present epidemic originated in Indonesia (1961), from where it spread to other countries in eastern Asia. It reached Bangladesh in 1963, India in 1964 and the Soviet Union, Iran and Iraq at the end of that decade. In 1970 it reached Africa where it spread rapidly – on this continent alone, it is estimated that there are 79 million people threatened with cholera, and some 120,000 deaths are calculated per year. In 1991 the disease reached Latin America.

When cholera breaks out in an area which is not prepared to deal with the infection, the mortality rate can be as high as 50% of the infected population. In 2004 there were new outbreaks of cholera in Burundi, Cameroon, Mali, Mozambique, South Africa and Zambia. In Senegal it has broken out again after a respite of eight years and in only two weeks 66 cases were confirmed. Even though the origin of the outbreak has not been confirmed, everything points to the shanty towns around Dakar as being fertile ground for the bacteria. These epidemics are caused by unhygienic living conditions and contaminated drinking water. When the rains come, the danger is increased because contaminated sewers and wells overflow and contribute to the spread of the disease.

UNICEF statistics show that cholera causes the death of 2 million children per year – some 5,000 daily in the developing countries, due to the fact that children are especially vulnerable to the dangers of contaminated water during crises, conflicts or natural disasters. For this reason, the reaction to this type of situations must provide for basic necessities. Thus, after the tsunami in South East Asia, UNICEF is asking that emergency aid should give priority to saving the children.

In industrialised countries, cholera, which was common in the 19th century, has been totally eradicated thanks to sanitation systems and to the treatment of drinking water. However, there have been recent outbreaks in Russia, Iran, China, Malaysia, India and Mexico, even though these countries do not correspond to a definition of risk.

The right to medication

Taking HIV-AIDS as our focal point, an analysis of the means of access to the drugs necessary for combating the disease provides a good example of the inequalities of our world and demonstrates the need to advance along the road to equality.

Data:
— In industrialised countries, preventive treatment with antiretrovirals, and by other means, has eliminated infection by HIV in suckling babies.
— 6 million people in developing countries need antiretroviral therapy but only 400,000 receive it.
— More than 90% of the people who need antiretroviral therapy are to be found in 34 countries with high death rates.
— Half the world's necessities related to antiretroviral treatment are concentrated in 7 countries: South Africa (15.8%), India (10.4%), Kenya (6.4%), Zimbabwe (6.2%), Nigeria (6.1%), Ethiopia (5.0%) and Tanzania (4.1%).
— With the introduction of antiretroviral treatment in Europe and North America, the AIDS death rate has dropped by 80%.
— In Brazil, the establishment of a programme aimed at providing universal access to antiretroviral treatment has succeeded in raising the period of survival of AIDS sufferers from less than 6 months to a minimum of 5 years.
— Even though AIDS is the main cause of death in Africa, it is the countries of this continent that suffer the greatest difficulties when attempting to acquire antiretroviral drugs.

In general, the problems associated with access to the necessary drugs are closely related to the restrictions deriving from international legislation on intellectual property — protected by trade agreements, their high cost, and the lack of investment in research.

Intellectual property rights, which in this case clash with the rights relating to safeguarding public health laid down by the WHO with the approval of the Agreement on Trade-Related Aspects of Intellectual Property Rights, have been a stumbling block for efforts to improve access to drugs which are fundamental for the survival of those affected by AIDS in the developing countries. Nevertheless, the WHO allows the granting of obligatory licences in the case of a national emergency. As an example, South Africa, with more than 3 million people infected, passed an obligatory licence law which allows them to grant licences to local firms for the production of generic anti-AIDS drugs at a low cost. The US pharmaceutical industry opposes this law, as it fears a reduction of its profits because of the production of generic drugs. The sector has appealed to the US government to defend its interests and has managed to apply sanctions against

India, and threatened to do so against Brazil, South Africa and the Dominican Republic.

In Brazil, where there are also local companies producing anti-retrovirals, the cost per month of the continuous double therapy is €80. In Uganda, where it is impossible to obtain generic drugs, the cost is €346 per month for the same treatment.

The problem stems from the fact that the patents for these drugs are controlled by large multinational pharmaceutical companies. This is the case – to take just one – of 'Zidovudine', which was first produced in synthetic form in 1964. Glaxo Wellcome acquired the patent and began to commercialise the drug in 1987 as one of the most expensive ever made. Today this company still has absolute control over its commercialisation. In general, research into these drugs has been carried out with public money, but later, and in spite of the fact that the patents are in the hands of public authorities, the commercialisation of the drugs has come to be controlled by private entities. This situation, along with all the other factors that we have been analysing, is the cause of the scandalous differences in the life perspectives of those infected depending on the country they live in, basically because of the difficulties the developing countries have when attempting to acquire the most effective drugs. We are not speaking, therefore, of a strictly medical matter, but rather of a question which is social, economic, political and, very deeply, moral.

With hunger as a backdrop

Hunger, being as it is inexistent for some, and a weapon of massive destruction for others, is a fact that makes us face up to the shame we should feel as social beings theoretically committed to the defence of the future of our species. Hunger could be defined as another pandemic, in addition to those dealt with above, but it is also important to emphasise that it exists as a backdrop to the diseases that ravage so many human beings. It is obvious that both poverty and hunger are variables that increase the vulnerability of the population and they become important risk factors with relation to these diseases. If we can forget for a moment that every five minutes a child dies of hunger, we must still face up to the fact that chronic hunger and malnutrition facilitate the spread of all types of disease.

It is even more difficult to fully understand the problem, when we realise that the solution is not out of our reach. A solution is possible because we have the appropriate technical, economic and scientific means. International commitments to this end have been made and renewed (the Millennium Development Goals are the most recent). However, reality does not allow us to be too confident about realising this aspiration, when data gathered over the past few years show only minimal advances which are clearly insufficient to achieve success. The most recent spark of hope came again from the UN, in whose

General Assembly of 2004 support was given to the campaign against hunger activated by the Brazilian president, Lula da Silva. Lately, and in line with that statement, a total of 113 countries signed the final declaration of the Meeting of World Leaders for Action against Hunger and Poverty, in which, alongside Brazil, figure especially Chile, France and Spain.

As is the case with other matters pending on the world's agenda for development, the solution to this problem is not merely a question of money, but first and foremost of other priorities such as education or the rights of women. To summarise, it is a question of fighting for the creation of societies which are democratic in the most profound sense of the term, a sense which obviously goes much further than holding regular elections. The promotion of a State of Law, the consolidation of free media and the growth of an active and autonomous civil society are, as we have always argued with deep conviction, the main elements in the fight against poverty, hunger and, in this case, the diseases which cause so many avoidable deaths.

There is hope

Haiti is the poorest country in America and one of the most badly affected by AIDS. Life expectation has dropped from 57 in 1993 to 50 in 2002.
In 2002, 30,000 Haitians died of AIDS and it is estimated that there are 250,000 infected, half of them women. The crisis of Haiti, like that of all the other countries affected by the pandemic, is not irremediable. Proof of this is the recovery, in the midst of social and political turmoil, of two Haitians who are receiving antiretroviral treatment.
Joseph Jeune is a young country worker aged 26, from the town of Lascahobas. His health began to decline in August 2002, with high temperatures and loss of weight as the first symptoms. His family took him to various health centres, but his state deteriorated so much and so quickly that he soon had to remain in bed. His parents were so resigned to losing him that they bought a coffin in preparation. In 2003, when he was on the point of dying, they moved him to the clinic at Lascahobas, where he was given antiretrovirals and treatment for tuberculosis. Joseph spent two months in the hospital and regained 18 kg.
Now, he is again working in the country and earns extra money as a bootblack.
Anna Vincent is 36 and is also from Lascahobas. In 2002, after going from hospital to hospital, she was diagnosed as suffering from AIDS and tuberculosis. Anna was attending sewing classes when she became infected. Her husband, who worked in Port-au-Prince, travelled to Lascahobas to visit Anna in the hospital where she stayed for three weeks receiving treatment for the two diseases. After treatment with antiretrovirals she has recovered, has put on 16 kg, and today she is to be found in the local market in Lascahobas.
Support given to local health systems and the introduction of antiretroviral therapy are the fundamental elements underlying the hope that these two cases represent. The therapy was first applied in 1998 in the hospital of the village of Cange and has been extended recently thanks to the project headed by the World Fund and Partners in Health and aimed at supplying antiretrovirals to some 55,000 infected people, with the idea of eventually reaching 260,000. The project is based on four courses of action:

· Antiretroviral treatment and preventive therapy
· Identification and treatment of cases of tuberculosis
· Identification and treatment of sexually transmitted infections
· Improvement of health services for women

The positive effects of the implantation of this project in local health centres have been multiplied by the arrival of specialist doctors, drugs and vaccines, and by the setting up of family planning and health information programmes.
The administration of antiretroviral treatment is also aided by the 'accompangateurs', community health visitors, who visit patients regularly. Since there are not sufficient beds to be able to hospitalise all the patients, only the most serious cases are taken in and the rest receive treatment at home, with the 'accompangateurs' being responsible for supervising correct administration.

It also depends on you

Without forgetting the need to activate our consciences when there is a cataclysm (whether it be the hurricane Mitch or the seaquake in South East Asia), the solutions to the problems must be structural. To deal with them from the point of view of an emergency is not enough to achieve substantial progress in the fight against pandemics.

In order to combat these diseases it is necessary to develop strategies which will only be successful if they emphasise prevention and the persistent, long-term collaboration of many people. This, in practical terms, means contributing with our technical and financial resources in a more sustained and less irregular fashion. The response activated by our emotions will always be positive in that it will show us to be people who are sensitive to the problems of our fellow beings, but a rational response will be even more so in that it will demonstrate that we understand that our individual effort, however anonymous and tiny it may be, will contribute to the planning of a strategy against ills and problems which needs the collaboration of many over a long period of time.

Document produced by researchers from the
Institute of Studies on Conflicts and Humanitarian Action (IECAH)
Madrid, January, 2005

Boris Mikhailov

'Here and now': this is my principal credo in photography. I remained faithful to it during the Soviet era and beyond, through the dismantling of the Soviet Union. And now too, I continue to hold fast to it.

If one looks into the eyes of a poor person, the right to freedom is defended. But if one doesn't look, tranquillity is safeguarded, tranquillity, inner calm, harmony. This is a phenomenon that is related to a cultural question.

Could it not be argued in defence of this peculiar aesthetic behaviour that a minimal commitment involves not photographing, not showing that which is bad? And yet this commitment may not be enough when the weight of that which is bad increases and can no longer be ignored, and more so when it becomes necessary to know how this situation has come about. Further, I should add that in a country where everyone was always being manipulated, we were morally obliged to portray the utter defencelessness and the lack of rights that people suffered. And in my book "Case History" that is what I tried to convey.

Not long ago, I accidentally found myself participating in a debate about the role of the 'left' and 'right' in art. I'm no expert in this matter, but the discussion made me consider a very serious question: it seemed to me interesting to try and understand the sources of the shift from 'left' to 'right'.

I'm interested in understanding the causes of the drift from the 'left' towards the 'right'.

I'd like to examine it through three books I produced in the '90s. The first two ("*U zemli*" ["On the Ground"] and "*Súmerki*" ["At Dusk"]) referred to the general situation, the worsening of the general standard of living. The final book ("*Istoriya Bolezni*" ["Case History"]) deals, in large part, with the homeless. Why did "Case History" provoke a double reaction? Why did it receive positive and negative reviews? Because in this book something new appeared. But it's not a question of depicting that which is bad, but rather the appearance of personality. "Case History" marked a transition from a general vision ("On the Ground", "At Dusk"*)* to the observation of the private, the particular. At this level, personality becomes more evident. For me, personality does not mean the personality of a particular person. For me, the individuals I photographed represented collectives. I have always been searching for the model of that which is Russian, of that which is local, of that which forms part of the folklore, for the kind of person whose image best expressed the general situation. But the viewer could interpret these images in the sense that the rights of a particular person were being infringed. In effect there does exist here the possibility of thinking about the inviolability of personality and the inviolability of that which is private. Though, as far as I'm concerned, at that time and in that place, personal space still did not exist for anybody - time had not yet created it. The homeless had no passports, lacked documents and private space. They did not possess what is understood, here in the West, to be personal. However, I have the impression that I did not destroy that which is personal, and not just because it did not yet exist. The possibility of perceiving the violation of a person's rights was enough to lead to an outcry from those who did not wish our dirty washing to be done in public, those who had seen no reason to protest against "On the Ground" or "At Dusk". It is a dangerous zone in which the left can begin to lean towards the right.

I do not consider that "Case History" crossed this limit for, when you see the enormous number of shrunken, shrivelled people and the huge amounts of pain, the personal defencelessness of the homeless only contributes to seeing the tragedy more acutely. And for me, this is the path 'away from the left'.

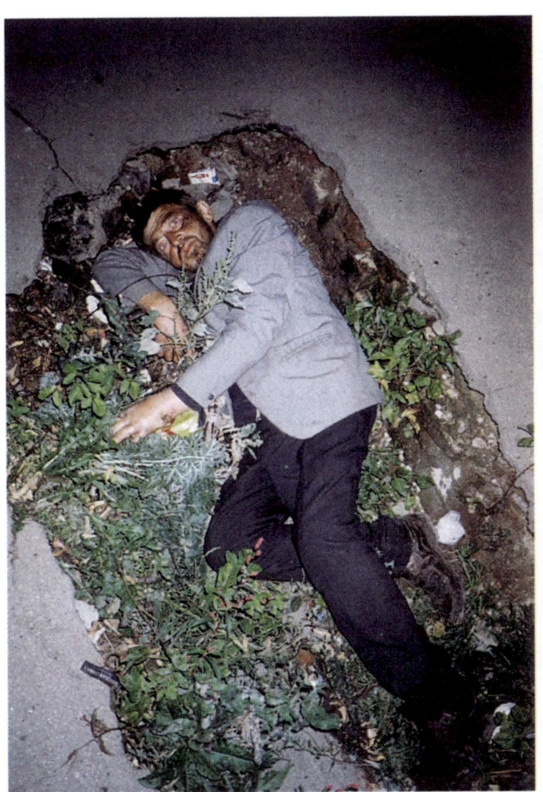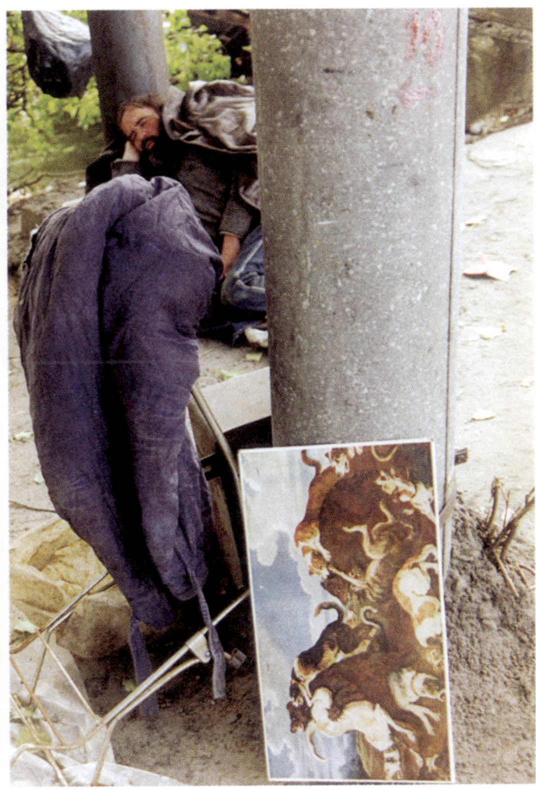

Boris Mikhailov
"Untitled", from the series *Case History*,
1998-1999
Colour photograph
150 x 100 cm

"Untitled", from the series *Case History*,
1998-1999
Colour photograph
150 x 100 cm

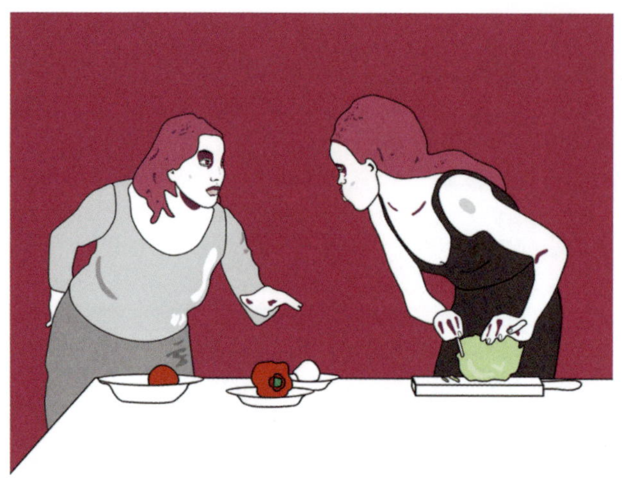

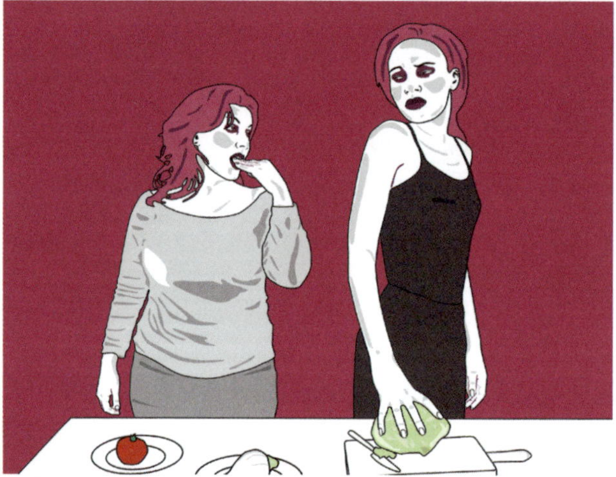

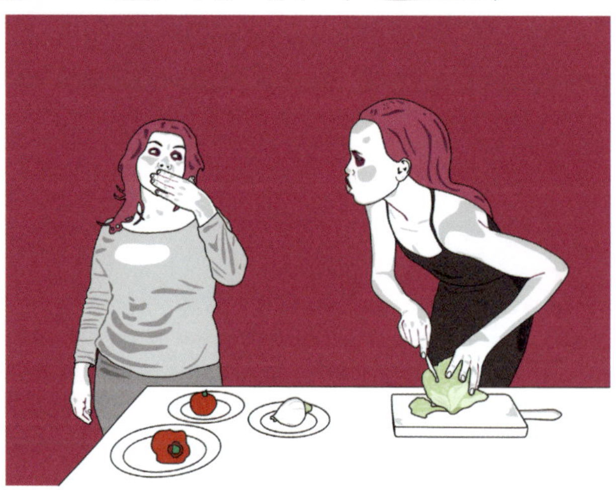

Ruth Gómez
Te sobrealimentas, 2003
Animation. DVD colour video with sound
23'' looped

Further reading

BERGHAM, G. (2004): *The Invisible People; How the U.S. Has Slept Through the Global AIDS Pandemic, the Greatest Humanitarian Catastrophe of Our Time*, New York, Free Press.
GARRETT, L. (1994): *The Coming Plague*, Penguin Books, New York.
GOSTIN, L.; KIRBY M.; GOSTIN, L. (2004): *The AIDS Pandemic: Complacency, Injustice, and Unfulfilled Expectations*, University of Carolina Press (US).
HOGG, R. (2002): *Time to act: global apathy towards HIV/AIDS is a crime against humanity*, The Lancet. Vol. 360. N. 30.
KATIN K, HEALY E. (2000): *The new drug approvals of 1996, 1997 and 1998: drug development trends in the user fee era.* Drug Inform J.
LEVY, J.A. (1993): *Pathogenesis of HIV Infection*, Microbiology Review, 57.
MITSUYA, H.; WEINHOLD, K.; YARCHOAN R.; BOLOGNESI, D.; BRODER, S. (1989): *Credit government scientist with developing anti-AIDS drug.* The New York Times, 28th September.
MORSE, S. S. (*ed.*) (1993): *Emerging Viruses*, Oxford University Press.
FEACHEM, R (2003): Conférence Mondiale sur Le Sida. Paris (14-16 juillet).Le Monde. Dossiers & Documents. N. 323, Sep-03, Dossier 3, p. 2.
ZWI, K.; SÖDERLUND, N.; SCHNEIDER, H. (2000): *Cheaper antiretrovirals to treat AIDS in South Africa*, BMJ.

Websites of interest

- FAO: http://www.fao.org
- The World health report (2004): http://www.who.int/whr/2004
- Doctors without Borders "Campaign for Access to Essential Medicines": http://www.accessmed-msf.org/index.asp
- UNAIDS: http://www.unaids.org
- World Health Organization: http://www.who.int
- Global Call for Access to Treatment: http://www.globaltreatmentaccess.org/content/camp/gcall/gcalleng.htm
- AIDS and Human Rights: http://www.hrw.org/doc/?t=hivaids&document_limit=0,2

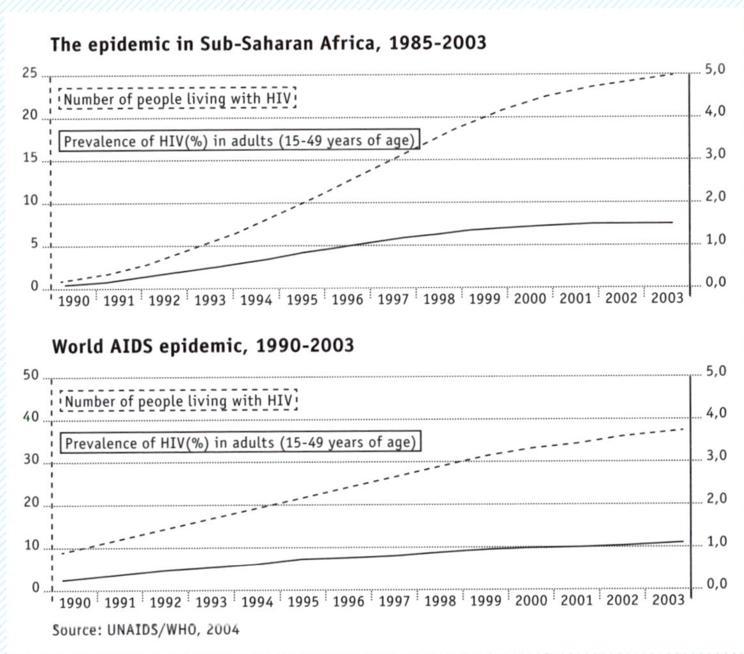

Access to education and culture is a basic requirement for development, be it individual or social. The conception of both dimensions has evolved from merely instructive visions of missions based on the acquisition of knowledge – in the case of education, or the promotion of the fine arts – in the case of culture, to more open approaches that cover a large part of human development.

Although it is a concept so widely handled every day, it is not easy to exactly establish its profiles. For the effects analysed here, it is enough to understand it as a complex magnum that includes knowledge, beliefs, art, morale, law, customs and any other habits and capacities acquired by human beings as members of society. Following its etymological sense – from the Latin, *'cultivo'*, culture, or rather cultures, are other forms in which we human beings responsibly cultivate our relationships with each other, with our context and with nature. Education from this perspective is fundamental for developing the capacity that will lead us to relate with each other in one way or another.

For its part, the UNESCO defines culture as 'the series of definitive spiritual, material, intellectual and emotional traits that characterise human groups and which includes, beyond arts and letters, forms of life, human rights, the value systems and beliefs'.

For its part, the term education has two complementary origins. On the one hand, it comes from *'educare'*, which means to lead, and in this sense it would consist of indicating the correct path, marking the route and ensuring that it is followed. An educated society is an organised society. However, etymologically there is second route to the term educate, more suited to the way it is understood today. *'Educere'*, which means to extract, indicates that educating is helping the educated person to extract and develop their own capacities and human potential, and with this, being able to take decisions freely and responsibly.

Cultural Freedom in different societies in the 21st century

Co-existence in different societies makes it necessary to recognise cultural freedom, which is what allows people to choose their identity – who they are – and to live without losing access to other options that are important to them. Cultural freedom is violated when there is no respect for or recognition of the values, institutions or lifestyles of certain cultural groups and when people are discriminated against because of their cultural identity, provided these signs of identity do not transgress the framework defined by human rights.

As Will Kymlcka rightly indicates, there are two basic forms of exclusion: exclusion from lifestyle and through the degree of participation in common life. In the first case, the cultural manifestations of a group are denigrated or repressed by the State – prohibition on the use of language, of a certain religious practice, of certain clothes. In the second case, there is social, political or economic marginalisation for the simple fact of being ethnically, linguistically or religiously different from the dominant group.

The UNDP report on Human Development in 2004 pays special attention to this subject, by including as a title 'Cultural freedom in today's diverse world'. Its pages deal with the fundamental idea that cultural freedom must be considered another human right, understood as a basic pillar for achieving development in 21st century societies. At the same time, it quantitatively evaluates the number of people who suffer from these main forms of exclusion: 518 million excluded because of their lifestyle, 750 million for economic reasons and 832 million for political reasons.

Some voices on the international scene have sung out to express what cultural freedom means for them:

Nelson Mandela (former President of South Africa) declares that 'once we won power, we chose to conceive as a strength the diversity of colours and languages that had been used to divide us.'

Shirin Ebadi (Winner of the Nobel Peace Prize in 2003 and an Iranian activist lawyer) understands that 'all cultures share some principles.'

John Hume (Irish politician and Winner of the Nobel Peace Prize in 1998) maintains that 'the European Union has achieved that a wide range of traditions are no longer a reason for conflict and have become a seed of unification.'

It is unfortunately obvious that some communities see their cultural freedom threatened on a daily basis, and this threat can become a problem for their co-existence:

— In the world there are some 150 countries with significant ethnic minorities and only 30 with none, which means less than 10 per cent of the population.
— In Indonesia, the Chinese population is three per cent of the total, but controls 70 per cent of the private economy. Despite their economic power, it is difficult for them to be educated in Chinese.
— Some 300 million people around the world belong to indigenous groups distributed in 70 countries and speaking 4000 languages.
— The 50 million indigenous people in Latin America represent 11 per cent of the population. In Bolivia and Guatemala, they account for over half the population of the country.

In the light of such realities it can be stated that in general terms we find a broad majority of multicultural societies made up of various ethnic or linguistic groups. To deal with the co-existence between these communities, we must have a flexible socio-political model that gives space for the autonomy for each of them and which, at the same time, enables the consolidation of common spaces on the basis of shared values and principles. It is essential that the public authorities must nurture and guarantee the fundamental freedoms of the person and that any form of discrimination on the grounds of gender, religion or ethnic origin must be prevented. This means that in certain circumstances, it will not be possible to discard measures of positive discrimination aimed at compensating initial collective disadvantages, but always under careful control to avoid them becoming negative discrimination.

With resources and without investing in education

Intermon-Oxfam has created an indicator – the Education Performance Index (EPI) to measure some aspects of the educational differences between developing countries. The aim is to identify which factors have the greatest influence in a national educational output. The EPI calculates the average difference that separates a country from the ideal educational level: 100% enrolment and completion of studies on each level and 0% difference between sexes. The countries with the lowest IDE are therefore those in a better situation.

A line of extreme deprivation has also been established, under which lie the countries with a deficit of over 33%. This figure means that more than one-third of the children have no school education and that an even lower percentage complete their studies, with the difference between the boys and girls being also over 33%.
This indicator also relates the educational data with income levels, so that it allows the existence to be observed of countries with serious economic difficulties which, however, achieve educational achievements far higher than those of others with a better income level. Obviously other cases are given where the opposite occurs. These latter would include Brazil, Colombia, Venezuela and Guatemala, which occupy a place between 15 and 45 times lower than the one that should correspond to them according to their income levels. Other countries with a deficient level of education according to their income levels are Pakistan (with a difference of 38 places), Kuwait (with 54) and Saudi Arabia (with 48).

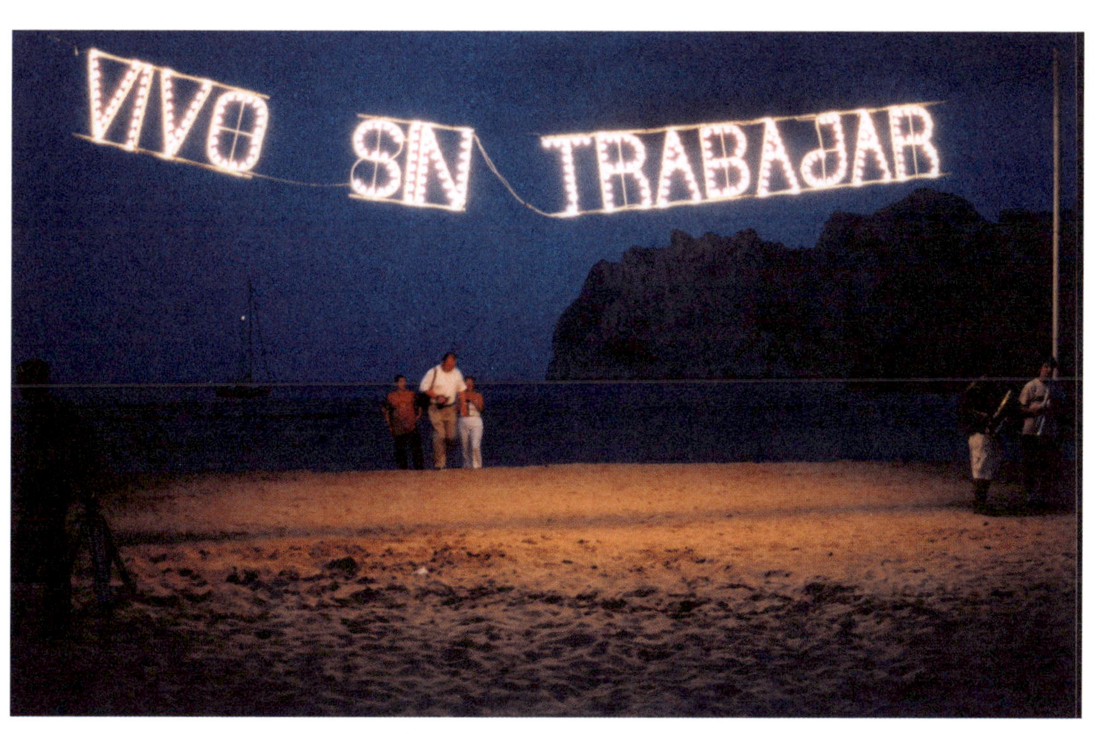

Fernando Sánchez Castillo
Vivo sin trabajar, 2002
Lit-up sign
80 x 1000 x 15 cm

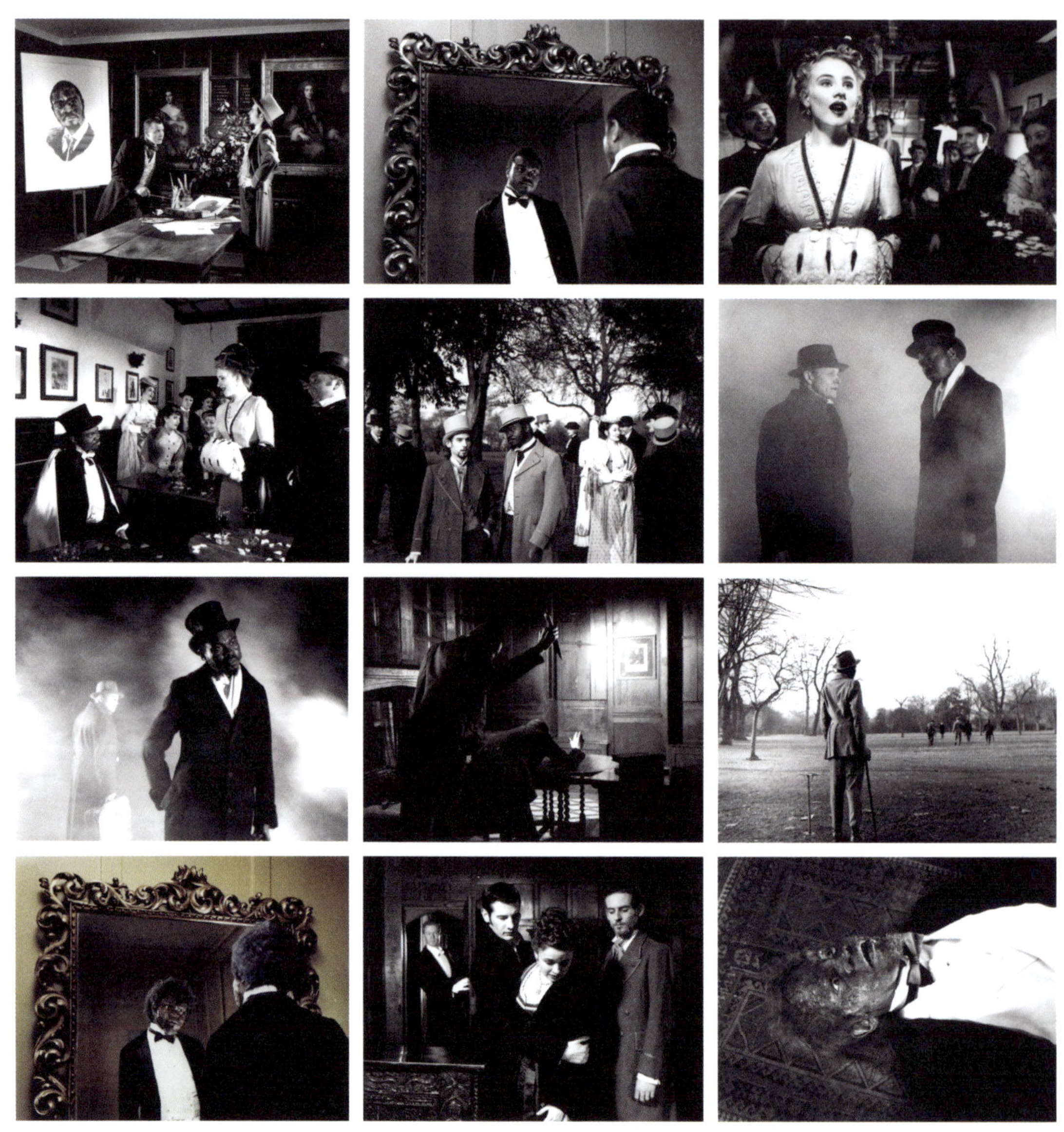

Yinka Shonibare
Dorian Gray, 2001
Installation consisting of eleven black-
and-white photographs and one colour
photograph (122 x 152,5 cm each)
Variable dimensions

140

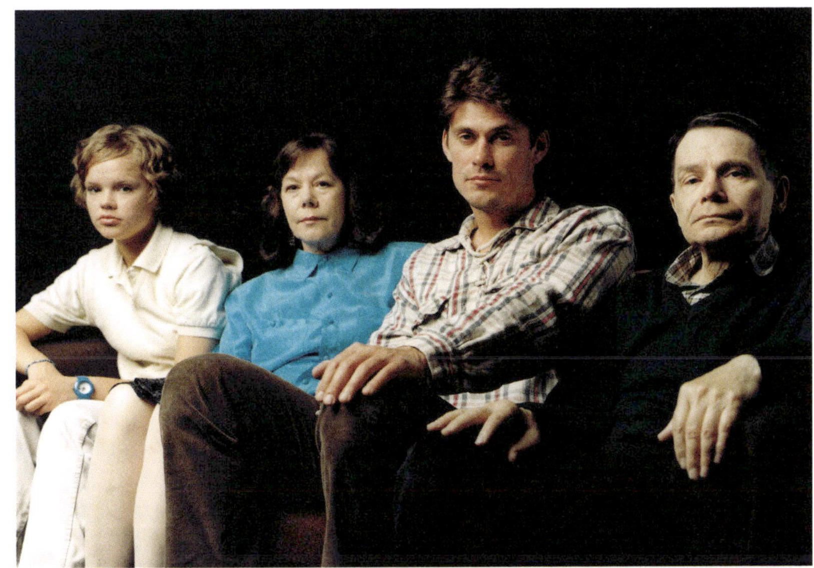

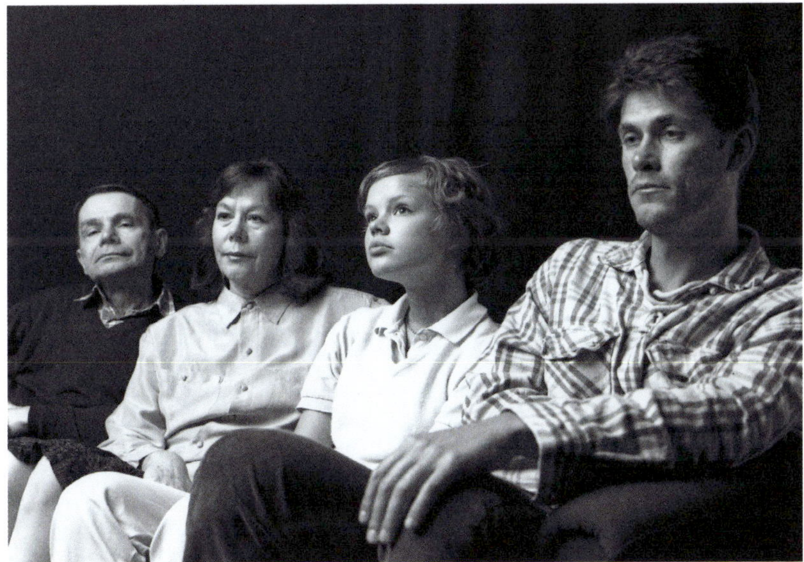

Eija-Liisa Ahtila
Tänään/Today, 1996-1997
Video installation comprised of three
projections (Film S-16/35 mm transferred
to DVD, 10' looped)
Variable dimensions

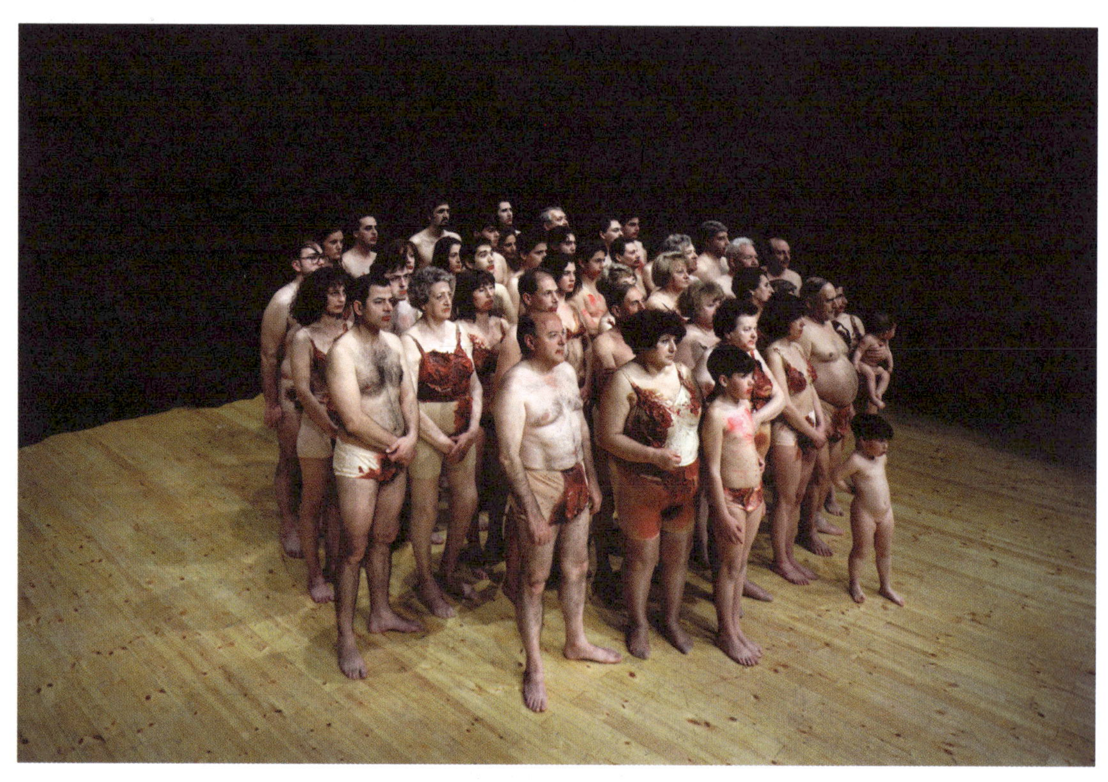

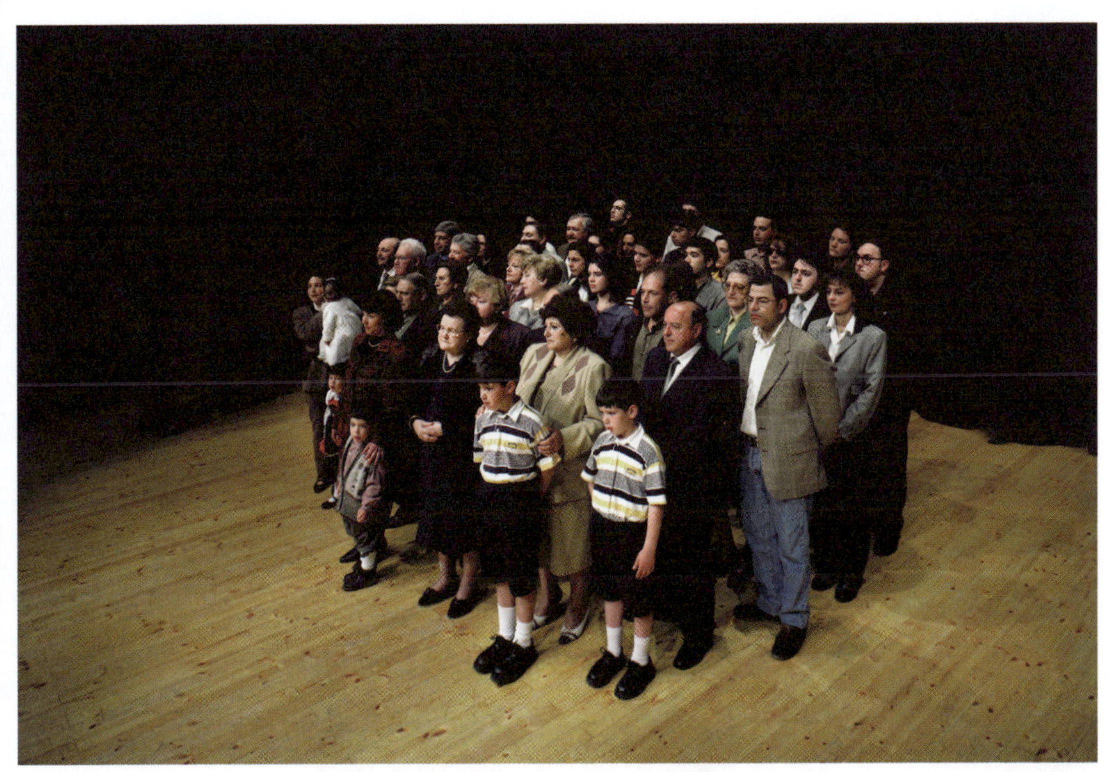

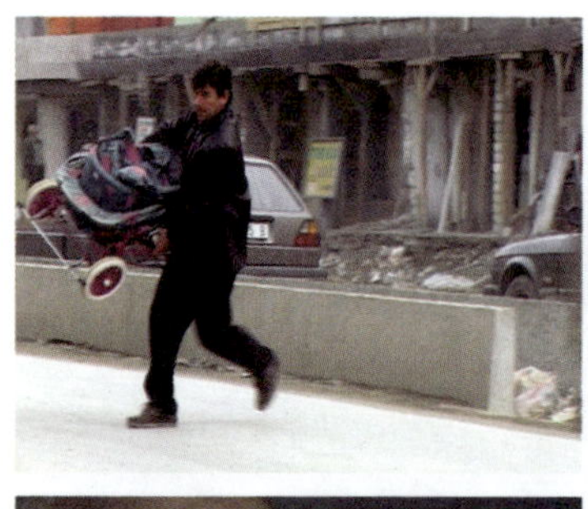
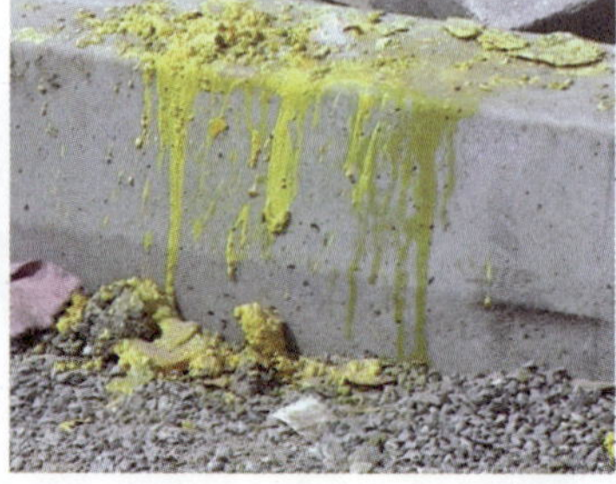
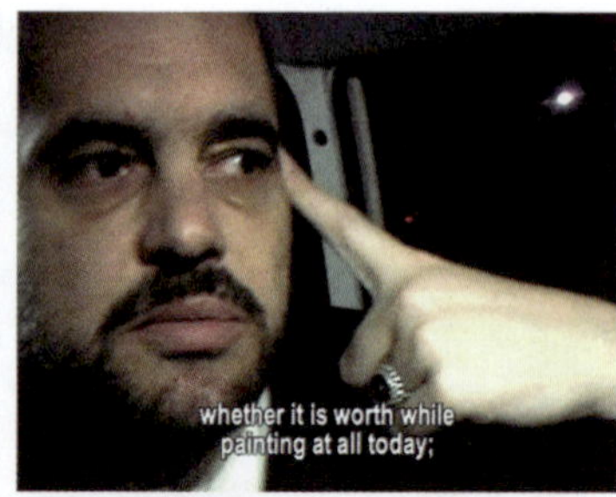
whether it is worth while
painting at all today;
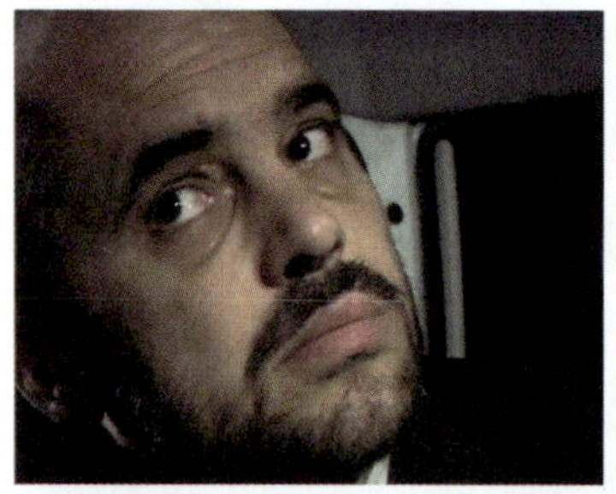
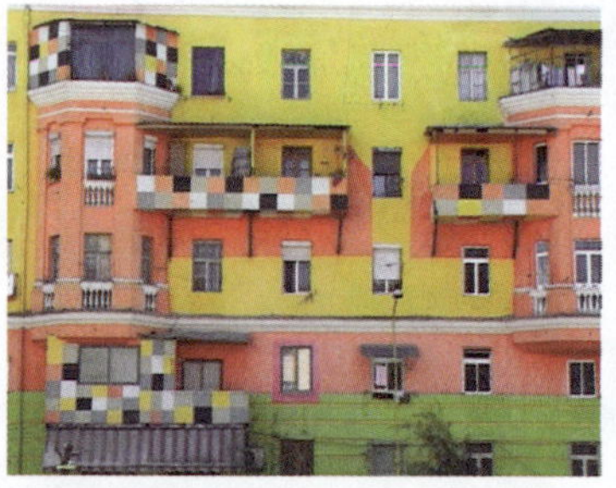
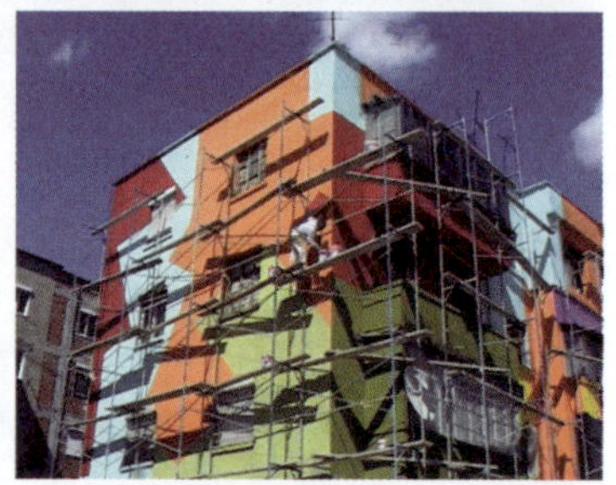
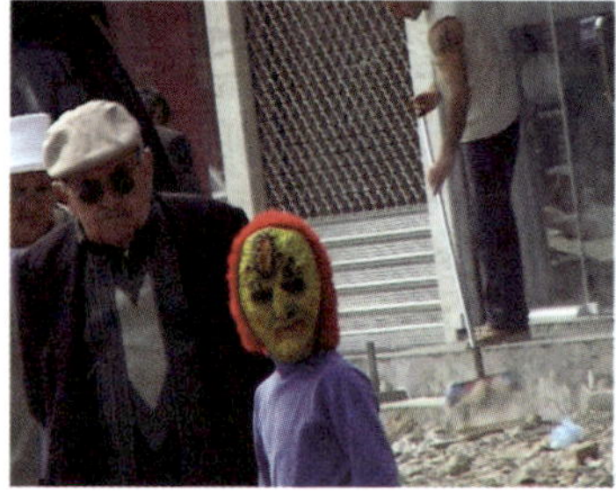
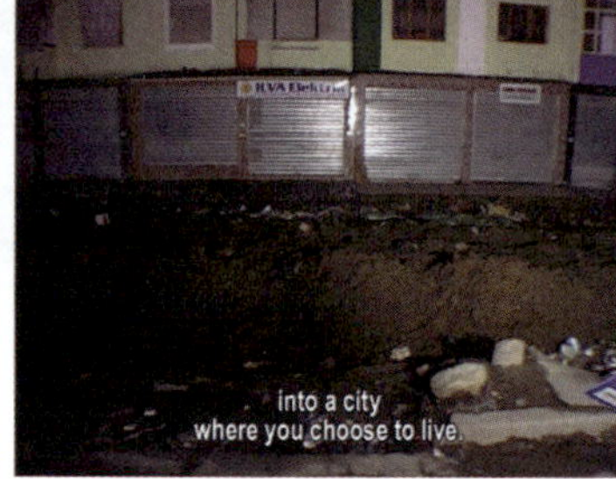
into a city
where you choose to live.
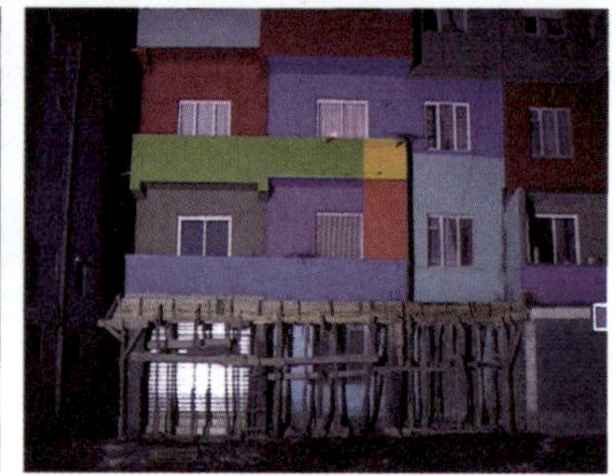

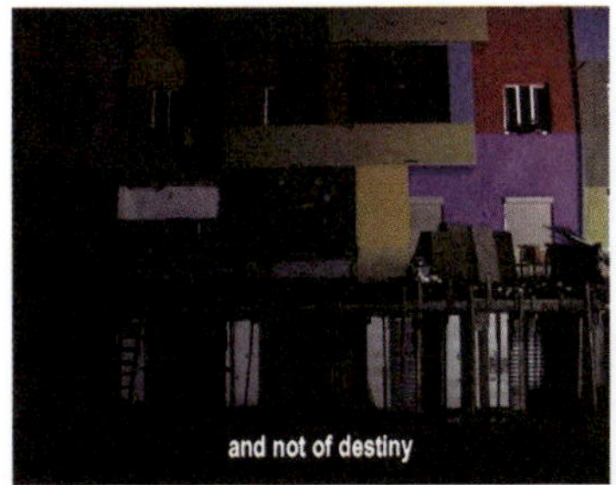

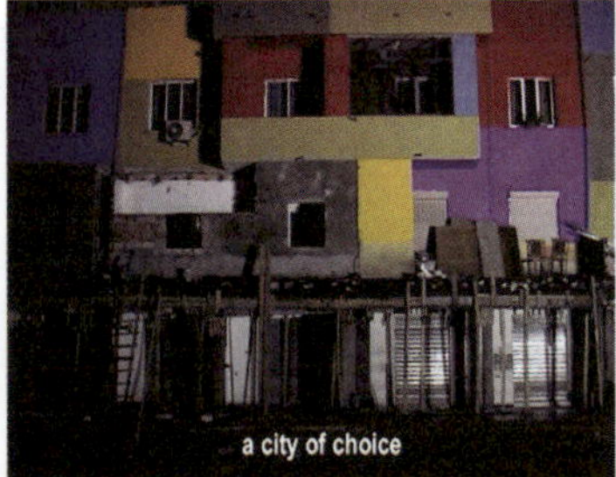

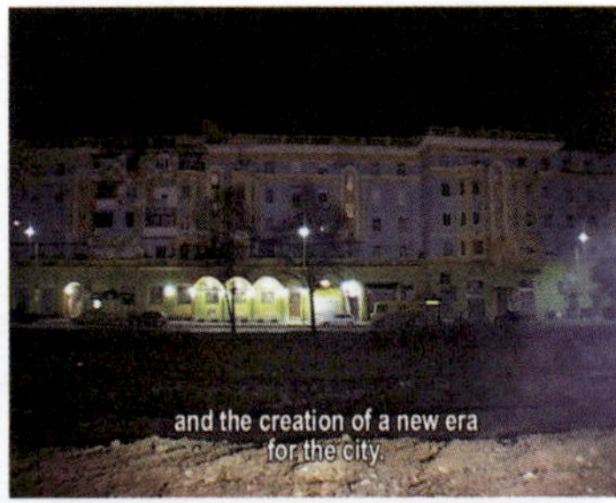

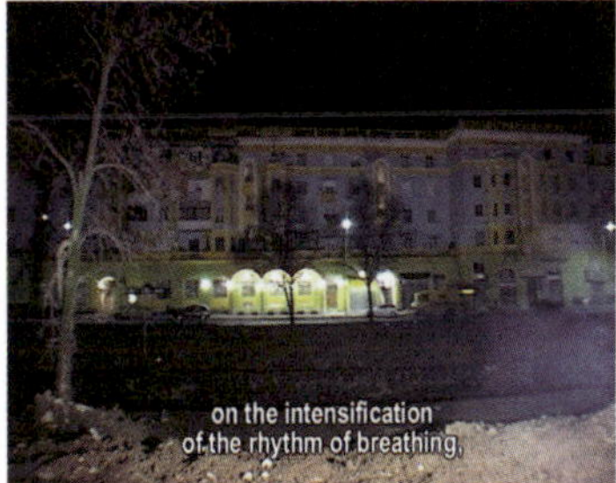

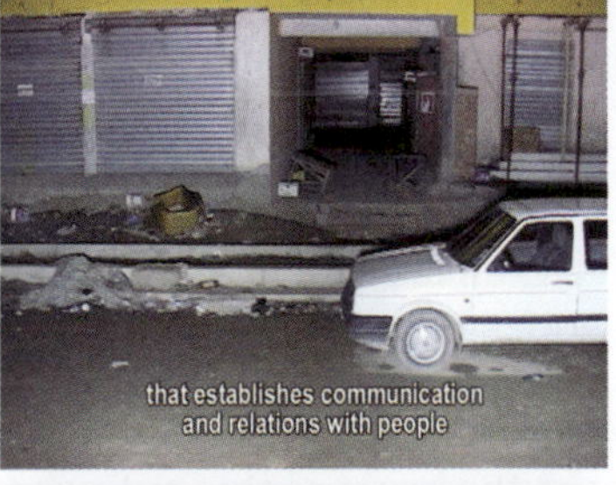

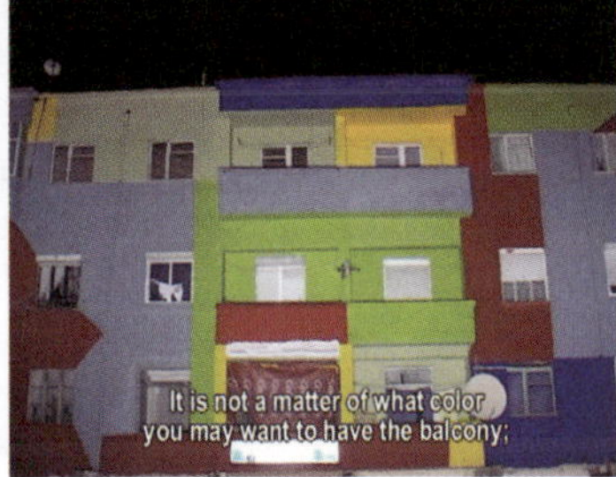

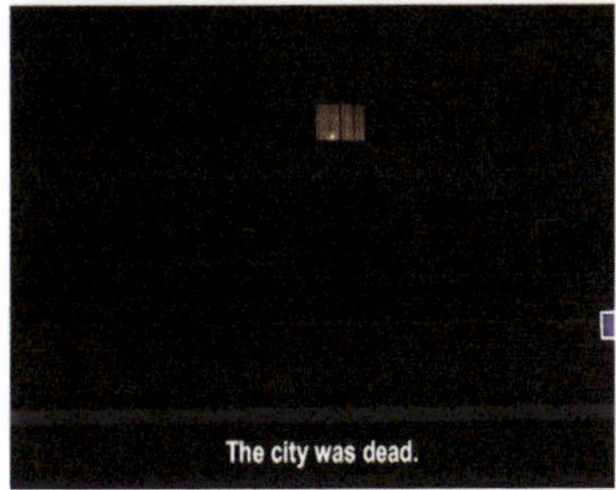

Anri Sala
Dammi i colori, 2003
DVD colour video with sound
15' 24"

Myths concerning cultural freedom

There are certain presumptions, many based on well-established prejudices, concerning cultural freedom. In a certain way to face the challenges of the 21ˢᵗ century concerning co-existence in diversity, it is important to overcome them, and discover the fallacies that have enabled them to become sustained myths, in many cases, in the most elemental lack of analysis:

Some cultures have more chances of development than others

In the face of this idea, the already mentioned UNDP 2004 Report insists on confirming that it is factors such as economic growth, economic policy, geography and the number of illnesses that have conditioned the level of the country's development, while cultural variables have been of little influence.

The example of Islam and its supposed incompatibility with democratic values is a recurrent case in which, in addition to appealing to pretended deterministic attitudes and commonplaces – 'they are people who are not prepared to choose for themselves' – it is forgotten that at the heart of this culture there are some components that could contribute to the true development of open societies – consultation ('*shura*'), independent reasoning ('*ijithad*') and consensus ('*ijma*'). Neither should we forget the commandment of the Koran by which, concerning religion, there may be no coercion.

In many cases, this interested confusion is applied, for instance, to the Islamic religion, using negative stereotypes that present it as radically opposed to democratic principles – as if the other two great religions 'of the book' were, by contrast, shining examples of the contrary. One thing is, in short, that practically all Arab countries today and lack democratic structures. Another, very different thing, is to interpret this as the direct result of religion and not of rulers interested in maintaining a firm grip on their populations, with Islam, amongst others, as an instrument in their service. Aside from the fact that there are countries with Islamic majorities with models comparable with others we consider democratic, the important thing is to understand that power in closed societies always tends to use the control mechanisms it has within reach, without this necessarily leading us to make value judgements on the relevant religion.

Cultural diversity inevitably leads to conflicts on values
This is the central approach of the 'clash of civilisations' model drawn up by Samuel P Huntington. It is true that many conflicts have a cultural component as a backdrop, confronting groups struggling to achieve their autonomy. In general each band in conflict considers that it forms part of the same culture. However, it has been shown that although this factor might influence the conflict to a varying extent, the main causes behind it are usually others. These are the variables of economic, resource control, power or territorial domination, when they are not derived from the inequalities between different social groups obliged to share the same territory, which fundamentally explain the immense majority of cases of organised violence and the current armed conflicts.

There are many examples of conflicts in which the political, social and economic components are identified as the main causes, although some would wish to present them simplistically as cultural clashes. Amongst these, we might mention those in:

— Malaysia: The attacks against the Chinese in this country in 1916 were result of the economic domination of the Chinese majority over the politically dominant majority.
— Uganda: Despite their undeniable economic power, Bantu speakers are marginalised in political terms compared with non-Bantu speakers.
— South Africa: Before 1994, the black majority suffered a very serious social, economic and political exclusion and this is what basically caused the uprisings after 1976, which produced the fall of apartheid in 1993.
— Nepal: The Maoist insurgency that started in 1996 may be related to the marginalisation suffered by certain ethnic groups, castes and women.

Diversity is not an obstacle on development

There is no obvious link a priori between diversity and development. Traditionally it has been considered that within the framework of the nation states it is easier for public matters to function and be co-ordinated if they start from a single cultural identity. In fact, it is a very complicated task to organise states based on cultural diversity. As has been seen before, when referring to the links between conflicts and cultural diversity, in this case it is not a question so much of placing the emphasis on the cultural diversity-development relationship, as understanding that the social, economic and political differences between the various groups co-existing in a society may make their joint development difficult. The priority therefore, if we intend to prevent any confrontation, will be to reduce and eliminate the said inequalities.

Furthermore, there are examples of countries such as the United States or India, with severe cultural diversity and which, however, do not present acute level of conflict between the different groups. In fact, India, with its 15 different official languages and its varied religious image, has no doubt in presenting itself as the largest democracy on the planet.

The challenge of universal education for 2015

Education is a fundamental right recognised as such in Article 26 of the Universal Declaration of Human Rights, according to which 'all people have a right to education'. It also appears thus in the Convention on the Rights of the Child approved in 1989, which in its Article 28 states:

- States Parties recognise children's right to education and with a view to achieving this right progressively, and on the basis of equal opportunity, they shall, in particular:
  — Make primary education compulsory and available free to all (...).
  — Take measures to encourage regular attendance at schools and the reduction of drop-out rates (...).

- States Parties shall promote and encourage international co-operation in matters relating to education, in particular with a view to contributing to the elimination of ignorance and illiteracy throughout the world.

From these two articles, certain responsibilities are derived to guarantee the achievement of this fundamental right. The task, in any case, is arduous if we bear in mind the situation reflected by the data given to us by the United Nations on enrolment rates in primary education and literacy rates, particularly in developing countries. The minimum objective to be achieved is clearly defined within the framework of the Millennium Development Goals 2000: to guarantee universal primary education by 2015. What remains to be seen is how far the real commitment goes of 191 member states of the United Nations organisation in fulfilling it.

The difficulties of fulfilling this objective, which UNICEF also considers priority in its 2004 Report, obviously do not lie in bringing together the necessary financial funds to cover the costs of the programmes that must be started up, or in designing such programmes. The key lies in managing to convince the governments of the countries with the greatest deficiencies in this area to commit themselves sincerely to improving it, something that can not always be taken for granted. Secondly, it is also necessary to mobilise political will in the most developed countries to increase their degree of involvement in the process, which, to judge from the results to date, will not be easy. In addition to universality in primary education, the most immediate priorities involve placing even more emphasis on the schooling of girls, and on allowing access to primary education in the mother tongue.

In this last aspect, different studies have shown that failure to study in the mother tongue in the first six years of life may negatively affect development. If this is the case, then the situation in Africa is still more alarming, where only 13 per cent of girls have access to education in the mother tongue. A continent, furthermore, where 2500 languages are spoken and where many people have great difficulties in expressing themselves in their language in the area of education or in their relations with the administration.

Some problems of education and culture in the 21st century

• **The path to interculturality**

The 20th century, and nothing has changed in this sense in our times, was characterised by the massive arrival of immigrants in Europe from Asia, Africa and Latin America. For their part, the United States and Canada received migratory flows from the south of the American Continent.

One figure that reflects the consequences of this phenomenon is that more than 300 languages are spoken in the schools of London. In these cases it seems a basic need to allow immigrants to live in their adoptive countries without giving up their origins. Therefore, it is necessary to go beyond the classical debate between integration and assimilation to apply policies of cultural recognition in a framework of unquestionable diversity. In this context, for the application and development of suitable educational policies, we must identify what is understood by cultural identity and by multicultural or intercultural societies. The educational model to be developed will depend on this.

In 2001, UNESCO, with the unanimity of the 185 member states represented at the meeting of its general conference, approved a declaration on Cultural Diversity. For first time, the international community had a regulatory instrument based on the conviction that respect for the diversity of cultures and intercultural dialogue is one of the greatest guarantees of development and peace.

To define today what is understood by multiculturalism, cultural pluralism or interculturalism is a central need. Only from here will it be possible, on the one hand, to suitably deal with the socio-cultural and educational management models and, on the other, the policies recognising difference.

Multiculturalism and interculturality have been shown as two forms within culturally plural societies. If in the 1960s the idea of cultural pluralism was introduced, the 70s gave rise to the idea of multiculturalism while the 80s saw the emergence of the theories on interculturality. The last of these theories were born out of the limitations of the multicultural focus, which was considered insufficient to deal with models of social cohesion of the political community. Interculturality is fundamentally based on the interaction between subjects or entities that are culturally different. It is not sufficient to recognise difference – multiculturalism, we must also consider mechanisms to promote the relationship between the said diverse entities. We must pass, therefore, from naming the differences to seeking points of convergence.

At the same time, interculturality as applied to the area of education means, on the one hand, overcoming exclusion and respecting the cultures and identities present in the educational area and, on

the other, focusing education in such a way that mutual learning
and exchange is encouraged with specific training in diversity and
democratic values.

- **Education, culture and ideology**

Education is not, in any case, an aseptic question. Its benefits are in-
numerable in all orders of individual and social life. It is undeniable
that education provides capacities to be able to aspire to a decent life
and to express opinions, know their rights and demand their compliance: in short it allows one to be heard and to participate more fully
in public life as a fundamental factor for human development.

But there is also a negative side, insofar as it can be used as
a form of cultural imposition of one over another. History is full of
examples of the manipulation of educational systems and cultural
manifestations in the service of reactionary, discriminatory causes
and discourses, when not directly aggressive. Nazism in Germany,
and Apartheid in South Africa are unfortunately only two examples
of many. The capacity of those in power to use the instruments of the
State in their favour, from religious approaches or any other kind,
is a reality that obliges us to be vigilant in order to avoid errors or
tendencies dangerous for co-existence. In this sense, the attention is
not restricted to the area of formal education but to any other artistic
or public information manifestation that might be contaminated by
intolerable principles.

To reply to these kinds of movements, it is only necessary to
establish a firm will to remain within the framework defined by all
of the human rights and by the promotion of democratic values, imposing, when necessary all relevant sanctions. To specify this in
one principle, we must not be tolerant with the intolerant and with
those who intend to create their own spaces outside of the rules of a
state of law. The effort must be applied in promoting the processes of
democratic co-existence both in the field of education and in general
culture, helping to identify and enhance shared interests between
different communities and rigorously pursuing any activity that
might feed confrontation or hatred between citizens from different
cultural communities.

- **The development of cultural homogenisation**

It is estimated that there have been some 10,000 languages spoken in
the world, of which today only around 6000 are spoken. The forecasts,
all pessimistic, are that this figure will fall by 50 to 90 per cent in
the coming 100 years. What was once considered divine condemnation is today recognised as an immense human capital, a sign of our
diversity and our ability to adapt to the environment. This process
of linguistic concentration is also happening fast in other areas of
cultural activity – the written press, radio and television, cinema,

music, literature. It seems as if the attraction of what is large and simple (unified by a dominant universal rule) is irremediably being imposed.

At one time, when almost nothing seemed to escape the powerful influence of the economic laws, the perception of culture was accentuated as a mere product of the leisure industry, understood in many cases as an object of luxury reserved for the wealthy. The marketing of culture, and of education, is an obvious trait of our societies, as has been indicated by José Saramago who complained that "the great threat is that of the market law, which sets out to transform the cultural product into merchandise. The pressure of the great multinationals of the sector, or clearly dominant countries such as the United States, poses the need for a response from a European Union that aspires to produce a different model of development that is respectful and enhances its original diversity".

What is discussed in essence is whether culture is a right which, in order to be exercised, needs the approval of protectionist laws against these dominant and mercantile tendencies or whether, as others think, it should be a matter simply submitted to market laws. Is it pure coincidence that the television programmes and films from the United States represent two-thirds of the global market? Is it too that their music, their fashions and even their feeding habits are imitated throughout the world? And what about the fact that every year more than half a million of the best foreign students enter their university system?

It is in this context that a large meeting of the UNESCO has been called in Paris for February 2005. The 190 countries represented will discuss the convenience of setting up a treaty to protect cultural diversity. The initial positions already indicate that any development will be very difficult. On the one hand, countries such as the United States and Japan, but also Holland, do not even support the idea of this meeting, considering that no regulation is necessary in the subject. Others, and particularly France, but also the majority of the states of the European Union, turn their efforts towards a framework to confront this destructive penetration, without excluding the need to impose limits on the cultural penetration of a certain country or medium. Although it is early to discern an end to this process, we can already see how some countries, such as the United States, are trying to anticipate what could hypothetically be harmful to them. In its agreements with Morocco and some Latin American countries, the United States is contemplating that the concession of the preferential entry of exports from these countries is linked to the free access to these markets for the United States' cinema and communication industries, including the purchase of packages of films. What are we to expect?

It also depends on you
We are undoubtedly faced with the challenge of overcoming obstacles that threaten co-existence between plural and diverse societies. In education, an intercultural approach is needed and one aimed at overcoming any form of exclusion. Also in the cultural field, one of the fundamental questions is the transmission of values and principles that enhance co-existence and tolerance of those who are perceived as different and which enable the peaceful resolution of controversies that inevitably arise in any collective framework.

The discussion over how to face cultural diversity is certainly not a matter exclusive of our times. Already in the 17th century Joseph-Marie de Maistre tried to call our attention to the need to change the focus on matters of co-existence and diversity when he said that he knew 'Frenchman, Englishmen and Germans but not men'. Montesquiu, for his part, had no doubt in saying that 'if I find something that is useful for my nation but were dangerous for another, I would not propose it to the Prince because I am a man more than just a Frenchman'. Maybe this is a good starting point to look at 'others', in the search for structures that bring together the affective, the rational, the intuitive and the dreamed to build a framework of co-existence that respects cultural diversity in all its manifestations and which educates respect for differences. Culture, effectively, cannot remain just a luxury or a saleable good because it is, in short, what raises us above the animal kingdom, enabling us to answer with dignity to our name.

Document prepared by researchers from the
Institute of Studies on Conflicts and Humanitarian action (IECAH)
Madrid, January 2005

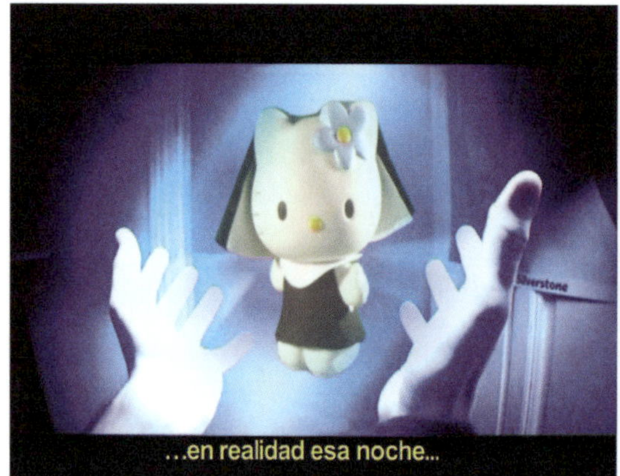

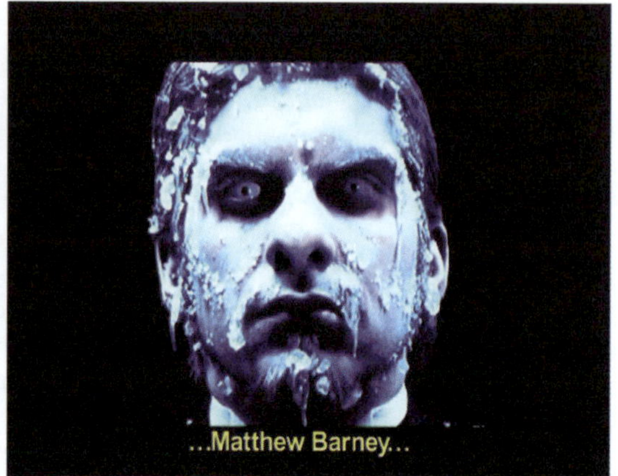

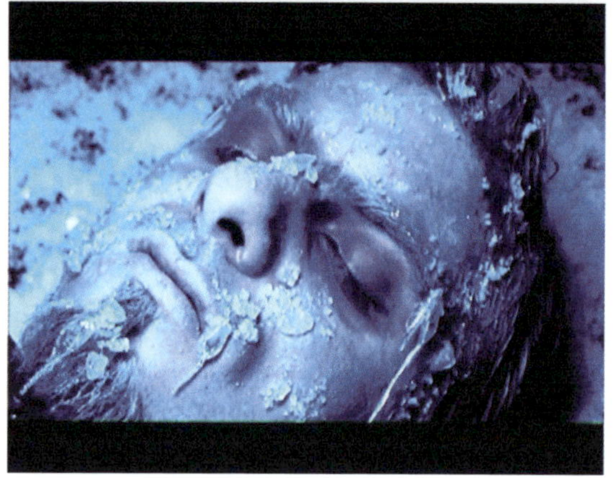

Martín Sastre
Videoart: The Iberoamerican Legend, 2002
DVD colour video with sound
16'

154

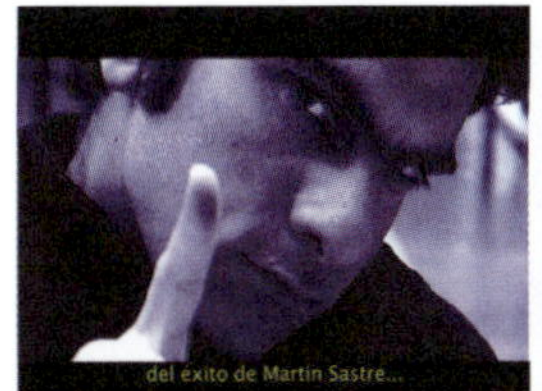

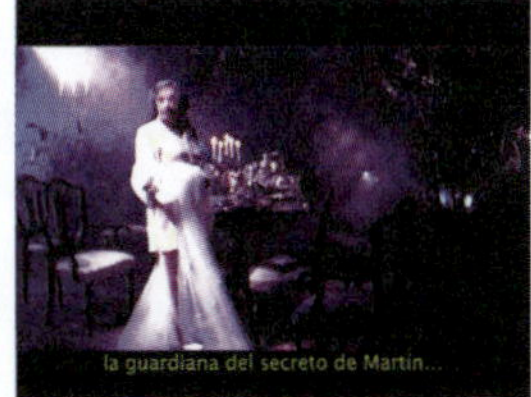

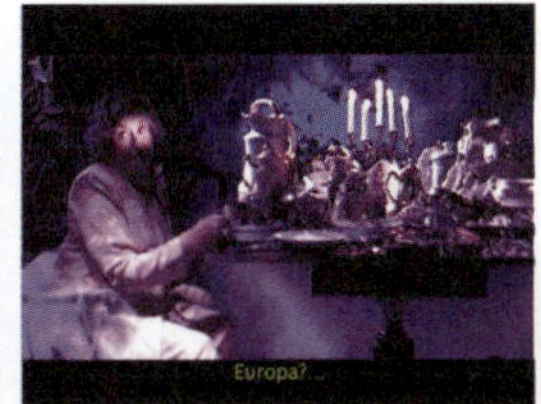

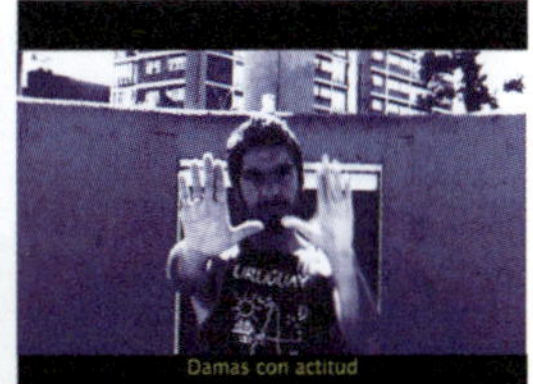

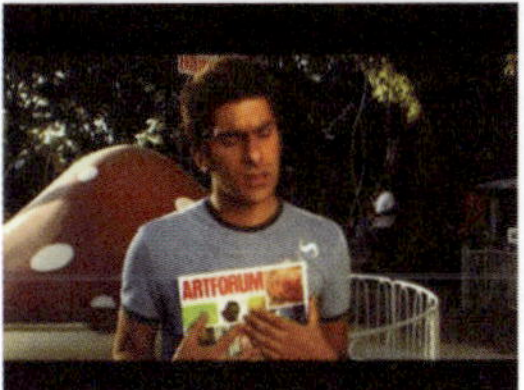

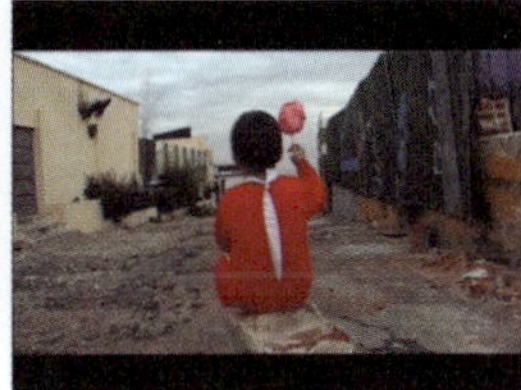

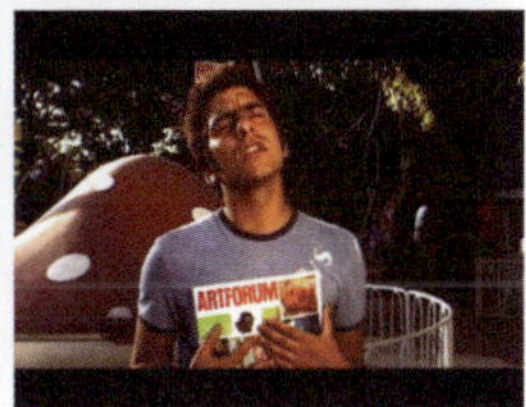

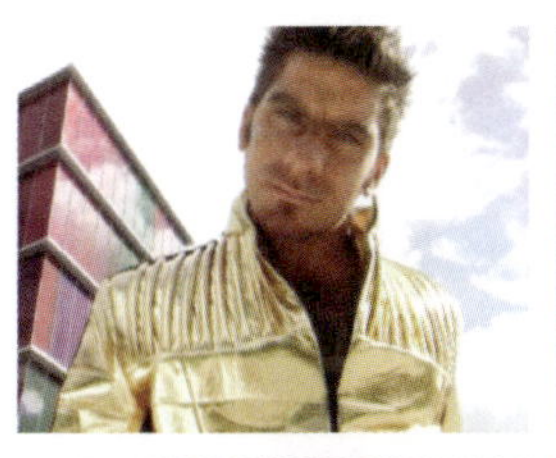

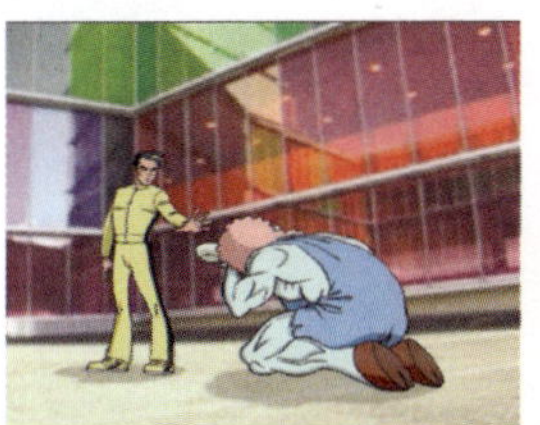

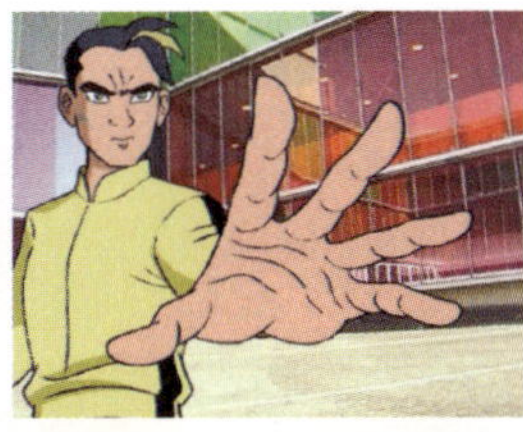

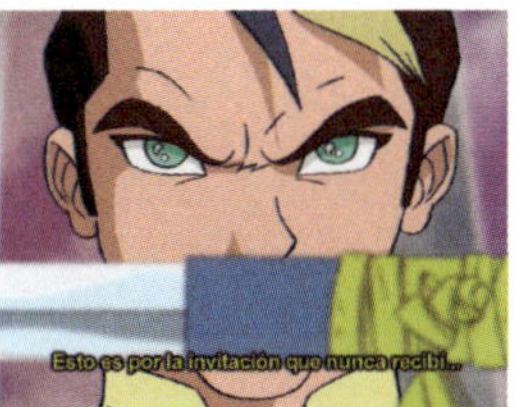

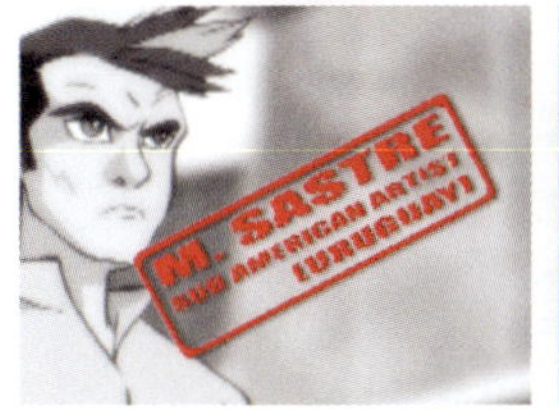

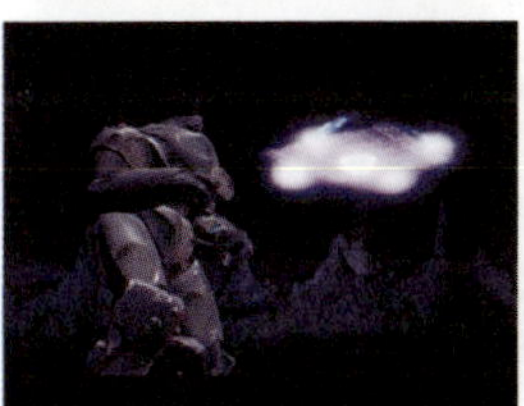

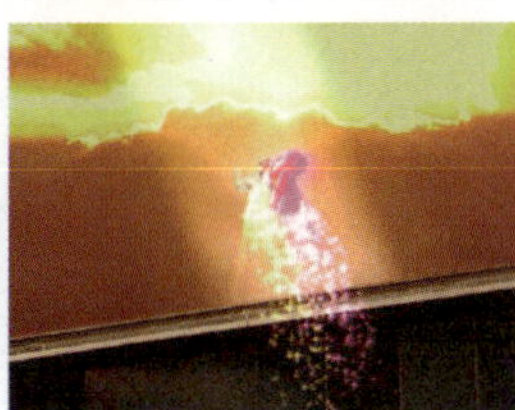

Montevideo: The Dark Side of the Pop, 2004
DVD colour video with sound
13' 26"

Bolivia 3: Confederation Next, 2004
DVD colour video with sound
10'

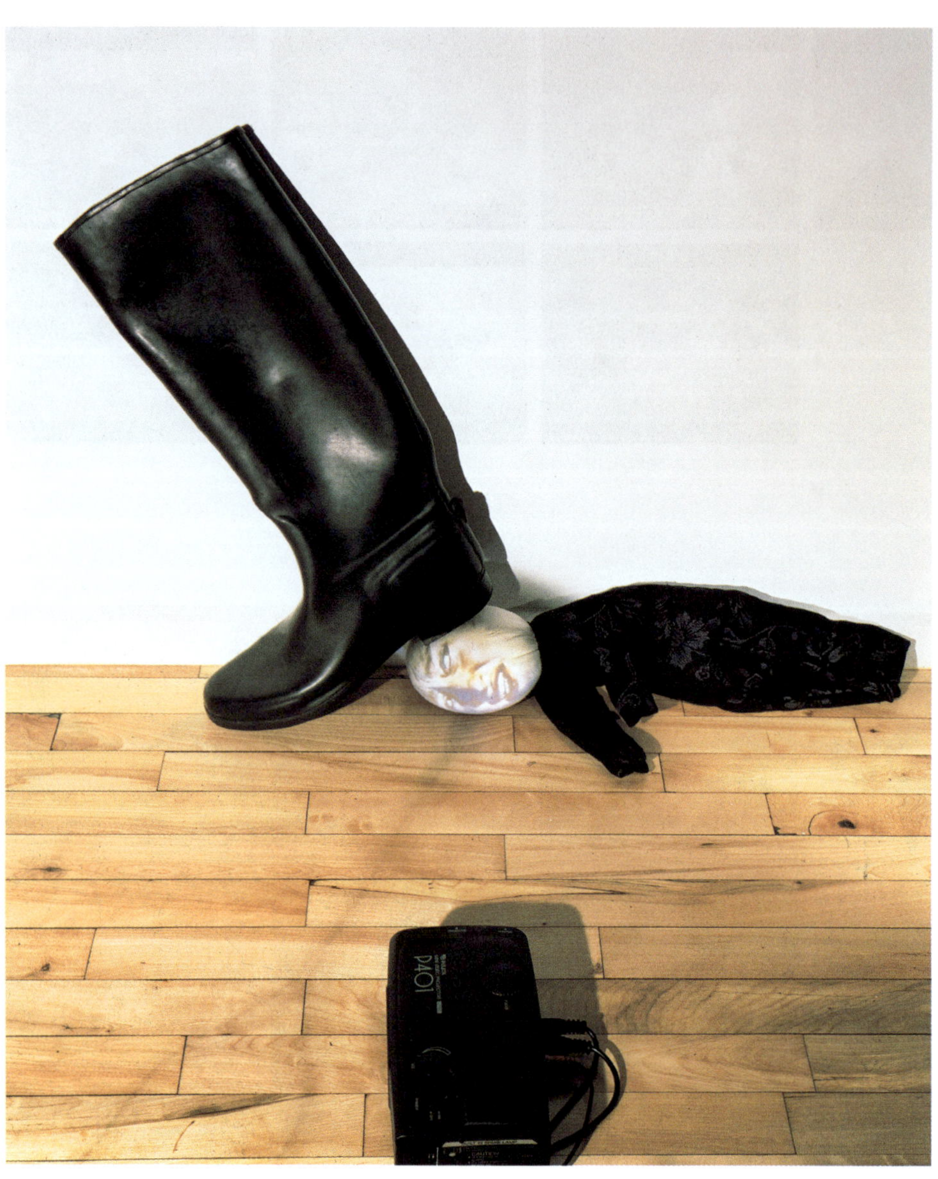

Tony Oursler
Boot, 1995
Video projection on a rag doll and a boot
62 x 31 x 31 cm

156

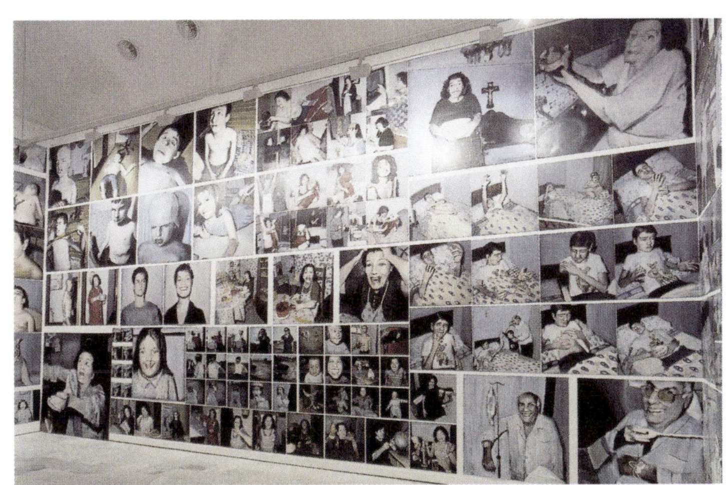

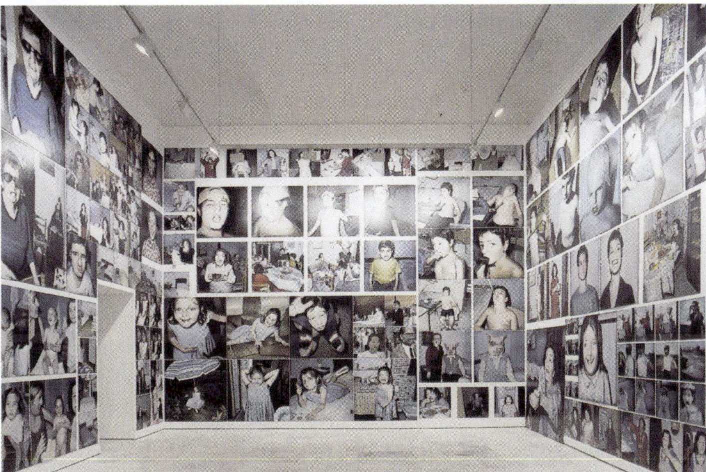

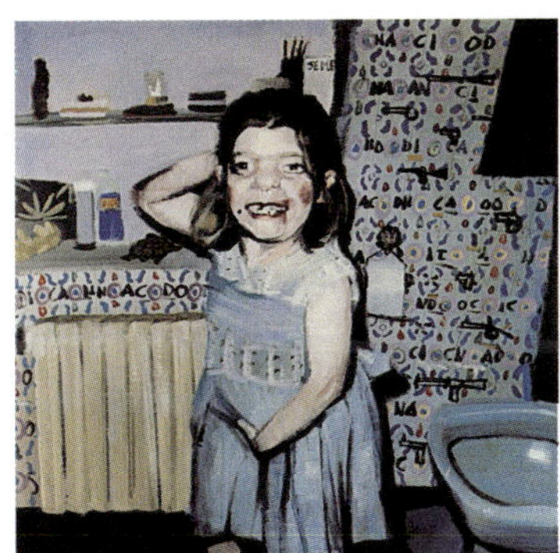

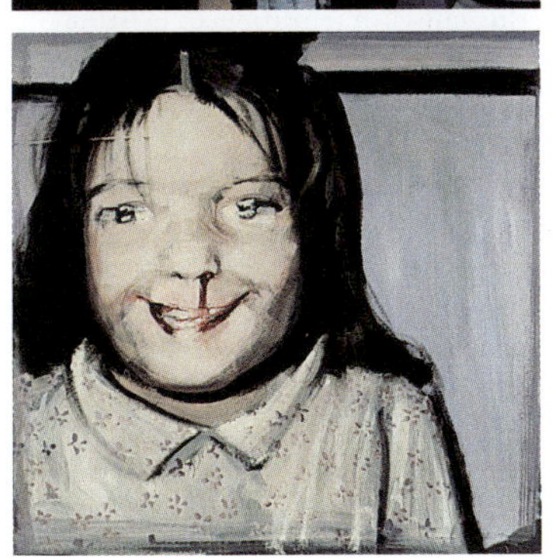

Enrique Marty
La familia, 1999
Installation consisting of one hundred oil
paintings on board
Variable dimensions

157

Sandra Gamarra
LiMac at the MUSAC

The Museum of Contemporary Art of Lima presents at MUSAC a selection from its collection, which currently consists of more than a thousand works. The LiMac, inaugurated in the year 2002 and constituted as a moving museum, works in different locations, its headquarters being the city accommodating it at any given time. For this show, in collaboration with the MUSAC, we are presenting a set of works arranged in the space in such a way that the visitor who is unfamiliar with the museum can get the best possible sense of the atmosphere pervading our art centre.

The museum within the museum

A museum is, by definition, a space devoted to storing varying types of collections. How then can a museum inside another museum be explained? Is it possible for a museum to belong to another museum's collection? Can a museum be part of an artist's work and not vice versa? LiMac is presented as a museum of projects and, at the same time, as a museum project. LiMac is a project whose purpose is, precisely, to project. This museum proposes the exhibition of the relationship between objects rather than the objects themselves. In a country where cultural institutions are scarce and galleries and art venues fulfil the role of the museum, a *mask* is needed to unite all

these efforts, in addition to the unfulfilled projects, the unpublished texts and the unprinted critiques. This museum aims to fill the institutional void created by the work effectively carried out in Lima. It does not work with the absence of the museum itself, but, on the contrary, that very absence compels it to exist and to function freely. This type of museum neither seeks to establish a new kind of museum, nor does it wish to be a virtual space or by no means an online museum. It really doesn't expect to possess a physical space at all; though it does indeed have an architectural project. LiMac does not wish to be a different museum; it just wants to be recognized as a museum, period. LiMac is one more museum project, like so many others. When imagining LiMac one should conceive a museum just like any other. Its characteristics are the same: it has a representative image, a collection, a catalogue, a website. It is not, then, a sort of ideal museum. Far from being a so-called imaginary museum or personal museum, this museum wishes to be the reflection of what a contemporary art museum would be in Lima, with all its aspirations and defects.

LiMac outside Lima

LiMac is presented as a real museum through the different ways in which real museums reach Lima; in other

words, through *souvenirs*, catalogues and printed material. A fake museum or a faked museum, the *souvenirs* and the catalogues produced by the LiMac give rise to false future memories, false future visits. Both objects and memories; those of LiMac are projected, ironically, in two directions: they arrive from a non-existent past experience and, given that their present is constantly under construction, they are directed toward a future experience of unattainable concretion. Hence it can be said that our museum has begun to build itself from the end; it begins by being a memory of what has not yet been lived. Its collection consists of works that can be found in museum catalogues or in the compilations of books on contemporary artists. The selection of the works belonging to the LiMac collection arises from previous selections. To be sure, LiMac's selection capacity exists because of an external filter. It feeds on the dynamics of selections: as generator of its own filter, this museum reintroduces existing selections into a different collection, which does not deny or supplant the original ones. From abroad, the works reach Lima as printed images. In most cases, those 'works' never really arrive. Nevertheless, the LiMac collection, materialized through painting, is real. Painting is the medium chosen for creating real works from printed images of 'original' works. Thanks to painting, the works making up our museum's collection obtain their own patina; they are all brethren belonging to a family of copies.

Taking advantage of the materiality of painting, this collection of copies becomes true. Painting ends up being a weapon of reality that supports the falsehood of the collection of a nonexistent museum. The catalogue turned painting, the painting turned catalogue. The museum catalogue is a mass reproduction of the original works from its collection; at LiMac, it is the original work itself. Our catalogue consists, not of reproductions of the works, but of appropriations of these works, which through painting become part of the collection.

Which is the original and which is the copy? Does an original model exist? Whether it is original or not, the LiMac collection exists, as do the works and the artists. This is a collection that expands toward reality inasmuch as it is directed toward the memory we have of what the museum collection is, and it is validated by the 'museum' that presents it as well as the observer that recognizes and endorses it. Consequently, LiMac starts with a book. This book, which contains the catalogue of its works, serves to create the collection and not the opposite. Its *souvenirs* serve to create a memory and not the opposite. The LiMac catalogue befits the catalogue form and its space, the projection of a remote memory.

The projection of the museum is so real that with the speculation it has stirred up, an imaginary collective can be built around it. Speculation simultaneously generates the idea of what the museum would be if it 'really' existed. We can begin to criticize it without having set foot inside it, and this proliferation of criticism is a reflection of a city's need for a space that 'somehow' unites the work produced within it. LiMac points out the capacity a city such as ours has to accommodate a space that serves as a real meeting and breaking up place, even though nobody can visit a contemporary art museum in Lima. LiMac's is an 'opportunistic' project insofar as it takes advantage of the absence of a contemporary art museum in the city to make manifest the fact that the criticism generated by museums, art centres, biennials and other similar institutions ignores the apparently simple fact of existence. It is taken for granted that cities have museums, inaugurate art centres and celebrate biennials. Whether they do so successfully or not, these institutions seem to provoke the existence of a space for reflection. The 'reality' of these spaces is so powerful that it is forgotten that the existence of that reflection is precisely what permits the foundation of the museum.

Criticism through absence or through presence, since the LiMac is fiction, a copy of existing museums (an amalgam of them); any museum could fit its description. The LiMac could be any museum, just as long as the real museum is capable of seeing the reflection it projects on ours.

I lie, therefore I exist

The LiMac has been physically presented inside another museum, a gallery or an art centre, whether in Lima or abroad. The museum presents a museum as exhibition object; the museum bites its tail. The MUSAC is converted into a greenhouse where the existence of another museum, which would otherwise not really exist, is possible. The real museum is exhibited to itself; the fact of observing becomes the object observed. The museum space and the museum object are presented in a game of mirrors where the observer is subject and reflection at the same time. In the greenhouse game, the observer is the only witness of the manipulation that makes this 'reality' possible and he is also responsible for maintaining the relation of coexistence of lie and truth.

The existence of a MAC – contemporary art museum- in Lima is a dream for us, but it is, paradoxically, a reality for those who live in other places.

It is not a surprise that *souvenirs* or news of its existence reach them, what does turn out to be a surprise is that LiMac is a fiction. Perhaps because there is no conception of another way of presenting locally produced art to the public, or, what would be even more terrible, because this would mean that the art produced abroad does not reach Lima, because while art is shared "culture will be reaching the cities of this world". For us, to have it would be only one way of existing in the 'world', as we exist sometimes for having *Hard Rock Café* Lima – as Ximena Briceño says in her story "ONE".

LiMac uses the predetermined museum form to create the illusion of a known space and, from there, encourage a dialogue in equal conditions. LiMac desires this only, like its collection, like its artists. It does not wish to be an 'exotic' or 'different' museum, but only desires to present itself with its differences and peculiarities, just as any other museum from any other region would do. The difference that exists between the creative production in Lima and that produced in other parts of the world does not lie in its shortcomings or its needs, but in the way we face those deficiencies and in the way we have to work with them, on such universal themes as war, pain and love. We participate in a dialogue and not a local monologue.

Lima is not a city where misery is all that can be found; the terrible thing about a city like Lima lies precisely in the opposite. Lima has it all, like a terrible display in which the needs are all mixed up, where needs such as the artistic ones remain hidden, as if ashamed, in so many others, without a possibility of finding an outlet. Perhaps this is why this 'claim' is made as inconspicuously as possible, almost like an ironic and paradoxical game. How many of us want a museum? How many of us could use one? Would we want to maintain it? The museum is not in itself the space that opens to the public, or the works, or the artists, or the critics, or the curators, but the way in which this set of stimuli work on the beholder and make the museum exist through the dialogue generated between them. Events such as the former Lima Biennial, some fine art competitions or venues with certain tendencies, generated a real dialogue between the parties; their disappearance has led to a set of monologues cut short, isolated phrases that only a devoted observer is capable of understanding. One might think that LiMac serves the purpose of planning its future, yet Lima does not work this way. The city devours everything in a long, endless digestion resulting in a rarefied mixture. Because Lima is not one way, it is the way it mixes things and makes them one.

The only thing the museum offers is a certain impression of order, a certain aspect of homogeneity and familiarity among the things it exhibits. Lima does not need a new battlefield for the different cultures within it, but rather a possible via for their pacific coexistence.

sussicraN

LiMac is putting its stakes on the multiplicity of dialogue. This is the greatest risk it runs. Because LiMac is open to a dialogue from its own space, toward others, with the flag of appropriation. The space for statements from Lima, due to its capacity to cannibalize everything, is naturally a space whose identity is ambiguous. This ambiguity is generally understood as a handicap. LiMac, from that circumstance, opts to make that capacity for appropriation its characteristic within a dialogue established between pairs. The premise it is based on is that of replicating the mechanisms and forms of existing museums, mirroring them. The LiMac project is promoted because the idea of museum it represents is not needed in Lima alone, but also in other cities. The reality of LiMac is not just fuelled by the needs of this city, but also by the imagery from abroad, in which each country's capital has its own contemporary art museum. LiMac is not presented as an alienating simu-

lacrum for the artists from Lima city; it is more like a simulacrum for those abroad. It is bait to attract them to work that exists, but that is not gathered in an easily visible fashion. It is bait in the form of that which seeks to attract, in a way similar to that in which, when we are in love with ourselves, we seek a form that agrees with us, a reflection of ourselves that makes us more real.

(Do It Yourself)

In LiMac inside MUSAC, the miniaturization of the exhibition space plays an important role in the spectacle of refraction, since the observer maintains its true scale and all the fake and real vanishing points are sustained. The observer is in charge of creating this double reality, which is opened from a perspective that includes the observer inside the LiMac inside the MUSAC.

As we said of LiMac at the beginning, this is not a separate museum; it is not a different museum. It answers, as do real museums, to the desires of a few. The museum makes tangible a space where discussing, creating and exhibiting art has real meaning; where utopias come true, allowing us to think that they are necessary.

The construction of a museum always takes place on quicksand. Perhaps this is why there is never total agreement about them; nothing is ever done

right; we are never all involved; those who should be are never included. They are dreams projected onto a limited real space. In this sense, LiMac is closer to reality than is expected, for as it has no limits, everything can fit inside it.

Like the lack of a cemetery, the lack of a museum results in the disappearance of the past, in the negation of a process. The absence of a place to commemorate the past affects a present that is constantly recreating itself, prevented from projecting a future. What happens then is that the works of local artists end up in foreign collections because Lima is incapable of housing them. The past is perverted and rearranged into a permanent present. The present is superimposed and multiplied in a disarray of incoherent layers. LiMac aims to order these times, although this would mean its own interment in the past.

The creation of a museum in Lima would not put an end to the fiction of LiMac; at most it would serve as a natural boundary paving the way for similar entities that can create a dialogue, which in turn convenes more participants.

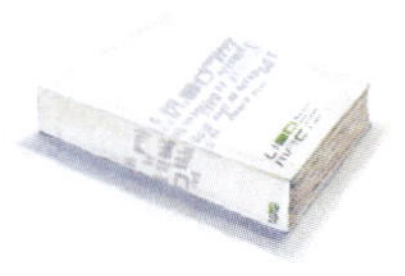
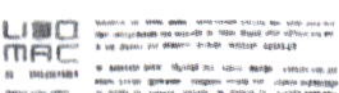
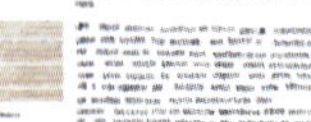
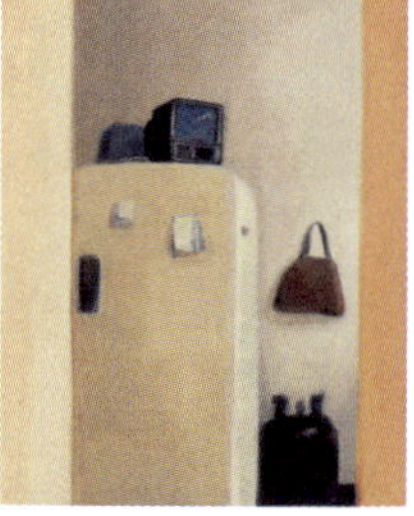
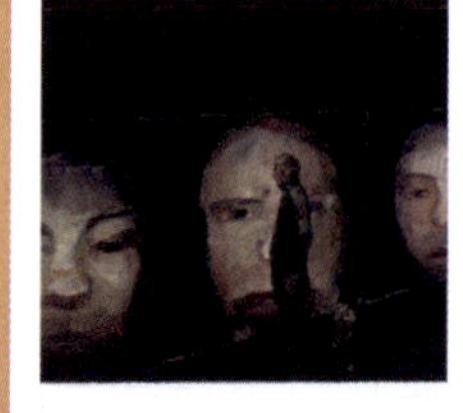
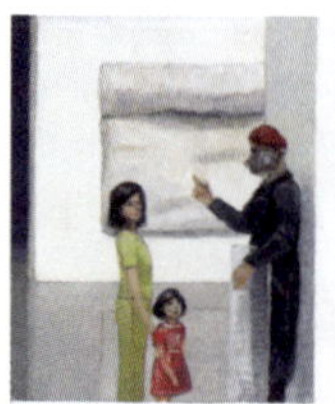
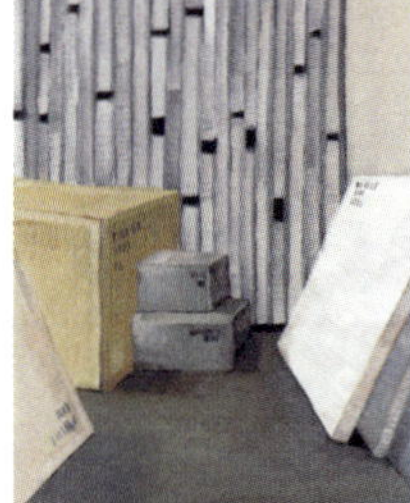
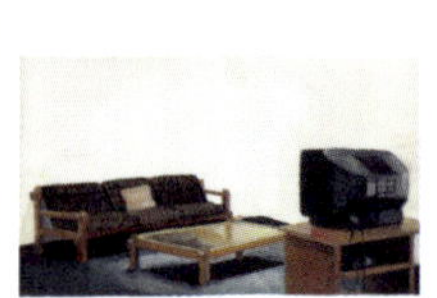
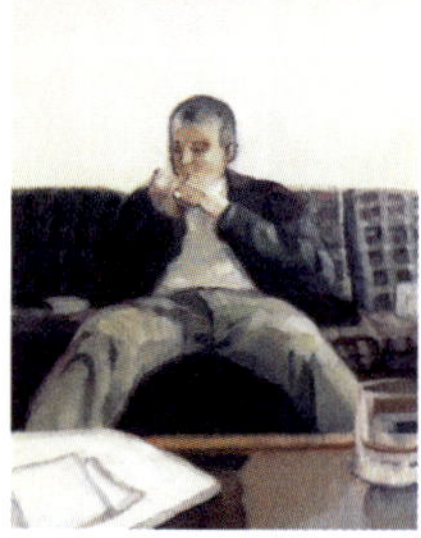
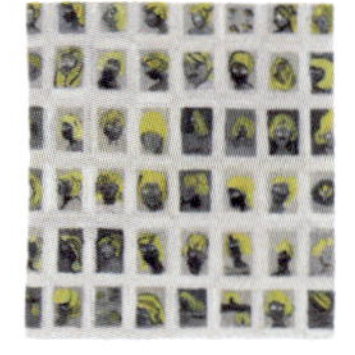
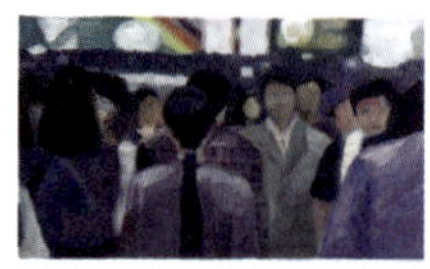
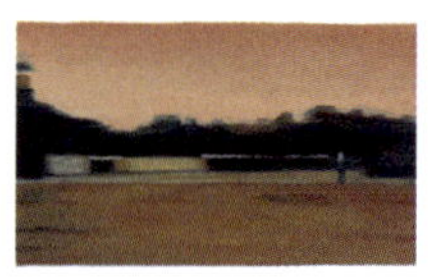
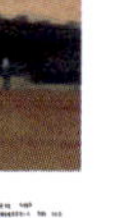
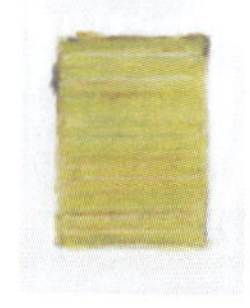
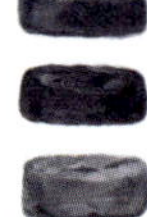
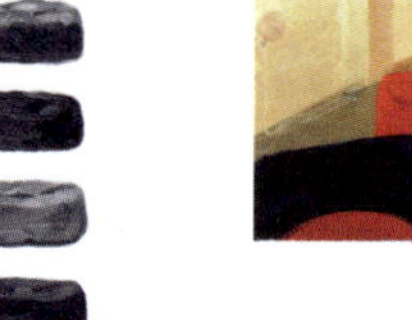
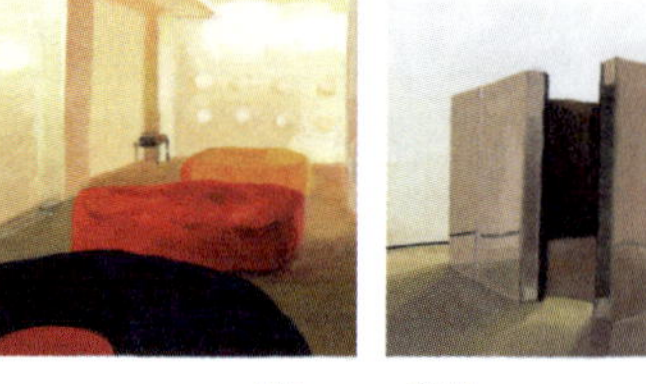

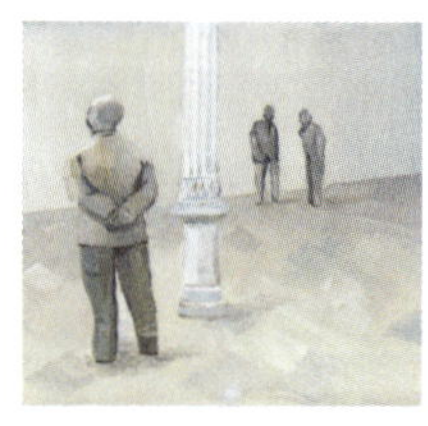
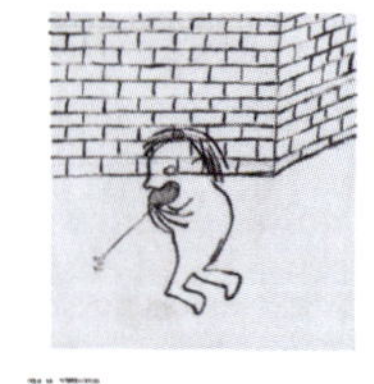
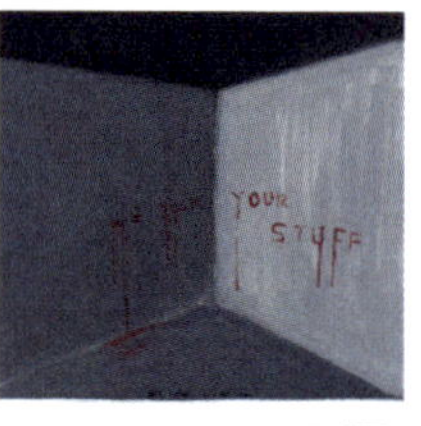
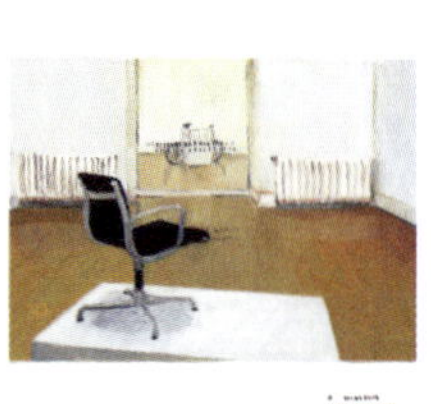
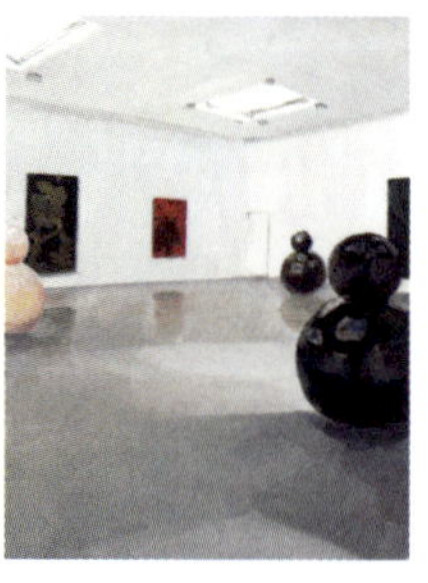
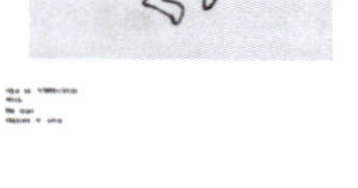
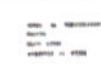
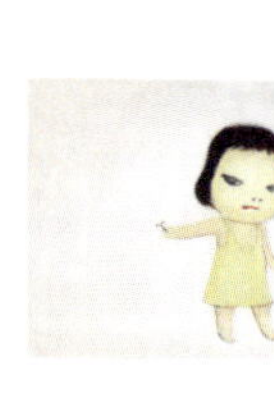
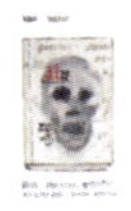
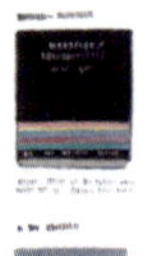
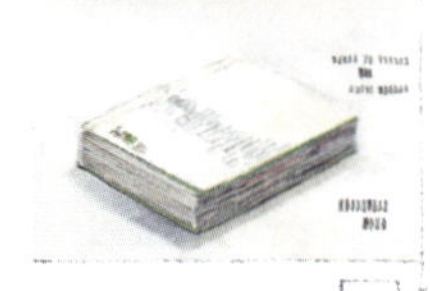
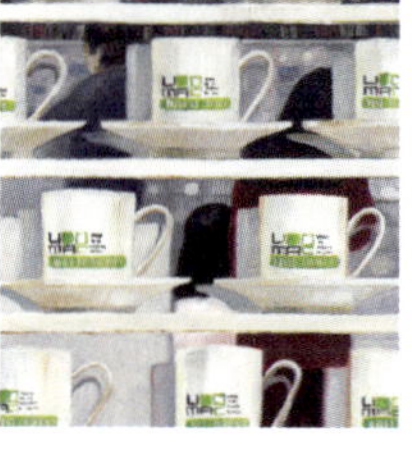
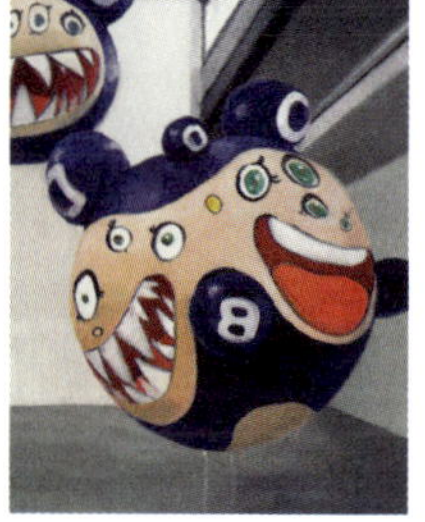
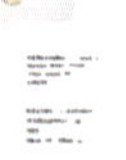
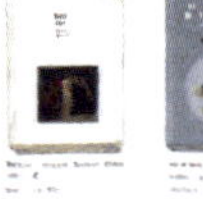
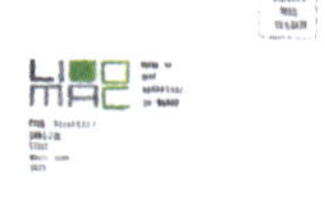

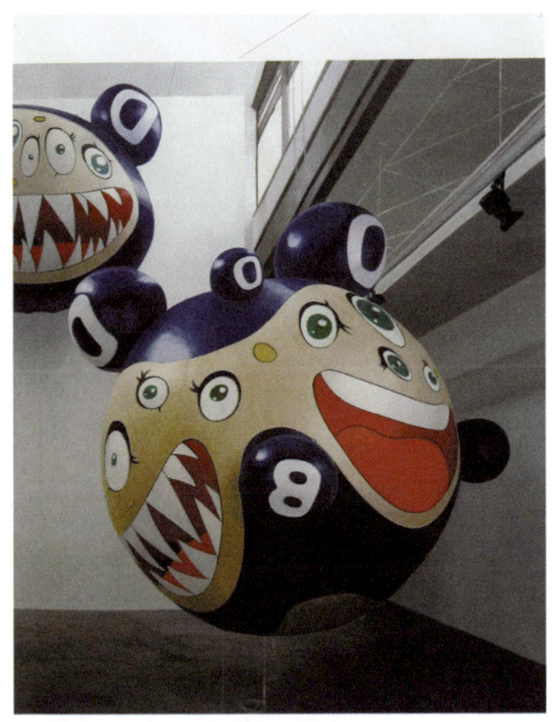

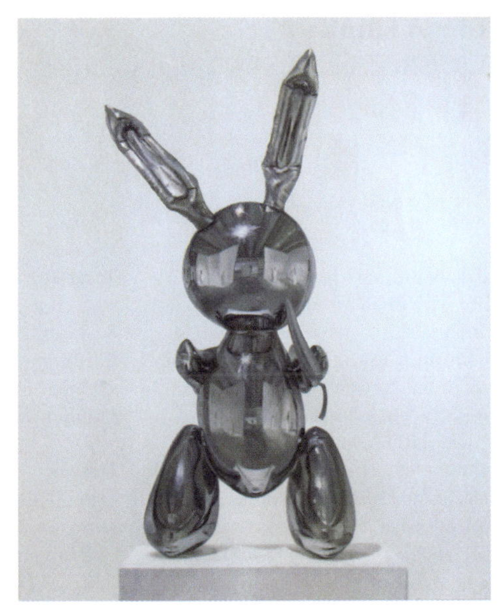

Sandra Gamarra
Murakami, 2004
Oil on canvas
195 x 146 cm

Koons, 2004
Oil on canvas
162 x 130 cm

Visita Guiada (Catálogo Li-Mac), 2003
Book composed of one hundred and twelve
oil paintings on cotton paper
23 x 17 cm each

Part of my work has been to go out with small groups of artists and political activists who try to contribute to changing the world in small but very creative and inspiring ways. What follows are excerpts of conversations with some of them about emergencies in our environment and the solutions they found.

John Jordan is an artist-activist who spends his time trying to find a space where the imagination of art and the social engagement of politics can be brought together. Since 1994 he has worked in direct action movements, principally with Reclaim the Streets. (www.weareeverywhere.org)

My Dads Strip Club tackles a variety of issues but is best known for filling the gap between the dissatisfied shopper and consumer culture. Recent work has been placed in the commercial zones of department stores, supermarkets, chain-store windows and banks. The Strip Club actively promotes networks of associations for creative resistance. It showcases the international effort of various commercially zoned workers from prison labour to sweatshops. (www.mydadsstripclub.com)

The Space Hijackers are a group of Anarchitects who have initiated actions such as the Circle Line Parties on the London Underground, attracting several hundred people each time, and who have challenged business people to matches of casual 'Midnight Cricket' using the empty squares in the financial district of London. (www.spacehijackers.org)

Demos

Immo Klink: The recent anti-war and Stop-Bush demonstrations in London made me doubt a little if marches can have much real political effect. Everything is organised and prepared for you, it has something almost consumerist about it. You just have to go along with the flow, hold a prefabricated placard delivered by a socialist group or a mainstream newspaper (obviously with their logo printed on it). Police control the movement of the crowd through central London along carefully positioned lines. At the mercy of the City Council people may gather in Trafalgar Square to listen to speeches about how successful and important the day has been. Everybody goes home and seems to be happy. The media is happy to report that the demo has been the biggest in history. The Police are happy stating that the success was 'testament to the professionalism of the Metropolitan Police Service'. George W. Bush and Tony Blair are happy to praise the

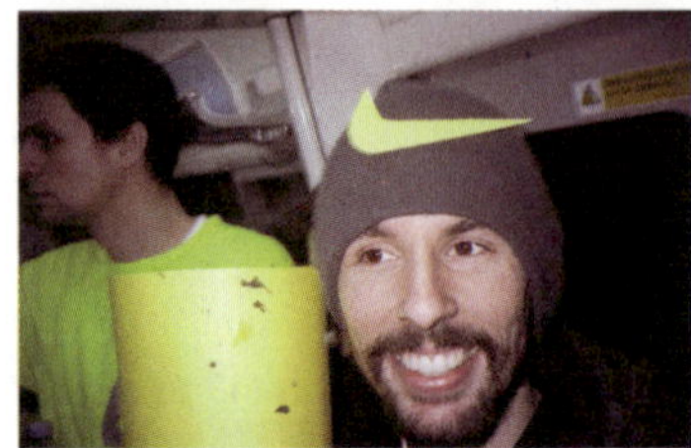

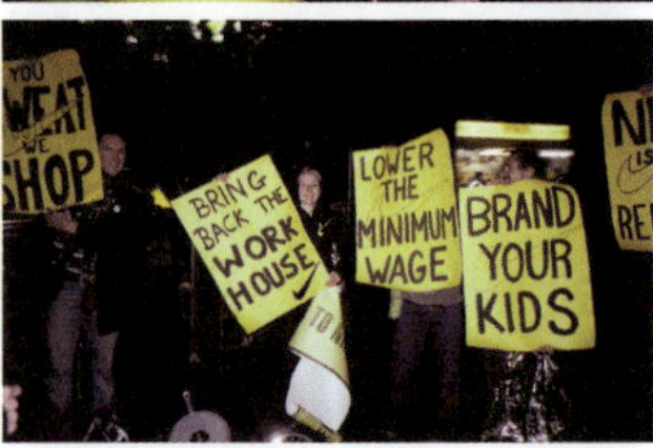

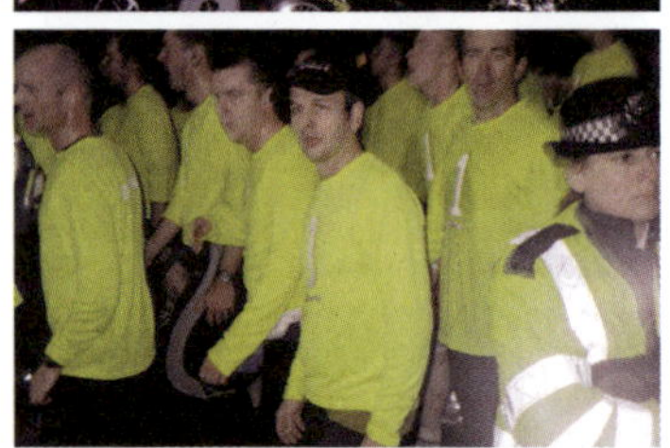

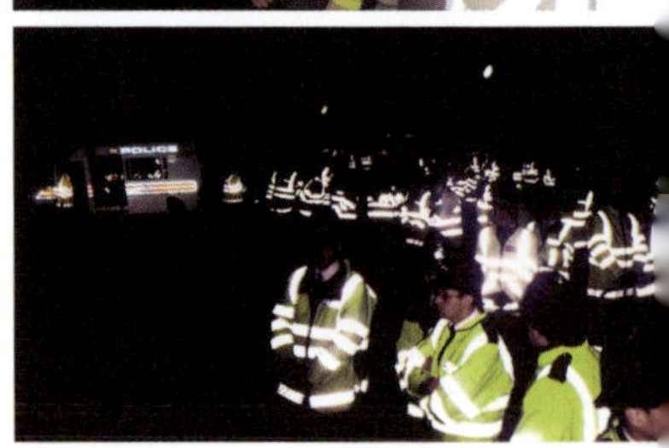

virtues of our democracy that allow us to express our opinions. So basically everybody is happy. But did anything change?

Space Hijackers: … a lot of people have become completely immune to protests. They switch off instantly and don't even listen. Which is why we did the pro-Nike protest at the NikeRunLondon event – a kind of pay-to-run marathon sponsored by Nike. If we'd gone there to do a normal anti-Nike/Sweatshop Protest, no one would have paid any attention and we probably would have been thrown off the finishing line area within minutes. Whereas doing something slightly different or taking it from a different angle – in the NikeRunLondon case carrying banners praising Nike and its use of cheap sweatshop labour – gives you this space to create enough confusion and discussion to get people to question things.

People don't take enough interest in what goes on around them in the city outside of their day-to-day routine. I think it's important to encourage more people to take an active role in the space and the city around them.

Direct action

John Jordan: What has been unique about the anti-capitalist movements and different to the anti-war movement was that the anti-capitalist movement or globalisation movement was promoting the idea of direct action instead of doing marches. Actions that in practice made a difference. The concept is: you identify a problem and you develop a means to respond to and alleviate that problem without going through bureaucrats and governments. You don't ask the authorities to stop the war for you, you do everything to stop the war yourself, you jam the gears of the machine with your body, your actions – you Do It Yourself. DIY.

Immo Klink: But if we resort to direct action, can we afford to bypass the established political parliamentary process? There are problematic issues of insufficient democratic legitimisation, lack of knowledge or self-righteousness amongst NGOs or Direct Action groups.

Convivial spaces

John Jordan: Direct action is not the only tool. We have to create spaces and events to reflect what we want. That is a cultural question and not only a direct action question. It is about creating spaces where human beings aren't relying on leaders and learn how to work in a horizontal way outside hierarchical structures or the market economy system. Sharing software and skills like peer-to-peer file sharing or Linux are now commonly known examples.

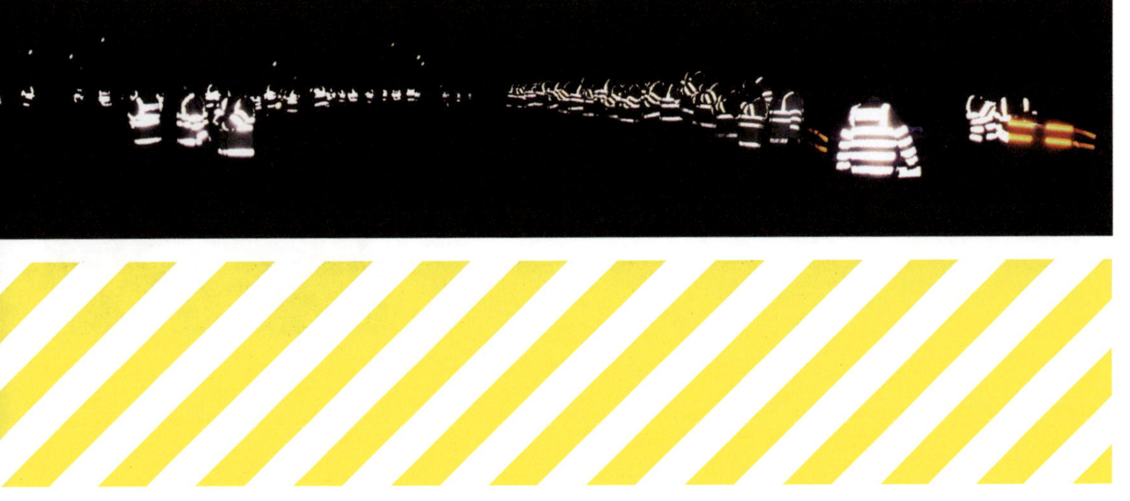

For me it is important to create
conviviality, especially within the
activist culture. Spaces that are
warm, friendly and non-hierarchical
where people can feel their own
empowerment. Fun and pleasure are
the key things in the new politics.
So much politics of the left has been
mostly tedious, boring and grey.
Preparing or creating a rebellion
has to be fun and pleasurable.
For me those are the values that hold
good in my work. But somebody
else might prioritise values about the
importance of deep ecology or gender
or race, etc.
The way something is organised and
the planning process are what already
represent the change. *Prefigured
politics* is about creating the space and
possibility to do it now, and showing
another model. It is not about seizing
power in the political system but the
process of empowerment. We cannot
change society until everyone feels
a sense of self-empowerment.
Of course we can't have a completely
direct democratic society where
everyone makes every single decision
that concerns them. But huge direct
democratic experiments have taken
place, such as the Spanish civil war:
They had horizontal systems to make
decisions in a consensual manner
involving tens of thousand of people

and this was well before mobile
phones and the Internet.

Non-linearity
<u>John Jordan:</u> I think what is really
beautiful about the globalisation
movements is that – unlike in the
past where there was one ideology and
one way of doing things – they are
an acceptance of diversity. Because
there are thousands of people doing
small things here and there and that
all builds up to changes which most of
the time aren't predictable.
<u>Immo Klink:</u> And the perception of
our world has changed and translates
into how we go about things. Vilem
Flusser suggests that mankind
developed from the three-dimensional
experience into the zero-dimensional
– from 3D space > to 2D images > to
linear text > to the pixel. We are now
leaving behind the one-dimensional
linear experience in the form of text,
which gave us our notion of history.
With the major impact of digital
media and the Internet, pixels pin our
zero-dimensional age.
We should therefore consider the
world much more as a collection of
independent particles or pixels in
space rather than as a linear flow of
events of cause and effect, and thus we
no longer see life as a movement that
changes the given reality, but rather as

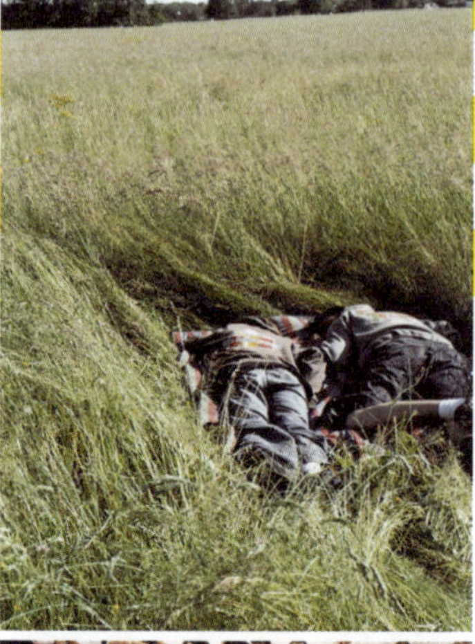

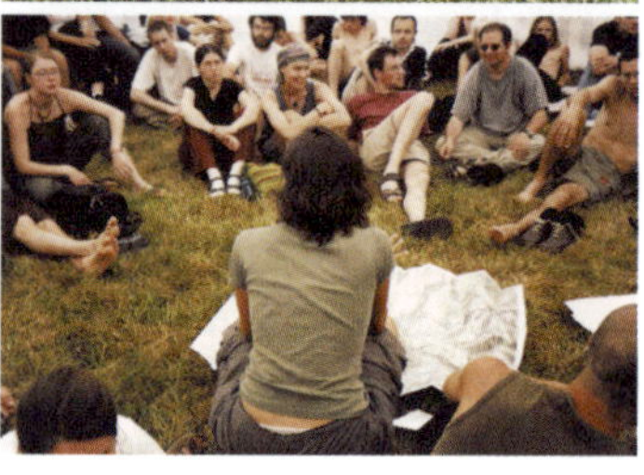

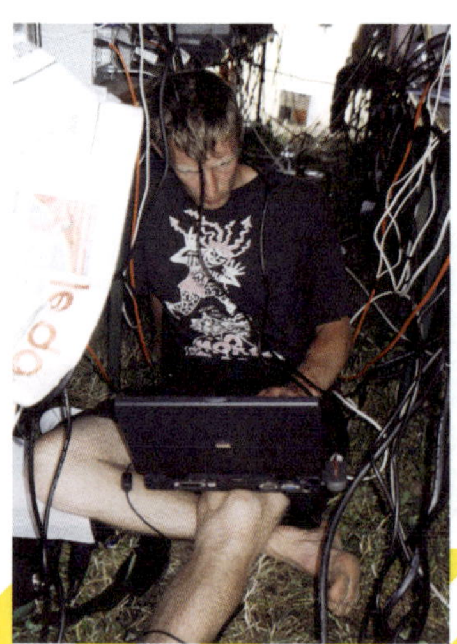

a tendency to realise given possibilities within and around us.

John Jordan: And I think we have to look at the beauty of the unexpected. We suddenly realise that everything is connected to everything else. And by that connection we cannot predict what we are doing. Ten years ago there was little criticism of capitalism. Capitalism was the norm, "The End of History". I'm talking post-1989, probably until the anti-capitalist uprisings in 1994 which declared: 'This is not the end of history, just the beginning.' And I think the Zapatistas for me really sparked this movement up. They are prime examples of the zero-dimensional world you were mentioning. The resonance from this little pixel of Chiapas in the jungle of Mexico has been enormous in the world.

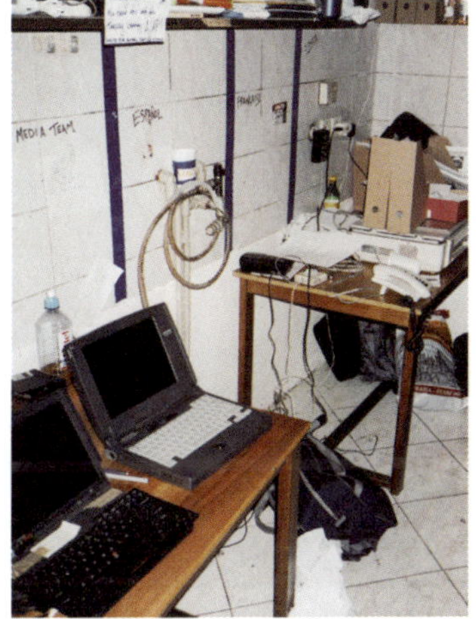

Distribute Myth

Immo Klink: And this pixelated view of the world works for us. You do something, you record it, and then send out some reports. You just create the feeling that something has actually been possible to do. Then others might take it on or do a variation of it.

John Jordan: Absolutely, and the new distribution systems like the Internet have really made that possible in a beautiful way because they create myths.

Interestingly, in the 19th century there was the myth of the general strike. What terrified the bourgeoisie was the idea of a general strike. In reality most people knew that you couldn't really have a general strike that would create a revolution. But the myth was terrifying. The Myth of Reclaim the Streets is interesting. After the first small street party, suddenly there was this Myth of a different way of rebelling across the world. Then, four years later there was a party that shut down the financial district of London on June 18th 1999, and simultaneously in 40 countries. We had no idea how successful it would be. But that event inspired people in Seattle to shut down the WTO. They thought, 'wow, if they can shut down the City of London, we can shut down the WTO'. And history comes out of all these moments. After the first emails we had about '… yeah let's do an action in the City of London…' – if at that moment you had told me that this action would inspire people all over the world and inspire the WTO shut-down in Seattle, which in itself became another myth! – then I would not have believed you.

Empowerment

Immo Klink: A lot of these actions used the idea of Carnival. Like 'Carnival against Capitalism' Mayday 2002. Various websites announced that Carnival has returned to Mayfair. Mayfair now is the most luxurious shopping area of London but historically the place where people used to gather in May for a wild festival. This was hundreds of years before May 1st was hijacked as Labour Day by the Communist movements. The power of Carnival is that for a short time people could change roles, ridicule and question authority and express their thoughts in a kind of playful way... It was a party and at the same time, a situation which could easily slip into a revolt if people were too discontented with the regime they were governed by.

John Jordan: ...and it has no hierarchy. In a Carnival there is no performer or audience. The spotlight has disappeared. It is not some people taking part while others watch. It kind of gets rid of the idea of the spectator. Exactly! There are many activities that people do together but so often they depend on some kind of mediator in the form of that spotlight, that big screen... Once you get rid of that, people feel empowered and they start creating this incredible energy.

Hijacking

We all use this word quite a lot these days. Like 'Come on! Let's hijack this!' to things like a space, a website, a conference or an ad campaign, etc. On the other hand we are also afraid of being hijacked by others. There have been strong claims that the World Social Forums or Protest Movements have been hijacked by socialists, governments or even corporations, as in the case of the Forum 2004 in Barcelona. Where does it all come from? Has everything become so virtual that it is so easy to turn everything into something else?

Space Hijackers: I think for us the Internet has been the great lever. The fact that James from the Vacuum Cleaner can take on Starbucks and turn it into ####FUCK### OFF## [starFUCKs'cOFFee] by just painting some letters over and then promote the idea by registering a similar website. This one person at home with a computer can have the same marketing machine as a massive company. He wouldn't be able to afford print media and things like that. In this way he couldn't compete in any way at all but, as an online presence, he is equally empowered.

Immo Klink: And maybe now the concept of hijacking websites in

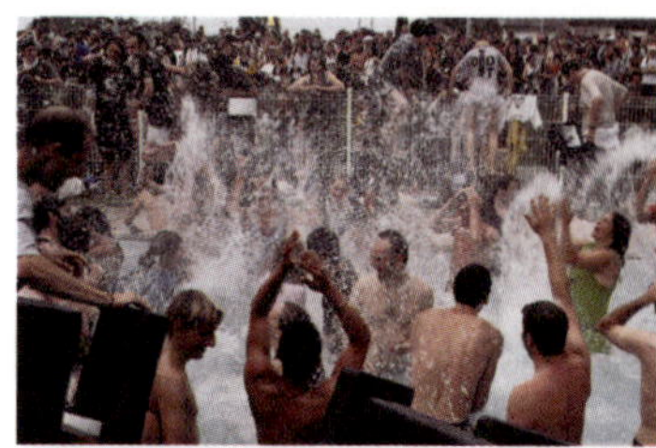

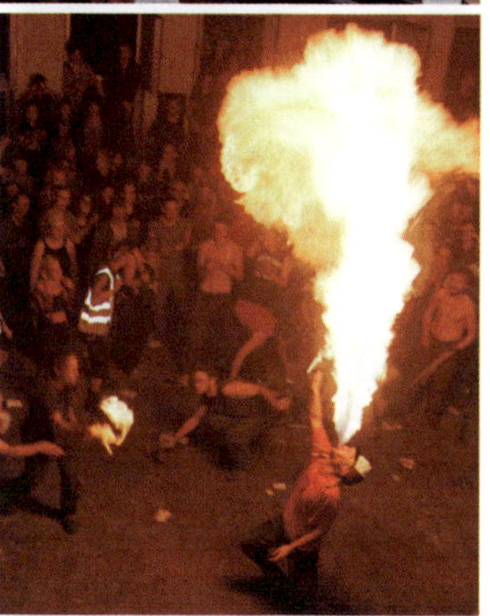

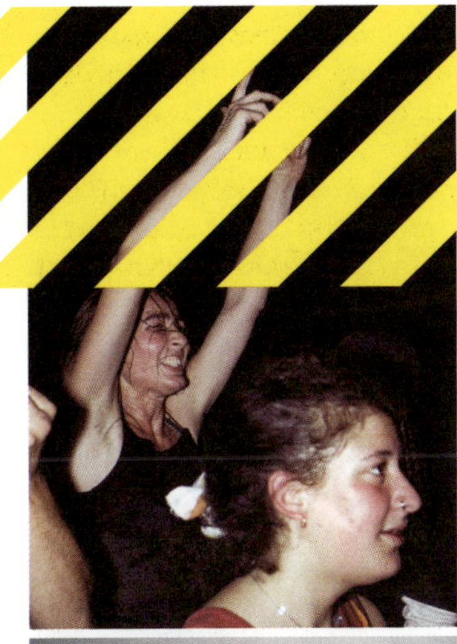

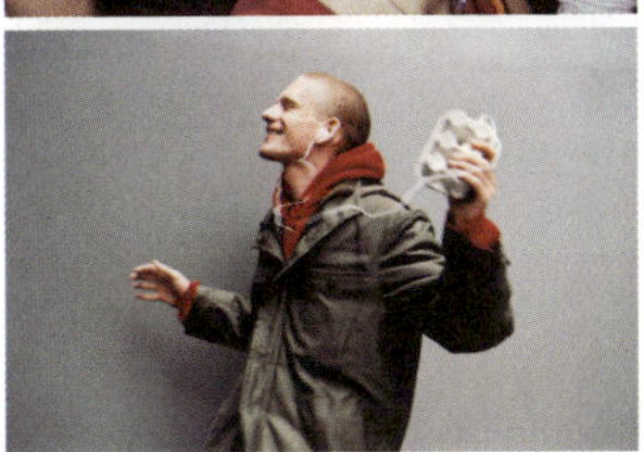

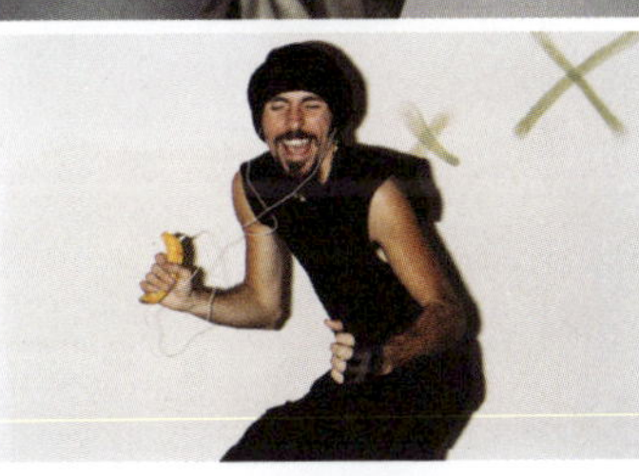

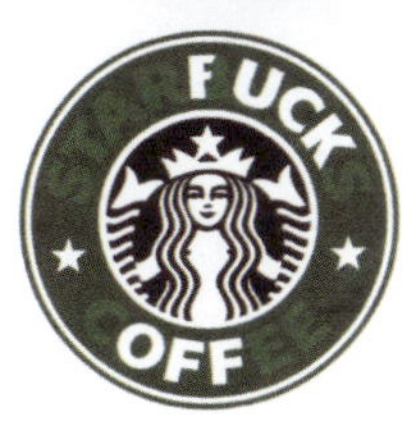

cyberspace translates back into real-world space.

Anarchism

<u>Immo Klink:</u> It's funny, I was about to say that you sound a bit like the Anarchists. But actually I hardly know anything about anarchism. Apart from some graffiti slogans and Black Block activities, most people remain in the dark about what anarchy, as a form of organisation, really means.

<u>Space Hijackers:</u> The word anarchy is so loaded and charged. The press talks about anarchism as if it just means chaos. But in fact it means almost the opposite – at least in some sort of weird idea that I have about anarchy – which probably isn't right either. I have this idea that one of the most anarchist things in the world is something like a bus-stop queue. Twenty years ago, say, if you went to Tottenham Court Road to catch the bus, people would queue for the bus. They would turn up and think 'We are here waiting for the bus, we stand in this line, it's equal and fair, everybody knows what's going on…' whereas now, it is often this mob-mess. The bus turns up and everybody just tries to get on it first. I think that is because there is too much control in public space.

Take the London Underground. People are ordered, controlled and guided around there so much that when they find themselves on a pavement where there is no control they don't self-organize anymore. And that's what for me anarchism is about: organizing ourselves without someone telling us what to do.

Alienation / Consumerism

<u>John Jordan:</u> To make political changes you have to work in cultural places to give people back their sense of autonomy and a sense of who they are, so they don't have to feel an emotional connection to the brand. Which is what capitalism wants. Capitalism tells people they have to work all their life. They then have to spend what little money they have made when working. Then they have to get into debt.

<u>Immo Klink:</u> But how can we be so sure we know better and occupy the high moral ground? Is everybody else really so alienated or are we just a self-righteous bunch of artist-activists driven crazy by the London marketing-madness?

<u>Space Hijackers:</u> I guess it is just a reaction to the fact that society is turning into a consumer society. And some change has to happen, it has to evolve somehow. But yeah,

maybe we are all just mental. haha!
… but that said, take things like
Starbucks. You might think there
wouldn't be so many Starbucks if
people didn't keep buying their coffee
there. But it's never as simple as that.
Starbucks has an active policy to go
out and close down small businesses
and take over. I think it's quite naïve
to think that it is just the people who
want to consume, so that's why there
is consumerism.

Immo Klink: I sometimes wonder
if our highly developed market
economies have shifted more to the
creation of new demands and desires
instead of satisfying the existing ones.

My Dads Strip Club: What kind of
annoys me is the patronising way that
advertising and marketing work.
They just think you're stupid because
the message that you get is: 'Come
and be an individual!' But what they
are asking you to buy is a product that
has been mass produced and you can
buy exactly the same product in every
city around the world.

Open a Gap

Immo Klink: PR and marketing,
especially direct marketing, have
come a long way since the humble
attempts at creating goodwill and
emotional attachment by classic
branding concepts. There are vast
amounts of hidden and subliminal
methods in place. Neuromarketing
is a new science where magnetic
resonance images of your brain help
to produce brain maps that show
which areas of your brain 'light up'
when exposed to a certain brand.
Increasingly common is Spyware –
illicitly installed programmes that tell
others about where you go and what
you do on the Web. Customer loyalty
cards gather information about your
browsing, from your eating habits to
your favourite contraceptives.
Take these methods, add your credit
card transaction details, and put them
together in a consumer database.
The result is that marketers nowadays
probably know much more about you
than you know about yourself.

Space Hijackers: Take supermarkets.
I read this book about how to design
shops to make you buy stuff.
It is really fucking devious the things
they do. There are supermarkets that
use slightly smaller tiles in more
expensive aisles. When you push your
trolley it clicks faster on the smaller
tiles so you think you are going faster
and you slow down and spend more
time in those aisles than in the other
ones. Milk and bread is put at the
very back of the stores so you have
to walk past everything else to get to
your essentials.

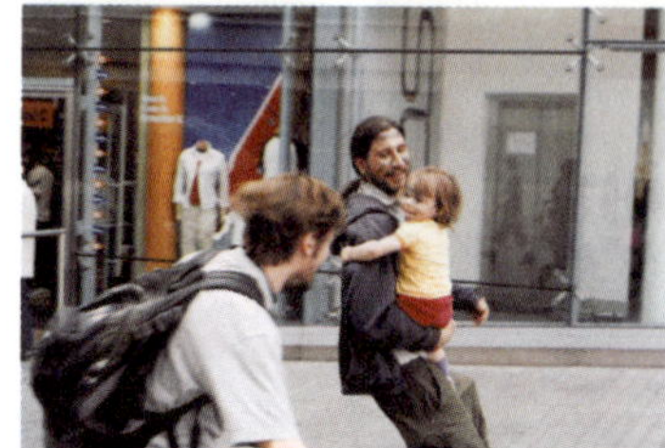

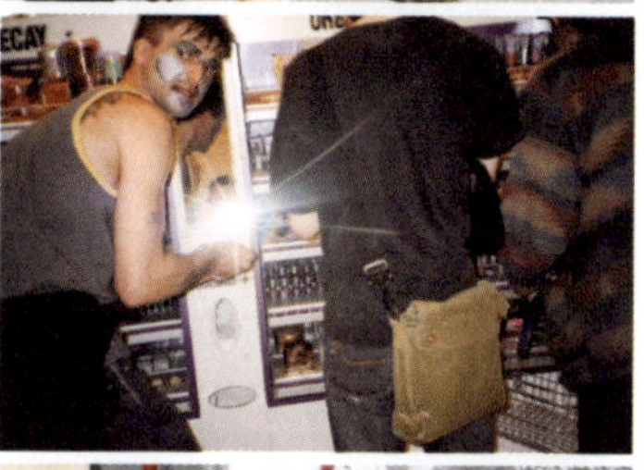

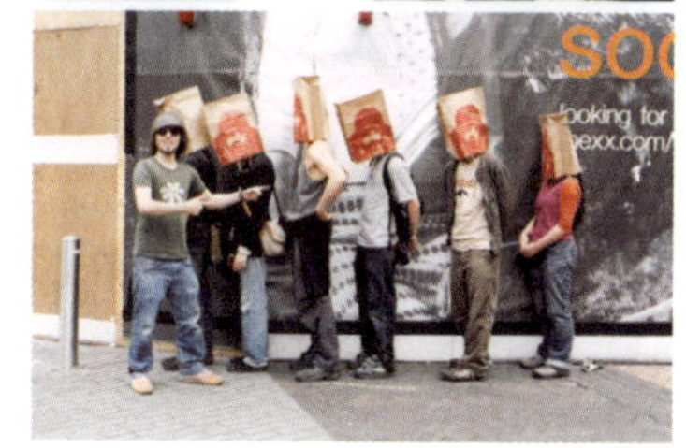

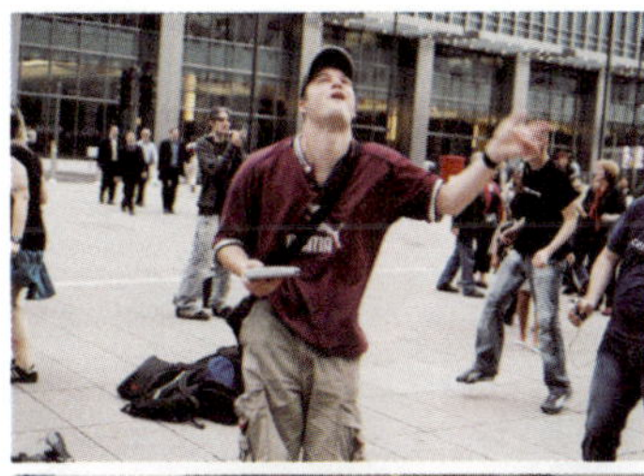

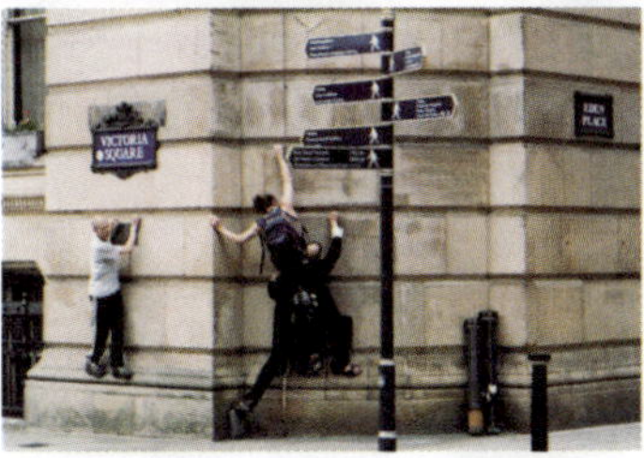

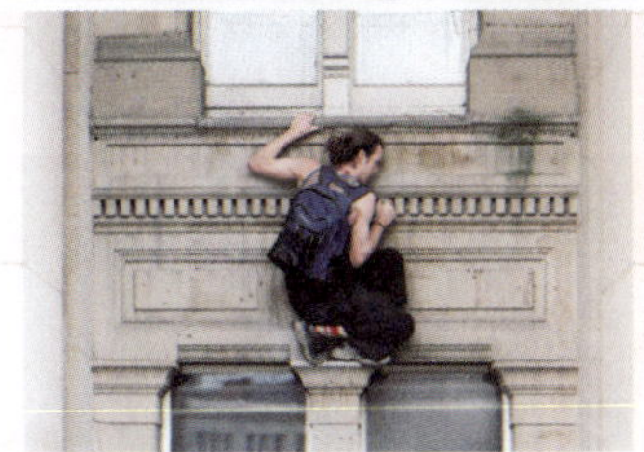

There is such a subliminal barrage of advertising that it is actually easier to consume it than it is to make up your own mind.

<u>Immo Klink:</u> Walking through the streets, sometimes you feel you can read all the hidden mechanisms behind the surface. It's like in *The Matrix.* Take a billboard image and what is behind it. All the marketing strategies, corporate objectives, focus group tests, digital image manipulation… Everything is run by the same commercial mechanisms and becomes predictable, boring and sometimes even absurd: If you go to the periphery of a city you will find that the areas where you have the most traffic congestion are plastered with advertising billboards inviting you to buy even more new cars. But these things have become so familiar that we have started to accept them as the way things work.

<u>Space Hijackers:</u> … yeah once you see it, you suddenly open up… and I think what we are trying to do is kind of open up a little chink in it for people to see through it and to see how these things work. Obviously they won't all follow it… but I think rather than saying 'we're right and you're wrong and lalalalala, it's much more about: 'have you looked at this? Have you thought about why this is how it is?' And some might be saying they like it like that. They might be saying: 'I'm really glad that they're gonna spend all this money on marketing to try to sell me stuff. Because that means it's cool. And then that means that stuff that I buy makes me cool…' They might go down that road. But then at the same time some might go: 'Hold on a minute!'…

Reclaimed space

<u>Immo Klink:</u> After I came along with the Space Hijackers or My Dads Strip Club to one of the large shopping mall areas like Oxford Street or the Bullring in Birmingham to do an action, I got this feeling 'I made this space my space!' not in an imposing or forced manner but just by playing silly games. Places with certain commercial functions changed into new functions for our games. And for us the whole area became some kind of adventure playground.

<u>Space Hijackers:</u> Exactly, I think that is spot on what the whole Space Hijacker thing is about. It's about finding a place and then making up your own set of rules for it. You are taking control of it on your own terms and then that can have a kind of knock-on effect within the other communities that use that

space. And then this space starts to change the way it works for everyone. In the case of a shopping mall, it means that someone going into the mall the day after he has seen us there playing something might have a different appreciation of it.

Immo Klink: It's kind of sublime. You just hint that everything could be different and create some kind of myth by spreading the idea or images of what happened.

Space Hijackers: It is like leaving mental graffiti, a kind of 'thought-graffiti', where you add extra ideas in these kinds of places. A company can only own the physical building, the bricks and mortar, but you can't own the meaning of the building and people can change it.
Same with the Nike tick: it has all these other associations now and Nike has no real control over it. Same with the Bullring mall or with your photos of the boarded-up places in Mayfair. You can change the way these places exist within the communities.

My Dads Strip Club: But entering these spaces on an individual level, it needs quite a psychological shift to get into that mindset. I still have to adjust when I start to do that sort of thing because of the whole security system and the unspoken rules

about the way you should behave in those spaces. I think people do get incredibly intimidated and scared by the idea of just slightly playing with these rules without doing anything illegal. But when you get into that head space there is a kind of rush that comes from it, similar to that on a fairground ride. Before, you might be a bit intimidated and feel like you want to back out when you're queuing up for the ride. But when you come out of it and you see that everybody is ok, you realize that actually these systems aren't so intimidating at all. There is a real sense of liberation.

Immo Klink: I really liked the Circle Line Party as well, because you just called out 'Everyone is welcome to come and have a party on a London Underground train. Nobody is in charge and if anybody asks, don't point at me!' And hundreds of people came, brought their own music and drinks and made almost three rounds on the Circle Line, having the party of their lives. There was no political agenda attached to it…

Space Hijackers: … but by itself it is very political. Not big politics. It's just that if people did start to actively become involved and actively use public space it would have a massive impact on the way things work.
As you said it's not about sweatshops

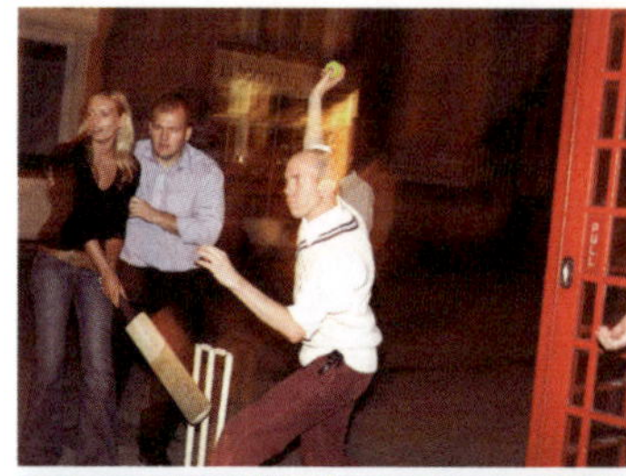

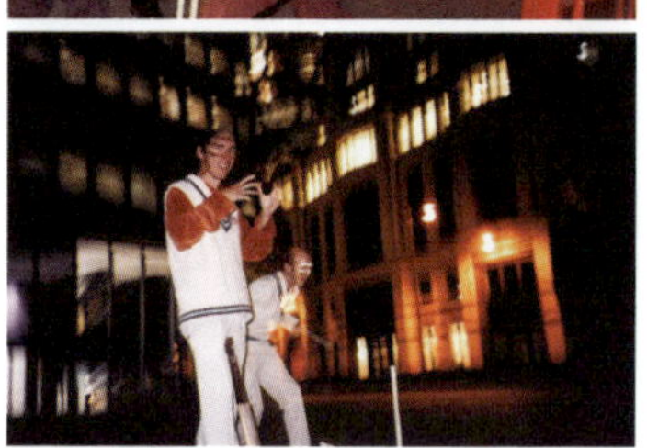

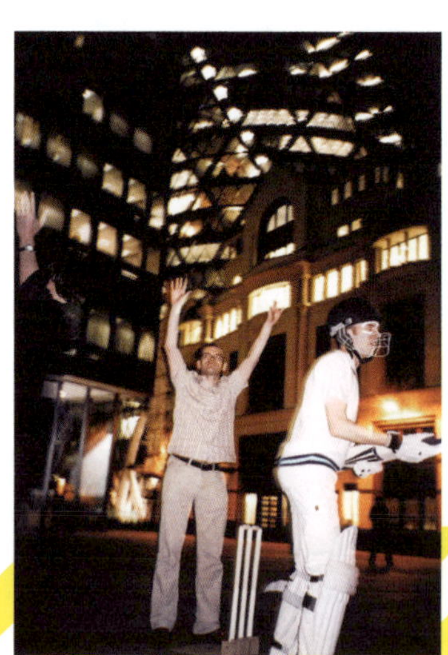

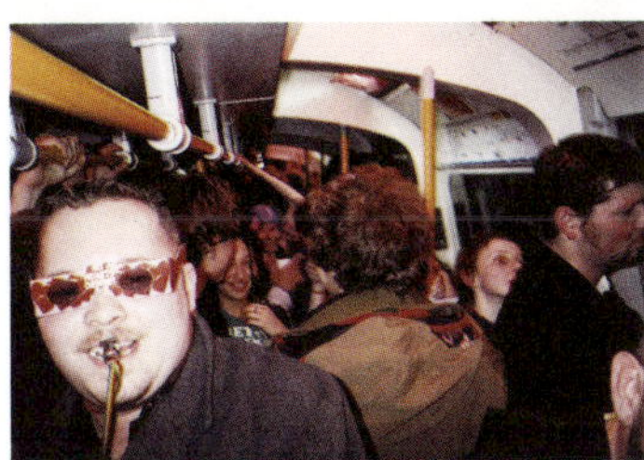

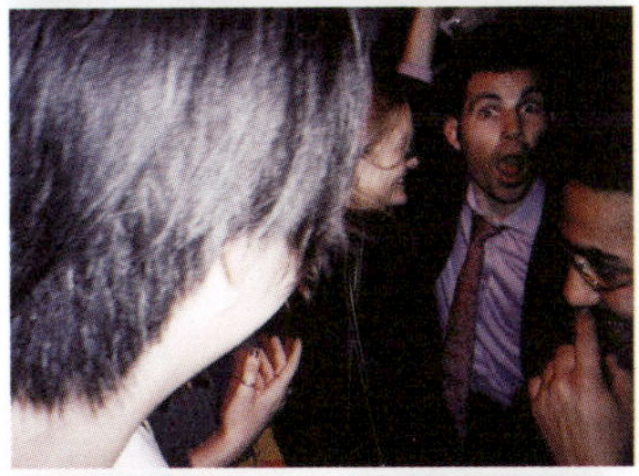

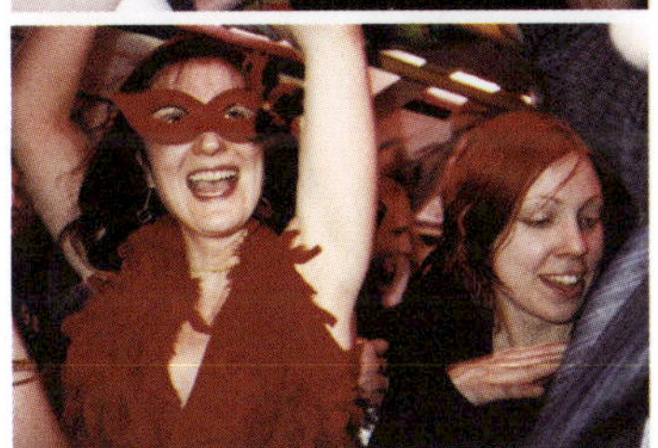

or privatisation and so on… it's about getting people active again… Most important with the Circle Line Party was that we weren't providing entertainment. People had to provide their own music, drinks or party outfits. They take control of the carriage and the area. They feel safety in numbers, but also the power that they have assumed.

Further links:
www.labofii.net
http://conglomco.org
www.immoklink.com
www.mobile-clubbing.com
www.freewebs.com/dedomenici/
index.htm
www.thevacuumcleaner.co.uk
www.theyesmen.org
www.yomango.net

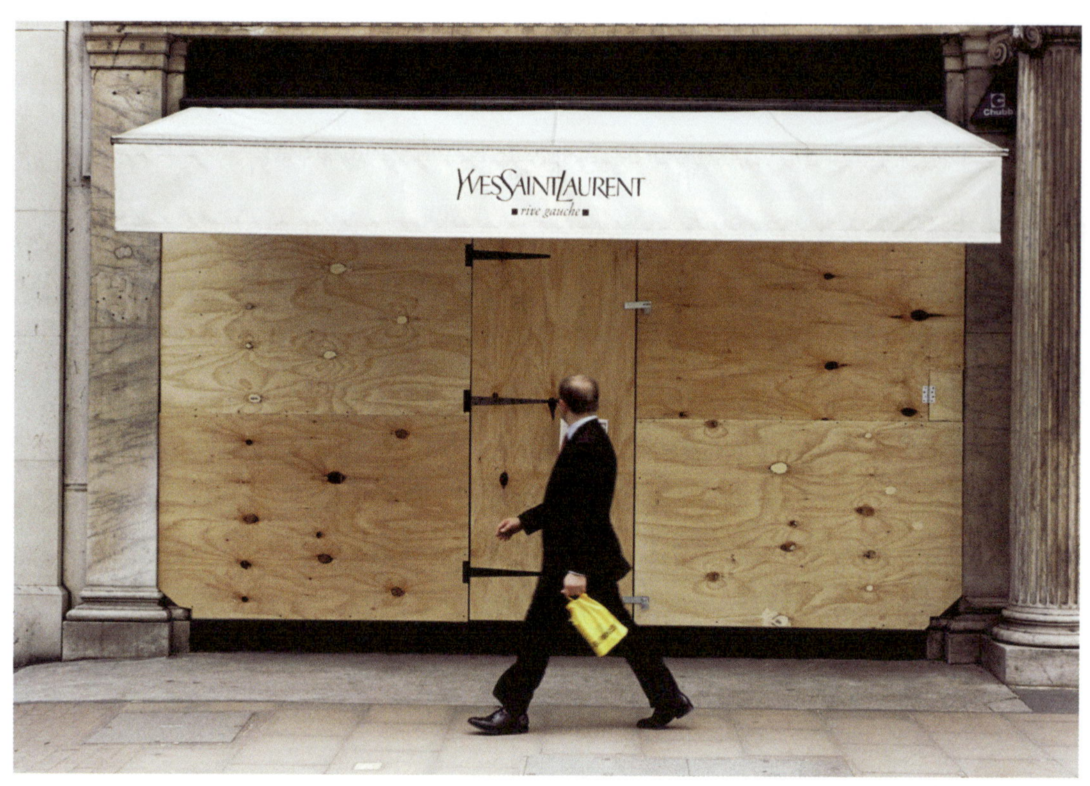

Immo Klink
"YSL", from the series *Mayday at Mayfair*,
2002
Colour photograph
120 x 180 cm

174

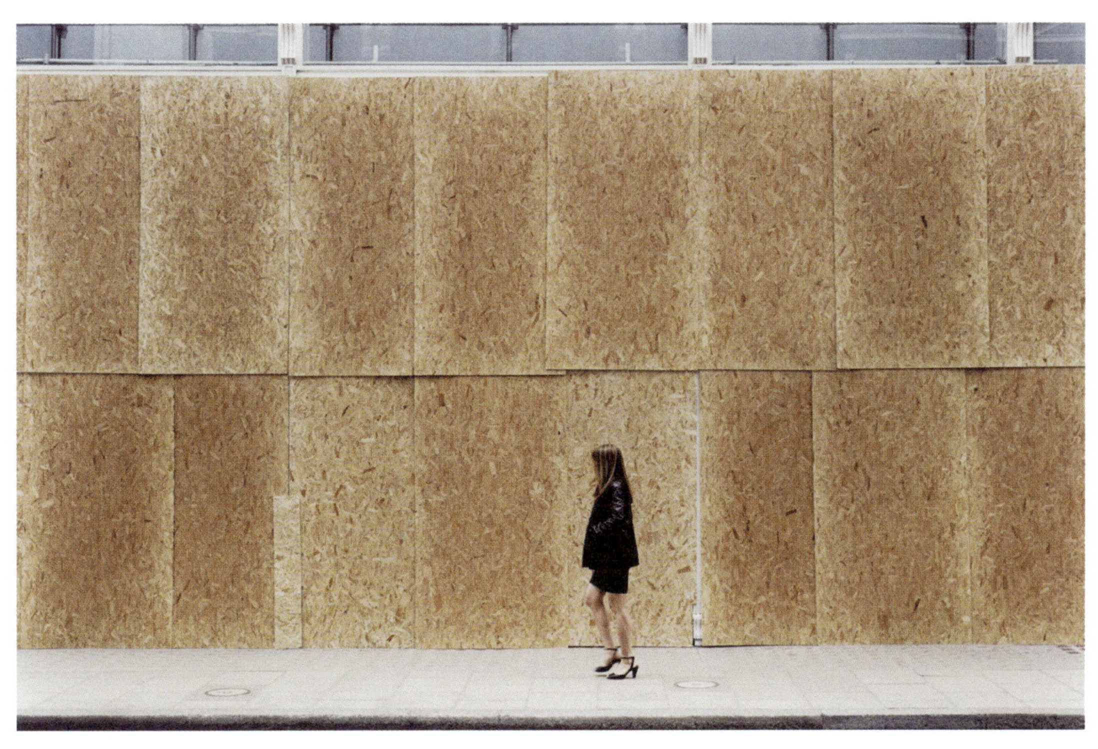

"Chanel", from the series *Mayday at Mayfair*, 2002
Colour photograph
120 x 180 cm

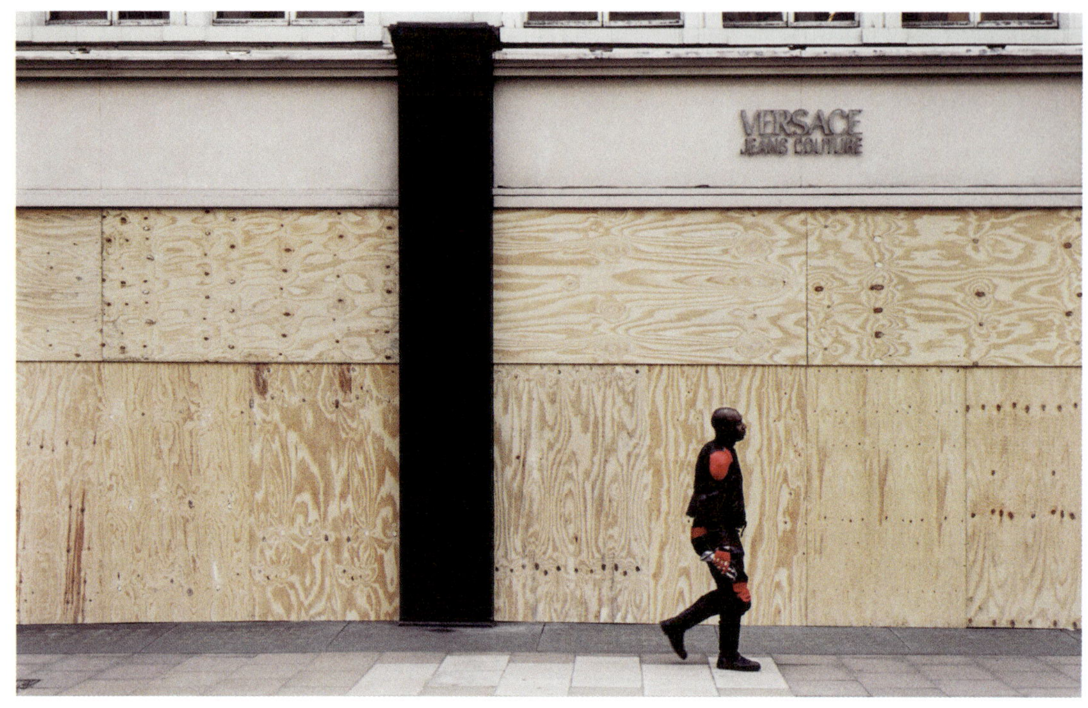

"Versace", from the series *Mayday at Mayfair*, 2000
Colour photograph
200 x 300 cm

176

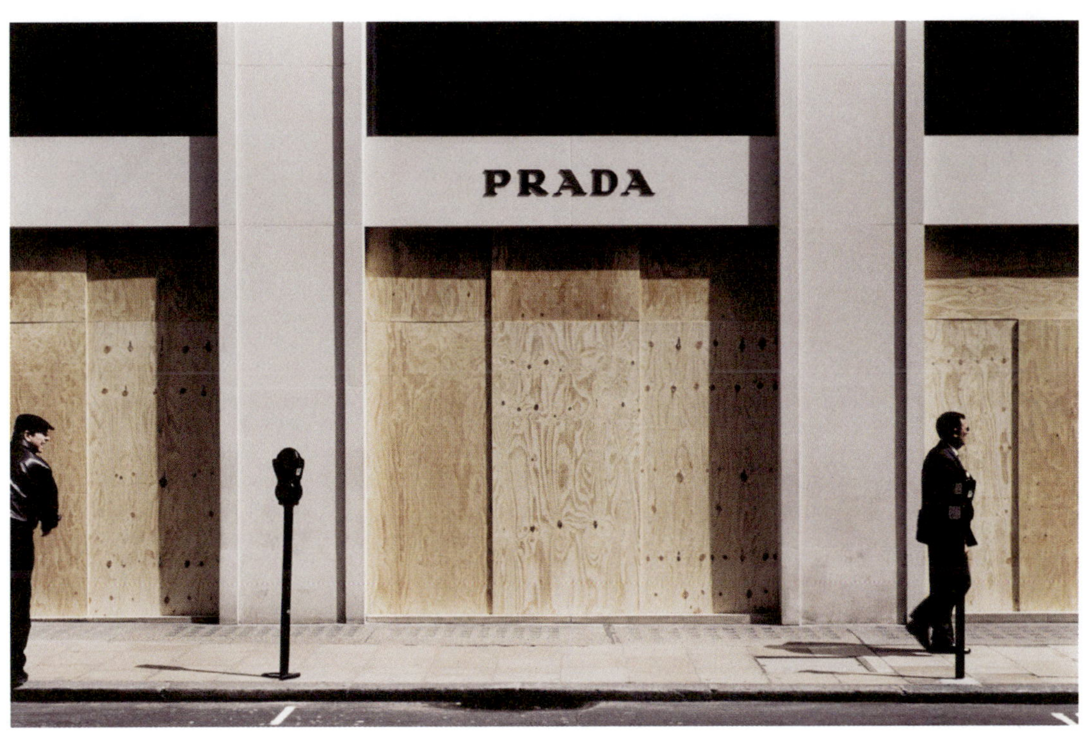

"Prada", from the series *Mayday at Mayfair*, 2002
Colour photograph
120 x 180 cm

Isaac Julien

I was in Philadelphia last week installing a double-screen film and video installation called "Frantz Fanon S. A." (1997), which was first shown at the Johannesburg Biennial in 1997. In the installation I abstracted a series of images from my feature film documentary "Frantz Fanon: Black Skin White Mask" (1996) that corresponded to a lyrical register in psychiatrist and revolutionary Frantz Fanon's writing. The vibrancy and sensuality of the images abstracted from my earlier film are represented in a condensed form – presenting a spin or ironic quotation on Fanon's piece 'There is no color prejudice here,' as the Fanon character in the film waves a South African ANC flag. The exhibition, curated by Mark Nash (my partner), is called "Experiments with Truth", a display of contemporary moving images intended to reassess the influence of cinema and documentary practice within contemporary visual art. In an increasingly troubled time of emergencies, war and disinformation, the work represents an alternative view – one in which images can play a critical role in shaping our understanding of the world rather than merely being used as a tool for propaganda.

The gallery, rather than the cinema, is becoming an important space for making interventions to review the differing cultural and political perspectives that make up 'moving image' culture from around the world. This shift brings with it a growing set of questions, including: How are we to consider the phenomena of contemporary artists working with film and video? How did a version of cinema become an increasingly common presence within the art gallery context?

This growing trend is marked in my own career as an artist and film-maker who, after Derek Jarman's death, witnessed the end of an independent (queer) film culture in the U.K. Regrettably, what Ruby Rich once rightly crowned "New Queer Cinema" was lost. It can be argued that elements from the genre have reappeared, here and there, in advertising, in mainstream television and in galleries. Through experimentation with film and video, the distinctions between narrative avant-garde and documentary practice have become blurred, along with shifts in the experiences of viewers – whose viewing habits and subjectivities are influenced by new digital technologies.

Distinctive experimental approaches to visual imagery, once the aesthetic hallmarks of the "New Queer Cinema", have transcended into the space of the contemporary gallery. The documentary turned into video art was perhaps hinted at a decade ago in Derek Jarman's 'imageless' feature film "Blue" (1994). With an anti-representational strategy, Jarman presented a blank screen of Yves Klein blue, which stood as a testament to a time now lost, by creating a blue frame where the spectator loses her or his sight into a sea of blue haze. The non-representational image retained poetic and factual information which Jarman sonically produced with precision – documenting his eventual blindness during his battle against AIDS. "Blue" premièred at the Venice Art Biennial as a video installation portraying the truth of his condition and, indeed, a part of our queer history.

Thinking about the representation of truth in the space of the city and notions of spatial temporality brings to mind my early research for "Looking for Langston", which also led me to Philadelphia, the very place of the "Experiments with Truth" exhibition. A connection between the past and the present is clearly evident, haunting my every step.

This city was home to two of the perhaps most important voices that created an impetus and interpolated my own art practice. I am, of course, referring to Joseph Beam, an activist and writer of the black gay anthologies "Brother to Brother" and to the poet Essex Hemphill. Indeed, Hemphill's poetic truth struck me again, as it did when I first read his poem in homage to Joseph Beam after his death 20 years ago:

When I stand
On the front lines, now
Cussing the lack of truth,
The absence of willful change
And strategic coalitions,
I realize sewing quilts
Will not bring you back
Nor save us.

It's too soon
To make monuments
For all we are losing,
For the lack of truth….

It was for the 'lack of truth' that Bush recently won the American election – as millions of voters lined up to vote against queer marriages it seems. But it was only 10 years ago that I first lived in New York to work on a four-part television series titled the "Question of Equality", a history of the Lesbian and Gay movement in the States, which chronicled the rise of the religious-right fundamentalism. This project was commissioned by Channel Four and ITVS for a program "Culture Wars" and in 2004 we are still deep in it.

In 1985 I first visited Joseph Beam in Philadelphia and it was in the same city where, in 1994, I last saw Essex Hemphill alive.

Next year will mark a decade since Essex Hemphill's death and it will also be the year "Looking for Langston" is re-released on DVD. The updated DVD will contain many surprises to celebrate Hemphill's work.

Looking back on the making of "Looking for Langston" (1989) and "The Attendant" (1993), I can see the creation of a discursive space for re-articulating the politics of queer-difference. This was a response to early developments in furthering what has now become known as "Queer Studies" in the States, and in Britain "Cultural Studies" (an already named and established discipline). I saw myself as a 'cultural-worker' who made visual imagery that translated theoretical concerns – either through the language of the cinema, or via progressive television programming, where the cultural and media revolution was taking place through Channel Four Television. Indeed it was Channel Four's lesbian and gay series "Out on Tuesday", in 1989 that commissioned and broadcast "Looking for Langston". The legacy of that intervention is a British version of "Queer Eye for the Straight Guy!" However, I think that the American original is much better – but that's where queer innovation has left us.

It is now left to artists and film-makers to make utopic interventions into spaces that seem to be more open and receptive to thematic and visual experimentation. Contemporary museums and galleries are certainly creative spaces where a queer legacy of innovation continues and aesthetic interventions are not only possible, but also recognized.

I don't want to claim it is a triumph, but it is a site where 'moving images' can explore 'queer aesthetics' receptively. Several projects, that have successfully used the space of the gallery come to mind – "The Orange and Blue Feelings" (2003) is a double-screen video piece by Glenn Ligon, who grapples with artistic creativity, growing up black and queer; the work invites the audience to explore the multiple significances of a 'lost queer painting' of Malcolm X. Francesco Vezzoli's "The End of the Human Voice" is haunted by cinephilia, re-enacting key moments in art cinema through the camp performances of Bianca Jagger. The piece references Cocteau, as Vezzoli casts himself, complete with iconic paper 'eye-lids', on one side of a bed and Bianca Jagger on the other. Both pieces can be seen in the "Experiments of Truth" exhibition at the Fabric Workshop and Museum in Philly, not in cinema proper.

The politics of the Museum were ambivalently signaled in "Looking for Langston" and "The Attendant". Both films explored spatial temporalities, queering history, transgressing racial boundaries and the space of the Museum. In "Looking for Langston", for example, sections of the black and white film show an art opening in New York from the 1930s. We see African American artists and their white patrons, while Stuart Hall reads a verse from Chaucer about history, 'the smiler with the knife under the cloak'. Here I was alluding to my suspicion of the art world and the possible dangers of

patronage for black and for queer artists. "The Attendant" is a story of (imagined) interracial transgression that occurs between a 'closeted' middle-aged black guard who works in a museum and, after closing hours, a younger white visitor.

Indeed the museum or gallery has become the site for my own re-articulations – an ironic relocation, I admit. Essex Hemphill was well aware of the contradictory nature of high cultural spaces, seeing them as sites for class and race wars ("Visiting Hours"):

The government pays me
Nine thousand dollars a year
To protect the East Wing
So I haunt it.

Visiting hours are over.
The silent sentry is on duty
An electric eye patrols the premises
I'm just here
Putting mouth on the place.

Modigliani whispers to Matisse
Matisse whispers to Picasso.
I kiss the Rose in my pocket
And trip through this tomb of thieves.

I'm weighted down with keys,
Flashlight, walkie-talkie, a gun

I'm expected to die, if necessary,
Protecting European artwork
That robbed color and movement
From my life

I'm a ghost in the Capitol.
I did Vietnam.
My head is rigged with land mines
But I keep my cool,
Waiting every other Friday,
Kissing the rose
Catching some trim.

I'm not protecting any more Europeans
With my life.
I'll give this shit in here away
Before I die for it
Fuck a Remb-randt!

And if I go off,
You'd better look out, Mona Lisa
I'll run through this gallery
With a can of red enamel paint
And spray everything in sight
Like a cat on heat.

This notion of treason and revenge of the multitude, hinted at by Hemphill, is a theme at work in "Paradise Omeros" (made for Documenta 11) and "Baltimore" (2003). The latter was a multi-screen video installation that developed from a documentary called "Baadasssss Cinema" (made in 2002). "Baltimore" deals with the cinematization of video art, on the one hand, and a 'queering' and 'racing' of the museum, on the other. I saw these video installations as interventions that attempted to address the 'creolizing vision' in the space of the gallery.

My emerging displacement of cinema, in an art context, can be seen as a continuation of some of my earlier independent cinema concerns.

It could be seen as a reconfiguration of sorts – this mutation, from one technology to another, from celluloid to digital, makes new interventions possible. Along with this come changes in the nature of spectatorship and subjectivity. Deterritorialization of the cinema into the gallery means that spectators who come to these spaces may have a different set of expectations, beyond the normative expectations of a general cinema audience. But, of course, that could be seen as a class difference as well, and that's why I like the idea of creating works that have an interdisciplinary approach. For example, "Baadasssss Cinema", the documentary I made for the Independent Film Channel, was shown on Cable TV, but "Baltimore", its sister project, was shown at Metro Pictures Gallery in New York.

These changes can also be viewed as a sign of the displacement of political demands which once took centre stage in the cinema proper, but are now relegated to a 'fine art' space. It is worth noting that many voices have been made absent in the cinema. It has been over ten years since Derek Jarman's death. His life is the subject of my next documentary – a project that is proving to be very difficult to raise funds for. To date, not one television station has agreed to support the documentary financially and I wonder, if Jarman were alive, would he join me in the call for a re-articulated cinema? Or, for that matter, would the political video work of Marlon Riggs be shown in a gallery as video art?

'Projection, it has been argued by some, reintroduces a more conventionally theatrical mode of spectatorship in which the audience remains outside the media feedback loop rather than participating as actors within it. Unlike Hollywood cinema, however, video projections, which are typically fractures across several screens, tend either to accelerate the pace of edits or to slow them dramatically, thus undermining any illusion of coherent action and serving to disrupt a viewer's smooth absorption within a narrative. Indeed, in this regard, as well as in its adherence to the planarity of the gallery wall, video projection is as much heir to the traditions of modernist painting as it is successor to closed-circuit video.'

Baltimore, the Video Installation

The aim of "Baltimore", a large-scale three-screen video projection, was to try and create a re-reading across three distinct archives, including that of Black action films from the 1970s. The installation aims to create a reflective 'third space' using both 'high' and 'popular' cultural motifs such as black science fiction and Afro-futurism.

The triptych component explores the aesthetics of the blaxploitation cinema genre and its contemporary references through a series of light-hearted citations from a number of movies. The work was shot in Baltimore – a city with a long history of black migration and settlement. Baltimore is also the home base of the NAACP in the States.

The prime locations of "Baltimore" are the museums of Walters Art Gallery, an important Renaissance art museum in downtown Baltimore, and the Great Blacks in Wax Museum (the equivalent of a Madame Tussauds gone wrong or a black Thomas Hirsh one installation - and one of America's African Americans' top ten history attractions). This is due to my own interest in archival spaces – including notions of power and memory and memorialization.

The blaxsploitation genres are profoundly imperfect, contaminated culturally, sexist yet queer. Certainly not everyone would call these films art, nor are many of them that compelling. I would argue this is irrelevant. The films are valuable and provide a rich starting point for my own imagery. They are involved with the aesthetics of the vulgar.

Video projection can draw attention to visual identifiers and codes, which I rework to produce a creolized vision of the museum. I hope the piece is received as a provocative and satirical intervention within the art world, critically re-arranging and untidying its curatorial endeavors. The idea behind this first part of the "Baadasssss" project was to place the documentary in a pedagogical relationship to the spectator. I wanted to show the archival process and the power of visual iconography in relation to the after-effects of the Black Power Movement, to people's lives – to their very representation. This attempt at queering blaxsploitation imagery is an acknowledgment of its ability to influence other genres such as Hip-Hop, Independent film and so on. I also wanted to consider the misunderstandings and complexities of the genre through interviews with black queer icons, such as Pam Grier engaged in debate and dissension. "Baadasssss Cinema" will merely enable the spectator to fully appreciate the spatio-temporality of "Baltimore's" multiple screens and sonic sound projections, allowing for a criticality that tackles the representational strategies inherent in blaxploitation films themselves, and approximates these aesthetics for the space of video art.

The scenes in "Baltimore" are shot with deliberate diegetic effects that work to disrupt the narrative telos. The camera, tracking movements within the frame, makes use of the sculptural potential of cinematic space. In the triptych format the images are not merely representations of certain people but representations of "the spaces of representations". Here identities are spatialized by collocated images across all three screens. The highway scene, for example, mirrors the visual ideas on perceptualization from the school of Piero della Francesca's "An Ideal City". This is achieved through pictorial montages in order to emphasize the politics of space. The "Sweet Sweetback's Baadasssss Song" is unique in allowing for a pan-black fairy queen to skip along to it. And although Melvin Van Peebles did not intend to make a queer black film, it is indeed a very queer and strange black experimental art film. It was for this element of the unexpected that he was chosen to play the protagonist, along with Vanessa Myrie, who plays the black femme fatale – part Angela Davis, part Foxy Brown, and part cyborg. Her character remains out of reach for Melvin – her sexuality is an enigma for some, but not for all. These characters are indeed haunted by the history of the spaces of the museum and their own filmic iconography.

At the end of "Heavy Breathing", Essex Hemphill writes:

At the end of heavy breathing
The dream deferred
Is in a museum
Under glass and guard.

It costs five dollars
To see it on display
We spend the day
Viewing artifacts,
Breathing heavy
On glass
To see
The skeletal remains
Of black panthers,
Pictures of bushes,
Canisters of tears.

I imagine he might have dreamt a few frames of "Baltimore" or prophetically dreamt my future.

Paradise Omeros
In this piece, a homage to Derek Walcott, I explore an adolescent's perspective on the mixture of English and St. Lucian cultures within both countries. A young man prepares to come to terms with a loss of innocence and at the same time there is an Oedipal reading of postcolonial and intra-ethnic relations enacted between the protagonist and the tourist/rasta male character. In England, the young man and his family experience both happiness and racial tension – which is shown through scenes of enjoyment, juxtaposed to ones of anguish. Other sections of the film are set in St. Lucia, where the rasta character quotes Robert Mitchum's performance in "The Night of the Hunter" (directed by Charles Laughton in 1955) to the adolescent. Here the dynamics of love and hate are explored – Mitchum's tattoo replaced by gold rings worn by the rasta.

I wanted to consider the representation of the Caribbean as a site of mythic cultural fantasy. One of the principal scenes, for example, is the submersion of the boy in the sea, intercut with historical images of riots and immigration in the UK. On his journey through the sea and the archive, our protagonist encounters traumatic images. Memories, both personal and public, lead him to the metropolis, London. Yet he returns to St. Lucia, and then back to London again, through the visual looping of the film, which is projected on the gallery wall. The effect is one of oscillation – as though the character continually travels back and forth in time. He refuses to be located, preferring to occupy another space – somewhere between the sea, the city and the gallery wall. Indeed, it is within the very walls of the contemporary gallery that artists remain free to explore such themes (which often sit outside mainstream interests). And, it is in this way that galleries are becoming an increasingly important critical and cultural site.

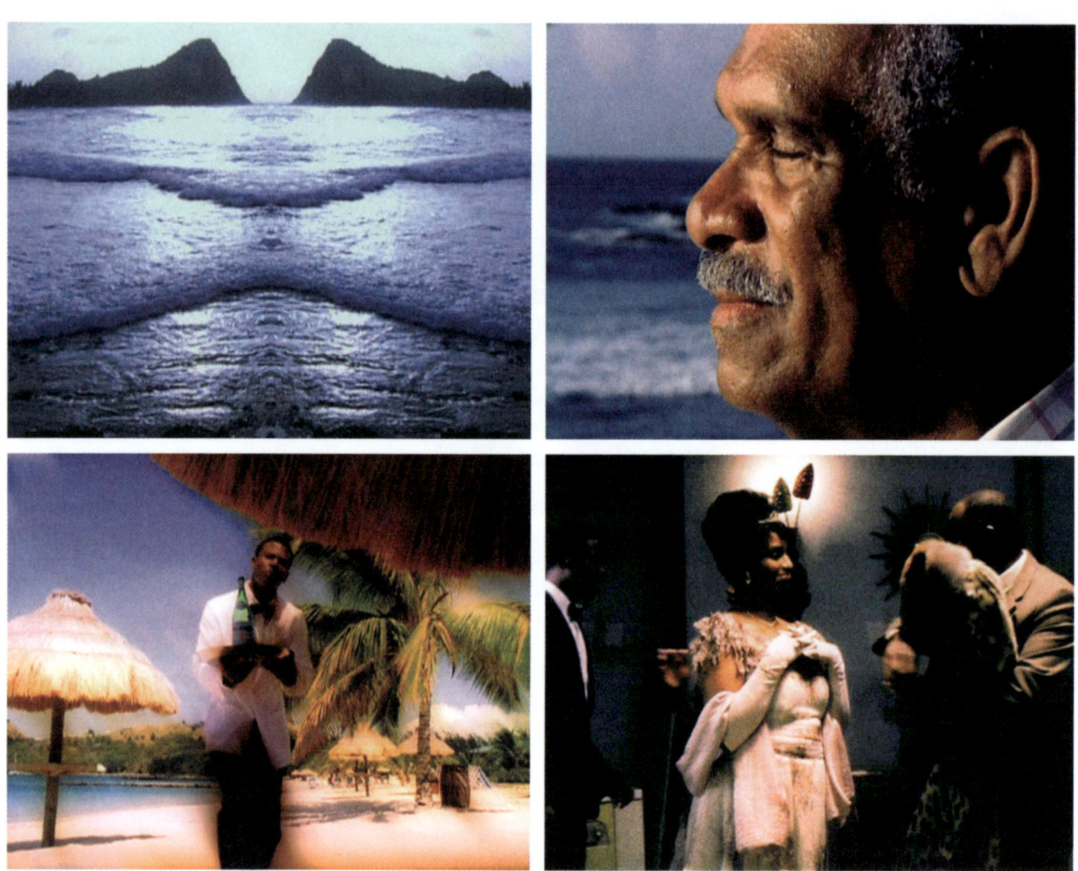

Isaac Julien
Paradise Omeros, 2002
16-mm film with sound transferred to
DVD
18' 51"

184

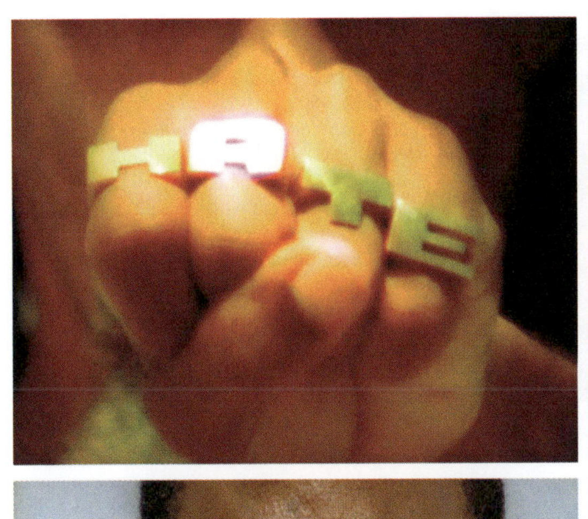

HATE

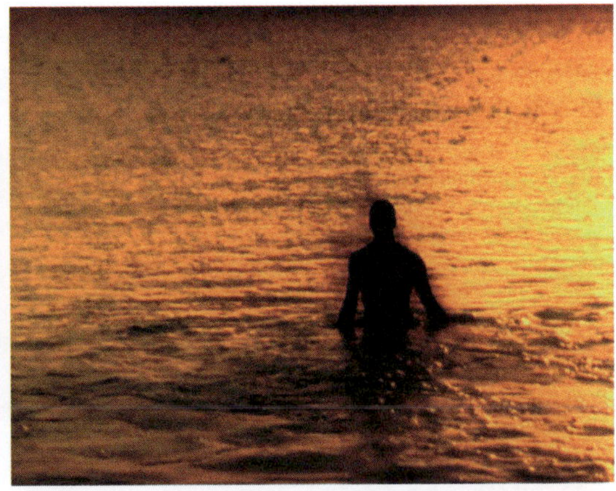
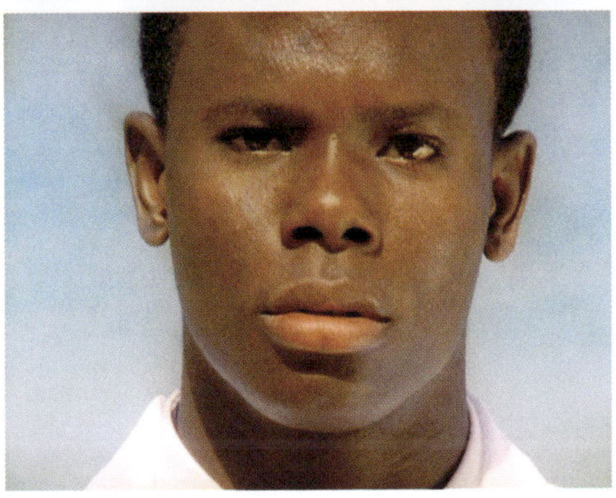
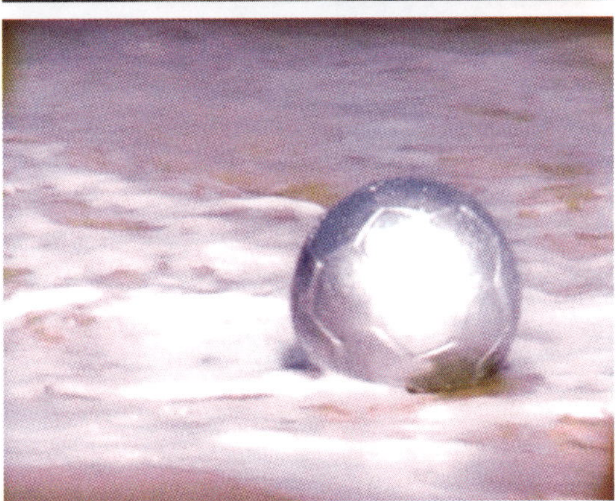

Further reading

ARANGUREN, L. A. (1998*): De la tolerancia a la intercul-
turalidad en un proceso educativo entorno a la diferencia*,
Anaya, Madrid.
FULLER, N. (2002): *Interculturalidad y Política.
Desafíos y posibilidades.*
GIMÉNEZ, C. (1998): *Migración y nueva ciudadanía*,
Temas para el Debate, 43.
HERNÁNDEZ, C. (1999): *Culturas y acción comunicativa,
introducción a la pragmática intercultural*, Octaedro,
Barcelona.
Hicks, D (1993): *Manifiesto de Sevilla sobre la Violencia*,
in Educación para la Paz, Morata, Madrid.
KYMLICKA, W. (1996): *Ciudadanía multicultural.
Una teoría liberal de los derechos de las minorías*,
Paidós, Barcelona.
LABAT, C., VERMES, G. (1994): *Cultures ouvertes,
Sociétés interculturelles, Du contact á l'interaction*,
L'Harmattan, St. Cloud: ENS, Editions Fontenary.
MEYER-BISH, P. (1995): *Culture of democracy or challenge
for schools*, UNESCO, París.
RINGER, B. Y LAWLESS, E. (1989): *Race-Ethnicity and
Society*, Routledge, London, New York.
STEVENSON, N. (2001*): Culture and citizenship*,
Thousand Oaks, Calif Sage, London.

Websites of interest

- Alliance for a Responsible, plural and United World:
  http://www.alliance21.org
- International Education and Resource Network:
  http://www.iearn.org
- Escola de Cultura de Pau:
  http://www.pangea.org/unescopau
- Asociación Internacional de Educadores por la Paz:
  http://catedradh.unesco.unam.my/aiesp/index2.html
- UNESCO: http://portal.unesco.org
- Edualter: http://www.edualter.org
- UNICEF: http://www.unicef.org
- INTERMON-OXFAM: http://www.intermonoxfam.org
- OXFAM: http://www.oxfam.org.uk
- Stockholm International Peace Research Institute:
  http://www.sipri.org

Enrolment in primary education by regions

2001/02	
North Africa	91,9
Sub-Saharan Africa	62,2
Latin America & the Caribbean	95,7
Eastern Asia	92,1
South-east Asia	90,8
Western Asia	82,9
Oceania	79,4

Source: UN Statistical indicators 2004.

Literacy index of the population between 15-24 years of age by regions

2000/04	
North Africa	78,5
Sub-Saharan Africa	76,6
Latin America & the Caribbean	94,7
Eastern Asia	98,9
South-east Asia	95,4
Western Asia	85,6
Oceania	81,3

Source: UN Statistical indicators 2004.

Population with no access to primary education in their mother tongue

Region or group	Number of languages spoken	Population with access to education in their mother tongue	Total population in millions
Sub-Saharan Africa	2.632	13%	641
Eastern Asia and Pacific	2.815	62%	1.918
Southern Asia	811	66%	1.480
Eastern Europe and CIS	625	74%	409
OECD countries	1.299	87%	912
Latin America and Caribbean	1.086	91%	530

Source: Human Development Report, 2004.

Proportion of national films	1984 (%)	2001 (%)
USA	97	94
France	45	42
Italy	34	19
Spain	22	18
United Kingdom	17	5
Germany	17	16

Source: IDH, 2004

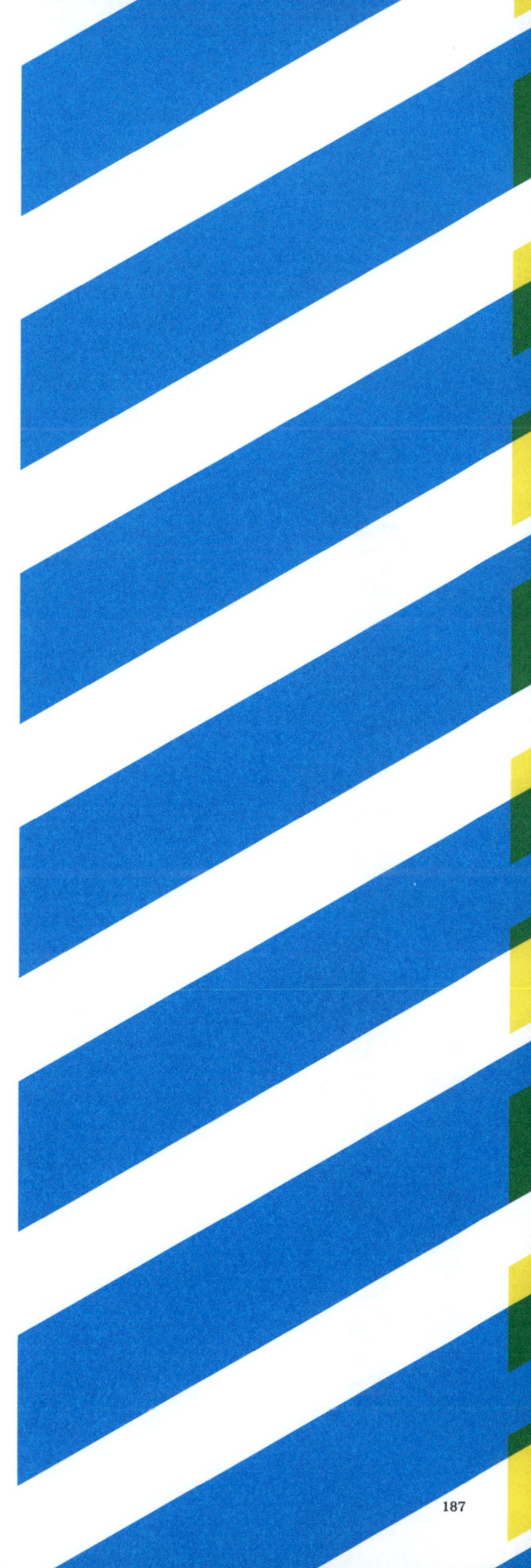

Secondary education for girls
Attendance of girls in secondary school as a percentage of boys 1995-2000.

Girls in secondary school
Countries where less than 25% of girls are enrolled in secondary schools 1997-2000.

Primary education
Percentage of boys and girls enrolled in primary education and who continue to attend in 1996-2000

Development objective for the millennium
Sex equality in education and training for women are essential for achieving universal primary education. When the school doors are opened to girls, both boys and girls benefit.

Primary school output
Percentage of boys and girls entering primary school and reaching fifth grade.
Survey data 1995-2001
Selected countries

Source: UNICEF Annual Report, 2004.

In the societies in which we are living, information plays an important role and each one of us is at the same time object of and subject to news and opinions. Access to information is a right, but in the same way, information is a product which is used to sell. The media are the best way for the members of a society or a community to find out what is happening around them in their social, cultural, political and economic environment. They are a channel through which information is obtained, processed and distributed on mass scale.

The media play a fundamental role in the formation of public opinion. The enormous difficulty of finding out first hand what is happening outside our more immediate environment is offset by the accessibility of the media, which make it possible for us to know what is happening, almost at the same time it happens, in any corner of the planet. In this way, the media make a decisive contribution to the creation of public opinion, a public opinion which is increasingly global and in which supposedly aseptic news and information is mixed with opinion, assessment and very often, rumours which are more or less justified.

The influence of the media is so enormous that their usual description as the 'fourth power', a real power of which there are copious examples every day, is no exaggeration. As happens with so many other things, take, for example, the simultaneous use of atomic energy in medicine and nuclear weapons, this enormous power can be used to broadcast, present, attack or defend a very different content. This is where we enter the field of professional ethics and the vision of the media as public servants, regardless of the line of thought of the owner, and basic instruments for the creating of a society with values and principles or, on the contrary, for self-interested manipulation in favour of certain arguments. In short, the media are anything but neutral factors in our social reality.

These days, it would not be an exaggeration to say that the media are undergoing a profound revolution, from both a technical as well as a political point of view. With regard to the former, it is clear that technological advances now allow an impressive volume of information to be distributed all over the planet. To the traditional supports, written press, radio and television – subject themselves to profound changes which have not only modified the way in which they are presented to the public, but also their contents, others have been added, Internet being the most significant, which have, in theory, made the preparation and monitoring of world-wide information a democratic process.

With regard to political aspects, it has been observed that the process of monopolising communication is accelerating – with the creation of large media conglomerates which are having a hard time properly combining their original vocation as public servants with their business and, to be more precise, political interests. Similarly, there is a notable attempt by public players, at any level, to become generators of news to promote their own image and further their own interests in order to obtain the permanent support of the citizens – the Berlusconi model is, perhaps, the most perfect example of this to date at a European level. In a world of image, public institutions are no longer content with being the source of news. They also seek to transmit their own interpretation through channels they can control, free of any kind of intermediary whatsoever. The instrumentation of this idea by the Nazi Regime decades ago was, in view of what has happened since, just the starting point in a process which cannot be considered over even with the fall of the Berlin Wall.

What has not changed at all, however, is the vision of the media as basic tools of the right-wing State, constant observers of the behaviour of public, but also private players, in contrast to the rules of play defining open societies. The level of freedom of the media is a direct sign of the more general level of openness and democratic maturity of a society and any attack which seeks to restrict their movements should be interpreted as an attempt to cut down one of the basic pillars of the democratic model of society. This is their great power, but also the source of their destitution, in that those in charge may find themselves tempted to use this huge potential for their own ends. The democratic health of the society as a whole depends, to a large extent, on the proper management of this power.

Some examples from history serve to remind us of the dangers lurking inside this powerful tool when it is used, for better or worse, to influence public opinion. Whilst in the case of the Vietnam war, the media played an important role in bringing about the ultimate withdrawal of the United States, in the Falklands war it was the very absence of any media activity which allowed the British Government – for whom the concept of journalists 'in the thick' of military operations was relatively new at this time – to run the campaign with no intervention from its own public opinion. A more recent example was that of the unprecedented world mobilisation against the war in Iraq, in which the media played a fundamental part. Although it is true that the intervention was not prevented, it is also true that the campaign sent a clear message to governments, by showing them the potential cost of falling into the temptation of making decisions which are out of line with those who are, when it comes down to it, the ones who have voted for them.

The information society and the power of the media

It is widely accepted that information is power. It always has been and it always will be in the foreseeable future. In view of this, it is essential that we know at least where we are and, where possible, that we start making room for the definition of a media framework which would avoid the risks arising from an excessive concentration of information collecting and distributing channels.

The toll on press freedom

World Press Freedom Day falls on 3rd May every year. It is an initiative which attempts to emphasise how important and what a vital factor the free movement of information is to the proper functioning of a democratic society and it dates back to 1991, when, within the framework of the 26th UNESCO General Conference, a resolution was passed entitled "Promotion of Press Freedom in the World".

This resolution acknowledges the fact that a free, plural and independent press is an essential component of a democratic society. Subsequently, on 20th December 1993, the United Nations General Assembly, on the recommendation of the Economic and Social Council, adopted a new resolution which decided to establish 3rd May as World Press Freedom Day.

In 2004, the motto for World Press Freedom Day was "Support for the Media in Armed Conflict and Countries in Transition", with the idea of defining the professional criteria and ethical standards which should guide the way in which the media report on wars and organised violence.

Past experience shows us that the way in which the information regarding these conflictive processes is transmitted has an enormous influence on the players involved in the violence – both victims and perpetrators – as well as on the alignment of governments and international public opinion. It is also a well-known fact that the information experts themselves have become, with no doubt whatsoever, the explicit objects of the perpetrators of violence. Either because it is important for them to be kept quiet or for what they say to be controlled, or because a specific alignment is being sought in favour of or against certain players, journalists have now been added to the list of targets to be knocked down. The report prepared in 2003 by Reporters without Borders leaves no room for doubt: 2003 was the year in which the most journalists were detained and the most were media censured.

Its description as a 'black year' is no exaggeration by any means: 42 journalists killed, 766 imprisoned and 501 media networks shut down or censured. In addition to stating that the violent pressure on the media and those working in the sector is still increasing – and the data for 2004 only confirm this trend – the reports emphasise the fact that attacks on freedom of expression have intensified as a result of the application of principles which advocate 'war on terror' and the anti-terrorist laws adopted by some governments after September 11th.

The following table shows the data reflecting the evolution of attacks against press freedom from 2002 until 2004.

On the other hand, the same organisation has also presented a report of press freedom in 2004, with data from 167 countries. Top of the list are the European Union Countries, monopolising – with the exception of Canada, Trinidad Tobago and New Zealand – the top 40 positions. The report refers to Russia, Central Asia and Caucasus as countries with serious problems in this area, while countries in East Asia and the Middle East appear at the bottom of the list. It is pleasantly surprising that countries with as many problems as El Salvador or Namibia maintain their traditions with regard to freedom of the press.

	2002	2003	2004
Journalists killed	25	42	120
Journalists detained	692	766	431
Journalists assaulted	1420	1460	366
Media networks shut down	389	501	178

Source: Reporters without Borders (reports).

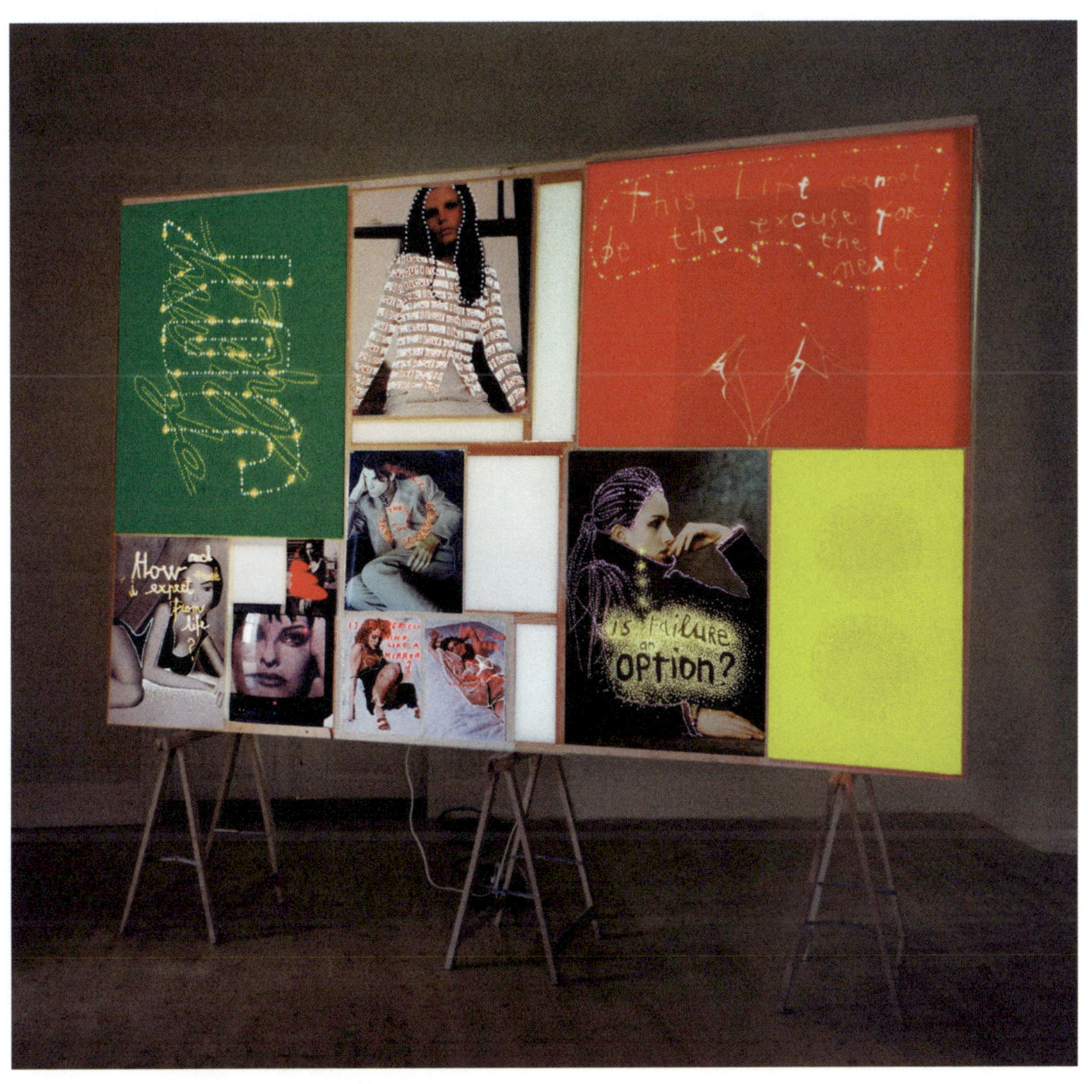

Daniele Buetti
Joy of My Life, 2001-02
Installation consisting of photographs,
monitor, neon lights, images and text
on PVC
270 x 300 x 50 cm

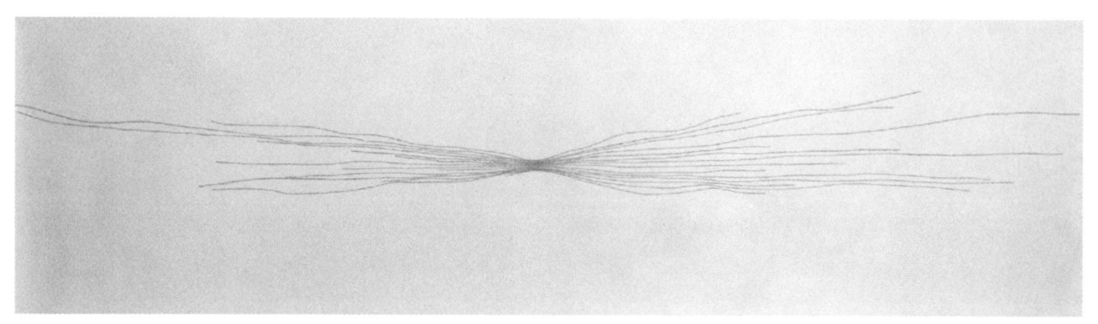

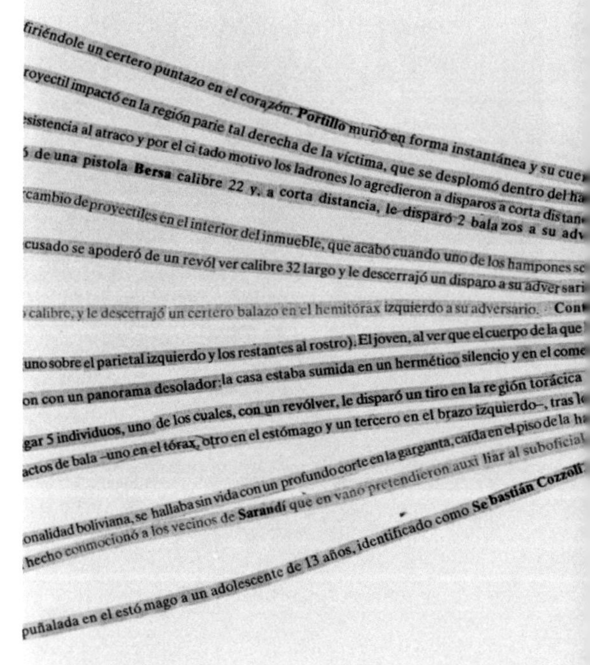
firiéndole un certero puntazo en el corazón. Portillo murió en forma instantánea y su cuer
royectil impactó en la región parie tal derecha de la víctima, que se desplomó dentro del ha
esistencia al atraco y por el ci tado motivo los ladrones lo agredieron a disparos a corta distan
5 de una pistola Bersa calibre 22 y, a corta distancia, le disparó 2 bala zos a su adv
rcambio de proyectiles en el interior del inmueble, que acabó cuando uno de los hampones so
cusado se apoderó de un revól ver calibre 32 largo y le descerrajó un disparo a su adver sari
o calibre, y le descerrajó un certero balazo en el hemitórax izquierdo a su adversario.   Cont
uno sobre el parietal izquierdo y los restantes al rostro). El joven, al ver que el cuerpo de la que
on con un panorama desolador; la casa estaba sumida en un hermético silencio y en el come
gar 5 individuos, uno de los cuales, con un revólver, le disparó un tiro en la re gión torácica
actos de bala –uno en el tórax, otro en el estómago y un tercero en el brazo izquierdo–, tras le
onalidad boliviana, se hallaba sin vida con un profundo corte en la garganta, caída en el piso de la h
hecho conmocionó a los vecinos de Sarandí que en vano pretendieron auxi liar al suboficial
puñalada en el estó mago a un adolescente de 13 años, identificado como Se bastián Cozzoli

do en medio de un gran charco de sangre. Trascendió que los sujetos comenzaron a la fatal reyerta por razones monetarias.

, en medio de un enorme charco de sangre. De inmediato los feroces agresores huyeron velozmente a la carrera, mientras que la mujer debió ser trasladada de urgencia al h

esplomó en medio de un charco de sangre y la oportunidad fue aprovechada por atacantes que huyeron rápidamente, luego de adueñarse de una suma de dinero y un aparato de

vó en medio de un gran charco de sangre y falleció casi en el acto como consecuencia del ataque. Los proyectiles impactaron en el tórax y en una mano del infortunad

a, en medio de un enorme charco de sangre. Mientras tanto, el otro individuo escapó a la carrera sin poder consumar el asalto, estableciéndose luego que había sido herido de un ba

mó en medio de un gran charco de sangre y pereció en forma instantánea —Horas más tarde el criminal se presentó en la comisaría de **Magdalena**, donde se entregó detenido

ió en medio de un gran charco de sangre, ocasión que el agresor aprovechó para huir velozmente a la carrera. Momentos más tarde la víctima fue llevada por un familiar

ja yacía en el piso sobre un charco de sangre, se llevó el caño del arma a la sien derecha y disparó, cayendo gravemente herido. Facultativos de un hospital de la zona acudieron en ayu

en medio de un enorme charco de sangre, se encontraban tendidos los cadáveres de los dos protagonistas de esta macabra historia. Una fuente consultada precisó que la muje

yó en medio de un gran charco de sangre, ante la aterrorizada mirada de **Guzmán**, que salió milagrosamente ileso. De inmediato los acusados fugaron velozmente a la car

ó en medio de un enorme charco de sangre. Rápidamente los criminales se apoderaron de la pistola de **Quinteiros** y del **Peugeot 405**, en el que escaparon. Luego el herido deb

dio de un impresionante charco de sangre. A unos metros de la trágica escena los investigadores se encontraron con otro detalle no menos estremecedor: una niñita de seis años pr

dio de un impresionante charco de sangre en el interior del Volkswagen Pointer negro, en el que se encontraba. Profesionales médicos que se hicieron presente en el lugar c

en medio de un enorme charco de sangre. De inmediato el menor debió ser trasladado a un centro asistencial de **Berazategui**, aunque luego pereció como consecuencia de s

• Throughout history, different milestones have marked the importance of the different types of media. If, in the written press, the reference point was Emile Zola's 'I accuse', something similar happened on the radio with Orson Welles' 'War of the Worlds' and on television with the first televised debates between Kennedy and Nixon. These three events had an impact on the citizens of the time and were turning points in the consolidation of each of these types of media. Nowadays it is not possible to identify a basic milestone of similar characteristics in the world of Internet, but this does not detract one iota from its central value as a representative icon, at least at the level of the three classic works, of the reality of the media today.

• The notion of the information society hatched at the end of the Second World War and became institutionalised during the seventies. In 1998, and within the framework of the World Trade Organisation, it was agreed that the resolution on the opening up of the national telecommunications markets should take effect, opening the door to the creation of large multimedia groups. In addition, in July 2000, the G-8 approved the Charter on the Global Information Society in Okinawa, in which, in addition to establishing a commitment to the defence of intellectual property rights, the fight against programme pirating and consumer defence, it supports maintaining the course towards total freedom of the media.

• In this context, the process of media concentration and the creation of large media groups is today already a fundamental characteristic, though still pending completion and affecting the information we receive, at the heart of the unequal globalisation we are experiencing. In the year 2000, AOL, the first world-wide Internet provider, took over the up until then number one among multimedia groups Time-Warner, which in turn owned well-known companies such as CNN. In addition, the US group Universal was absorbed by the French group Vivendi-Canal+.

These simple examples, among many others which are gradually making look small what seemed to us, in theory, to be highly powerful and dangerous platforms of social influence, not only reflect the acceleration in the world-wide process of media concentration, but also its interpenetration with the interests of the most- and best-globalised financial players. This clear monopolising trend eventually accentuates even more the dysfunctional effects of accepted lines of opinion and renders those hoping to lay claim to their radical freedom of thought increasingly helpless. In the same vein, the observation of an increasing lack of critical and independent thought, pushed aside by economic powers which take precedence over the promotion of culture (without instrumental interests) and freedom of the press (without prejudiced restrictions) is no coincidence.

• A similar process has occurred in the news agency field. Ever since Charles Havas started up the first agency (Agence Havas) in 1835, an accelerated race for concentration has developed. Often presented as the single result of technical necessity and the cold criteria of economic profitability, the process is in fact a response to far more ambitious interests. While in previous times, each State sought to have its own news agency with which to 'sell' its own interpretation of events and its image on the international stage, aspirations today already extend to toppling governments in power in order to become the top players in a planet-wide competition to design and shape the agenda for world-wide affairs.

Currently, no less than 85% of all news received and distributed around the world by the media comes from five press agencies: Associated Press, United International Press, Reuters, France Press and Tass. A small area in which other news sources can be identified remains outside their control, but the quality of these sources and their ability to present the news in a different manner to the larger exclusive group is becoming increasingly minimal. It is this reality which, to allude briefly to the Islamic world, must be taken into consideration when analysing the way in which this wide and heterogeneous universe is normally reflected in the Western media. Not even Islamic countries have their own means of presenting their visions at the same level as the aforementioned, although it cannot be said that these five agencies act as a single player in favour of one sole argument. Whatever the case, it is not difficult to spot a specific country behind each of them, a country interested in spreading its own interpretation of things in order to benefit its own ends.

• In developed societies, the information process is not a one-way concept. Although it is very true that the media have an influence on society, it is also true that citizens have the ability, in turn, to modulate certain perceptions and to command the adoption of certain positions within the public power and within the media themselves. It is the difference between published opinion and public opinion. The same concept of public opinion already incorporates the influence component which the social players, both individually as well as organised in a multitude of formats, have over the deciding powers and institutions at local, national and world-wide level. Public opinion is a cross-national force with an increasing capacity for effective pressure. This was directly acknowledged by the New York Times when discussing the world-wide emergence of public opinion as a new international player as a result of the extensive response by citizens and their eventual international mobilisation against the illegal military campaign in Iraq.

Public opinion intervenes in political affairs because it has an influence on governments, even if it is only by pointing out the range of issues and viewpoints from which those in charge must choose if they wish to maintain the majority vote. The other side of the coin, however, is that that same public opinion can be shaped and controlled by those who control the media – the published opinion. The merger of interests between the United States government and the main national media to create a state of opinion which would justify the need for military intervention in Somalia in 1993, is probably one of the best recent examples of this union.

•	In many developing countries, the situation is very different. The authoritarian zeal and the desire to prevent the people of a country from becoming 'contaminated' by what often tends to be presented as the outside enemy, mean that attempts to control all sources broadcasting news and information are intensified. It is not just a question of closing down a few rebellious corners among the media. It is done more discreetly, by using the fact, for example, that the printing presses are the property of the State, to allow it to control the contents of written press, and that people are frightened of upsetting those in power and being punished. In this same vein, governments make desperate attempts to limit what citizens, men and women alike, may be hearing or seeing on radio or television. Attempts by the Iranian or Saudi Arabian governments, for example, to prevent the spread of parabolic antennae - the fear is no longer only what the western channels may broadcast, but their own Al Yazira, which causes real inward and outward revulsion in the context of the Islamic world - or by the Cubans and North Koreans to limit access to Internet, are doomed to failure.

•	Internet has broken, once and for all, the moulds of hierarchical models for the production and distribution of news and opinions at a world-wide level. Now any one, in any far corner of the earth, can know what is happening thousands of miles away. And what is even more important: can also become an almost instant broadcaster of information! This reality clashes with government aspirations to control what its citizens, men and women alike, are able to find out and with the attempt by large media conglomerates to promote the control of the news channels in their favour.

•	This reality is not, however, free of shady areas. On the one hand, it is not entirely clear that a vast profusion of information channels would automatically mean more media democracy – what could happen is that those behind this apparent curtain of endless offers are still in fact the same large media organisations as always. On the other hand, the principle according to which the greater the number of information sources the greater the freedom of the consumer may not hold true if the sources become too numerous, not only because people can lose their sensitivity to certain issues, but because being saturated with information can be as harmful as having no information at all. Finally, the apparent lack of control over the news-producing sources damages credibility; the contents are not subject to any filters or selection criteria which means there is a risk that no distinction is made between information and manipulation.

• New information technology (NIT) has allowed the volume of information broadcast to be increased and a greater number of citizens to access the messages. In short, this NIT contributes to the democratisation of the information media throughout the world. It should be recognised, however, that this situation is not homogenous, since developing countries do not enjoy the same conditions as developed countries. Proof of this is the digital gap, which leaves behind a large number of people who, for financial reasons – it is no coincidence that the cost of accessing information is comparatively higher in less democratic countries – as well as technological and educational ones, are unable to keep up. At the same time as being able to know what is happening in the remotest community in Chiapas or Mozambique, we must also be aware that advances in NIT are giving rise to a new form of exclusion, involving increasing percentages of the world population.

The media as instruments of war and builders of peace
Historically, the media have played a relevant role promoting or legitimating war, but they have also contributed, and can still carry on doing so for a long time to come, to the prevention of conflict and the building of peace.

One of the classic instruments for influencing the enemy psychologically in armed conflict, or for bringing about certain reactions to specific events, is propaganda. Propaganda pamphlets were already being used during the Thirty Years War, by the German Protestant princes as well as by the Imperial Catholic authorities. The intention was, as always in these cases, to keep up the moral of one's own troops and weaken enemy resistance. During the American War of Independence, there were also several examples of the use of persuasion and manipulation, including public accusations of hypothetical atrocities committed by the enemy, exaggerating or distorting reality when it was considered necessary.

The 20th Century simply used the technological advances applied to the field of communications to extend the range of activity, both geographical, as well as thematic. No one can claim to have overcome the temptation to use this powerful weapon, whether it is the communist leaders – the famous 'agitprop' became a notorious tool of the Soviet foreign policy for many years – or western governments, which already used psychological warfare on a massive scale in the 1st World War in order to smooth out the way to war, overcoming the resistance of their respective public opinions to involvement in the conflict, or to mobilise the necessary human and financial resources, once the conflict began.

This is so much the case, that the majority of governments made propaganda just one more tool to promote their international relations, even creating specialised organisations and recruiting media experts to carry out the activity. It is sad to recall, but Goebbels and the propaganda machine he used for the Nazi cause, was, for many, a model to be adopted and perfected in the years since then. Propaganda, disguised on so many occasions as objective information, was thought of as just one more weapon of war not to be under estimated.

The current panorama is no different. Perhaps the most significant case is the role played by the Mille Collines radio station during the genocide in Rwanda. This radio station devoted itself to the promotion of a systematic campaign against the Tutsi population circulating, on a day to day basis, an argument which presented the members of this ethnic group as inferior beings and encouraging the Hutu population to move against them. We do not need reminding of what happened as a result.

The media are still very often used as vehicles for gathering support for the cause of one of the players in a confrontation. The different warring factions in Biafra and Ethiopia saw the advantage of sensationalist use of the news and allowed brutal images of victims to be broadcast in order to shock world-wide public opinion into favouring their cause and to gain the support of some governments. The same can be said of the Algerian government which, during the difficult years of violent crisis in the middle of the last decade, tried to win the sympathy and support of the West in its attempt to violently wipe out the radical Islamist groups which had taken up arms in response to their being illegalised.

Fortunately, and despite these examples, there is also clear proof of the role this very same media can play in the prevention of conflict and the building of peace. The terms should not be confused: the media are not humanitarian players they are media companies seeking to obtain financial and commercial benefits, using information. On the other hand, it should be recognised that information is an essential part of humanitarian action. At the point where these two agendas merge, it is possible to recognise the positive work of the media, serving, first and foremost and by handling information properly, as one more factor in the necessary early warning system which may prevent a subsequent outbreak of violence. In addition, they can also make a decisive contribution to the legalisation of political activities promoting dialogue and negotiation, as well as social mobilisation aimed at trying to diminish the harmful effects of uncontrolled violence. For those experiencing violence, this type of information can also be, more than anything else, an essential factor for survival.

For those operating in areas where there is violence, the contribution the media can make revolves around co-ordination with other local players and between themselves the humanitarian players, and the carrying out of sensitising tasks aimed at raising funds to care for victims or mobilising public opinion in order to pressurise governments into greater involvement in the attempt to stop the conflict. The media can also create bridges of communication between opponents and generate space for negotiation, debate, arbitration and the building of peace. Their activities include the creation of platforms promoting artistic expression – in a field which encourages the channelling of emotional aspects in the population subject to violence, the training of journalists – so that they in turn might use information to find ways of resolving the differences, or collaboration in order to involve the civil society in peace processes.

Some information groups have been created to promote peace. The following can be mentioned merely as examples:

• The 'Media Action International Foundation', founded by a group of Swiss and international journalists to defend the right of the victims of conflict and natural disasters to unbiased information. This Foundation created an information programme (the SPEAR project), intended for Kosovar refugees who fled towards Albania during the 1999 war. It provided them not only with information on the situation in Albania and Kosovo, but also with social and psychological support. When the emergency period was over, the project became a radio information and music programme for the young people of Kosovo, which dealt with issues relating to human rights, AIDS, drugs or culture.

•   The 'Internews' programme in Bosnia, which produced a weekly programme 'Fresh' aimed at overcoming the prejudices against adversaries left over from the times of war, in order to promote reconciliation among neighbours.

•   'Search For Common Ground' contributes, in turn, to the training of journalists so that they investigate beyond the official versions, encouraging contact with victims in order to obtain information. It also promotes mediation organisations for resolving conflicts, with specific action in Gaza and in the Ukraine, among other places.

•   The social radio stations – responding indiscriminately to many different names such as community, participatory or co-operative radio stations – which have the common objective of providing a channel of open expression to those who normally have no voice, serving as a spokesman for those oppressed on the grounds of race, sex or social class. Generally speaking, they provide useful tools for development, carrying out their activity for non-profit purposes. It is the community which controls and owns them and their most distinct characteristic is the participation of all members.

It also depends on you
We are, increasingly, the object of and subject to information, a fact that has prompted some of us to seek out those fifteen minutes of fame which Andy Warhol used to talk about, in whatever way we can. The role of news broadcaster (male or female) has now joined the traditional role of reader, listener or television viewer. We are all, men and women alike, open to the world and we have never been as sure as we are today that we live in a global village for which we are all responsible.

If there was ever a time when passivity in the face of certain situations could be defended with the words 'I didn't know', such a stand would be inconceivable today. However strong the monopolising zeal of some media companies and however serious the attempts by some governments to hide their embarrassments, alternative ways of finding out exist, which allow us to escape from this standardising mould. In developed societies, the breaking of these boundaries is no longer a question of technical ability, but rather individual commitment to those least favoured by fortune. Those who wish to know can do so.

For sensitised citizens, the media are not only an instrument of knowledge they are also a tool for action. The real power of NIT in the hands of people has been demonstrated in the case of the mobilisations against the war in Iraq, as well as previously when platforms were set up for the exchange of information and co-ordination of activities at international level – take, for instance, the succession of collective responses gradually produced from Seattle, as the regular meetings of the main international financial organisations take place.

In this unstoppable decentralisation of the focal points from which news and opinions are broadcast, the latest (?) advance are the blogs, which proved to be so useful at the time of the Asian tsunami that they allowed people to discover first hand, before the envoys of the international media were able to reach the area, what was happening and what kind of help was initially needed. Although they are open to manipulation and contamination, the ease with which they can be started up and their immediate nature could turn them into an important means of rounding off our knowledge on issues which interest us and, at the same time, of passing our own reality onto others.

Finally, it should not be forgotten, that not only are the media not the only source of knowledge in the world at our disposal – relations with our fellow men and women, school, our direct experiences and many other channels are at least as important – what we receive from them should not be assumed with uncritical eyes; it should be analysed, discussed and, if necessary, reacted against. As Umberto Eco took great care to show us, the 'semiological guerrilla' should be a constant frame of mind in a watchful population – is it worth mentioning that that is precisely what happened between 11th and 14th March, 2004 in Spain?

Document prepared by researchers from the
Institute for the Study of Conflict and Humanitarian Action (IECAH)
Madrid, January 2005

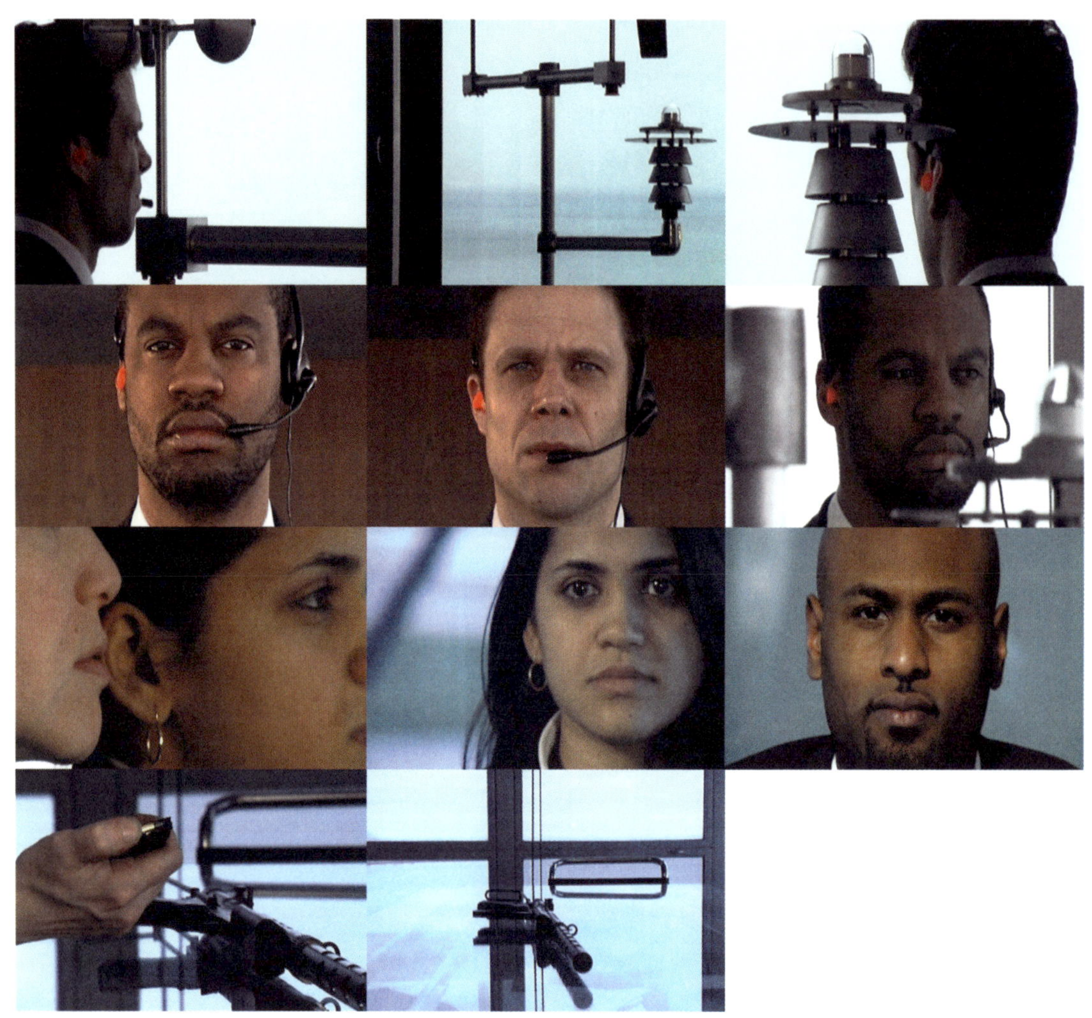

Íñigo Manglano-Ovalle
Climate, 2000
A video installation consisting of three
overhead projectors (DVD colour video
with sound, 23' 25'' looped) an aluminium
structure
1000 x 400 x 230 cm

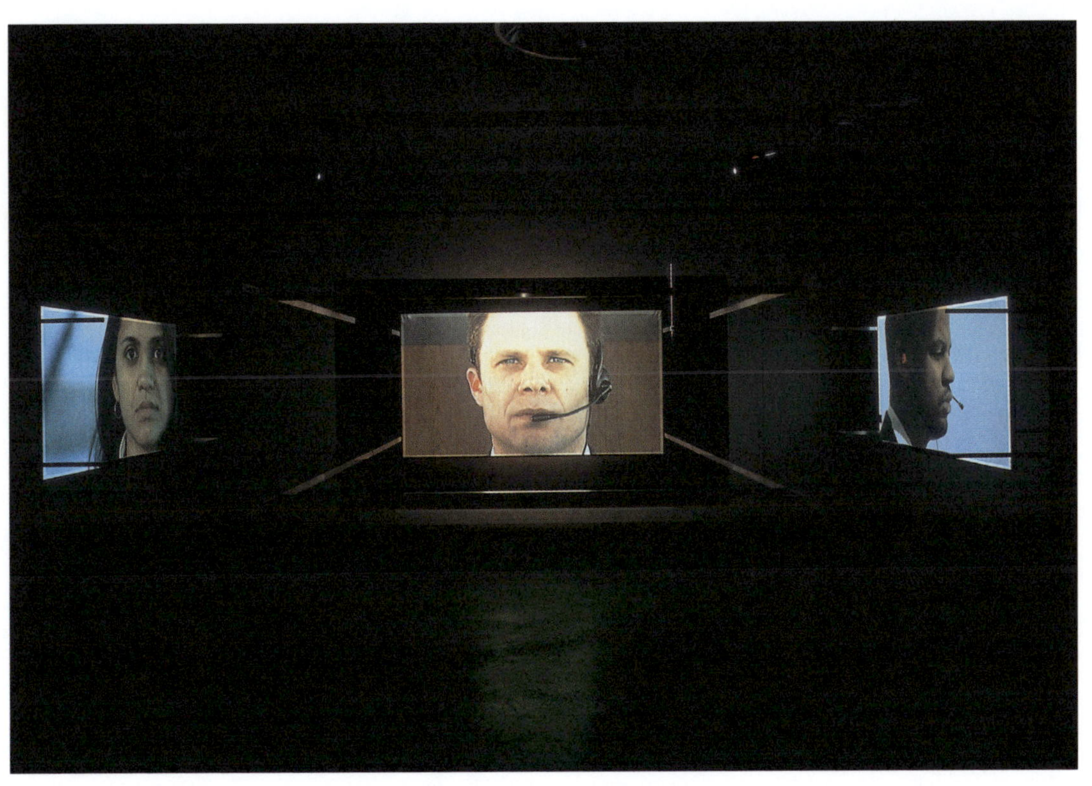

Rogelio López Cuenca

I was trying, uncomfortably, to explain for the umpteenth time what my work was about to someone amiably interested in it, and as I was plunging again into a quandary of paraphrase (which included such disparate references as the history of critical thought and the literary experiments of the avant-gardes to contemporary advertising technique), when my conversational partner interrupted me to propose a solution he believed he had gleaned from my confusing speech: 'Ah, un lavoro d'archivo'. An archival work. This is not a bad definition for an activity that, in effect, seeks nothing more than to read carefully, observe thoroughly, select recurring elements in diverse 'texts' and try to discover the intimate order, the inexplicit intentions that are answered to by the millions of images we contemplate every day – that contemplate us every day, those shadows cast at the end of the cave, shaping the world we live in, shaping the way we see it and the way we see ourselves: the images that shape us.

I write these pages during the last days of December 2004, in the context of the overwhelming news of a devastating earthquake that has razed much of Southeast Asia, causing tens of thousands of deaths. The newspapers came out on the 27th (the day after) with headlines such as 'The worst earthquake in 40 years ravages South Asia', and secondary headlines such as 'almost 12,000 dead as gigantic waves reached areas of Sri Lanka, India, Indonesia, Thailand and Malaysia', and the reports were hurriedly completed with an account of the other 'natural catastrophes' of the year that was coming to a close (Haiti, Madagascar, the Philippines and Morocco), as well as comparisons with preceding calamities (Chile 1960; Tianjin, China 1976; Iran 1990, India 1993 and 2001, Kobe, Japan 1995; Turkey 1999 and Bam, Iran 2003). During the following days, they focused on the death toll, and reports focused on the testimonies of survivors, preferably including statements by 'famous people' and informing of the humanitarian aid efforts set in motion to assuage the effects of the catastrophe: 'The UN deploys the *most important* aid operation of its history', 'The international community shows its concern by sending aid quickly'. During the following days, they continued with 'Epidemics now threaten Southeast Asia', 'The WHO fears that infections may cause more deaths than the tidal waves' and 'the refugees are the major problem'. All in all, Glen Maguire, the chief economist for Asia for the Générale Sociéte, made a statement to France Presse on the 28th that 'above all this is a human tragedy', coinciding with other analysts by diminishing the emphasis on the economic effects, which 'will be less than those of the Asian flu' (an epidemic that, for its part, 'took a toll of *only* 800 deaths'). Four days later, on the 30th, the front pages recounted that 'millions of survivors wander helplessly amid a desolate scene', insisting that '50,000 people may die of hunger and unsuitable sanitary conditions in the next three weeks', while, at the same time 'The UN considers 'its largest donation' ever'.[1]

The special circumstance that the tragedy took place in a popular tourist area (in Thailand, which receives twelve million foreign tourists a year, this industry makes for 12 % of the GDP) and the presence of Westerners among the victims – and witnesses- provided details – and ways of approaching them – quite different from most similar cases, and therefore allowing – in addition to the inclusion in T.V. news broadcasts of footage captured by the tourists themselves with their own amateur video cameras – the news stories to provide space for the personalization, for attaching names and faces to some of the victims: actors, models, businessmen or sports stars, who, as an exception, found themselves among the victims this time. Among the dead and missing, there are thousands of Europeans.

The term 'humanitarian catastrophe' – a gross oxymoron coined in recent times that has enjoyed a resounding acceptance and commands much respect in the mass media– is becoming a genre in itself, a specific section of the coverage of the South in that same media. The South (a concept that works like a soothing, depoliticized convention for referring to the *other*) is a portrait-stereotype limited by two always extreme simplifications: the South always appears confined between these limits – either a hell or a paradise[2]. Writhing in delight with the paradox, El Mundo newspaper has been publishing the section devoted daily to this event under the heading "Catastrophe in Paradise". Nevertheless, the representations of South-as-Paradise are restricted to tourist brochures and advertising. The *virgin lands* as places where more natural and exotic ways of living supposedly survive, removed from the exploitation of the climate customary in industrialized societies, are offered directly as holiday destinations in travel agency and vacation package advertising. The possibility of gaining access to the *authentic* experience is also oftentimes proposed symbolically, through the consumption of products (beverages, especially rum, or tobacco) associated with places (mainly the Caribbean) that evoke primitive and straightforward lifestyles, where people are uninhibited and leisurely, festive and gay, while also toying a bit with colonial fantasies of power over goods and persons: total availability inevitably personified by feminine figures (the myth of the mulatto woman as *sexual savage*). The South, sheer merchandise.

The presence in advertising of images corresponding to the South-as-hell is much less abundant and also more recent. It is in the consciousness raising campaigns of the NGOs where we encounter portraits of dark-skinned boys and girls looking straight into the eyes of the beholder, imploring compassion. Deserving of separate consideration are the controversial campaigns produced during the late 1990s by various companies purposefully associated with diverse NGOs (Pepsi, Médecins Sans Frontières, Fortuna and 7%, Unicef and Ericsson), companies that seek an image of goodwill in order to snatch customers from the competition through striking pictures and a strategy that have a direct precedent in the success – albeit also controversial - of Oliverio Toscan's photographs for Benetton.

To be sure, we must not evade protesting against this trend in the art field – especially in photography - toward the aesthetization of misery. However, in the international sections of newspapers, and in the corresponding sections of radio and television news broadcasts, South-as-hell is the official image of the impoverished countries. It is accompanied by a panoply of horrors where, as in an undistinguishable whole, natural

catastrophes are blended with famine, epidemics, endless 'tribal' warfare (Hemas against Lendus, Hutus against Tutsis), one dictatorship after another, endemic corruption…
The photograph of sorrow, desperation and despair, made into myth, depoliticized, presented as something 'natural'.
On the last day of 2004 the newspapers were blaming 'bureaucracy and the lack of infrastructures' for the 'hunger, pillage and epidemics' suffered by the tsunami victims. Old familiar phantoms took over the timeworn landscape. The tragedy became more explainable, routine and commonplace. Others informed that 'The fear of a new tidal wave unleashes panic in Southeast Asia'. The whole thing over again, the tragic wheel of wretched fortune to which most of the world seems to be doomed ceased to be an exception. The image of the third world *other* is shown to us within the framework of violence, of the presence or threat of violence. We, for our part, ensnared as we are by the hypnotic power of that violence, are invited to contemplate it as prey to a sort of fatality: typhoons, earthquakes, tropical storms and cyclones that lash *Earth's dark places* (*the heart of darkness*) as essential, immanent to that 'damned part' of the planet.

Save certain specific details, the aforementioned news stories could easily be exchanged for those referring to any other 'humanitarian catastrophe' – gross oxymoron coined by the mass media - whether they result from natural causes or are produced by humans, for they are ultimately presented as 'natural', though the magnitude of the damage caused cannot be explained without taking into account key aspects such as deforestation or the absence of infrastructures and prevention measures; all of which are hardly 'natural', but are instead manifestly political.

The perverse insistence on immovable hackneyed clichés ends up provoking, in the mind observer's mind, a nagging feeling of weariness, the suspicion that 'there is no remedy', scepticism with respect to our responsibility, doubts, inhibition and, finally, cynicism, which spreads, of course, to the people immigrated to the rich countries.

In the portrait of a South enchained by its own essence to underdevelopment, the not to be underestimated role the North plays in this is usually brushed off for self-interested reasons: the 'recommendations' of the IMF that hinder development in the local economies; the *pro domo USA* privatisations executed through merciless means by tyrants protected by corporations *sans frontières* that despoil the national resources – satraps with the blessing of the West in name of the international war on terror; human rights abuses and repression of any kind of opposition that questions the status quo and proposes democratic transformations to permit the redistribution of wealth. The most efficient aid we can offer the impoverished and oppressed of the South is none other than the recognition of their condition as equals, as human beings with inalienable rights, one of which is the right to decide their own future, their own 'development' and society model. This is the ever pending emergency – squashed over and over again by Western interests. Our collaboration has to consist, on the one hand, of supporting the self-organization of the different democratic movements of the South,

and on the other, in sabotaging, through anti-information, the gigantic machine forging meaning – forging destiny - that makes injustice acceptable.[3]

The frenetic flux characteristic of the information society (the production and renovation of an endless stream of novelties) paradoxically leads to the imposition of a non-historical, non-political form of non-interpretation. The mass media compose, produce and reproduce codes for reading reality that, ultimately constitute an 'image of reality' that is more visible and powerful than reality itself.

The dominating role conferred on cultural productions as mechanisms of social control in post-Ford capitalism, places the 'aesthetic operators' in a heretofore unknown situation with regard to the importance their work has when functioning as an alibi and ideological support system for 'putting the world into images' (for putting it on sale in the image market). Likewise, that work may – and ethically it should - serve to reveal that false simplicity, the apparent homogeneity, the tautological mode with which we are shown 'things as they are' and the mechanisms of domination and exclusion are naturalised.

This is an archival work up against the mind boggling ephemeral archive in permanent self-destruction that forever constructs and demolishes images of the present, according to the dictates of the blinding logic of consumption.

To politicize (restore the polis to) contemporary fine art, it is requisite that our realm of work be recognized, not as a channel for transmitting the messages of the varying interest groups, but rather as another full-fledged sphere of political action, of resistance and disobedience, in which to practice 'ways of seeing' and 'ways of making' that discredit, defy and break down the hegemony of the discourses that consecrate and justify the current map of the world.

1 The newspapers El País, ABC, El Mundo, la Vanguardia. December 27-31, 2004.
2 Fueyo Gutiérrez, Aquilina. (2002) De exóticos paraísos y miserias diversas. Icaria, Barcelona.
3 Latouche, Serge (1993) El planeta de los náufragos. Acento, Madrid.

Further reading

BALLESTA, J. (2002): *Medios de comunicación para una sociedad global*, Universidad de Murcia (Servicio de Publicaciones), Murcia.
BANGEMANN, M. (1999): *Which rules for the online world, The European Union Contribution*, in The journal of policy, Regulation and Strategy for the Telecommunications, Information and Media, Vol. 1, N. 1.
CHOMSKY, N. (2000): *Los guardianes de la libertad: propaganda, desinformación y consenso en los medios de comunicación de masas*, Crítica, Madrid.
COLARD, D. (1993): *Les relations Internationales de 1945 à nos jours*, Masson, Paris.
DUTTON, B. (2000): *Media studies an introduction*, Harlow Pearson Education.
FERNÁNDEZ, I.; SANTANA, F. (2001): *Estado y medios de comunicación en la España democrática*, Alianza, Madrid.
ECO, Umberto (2004): *Apocalípticos e integrados*, Nuevas Ediciones de Bolsillo.
IGNATIEFF, M. (1997): *Is Nothing Sacred? The Ethics of Television* in M. Ignatieff, The Warriors' Honour, Ethnic War and the Modern Conscience, Henry Holt and Company, New York.
MATTELART, A. (2002): *Historia de la sociedad de la información*, Paidos, Barcelona/Buenos Aires/Mexico.
RABOY, M.; DAGENAIS, B. (1992): *Media, crisis, and democracy mass communication and the disruption of social order*, Sage, London.
RAMONET, I. (1998): *La tiranía de la comunicación*, Debate, Madrid.
REIG, Ramón (2004): *Dioses y diablos: cómo manipula el poder a través de los medios de comunicación*, Urano.
SCHECHTER, D. (2004): *Las noticias en tiempo de guerra: medios de comunicación: ¿información o propaganda?*, Paidos, Barcelona.
SERRANO, A.; MARTÍNEZ, E. (2003): *La brecha digital: mitos y realidades*, UABC-FOECA.
VIDAL BENEYTO, J. (2002): *La ventana global*, Taurus, Madrid.

Websites of interest

- UNESCO: http://portal.unesco.org
- Reporteros sin Fronteras/ Reporters without Borders: http://www.rsf.org
- Centre of mass communication research: http://www.leicester.ac.uk/cmcr
- Observatorio de políticas de comunicación: http://www.portalcomunicación.com
- Observatoire français de médias: http://www.observatoire-medias.info
- European Audiovisual Observatory: http://www.obs.coe.int/medium/law.html.en
- Etcétera: http://etcétera.com
- Search for Common Ground: http://www.sfcg.org/
- El Portal de la Brecha Digital: http://www.labrechadigital.org/

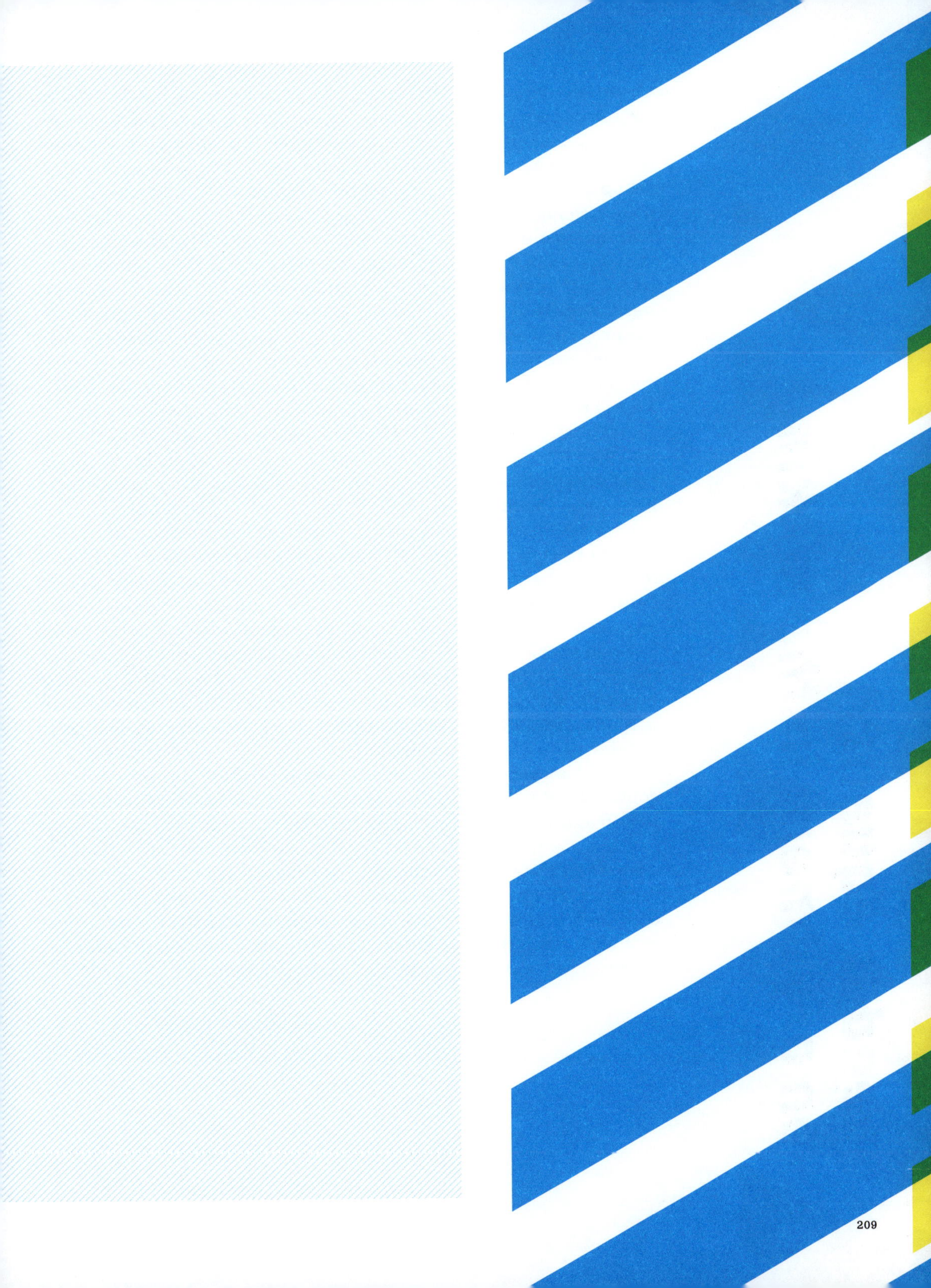

One of the most important social changes to occur during the 20th century was the elevation of women, in the private as well as the public domain. Ever since the initial drive by the suffragettes, at the heart of the movement The Women's Social and Political Union (WSPU), set up in 1903 by Emmeline Pankhurst, many other women and some men, although not as many as might have been hoped for, have been making a continuous effort to achieve full equality for women, and thus ensure that gender is no longer, under any circumstances, a factor for differentiation in social, political or economic life. It is not very hard to see that this goal has not yet been achieved and that despite the progress recorded, the situation is far from ideal. There are clear deficiencies, both in less advanced countries as well as in those which consider themselves to be living examples of what an open society should be, although the degree of differentiation varies notably.

Whilst the Integral Law against Gender Violence, which came into effect in Spain on 27th January 2005, is, obviously, a step in the right direction, it also shows that this problem is still a stark reality in Spanish society. In the case of other countries, the situation is even worse. In Morocco, for example, the reform of the personal status code (the *mudawana*) in favour of women has always met with resistance from extremely numerous and powerful sectors of society headed by the Islamist movements. Only the personal efforts of the current monarch finally got the reform approved in January 2004, although basic shortcomings can still be detected and fears are already creeping in that its implementation may be hampered by both the lack of human and financial means made available to it, as well as by the prejudices of a legal system which can clearly be improved upon, both in this and in many other areas.

The concept of gender, as used today, started in the sixties, in a context in which the differences used historically to justify discrimination against women were explained from another perspective: the feminist viewpoint, as a social and cultural phenomenon rather than a mere biological fact. The feminist argument uses the concept of gender as an integral part of an analysis which looks at the subordination of women, and attempts to explain its causes and the consequences of it and, since the objective is to change the position of women in society, tries to develop strategies for overcoming it.

The gender perspective, therefore, raises questions regarding the difference between the sexes and helps to define the characteristics of women (feminine) or of men (masculine) and the social and cultural prejudices attributed to men and women. It is neither a static nor a universal concept, but has a different meaning depending on the time or geographical setting being considered. Sex is biological, whilst gender is socially defined, by means of the different social roles which have been allotted to men and women throughout history. For this reason, we need to understand what Simone de Beauvoir was getting at when she maintained, quite rightly, that 'a woman is not born, she is made'.

One of the eight Millennium Development Goals for 2015 is the promotion of gender equality and autonomy for women. Whilst this can be seen as an achievement, resulting from the concern of the international community over this issue, we should first ask ourselves what the reality is in this field.

Death in the name of honour

In Pakistan, millions of women are forced to live in accordance with traditions which condemn them to isolation and total submission to men. Men have rights over them which are virtually absolute, including punishing them for any act which the men consider weakens their position as owner.

As Amnesty International points out, every year hundreds of women are murdered in the name of honour. Most of the perpetrators escape punishment and many others are not even reported. The situation of these women is often worsened due to the fact that the aggressor acts with the consent of the victim's own family, in collusion with the State and under an indifferent judicial system.

Nor do these women have any chance of escape. Those who dare are quickly hunted down by their families and very often tortured by the police when they are found. On the other hand, should they decide to try and escape the number of shelters or refuge centres to which they can go is just not sufficient. Even though murder committed in the name of honour is specified by the Pakistani penal code as a criminal offence, in practice, however, the passive attitude of the magistrates means that the State itself can also be considered responsible for these acts. The fact that people know there will be no punishment explains how a woman can be burned alive by her brother if he so much as suspects that she might be carrying on an 'illicit' relationship with a neighbour, or how a husband's just having dreamed that his wife is being unfaithful is enough for him to decide to put an end to her life. In these circumstances, suicide ends up becoming the only way out for many women.

Among the most aberrant forms of this type of murder for honour, those which stand out are the ones occurring:

Against women who decide to marry for love and a man of their choice:
In Pakistani society, the majority of marriages are arranged and therefore, for a woman to hope to choose her husband would be to challenge paternal authority. Those who attempt to do so risk being murdered by their own families.

Against women who want a divorce:
For a woman to ask for divorce is a public act of rebellion. In order to restore the honour of the man, punitive measures can be applied which can go as far as murder. This is what happened to 29 year-old Samia Sarwar.

No one stopped to consider the fact that her request was justified due to the degrading treatment she received from her husband - not only did he maltreat her on a regular basis, he also went as far has to push her down the stairs when she was pregnant.

After leaving home, she was shot dead by her own mother while she was at her lawyer's office in Lahore. Since it was an act corresponding to tradition, none of the perpetrators, neither her mother, or her uncle, or the driver who was accompanying her, were ever tried.

Against women who have been raped:
A woman who has been raped is an embarrassment to her family and swift measures must therefore be taken to restore tainted honour. Sixteen year-old and mentally retarded Lal Jamilla Mandokhel was raped several times. Her uncle reported the rapist who was held in police 'protection' but he also handed the girl over to her tribe (the *mazuzai*). The committee of elders decided that she had, in her position, committed an outrage against the honour of the tribe and that she should die in order to restore that honour. She was shot.

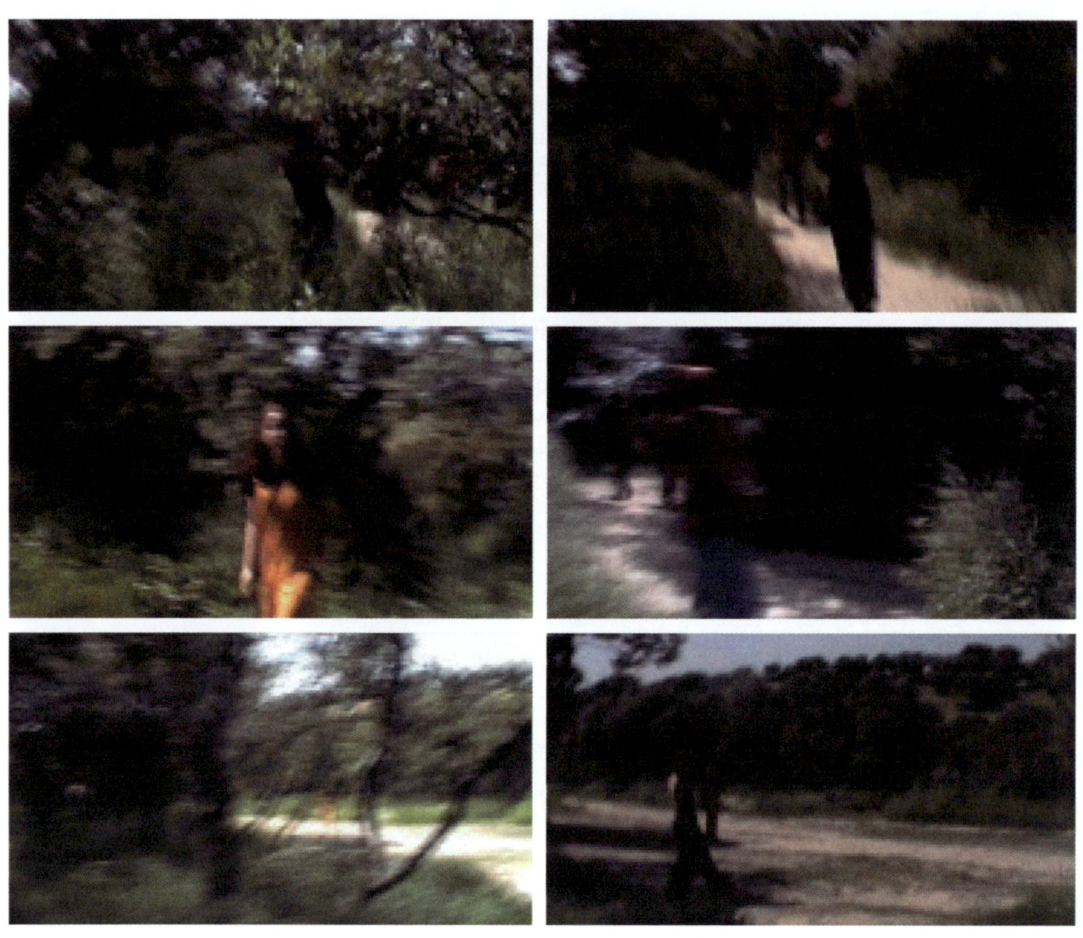

Carmela García
Untitled No2, 2000
DVD colour video with sound
4'

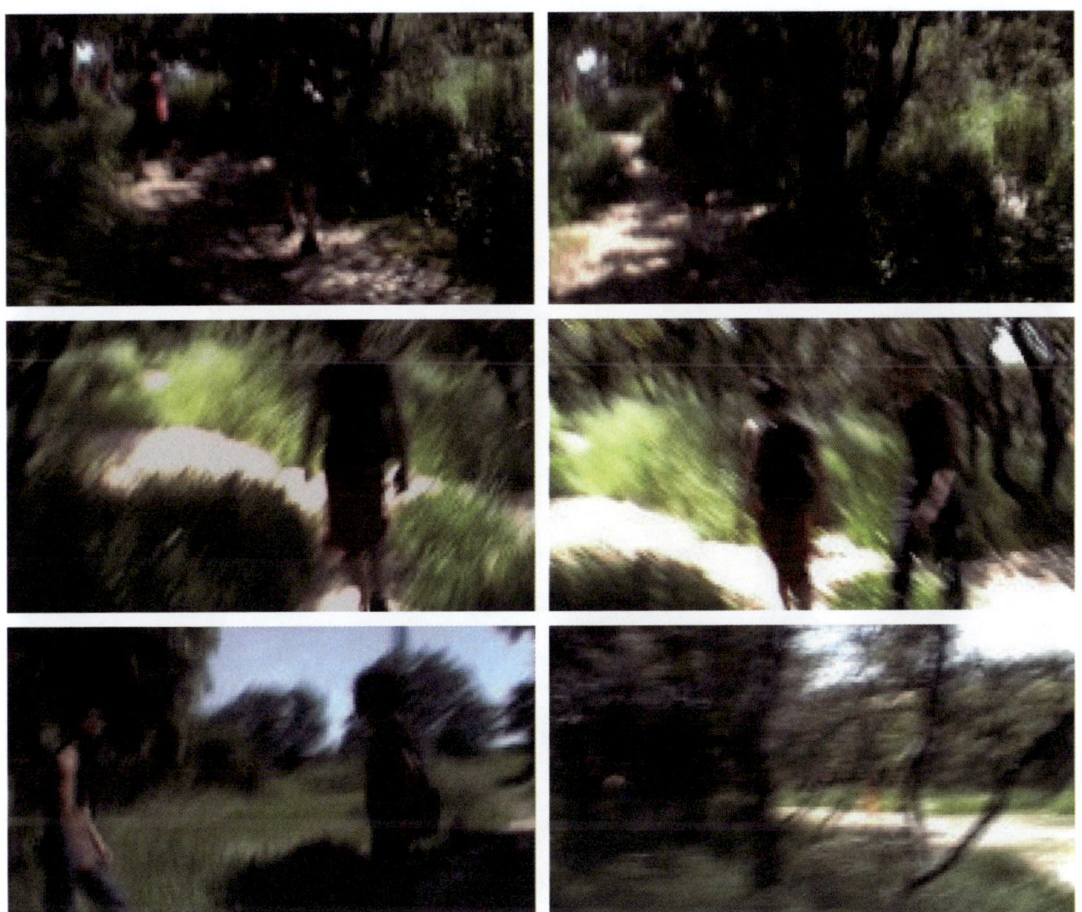

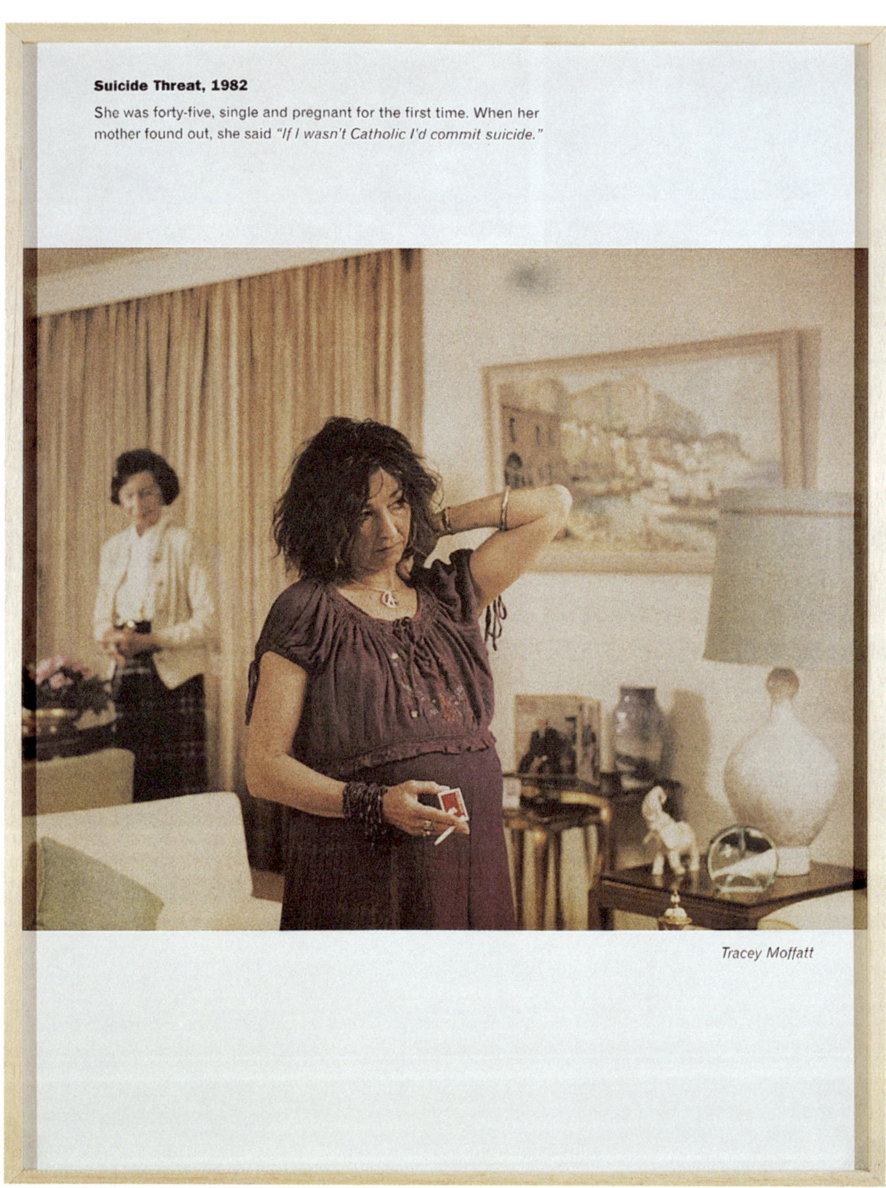

Tracey Moffat
"Suicide Threat, 1982", from the series
Scarred for Life II, 1999
Off-set print
80 x 60 cm

214

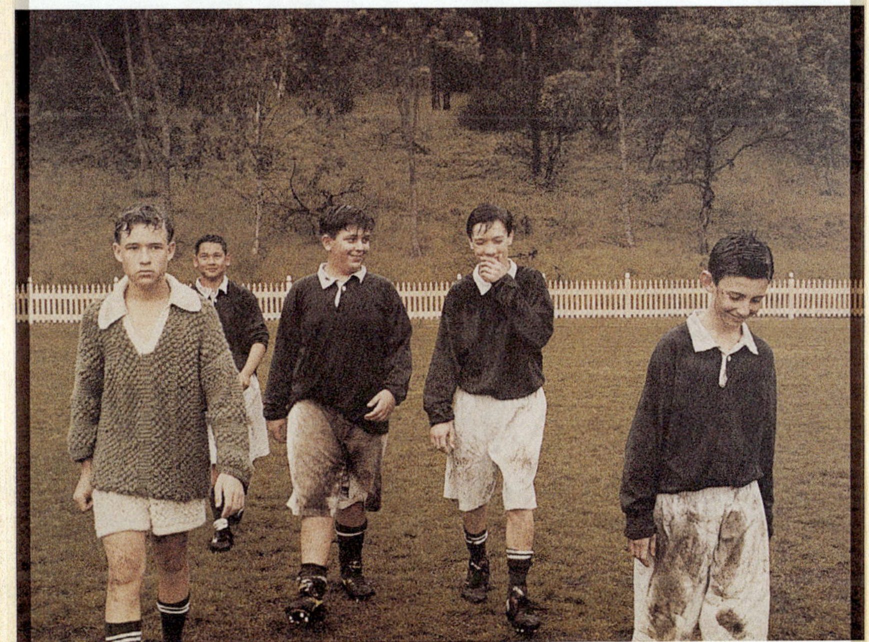

"Homemade Hand-knit, 1958", from the
series *Scarred for Life II*, 1999
Off-set print
80 x 60 cm

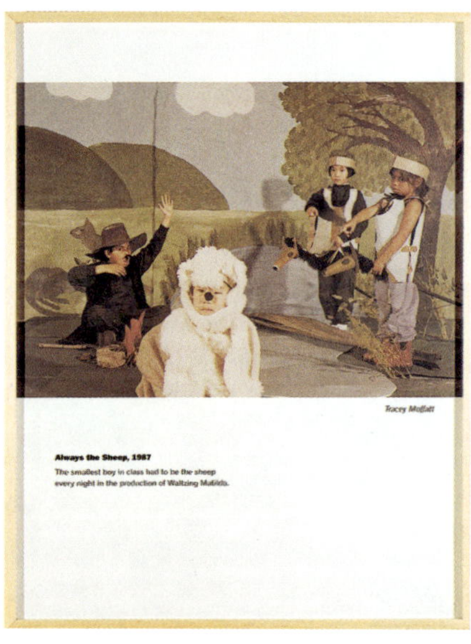

Always the Sheep, 1987
The smallest boy in class had to be the sheep
every night in the production of Waltzing Matilda.

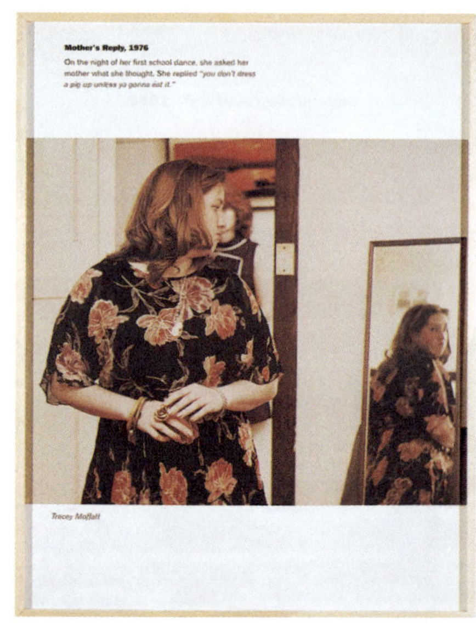

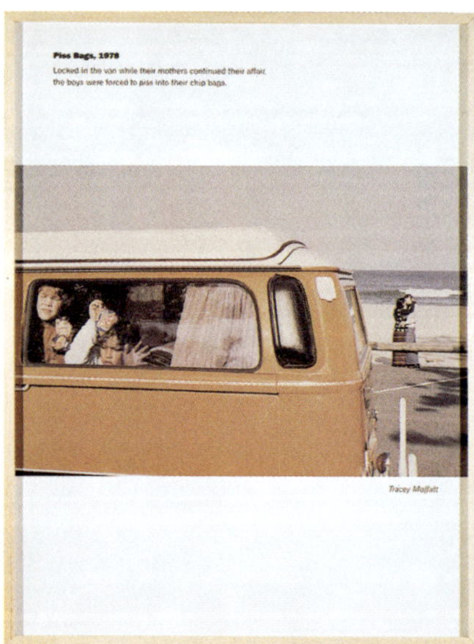

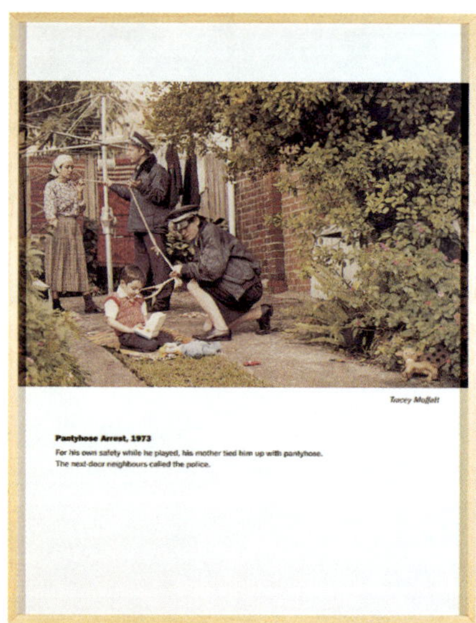

Pantyhose Arrest, 1973
For his own safety while he played, his mother tied him up with pantyhose.
The next-door neighbours called the police.

"Always the Sheep, 1987", from the series *Scarred for Life II*, 1999
Off-set print
80 x 60 cm

"Mother's Reply, 1976", from the series *Scarred for Life II*, 1999
Off-set print
80 x 60 cm

"Piss Bags, 1978", from the series *Scarred for Life II*, 1999
Off-set print
80 x 60 cm

"Pantyhose Arrest, 1973", from the series *Scarred for Life II*, 1999
Off-set print
80 x 60 cm

216

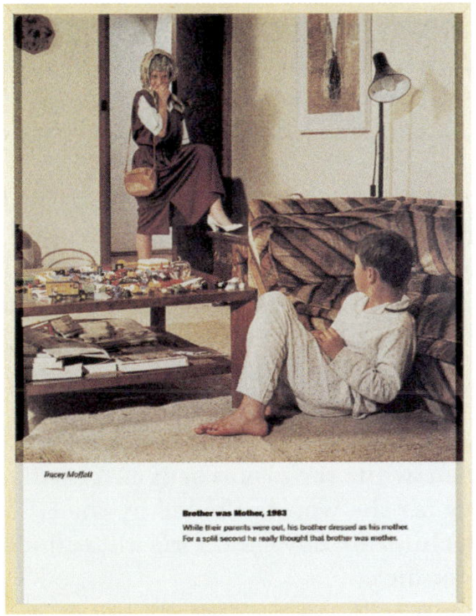

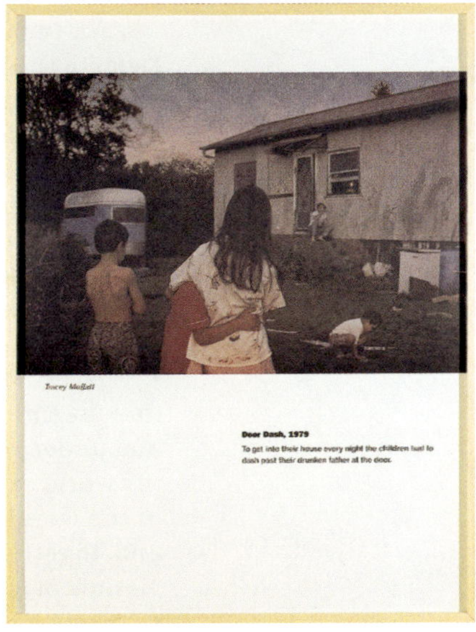

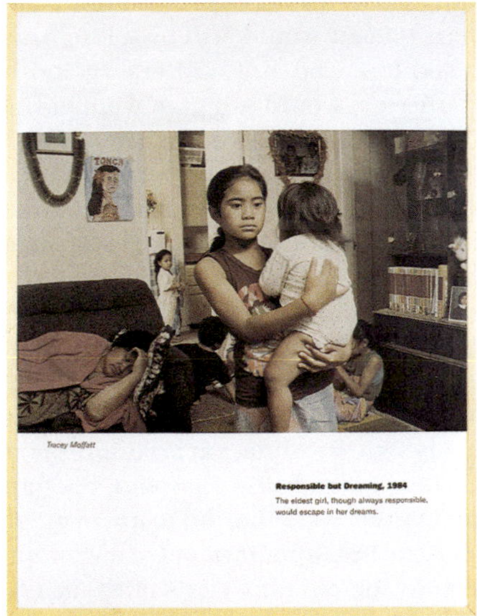

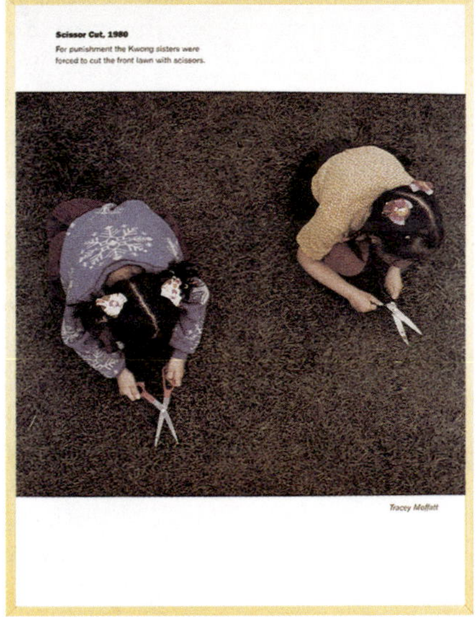

"Brother was Mother, 1983", from the series *Scarred for Life II*, 1999
Off-set print
80 x 60 cm

"Door Dash, 1979", from the series *Scarred for Life II*, 1999
Off-set print
80 x 60 cm

"Responsible but Dreaming, 1984", from the series *Scarred for Life II*, 1999
Off-set print
80 x 60 cm

"Scissor Cut, 1980", from the series *Scarred for Life II*, 1999
Off-set print
80 x 60 cm

An imperfect reality

Despite the difficulties of synthesising a reality which is so complex and for which the differences existing between one culture and another are so significant, some basic characteristics of the problem can be identified:

•   No country has yet achieved gender equality in the full sense of the word. In general terms, there is a favourable opinion towards the need for extending the effective presence of women outside the tasks they have been assigned traditionally, such as running the house and the reproduction and care of the children, boys and girls alike.

•   The differing rates of progress registered cannot hide the fact that, at a global level, women are the least favoured among the poor and underprivileged. Two-thirds of the 876 million illiterate people in the world are women, while they represent 60% of all the poor people in the world, are by far the worst affected by the HIV-AIDS scourge and, together with children, boys and girls alike, make up 80% of the victims of armed conflict.

•   Issues which can seem so elementary today, such as votes for women, were, as we all know, the front-line in a battle which sapped the strength of many generations. Even though New Zealand gave the vote to women in 1893, it would still be a long time before Spain (1931) or France (1944) followed suit. Others, including many of the Latin American countries, would not give women the vote until the fifties – once the UN approved the Convention on the Political Rights of Women in 1952. Even today, however, this right is non-existent, in practice, due to social or cultural decrees which, in many countries, allow a delegate vote, carried out by the patriarch on behalf of all the adult women in the family.

•   The process for increasing the presence of women in the parliamentary or governmental decision-making circles is clearly very patchy. From a total of 183 countries for which data is available, 15 have no women at all in parliament, while 72 have parliaments consisting of less than 10% women. Only two (Rwanda, surprisingly enough, with 48.8%, and Sweden, with 45.3%) exceed 40%. In Spain, the figure is 36%.

With regard to female participation in government cabinets, the figure has risen since the first appointment of a woman to this position in Denmark in 1924, to the current 11.3% (6.8% in 1996). Only Spain and Sweden have governments with an equal presence of men and women. On the other hand, only eleven women hold the position of head of government or state (5.6%).

•   One of the most silent violations of human rights is gender violence which, contrary to initial appearances, affects both developed countries as well as those which are less so and both people from upper social classes as well as those at the bottom of the ladder.

•   If we look more specifically at the situation in Spain, the first significant data we find is that there are 627,190 more women than men. This majority population, however, does not make it any easier for women to achieve the same level as their male counterparts in all the different walks of Spanish life. Female access to the job market is still restricted, – the unemployment rate for women is 16.8%, whilst for men it is a mere 7.8% – and women receive lower salaries for doing the same job – the average gross salary per hour for women being 86% of that for men.

• In the hope that solutions will gradually be found to other issues, gender violence is perhaps the issue which has the greatest social impact right now in Spain in relation to the position of women. The 109 deaths which occurred in 2004 are of great concern -and the situation for 2005 is not looking hopeful, since 9 violent deaths had already been added to this tragic number before January has come to an end. The recently passed Integral Law against Gender Violence already mentioned is an attempt to stop this negative trend, by combining preventative and educational proposals with measures to protect and assist victims, as well as new penal regulations for the aggressors. Although only time will tell whether this course of action is, in the end, the appropriate one, in the meantime, the announcements regarding the creation of specific courts of law to deal with these matters, the new legal figure for handling violence against women and the imme-diate increase in the number of permanent policemen responsible for taking care of the accusations and the protection of the victims are at least hopeful.

Women in Black

Women in Black, is the name of an international network of women who share the same clear-cut philosophy against militarism and violence. It is present in several countries and is neither a structured nor hierarchical movement. Instead, its members meet on specific dates in squares, they organise vigils, wear black clothing and invite women to participate. Their voice is a silent one. As they themselves say 'too much has already been said'. Their first silent demonstration took place in Israel in 1988, with the aim of bringing the women of Palestine together to assert their right to peace. In 1991 they occupied the square in Belgrade in condemnation of the war in ex-Yugoslavia. The campaigns in Belgrade continued in 1993, as well as outside the headquarters of the United Nations, in protest against the use of women's bodies as weapons in the conflict. After the terrorist attacks of 9/11, the monthly vigils in New York were held weekly. Subsequently, they have also demonstrated in Argentina against the military campaign led by the United States against Iraq. Similar movements have emerged in Azerbaijan, Canada, Scotland, Spain, Denmark, England, India, Indonesia, Italy, Switzerland, Colombia, the United States, Argentina and Turkey. They all clearly express their wish that political leaders withdraw from conflict and they ask that those responsible for violent acts be brought to justice and tried under international law. They wear black to mourn the dead and as long as there is violence and armed conflict, the Women in Black will continue coming out peacefully to accuse those responsible with their silence.

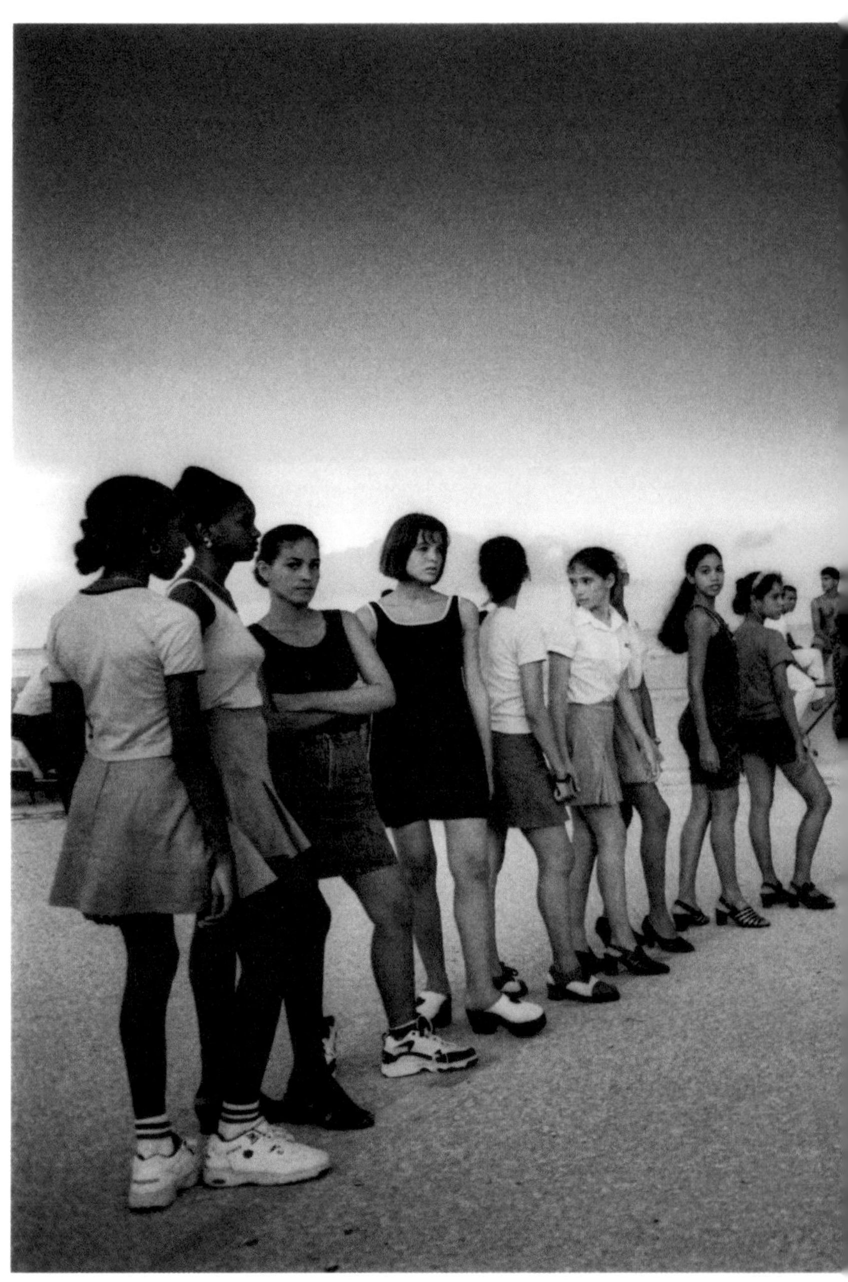

Cristina García Rodero
Escuela de Modelos. La Habana, Cuba,
1997
Black-and-white photograph
76 x 115 cm

220

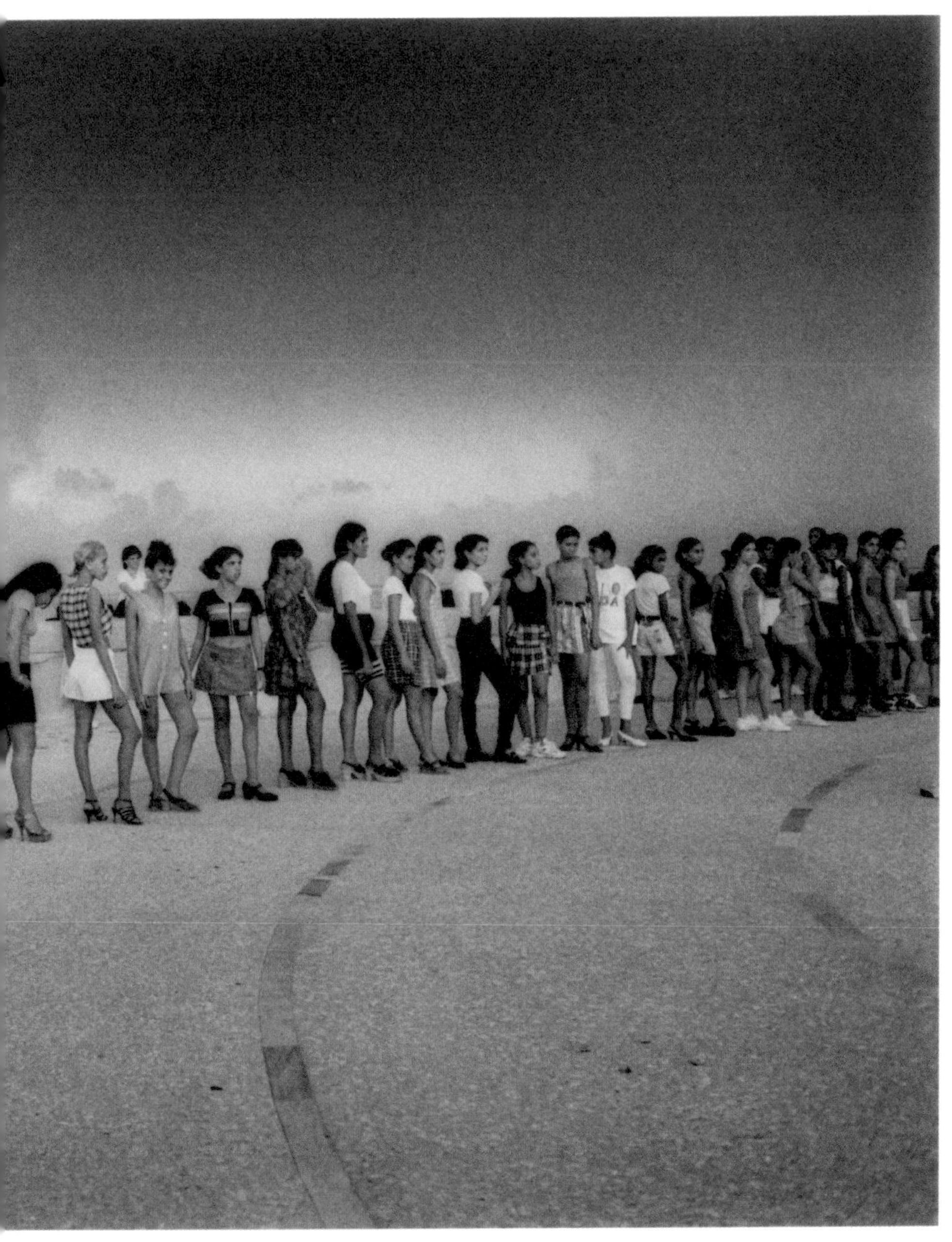

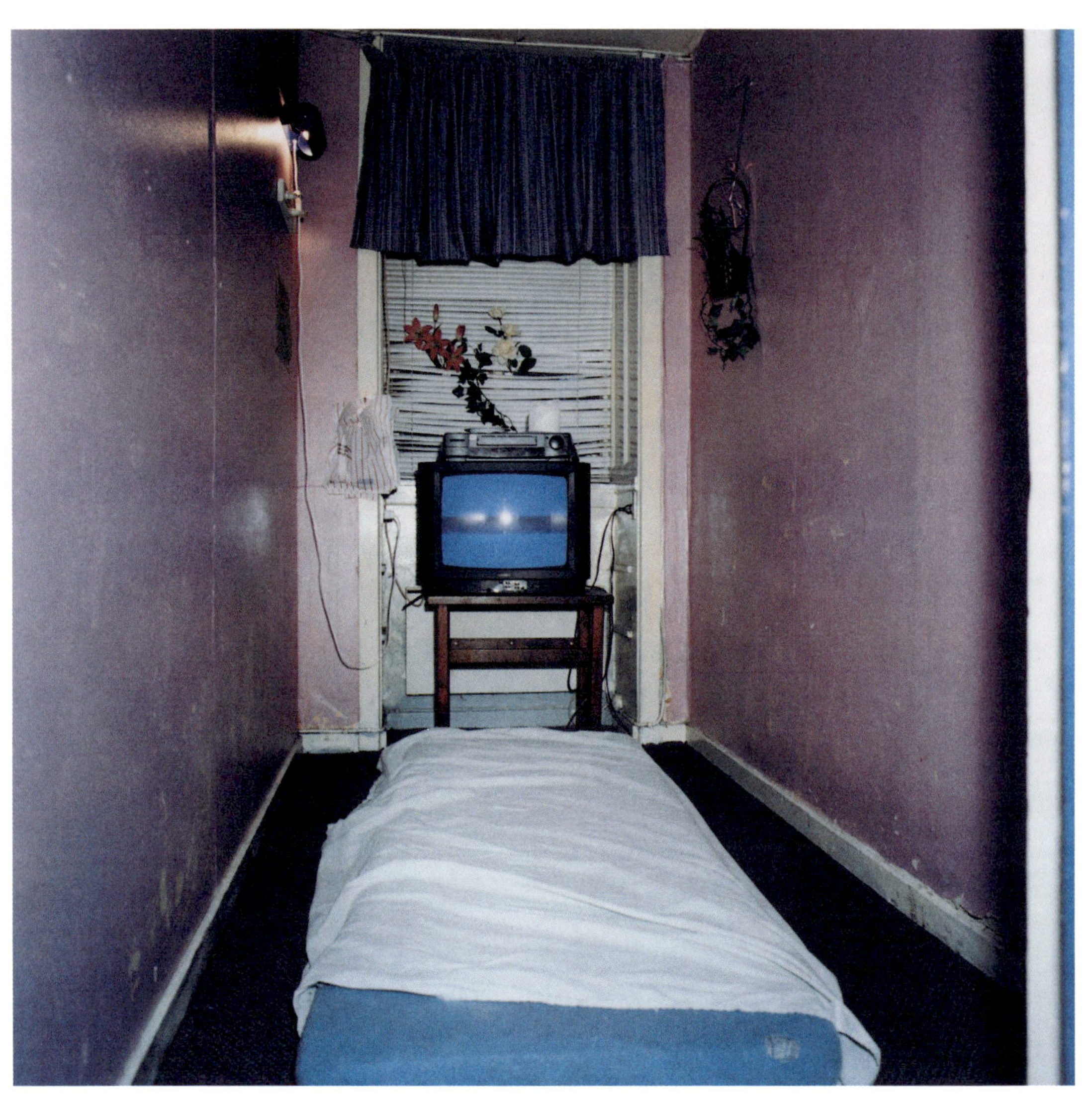

Trine Søndergaard
"Untitled", from the series *Now that You
Are Mine*, 1997
Colour photograph
100 x 100 cm

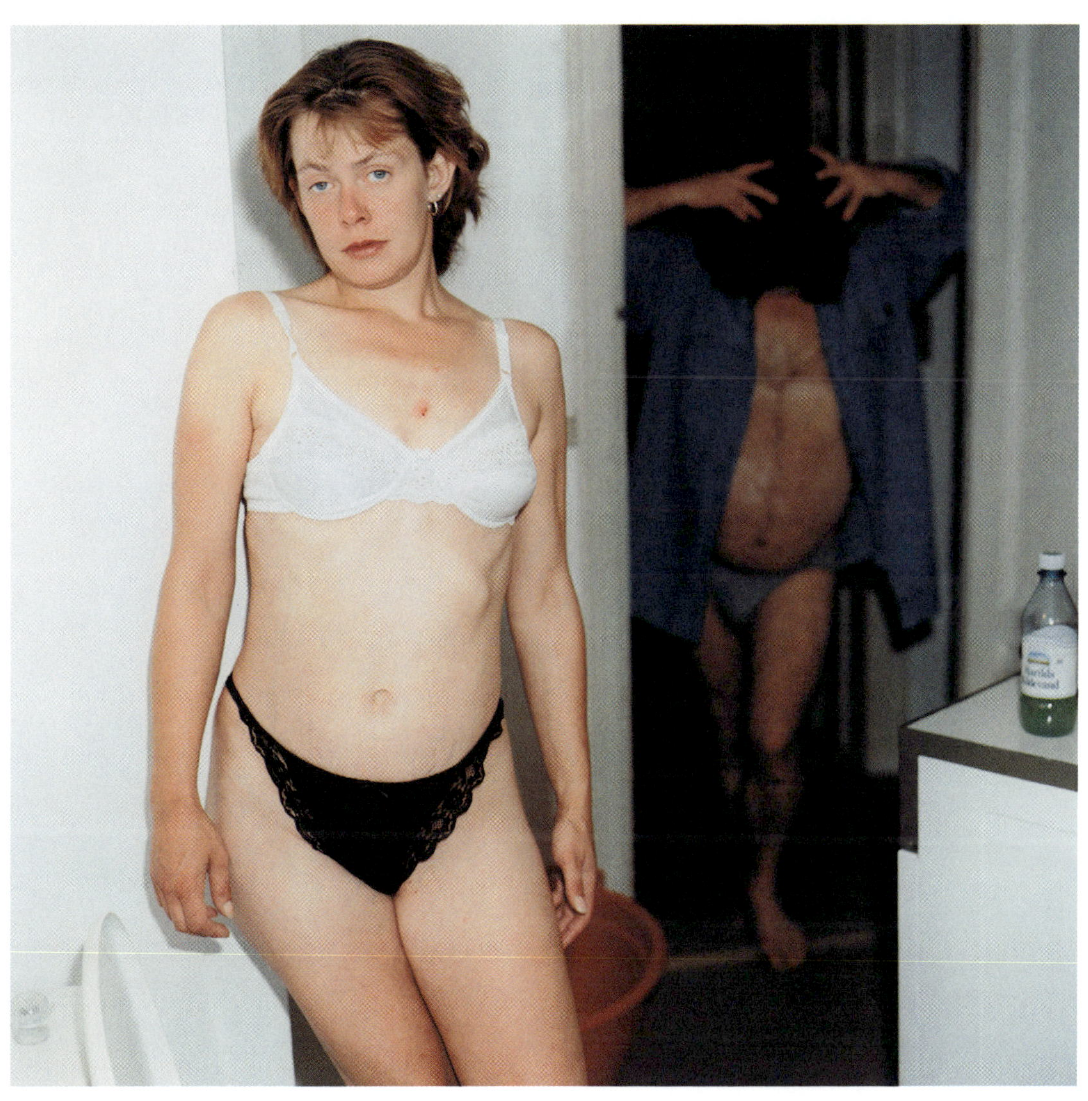

"Untitled", from the series *Now that You Are Mine*, 1997
Colour photograph
100 x 100 cm

223

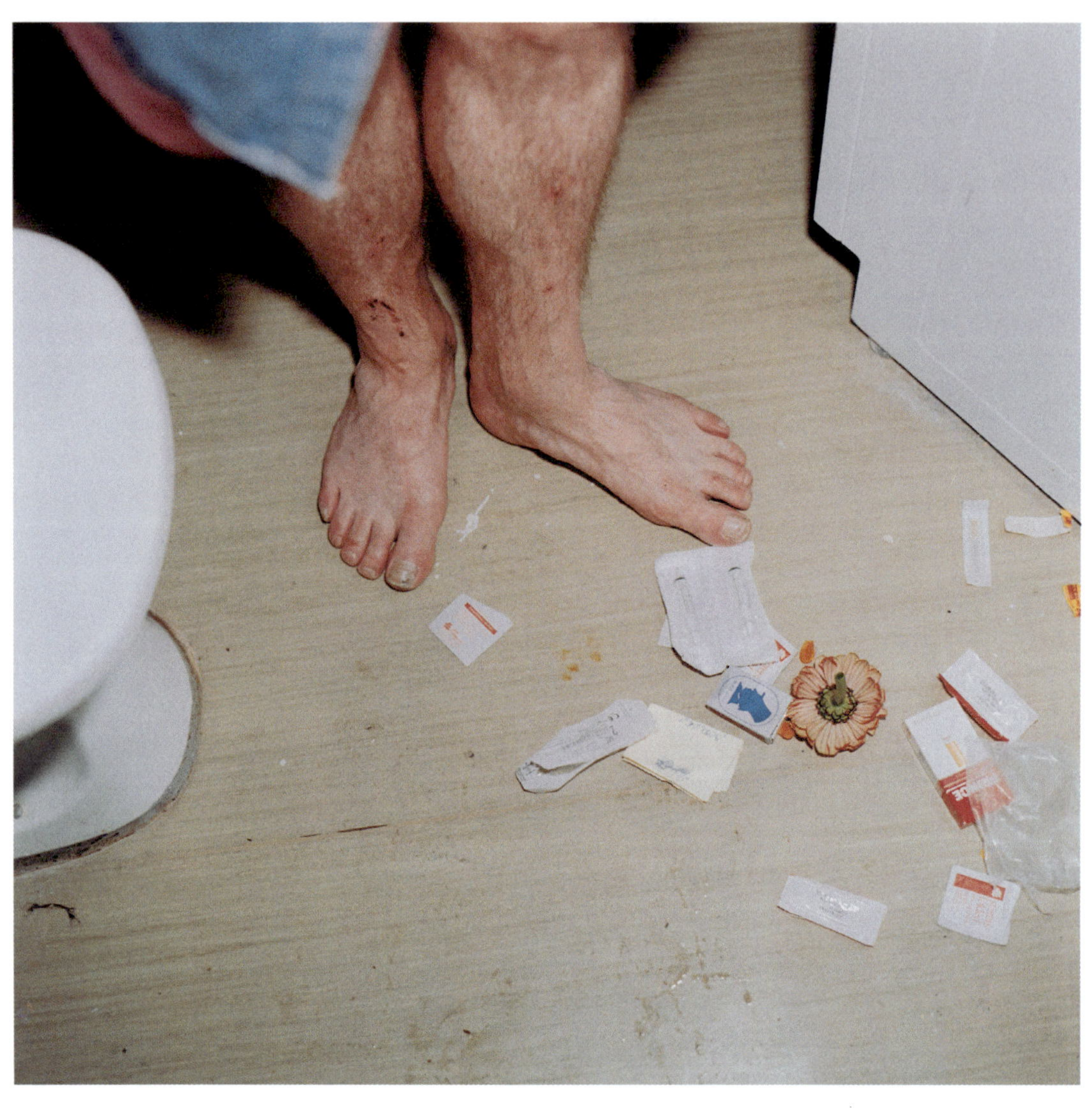

"Untitled", from the series *Now that You Are Mine*, 1997
Colour photograph
100 x 100 cm

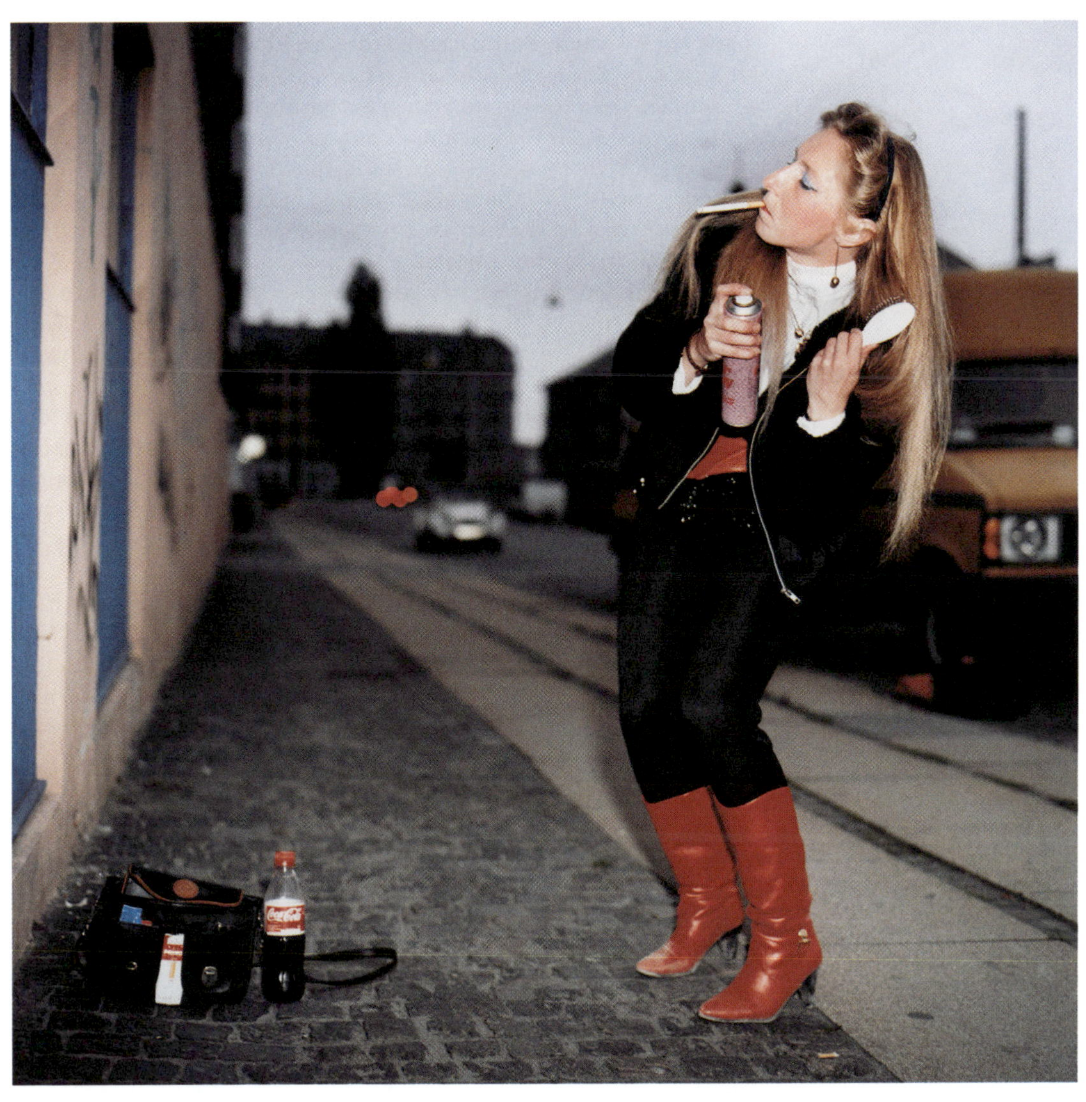

"Untitled", from the series *Now that You Are Mine*, 1997
Colour photograph
100 x 100 cm

Looking forward: Beijing as a starting point

In the long trek towards total gender equality, very different initiatives have been gradually put into practice and these can be divided, generally speaking, into two major courses of action: that which opts for carrying out institutional and political changes to allow women to be incorporated into the workforce and their participation in the centres of power and that which, in turn, opts for transforming the processes and institutions which generate gender inequality. Both courses of action are necessary, and relevant examples of both can be provided.

With regard to the first, and from an international perspective, the Fourth World Conference on Women (Beijing, 1995) should be considered the starting point. It was the culmination of three previous international events (Mexico, 1976; Copenhagen, 1980; and Nairobi, 1985), and it has already become a milestone which has contributed positively towards instilling greater awareness among the general public with regard to gender discrimination and also stimulating action on the part of the different national governments.

The 189 governments present approved the Beijing Action Platform, the object of which was to remove the obstacles obstructing female participation in certain walks of public and private life. In this document, twelve areas of particular concern were identified, as well as a series of measures which governments should adopt in order to remedy the situation:

— Poverty burdening women.
— Inequality in access to education and the lack of educational opportunities.
— Women and health.
— Violence against women.
— The effects of armed conflict on women.
— Inequality in the participation of women in the definition of political and economic structures and in the production process.
— Inequality in the exercising of power and decision making.
— The lack of sufficient mechanisms to promote the advancement of women.
— The lack of effective awareness promotion regarding the human rights of women.
— Insufficient mobilisation of the media in promoting the contribution of women to society.
— The lack of sufficient and supportive recognition of women in the management of natural resources and the protection of the environment.
— Girls.

In order to follow-up and monitor the commitments made, a follow-up committee was formed consisting of representatives of national governments, the UN, and the civil society, which for the very first time, assessed the results achieved after five years. In June 2000, and in the form of a Special Session, the international meeting Beijing+5 was held at the UN Headquarters with "Women 2000: Equality between the genders, development and peace in the 21st Century" as its motto. Those present (governments, UN agencies, and international NGOs) adopted new initiatives for strengthening legislation against the different forms of domestic violence and for making forced marriage and female genital mutilation a thing of the past. In addition, objectives were set to ensure compulsory primary education for girls and boys as well as to improve the health of women by extending their access to medical care to preventive programmes.

Challenges in the policies for the empowerment of women
In this same vein, the promotion of institutional and political changes which would allow equality between the genders to be achieved, the 2003-04 report by the United Nations Development Fund for Women (UNIFEM) puts forward four areas where work should be a priority:

• Reduce the feminisation of poverty – This means, among other measures, the articulation of mechanisms which would make it possible for women living in poverty to emigrate safely – with some support to help them become familiar with the employment laws of the places they are going to and find support centres for immigrants in the country in question, together with a drive towards achieving the adoption of common frameworks for managing the flow and integration of immigrants. It also demands the preparation and endowment of budgets incorporating gender issues in order to even out the unequal starting positions (UNIFEM has directly supported the preparation of this type of initiative in twenty countries).
• Put a stop to violence against women – The UNIFEM campaign "A Life Free of Violence: it's our right" ended in 2003. As part of this campaign, which took place in the Commonwealth of Independent States (CIS), a group of lawyers, psychologists and social workers in Kazakhstan organised the 'Train of Hope'. On a tour around the whole country, they talked to and trained police forces with regard to the need for putting a stop to violence against women; they also carried out educational activities for women and children, boys and girls alike, in the schools. This type of programme focuses on the direct involvement of men in the activities, assuming that men tend to pay more attention when the person talking to them about gender violence is another man.
• Counteract the spread of AIDS among women and young people – Attempting, on the one hand, to lighten the burden on the health sys-

tems. In Enugu (Nigeria), for example, 13% of the population in rural areas has AIDS and the health services are inadequate to the situation. UNIFEM has supported the preparation of some AIDS guidelines for health services which include the gender perspective – it should not be forgotten that women with AIDS are very often invisible in these systems and are condemned to life-long stigmatisation.

On the other hand, by directly addressing those people, men and women alike, responsible for preparing and developing the policies on these issues: The objective of this type of initiative ranges from obtaining low-cost antiretroviral drugs to supporting the children, boys and girls alike, of HIV-positive women, not forgetting the need for improvement in the distribution of educational materials. In short, the aim is for the voice of those women who are affected to be heard by those who are making the political decisions.

• Achieve gender equality in democratic management, both at times of war as well as in peacetime – Following the example of Rwanda, as mentioned earlier, which is today the world leader as regards the percentage of female members of parliament in its national assembly, UNIFEM supports the incorporation of women into politics in other places.

There is also a need to promote the adhesion of a greater number of countries to the Convention on the Elimination of all Forms of Discrimination against Women (CEDAW).

All-inclusive democracy

Parallel to the actions mentioned earlier, the efforts carried from other perspectives focusing on the transformation of the processes and institutions which generate gender inequality, should also be taken into consideration.

We need to start with the fact that in patriarchal societies, the centres of power are occupied by men and, as a result, it seems virtually inevitable that the institutions with the power and the decision-making processes will end up reflecting the values of those who are dominating these bodies. As the opportunities for women to participate in this field are increased, it would make sense to suppose that the decisions made within them will increasingly end up reflecting the true pluralism coexisting in society.

In its time, the fight for recognition of the right to vote was, with just reason, the centre of the political agenda for women. Subsequently, however, it was observed that a representative democratic framework did not by itself guarantee the effective participation of women in the political arena, even though they were officially entitled to do so. The right to vote alone was not enough to change the behaviour and blueprints marked out in accordance with the moulds which those who had monopolised this area up until then had been gradually developing.

The next thing that was needed, therefore, was the modification of the social contract and an end to the traditional division of tasks which assigned the reproductive activities to women and the productive activities to men. Both men and women must share the responsibilities arising in the private domain, allowing women to start enjoying the same opportunities as men in terms of entering the public domain.

Given the original situation, it did not seem likely that this process was going to happen on its own in the short-term and the quotas system was seen as a necessary option for accelerating it. Among the different international initiatives directed at this issue, the ones which stand out are those promoted by the European Council, which already recognised the right of equality in its founding treaty in 1949. In 1979 it set up the Committee for Equality between Men and Women, proposing two courses of action in order to guarantee that equality: parity democracy and positive action.

Organisations have continued insisting, from various camps and with varying degrees of success, on the need for the modification of the bases of the prevailing model of parliamentary democracy, in order to meet the demands of a very wide sector (women), which believes that its full incorporation into political life would strengthen the options for active democracy. The aim is not only to ensure that their rights are respected and fulfilled in practice, but also to make it clear to people that this situation would be to the global advantage of the society. It is all citizens together, with no exclusion or discrimination, who should participate in the decision-making processes, in the local as well as the regional, national and international environment. In order to be effective, democracy must be an all-inclusive system.

This model of all-inclusive democracy could be seen as an alternative to that of representative democracy. Its main and most important characteristics include a determination to ensure the presence of minorities, to perfect the traditional, although not always developed, divisions of power and give a greater degree of protagonism in the decision-making process to social players.

When viewed from the perspective of gender, this political profile approach advocates an increase in the presence of women at all levels of political decision making, since it considers that women tend more towards negotiation and consensus. Whatever the case, and on the assumption that there is a need to balance a situation as unequal as the current one, it is perhaps not as helpful to focus the attention on the sex of whoever is making the decisions, but rather on the kind of values they are defending. It is in the field of education, like many other issues in need of radical improvement, that we must try and establish ethical values and principles which direct future political leaders, men and women alike, towards fairer, more sympathetic and sustainable courses of action than those promoted by their predecessors.

Last of all, this task must evidently not be undertaken exclusively from inside the political parties. All bodies of public activity must involve themselves in it, from the neighbourhood associations to the trade unions, non-governmental organisations and any other collective platforms from which, day by day, our model of coexistence is constructed/destroyed.

It also depends on you

How easily men – and women too – adopt sexist stereotypes! Either because of the education they have received, their customs and traditions, a lack of sensitivity or by express desire. Our language and our actions include many discriminatory habits which are detrimental to women and which even make it compatible with an argument which is officially egalitarian. It is precisely at this initial level where we must focus our attention. It is our subconscious and our semi-conscious attitudes, which although hidden in our minds, must be reviewed immediately in order to question certain frameworks which, at the very least, are strengthening situations that really should not be allowed. It is about the very words we use to refer to certain matters, the jokes which we not only accept from the mouths of others, men and women alike, but also laugh at together, with attitudes which deny in practice what we claim to support with our ideas about equal distribution of the tasks to be undertaken in our own family environment.

We then need to look outwards, and realise that the educational system, the media, political leaders and many other players have a great deal to say on this issue. It is part of our work as citizens, men and women alike, committed to improving the social, political and economic models we have all had a hand in supporting, to involve ourselves in the eradication of these abscesses.

In this same outward glance, we should also look beyond our borders, at those who are expected to 'hold up half the sky', at least if we adhere to the teachings of Mao Tse Tung, at those who are still, in many parts of the planet, deprived of their basic rights and condemned to a life of indignity for the simple reason that they are not men. While history is full of abominable procedures, promoted, among others, by religions, the cores of which still fall seriously short when it comes to meeting the demands made in this area, this is no excuse whatsoever for rejecting the need for change. A mistake does not stop being a mistake just because it has been made on a continuous basis over a long period of time; it only serves to show us once more that human stupidity can be infinite when it tries to preserve that which has allowed some people to live on the basis of the exploitation of others.

Document prepared by researchers from the
Institute for the Study of Conflict and Humanitarian Action (IECAH)
Madrid, January 2005

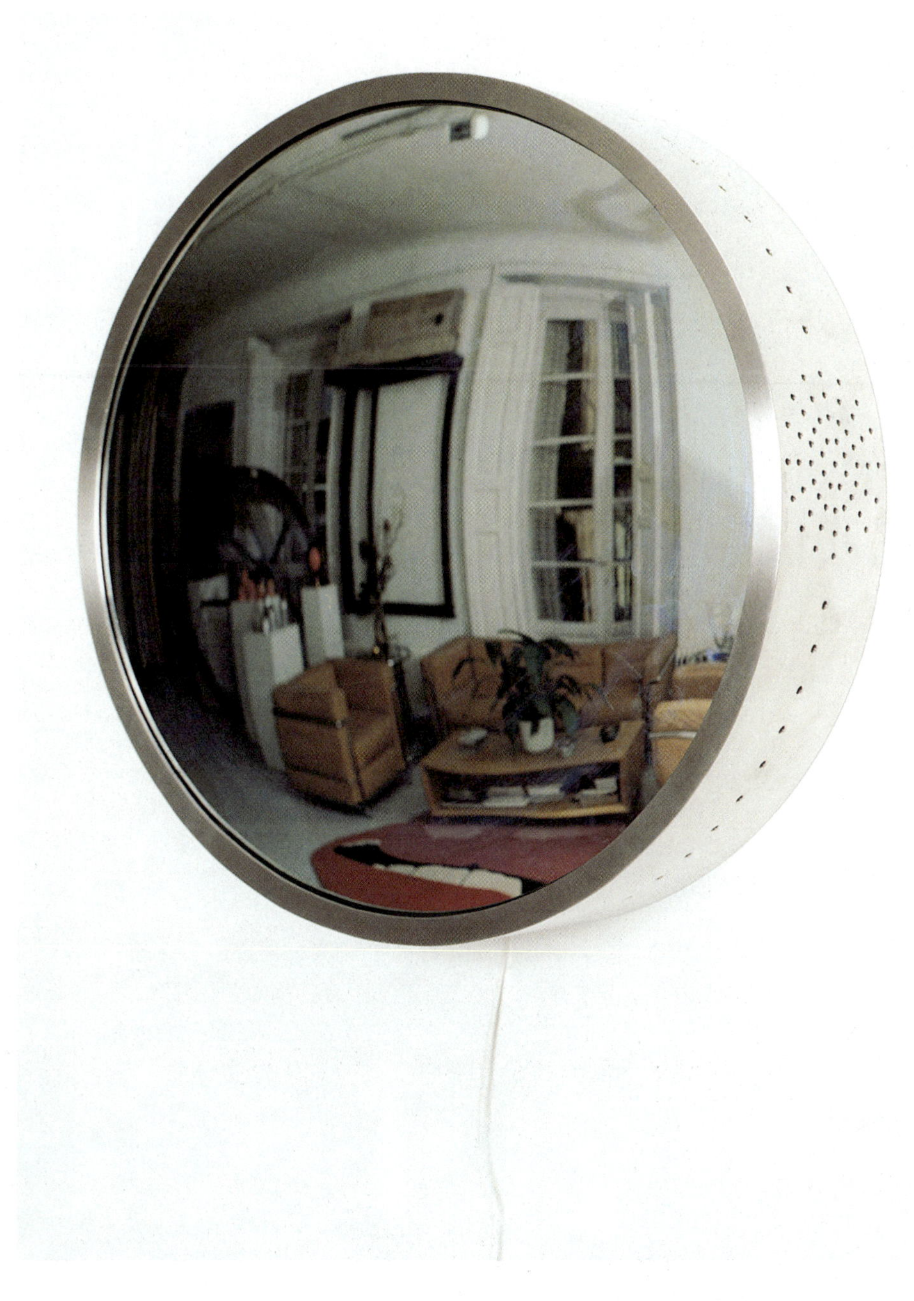

Pilar Albarracín
Espejito, 2001
Mirror and installation with sound
Ø 61 x 11 cm

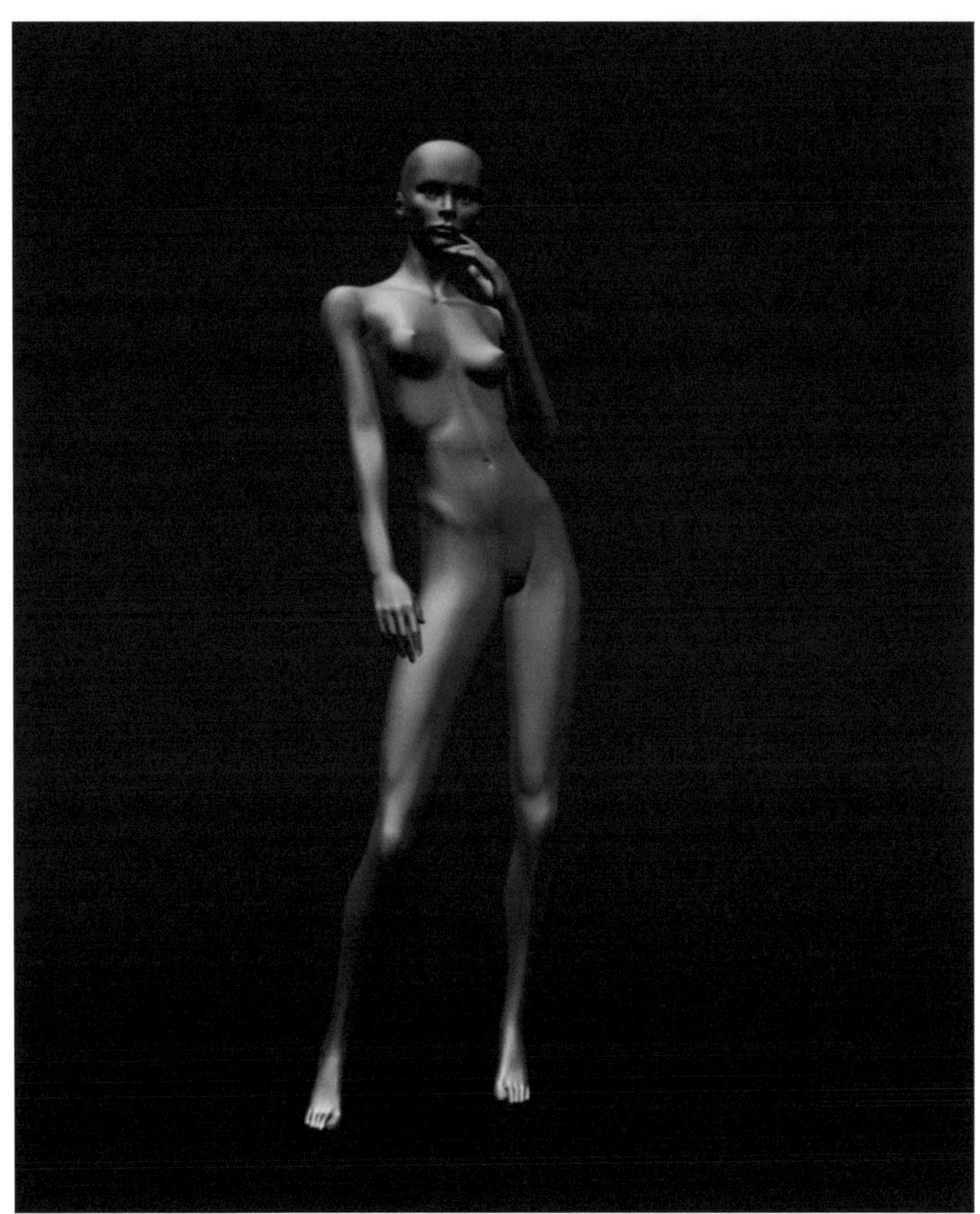

Kirsten Geisler
Dream of Beauty 3.1, 2003
DVD colour video with no sound
4' looped

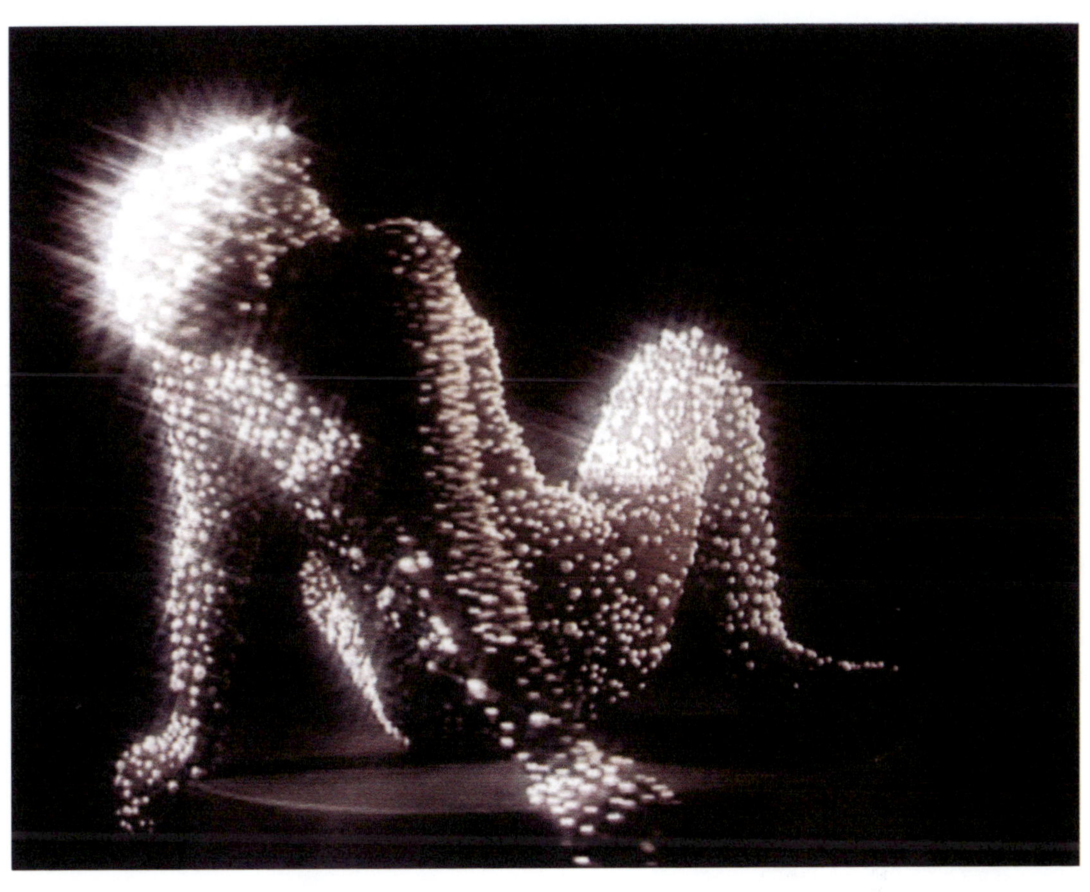

Julia Montilla (+ Juande Jarillo)
Flame (Capriccio), 2001
DVD colour video with sound
1' 48"

233

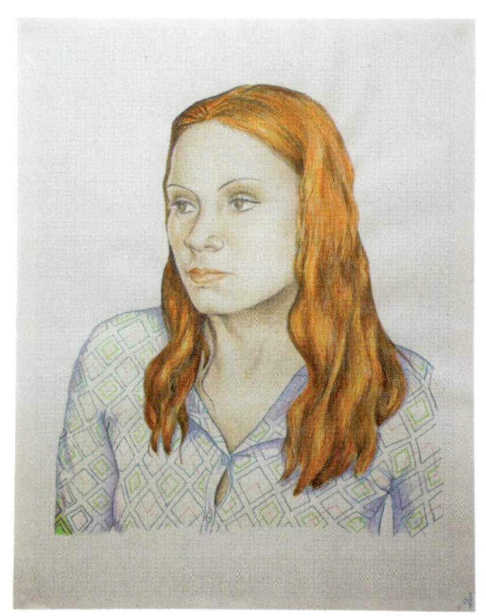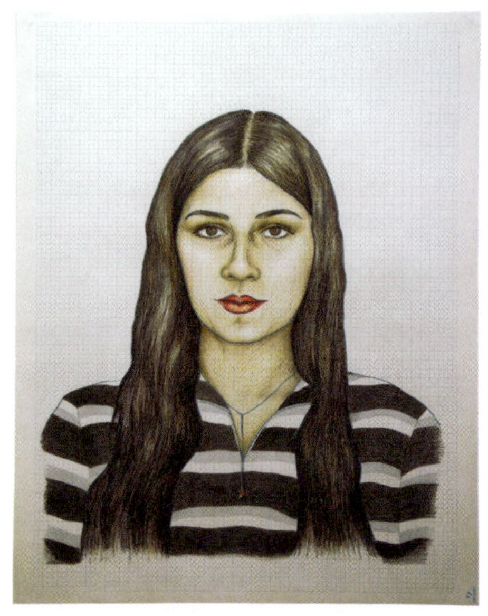

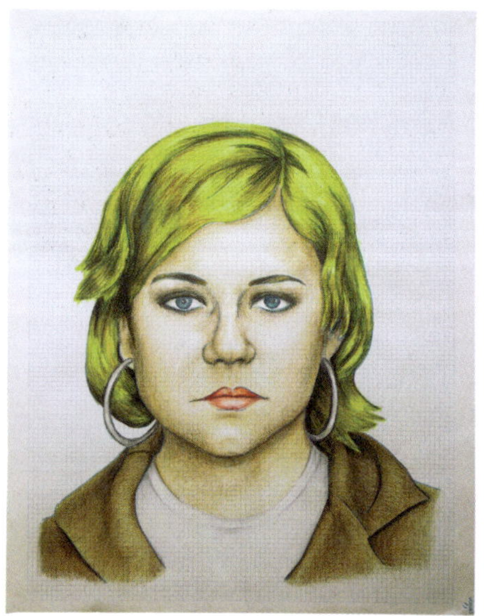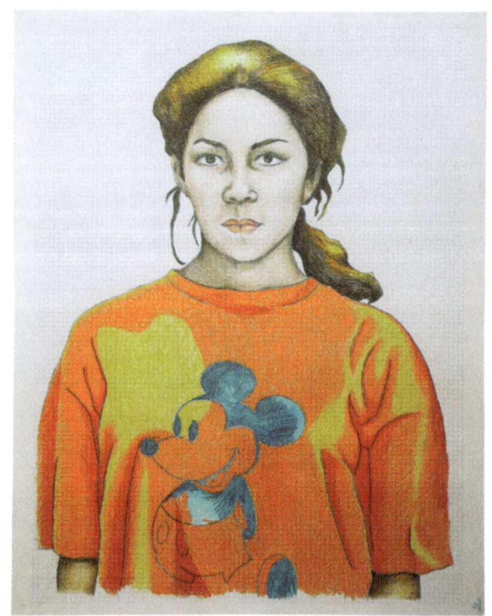

Gilda Mantilla
"Lilliam Enid Medina Hernández",
from the series *Mujeres peligrosas*, 2004
Pencil drawings on squared card
49.5 x 64.5 cm

"Gilda Mantilla", from the series
Mujeres peligrosas, 2004
Pencil drawings on squared card
49.5 x 64.5 cm

"Samantha Marson", from the series
Mujeres peligrosas, 2004
Pencil drawings on squared card
49.5 x 64.5 cm

"Kelly Kuriyama", from the series
Mujeres peligrosas, 2004
Pencil drawings on squared card
49.5 x 64.5 cm

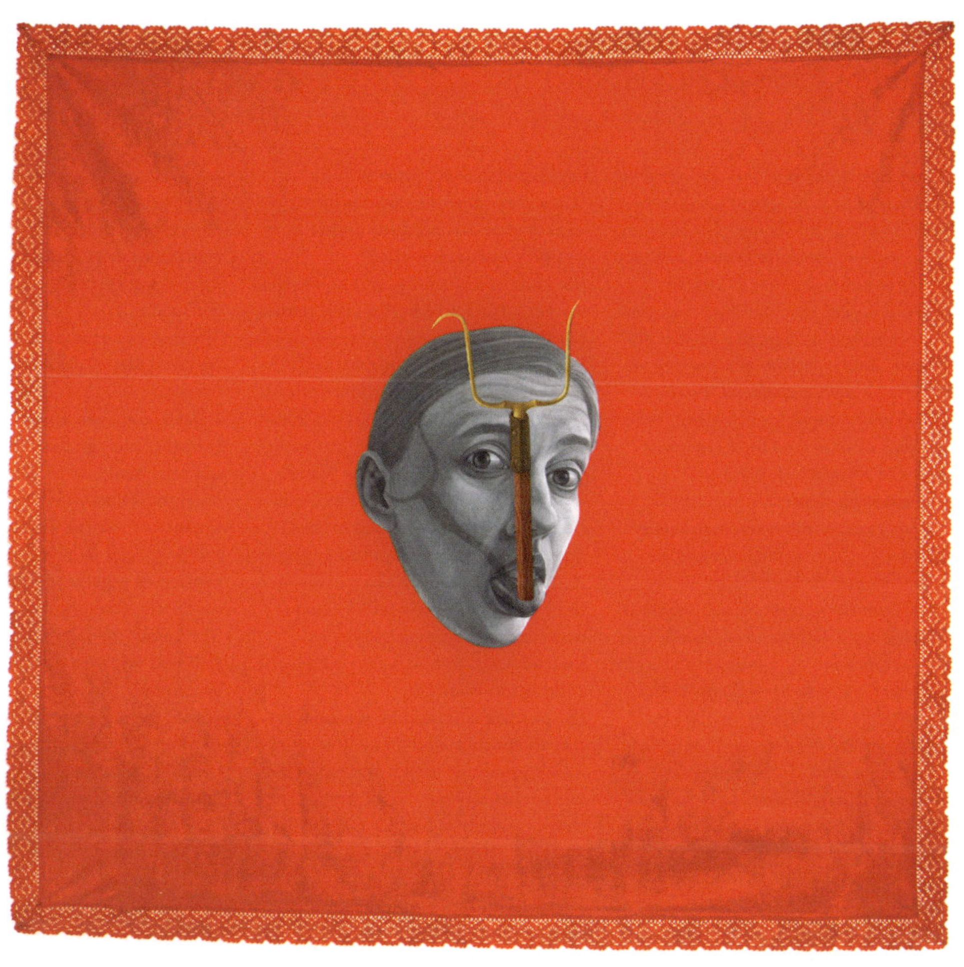

Marina Núñez
"Untitled", from the series *Locura*, 1996
Oil on canvas
155 x 155 cm

Some little heads of women emerge from the haze of an explosion of what seems to be a nuclear mushroom, but turns out to be a sperm bomb. In keeping with the metaphor, they confront it, saying: 'fuck you! fuck you! fuck you! fuck you!' In the midst of a disgusting jumble of leftover food suggestive of a country picnic with a nightmarish end, some eyeglasses that have fallen into vomit reflect a naked woman wearing a grotesque grimace, thrown onto the floor, and probably dead.
A woman is getting cocks stuck into her, all over her face, as far as we can see. In her mouth, in her nose, in her eye, in her ear. Since these are not adequate orifices, most of them bleed. As the woman does not seem to enjoy it, a voice tells her: 'try to be more comfortable'.
A naked woman is lying on a table, with her head inside a bag that is tied around her neck. Surrounding her, a gang of small children, with sinister expressions, watch her impassively, waiting for some sort of ritual to take place.
A woman crawls tiredly and wearily along the floor on all fours, dragging a long string of shit that is coming out of her arse, which is soiled with excrement. Some women warriors surround a man whom they have caught, while one of them proceeds to cut off his penis. It is an imaginary vengeance, as opposed to the imaginative but very real atrocities to which women have been and continue to be subjected, which include castration.

And so forth, and so on.
To start with something shocking not only increases the audience's incredulity, but also their expectations: What sort of world can produce a society that can produce artists[1] that can produce such works?
(Be careful not to slip into a dream world: it is science fiction, not fantasy. I will have to compensate the unlikelihood of biology, philosophy and ethnology with convincing descriptions.)
On 'Earth', nature will not work according to the cooperative processes that are customary on most planets with life. On the contrary: its evolutionary logic will be based on isolation. Symbiosis will seem so strange that it will be viewed as an invasion. In other words, there will be no genetic exchange between species. Instead, each one will vary its genetic code autonomously.
(Be careful: it would be too unscientific to speculate on an evolutionary development in which symbiosis had not played any part at all. Let us say that originally it had been minimal and that currently it is virtually nonexistent. And there will still not be any consciousness of its being inscribed on each and every cell.)
The same lack of intuition about the genetic processes will hinder the basic metamorphic capacities. Therefore, even in the organisms with the most highly developed intelligence, the derivations of the genome will not depend on voluntary testing orchestrated in terms of one teleology or another, but they will be erratic events dependent on minimal random mutations. As if this were not enough, it will be a slowly evolving biosphere: knowledge will not be inherited from forebears, whereby each generation's psycho-cognitive know-how will be perpetually crude.
(Be careful, don't overdo it: allow the transmission of some instincts or habits that are essential for the survival of the species.)
The lack of communication will not be corporal alone, since there will be no telepathy whatsoever between species. Indeed: not even among members of the same biological variety. Consequently, madness will be unleashed: outright, blind competition between organisms not connected to their fellow species, without the least conception of togetherness, to exclusively secure the ecological niches available. The law of the survival of the fittest will also apply to the brief lives of specimens: the majority of whom will obtain their energy from the ingestion of other living beings, thus creating cycles of death and regeneration that are as surprisingly effective as they are perverse.
We will therefore have an evolved society, paradoxically constituted by beings that seem to be the result of a backward process: isolated, violent, hierarchical, immature and forever trapped in a genetic code. In these conditions, empathy will be nothing more than an odd, chance phenomenon. Most goodwill will simply stem from evolutionary logic: effective in terms of the survival of the race.
A confrontational philosophy befits a confrontational nature: the logic of 'humans', my protagonists, will not be multiple but dualist. Instead of the habitual profusion of concepts that result in the exchange of fragments and positions when approaching a matter,

there will be two main concepts only per theme, let us say A and B. And they will be considered perennial and in opposition to each other: immobile and separated by insurmountable gulfs, without recognizing their mutual dependence. Either A or B. Furthermore, A is not only against, but superior to B, wherefore B is scum. Also at this level, the isolation of individuals will impede perspective: they will believe fanatically in their small subjective realities. These disparate points of view will vary drastically from specimen to specimen, by virtue of highly personal cruses, oftentimes reaching extremes of delirium. In any event, they will be mistaken for universal laws, and preached, therefore leading to all sorts of fundamentalisms.
(Be careful not to exaggerate: it would be too absurd if they did not conceive normal thought. Something will be known about non-linear processes, multi-perspectivism and diffuse logic. But this will be rare knowledge that will not affect overall epistemological dynamics.)
Clearly this tendency will hold true on an ethical level. There will be no harmoniously self-organized systems whatsoever: dogmas, hierarchies and leaders will be imposed. Specimens will be divided into A and B, in accordance with a classification that is as incongruent as it is blatant: I am A and the other is B. It will matter little to individual A that B is also an 'I' and has the same idea of himself: if the power structure is momentarily opportune, A will try to subjugate and use B and, if things get complicated,

A will consider B's disappearance, whereby A will provide whatever means are necessary for the extermination of B, or masses of Bs.
To specify the duality upon which I will focus: among humans there will only be two types of sexual functions. They will not depend on context or desire, wherefore, again, they will lack any flexibility: a person will have the same ones throughout his entire existence. Furthermore: there will be no more than two genders, both inevitably associated with its sex-source, and proclaimed as a natural fact in order to oblige its implantation.
So we have the human males, the 'men', who should be "masculine", and the female humans, the 'women', who should be 'feminine'. In that order of power. With a closed genetic source-code, there is no possible sex change or experimentation with new sexes. Heterosexuality is the law. With a strict set of atavistic sexual laws, there is no possible gender change or experimentation with new genders. The masquerade will be the rule.
People who accidentally or wilfully escape this rigid stereotyping, whether in a corporal sense (different levels of hermaphroditism) or a social sense (nonalignment of official sex and gender, or relations between individuals of the same sex) not only will not be worshipped (insist on the fact that the tiring repetition of The Same Old Thing is rewarded) but they will be abhorred and punished, for being mutants and degenerates. In this world, these words will clearly be understood as insults. On the other hand,

for heterosexual women, well-adjusted to the standard definition of femininity, it will not suffice if they comply with the rules of sex and gender: they will be abhorred and punished nevertheless. By Bs.
(Be careful: without symbiosis, without metamorphosis, without telepathy, without empathy…,
and with the psychosis of control heightened by these mutilations, it would not be difficult to conclude that, on this ominous planet, women will simply be eliminated. But the solution is easy: extermination en masse cannot be carried out for reasons of self-preservation.
At that technological point, only the women will be receptacles of their offspring, whereby the violence will be controlled and the As will make do with some lesser exterminations and varying forms of exclusion and torture. Furthermore: I will make sure this biological advantage is at the root of their misfortune.)
I still do not know what plots will involve the artists with whom I begin the work, but there will be a surprise: in the end it will be discovered that the women who imagine these overwhelming scenes are not exemplary of particularly harsh lives, of that group that has been discriminated against and harmed over the ages. On the contrary: they will be part of a privileged minority that will have finally gained access to certain rights, such as the power to communicate through those images or any others.

1 I have the names: they are called Nancy Spero, Cindy Sherman, Sue Williams, Marlene Dumas, Kiki Smith and Nicole Eisenman, respectively.

Further reading

AMNESTY INTERNATIONAL (2003): *Mujeres invisibles, abusos impunes*, Amnesty International, Spain.
ATTIYA D. (1999): *Karo-kari: A question of honour, but whose honour?*, in *Feminista*, 2 (3/4), April.
BEAUVOIR, S. (1949): *Le Deuxième sexe*, Ed. Gallimard, Paris.
BOULDING, E. (1988): *Warriors and Saints: Dilemmas in the history of Men, Women and War.* Isaksson, Eva (ed.), Women and the Military System, St. Martin's Press, New York.
GILLIGAN, C. (1982): *In a different voice. Psychological Theory and women's development.* Cambridge, Harvard University Press.
LEIBOVITZ, A., SONTAG, S. (2000): *Women*, Random House, United Kingdom.
MAGALLÓN, C. (2003): *Pacificar violencias cotidianas*, Zaragoza, Seminario de Investigación para la Paz, Zaragoza.
MERNISSI, Fatima (1991): *The Veil and the Male Elite: A Feminist Interpretation of Women's Rights in Islam*, Perseus Books, Philadelphia.
NAFISA S. (1998): *A story in black: Karo-kari killings in upper Sindh*, Oxford, Reuter Foundation Paper 100.
NOVO, María (2001): *Ellas, las invisibles*, Algaba Ed.
PONIATOWSKA, Elena (1996). *Paseo de la reforma*, Plaza&Janés, México.
PHILLIPS, A. (1997): *Engendering Democracy.* Polity Press.
REARDON, B. (1990): *Feminist concepts of Peace and Security*, in A reader of peace studies, Oxford, Pergamon.
SHIVA, V. (1992): *The seed and the Earth: Women, Ecology and Biotechnology*, in The Ecologist, Vol 22, N. 1, January/February.
TUBERT, S. (2003): *Del sexo al género, los equívocos de un concepto*, Cátedra, Madrid.

Websites of interest

- The White Ribbon Campaign in Europe:
  http://www.eurowrc.org
- 4th World Conference on Women (Beijing, 1995):
  http://www.un.org/womenwatch/daw/beijing
- Millennium Declaration:
  http://www.un.org/millennium/declaration/ares552e.htm
- Globe Women: http://globewomen.com
- Human Development Report (2004):
  http://hdr.undp.org/reports/global/2004/
- ISIS International: http://www.isis.cl
- Red Feminista: http://www.redfeminista.org
- UNIFEM: http://www.unifem.undp.org
- Women's human rights: http://www.whrnet.org
- Women Action: http://www.womenaction.org
- Women in Black: http://www.womeninblack.net
- Women's movement: http://www.nwhp.org
- Women Watch: http://www.un.org/womenwatch

Main United Nations Organisations for Women

INSTRAW: The UN International Research and Training Institute for the Advancement of Women, dedicated to research into and preparation of training programmes which contribute to their advancement.

UNIFEM: The United Nations Development Fund for Women. Set up in 1976 to give technical and financial assistance to programmes which promote the rights of women, their participation in politics and their financial security.

DAW: The Division for the Advancement of Women is part of the Department of Economic and Social Affairs and is the main body supporting the work carried out by The Commission on the Status of Women (CSW) and the Committee for the Elimination of Discrimination Against Women.

OSAGI: The Office of the Special Adviser on Gender Issues and Advancement of Women is responsible for providing incentives for the immediate fulfilment of the Millennium Development Goals and adherence to the documents and plans of action included in the conference Beijing and Beijing+5.

IANWGE: The Inter-Agency Network on Women and Gender Equality acts on the basis of focal points allowing exchange and monitoring of these issues by the players involved.

Deaths from Gender Violence in Spain (2004)	
Within family environment	94
Sexual aggression	6
Trafficking of women and prostitution	3
Other indirect victims	6
Total victims	**109**

Source: redfeminista.org

Gender-related Development Index (GDI)

Measures the achievement of a country in three dimensions (like the HDI): long and healthy life, knowledge and extent to which life is dignified. This indicator introduces the unequal achievements of men and women. The greater the gender disparity as regards basic human development, the lower the GDI of a country in relation to its human development.

Ranking according to the GDI (144 countries)

Top 10	Bottom 10
Norway	Chad
Sweden	D. R. Congo
Australia	Ethiopia
Canada	Central African Rep.
Netherlands	Mozambique
Iceland	Burundi
Belgium	Guinea-Bissau
USA	Mali
United Kingdom	Burkina Faso
Finland	Niger

Source: HDI (2004)

Gender Empowerment Measure (GEM)

Shows whether women can participate actively in economic and political life.

Ranking according to the GEM (78 countries)

Top 5	Bottom 5
Norway	Sri Lanka
Sweden	Egypt
Denmark	Bangladesh
Finland	Saudi Arabia
Netherlands	Yemen

Source: HDI (2004)

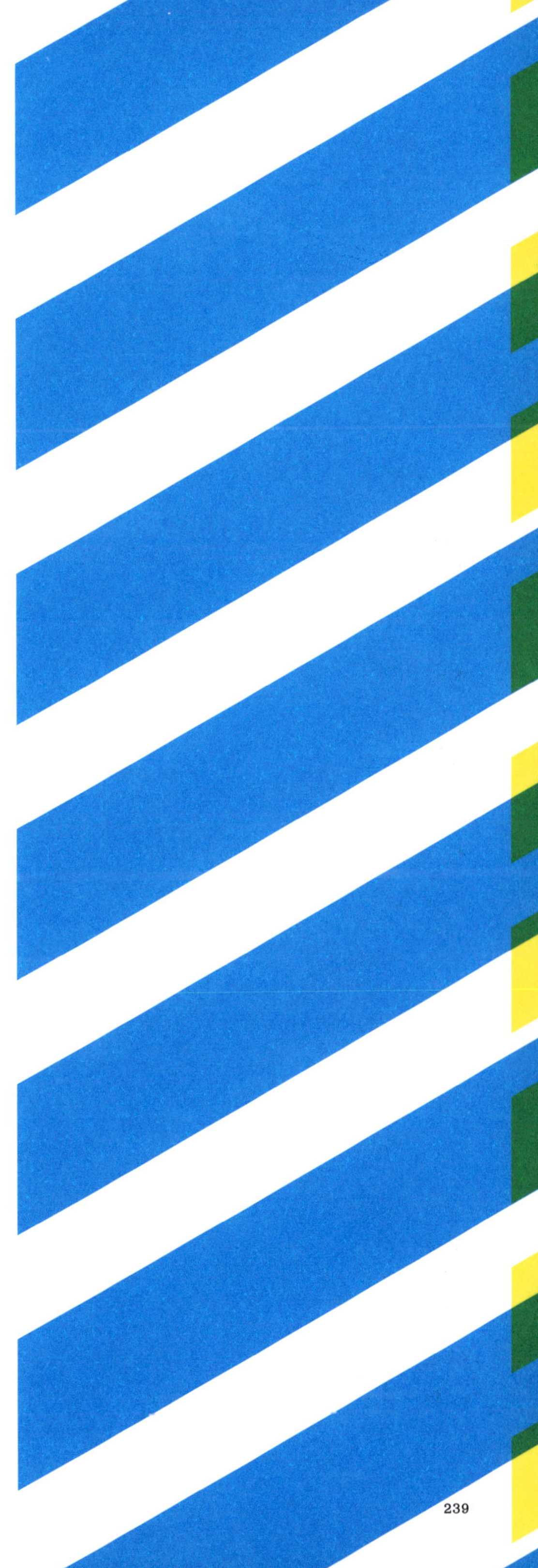

The history of humanity is accurately reflected in the aspirations of human beings to achieve more dignity and to see this realised through the recognition of their rights. However, what these rights are, what obligations they imply, in short, what we understand as human rights, is not a question free of controversy.

Although the process of constructing the basic framework of human rights has already gone through various stages, in no case should it be considered that these accomplishments are irreversible. Every day, we see these rights violated, and how they have become simple rhetoric that does not guarantee even a minimal protection of human dignity. How, then, can we move forward to a world that is based on human rights and justice?

The juridical revolution

The first declarations that deal with fundamental human rights are of a national nature: the Declaration of Rights of the State of Virginia at the time of the United States independence (1776), and the Declaration of the Rights of Man and of the Citizen after the French Revolution (1789). In both these situations, a series of fundamental rights that are political and civil in nature were recognised. These would be rounded out later on in the 19th century with specific contributions in the context of economic, social, and cultural rights. These particular rights are collective in nature, are exercised on a national level, and are exacted from the powers of the State.

However, the human rights juridical revolution, the emergence of human rights, would begin with the Universal Declaration of Human Rights (1948) and with the signing of the Geneva Conventions on international humanitarian law (1949). It is no coincidence that Elie Wiesel defined the 1948 Declaration as 'a world-wide secular religion', while Kofi Annan considers it to be 'the standard by which we measure human progress' and, to add just one more quote, Nadine Gordimer has described it as 'the quintessential document, the touchstone, the creed of humanity that, without a doubt, sums up all of those creeds which guide human behaviour'.

Other documents have been added to these two, such as the Convention on the Status of Refugees (1951), the Convention on the Prevention and Punishment of the Crime of Genocide (1948), and the European Convention of Human Rights (1950). The culmination of this process - by definition, always incomplete – has meant an important step in terms of protection. The classical notion of International Law, under which the protection of the citizens is subject to the laws of the national State in which they live, has given way to a framework of international protection – universal as well as regional. As the driving force behind this dynamic, it is necessary to point out the impact of the massive and systematic violation of basic human rights practised during World War II, and especially in the Holocaust.

In the ground covered up to this point, it is customary to identify three generations of rights: a) civil and political; b) economic, social, and cultural; and c) those concerned with solidarity (the right to development, to the environment, to peace). All of these are governed by the principles of interdependence and indivisibility, which means they are not hierarchically ordered, even though their real application might be unequal.

Traditionally, a certain idea has existed that the mere signing of the Universal Declaration or any other international treaty does not in reality imply any responsibility. This has led many of the signatory States to continue with their oppressive domestic practices. The international system, however, anticipated this with a series of instruments to guarantee human rights protection. On the whole, these are dealt with by the agreements adopted in Resolution 2200 (21) of the General Assembly (16th of December of 1966): the International Covenant on Economic, Social, and Cultural Rights; the International Covenant on Civil and Political Rights; and the Facultative Protocol attached to the International Covenant on Civil and Political Rights. At the same time, two types of international guarantee measures were instituted: the obligation for States to implement in their territory all that is stipulated in the pacts, and a system of international control covering compliance (with the presentation of reports before the Secretary General of the United Nations).

In the case of civil and political rights, the control mechanism is even more precise. The Human Rights High Commission, through its Committee for the promotion and protection of human rights, receives reports produced by States as well as individual reports of violations. On a regional basis, the existence of the European Court of Human Rights, set up in 1950, should also be noted.

A true universality
The human rights doctrine has historically been criticised as being Euro-centric in nature, which brings into question its universality by perceiving it as yet another instrument in the supposed Western pretension of moral imperialism. In the context of the moral dispute between the West and the rest of the world, both parties tend to commit the error of taking for granted that the other side speaks with a homogenous and uniform voice. In order to avoid these types of conflicts, alternative proposals have been made within the wide reaching concept of a culture of peace. Some have been inclined towards what has been called 'deliberation', proposing that the Universal Declaration of Human Rights become a type of common linguistic departure point that would serve as the basis for an open debate. Others, using what they call 'minimal planetary ethics', are trying to make possible the right of free expression for all human beings concerning that which affects them. This minimal ethic incorporates values such as

justice and solidarity and is not limited to proclaiming individual responsibility but instead it argues that, as Kant warned, 'the violation of the law in one part of the world affects the whole planet'.

RPP: three basic pillars for human rights

The aspiration to convert human rights into an effective reality requires the simultaneous satisfying of three requirements: recognition, protection, and promotion.

Recognition: This happens when States begin to be aware that human necessities exist which have to be raised to the category of internationally defendable rights. The Universal Declaration has become the principal reference in the area of recognition. The objective of human rights is 'the protection of the human agency [this refers to the existence of a responsible agent] and, therefore, deals with protecting human agents from abuse and oppression'.

Despite the non-existence of coercive measures to guarantee its application, recognition is the starting point in any attempt to achieve respect for human rights. Assuming in part that, as Thomas Hobbes sustained pessimistically, 'agreements without force are no more than mere words', the recognition of rights provides people with the right to protest against abuse and oppression, outside as well as within their borders. This has led to active campaigning by citizen groups in support of the demand that States practise what they preach.

Protection: This is effected by means of the tribunals and specific courts created in order to demand responsibility from those who violate human rights. In this sense, it is also important to point out that, besides the universal character of protection, the existence of particularly vulnerable collectives has brought about the emergence of specific protection measures for women, children, refugees, displaced people, and other groups.

Promotion: This is developed, among other ways, by means of activities, conferences and international committees which foster the protection of human rights. Alongside these, it is fundamental to emphasise education in values and the diffusion of human rights. This should happen not only in academic centres, but also in more private contexts such as the family, with the goal of promoting human rights being part of our daily lives.

The encouraging of the recognition, promotion, and protection of human rights, on the international as well as the national level, has meant an evolution in their contents. Because of the new risks and threats hanging over humanity, human rights have taken on a new dimension with the formulation of the so-called solidarity rights. These are dealt with separately because their application and recognition depend on the joint effort of the States and other members of the international community, including the civil society.

Forced evictions and the right to housing

One of the many issues that affect ESCR is that of the forced evictions from housing. The COHRE (Centre on Housing Rights and Evictions) has been a point of reference in this area since 1994. In its 2004 report, emphasis is placed on the increasing pattern of forced evictions that are put into effect outside of international law, violating basic human rights and fundamental legal principles as understood by the members of a developed society.

The right to housing is a basic human right and its violation denies, theoretically, the possibility of a dignified life. Although this idea is recognised legally within the framework of ESCR, the situation is not favourable at all when one considers that seven million people were objects of forced evictions by their own governments in the period 2001-02, and more than six million are currently under threat.

The report analyses more specifically the forced evictions realised on the occasion of international events such as the Olympic Games. The last Games in Greece (2004) are a good example. The obsession to avoid any factor that might cast a shadow over the staging of these types of celebrations, aside from other economic interests of a speculative nature, ends up eliminating any kind of resistance or troublesome element. In the Greek case, thousands of people, among whom were members of the Marosi Community (Gypsies), were threatened with forced evictions in the area of Greater Athens in the two years prior to the games. Of these, 140 members of the aforementioned community were finally evicted.

The problem is neither new nor limited to the Olympic Games. In general terms, these operations are too closely tied to the development of big infrastructures, to the urban investment made by large multinational companies, and to the potential profits that can be obtained by activity in the tourist sector.

A classic precedent of this kind can be found on the occasion of the Berlin Olympic Games (1936), when the Nazi government used all kinds of means to 'clean' the streets and eliminate any sign of poverty in the capital.

This practice, in short, is one indulged in by many regimes that are not very respectful of human rights, as well as others who are technically more committed. The COHRE reports attest to the forced removals that have been carried out in the area of Olympic villages, stadiums, or the entrances to subways by means of 'homeless cleansing' operations, but which also affect other people who live on the edge of extreme poverty. It happened in Barcelona (1992), Atlanta (1996), in South Korea (1988) - with the removal of about 720,000 people in the areas of Seoul and Inchon, to a lesser degree in Sydney (2000) and in Athens (2004). In Peking, 300,000 people have already been evicted as a consequence of the preparations for the 2008 Olympic Games.

Political and civil rights after September 11ᵗʰ

The terrible events of the 11ᵗʰ September 2001 have also affected the international legal system. In the context of the ill-named 'war against terror', a curtailing of rights and liberties has begun, which in general is being accepted with excessive passivity by frightened citizens who are willing to accept reductions in exchange for supposedly greater security. This situation has upset the international system, as Amnesty International has been warning in its annual reports that show how millions of women and men suffer persecution for no other reason than their ethnicity or creed.

This retrocession is generalised and accepted. On one hand, those that should be the principal guardians of human rights, being representatives of open, democratic, and developed societies, are now the first to be submerged in a process of identity loss as they become more and more like those they condemn for their use of violence. This is the explanation for the aberration that is the existence of the Guantanamo installations, which defy the framework of international legality and human rights, or the process by which any foreigner can be considered, by definition, a suspect. Neither should we forget the existence of secret detention centres, outside any police or judicial control.

On the other hand, and on the basis of that previously mentioned, it is hardly surprising that other political leaders, barely democratic, are taking advantage of the current trend established by governments

The International Criminal Court: hope in action

The last few decades have been witness to serious violations of international humanitarian rights and international norms concerning the protection of human rights. On too many occasions, those responsible for these crimes have avoided prosecution in their respective countries, protected by the so-called 'full stop laws', which impede the investigation of the acts in question and the punishment of those responsible. For too long, the international community has lacked the adequate instruments to charge and sanction the authors, instigators, or accomplices of these crimes, and was condemned to remain powerless in front of them. In order to tackle this problem and rectify these deficiencies, a diplomatic conference was held in 1997 in Rome under the auspices of the United Nations participated in by delegates from 160 States, observers from 31 institutions and international agencies, and 133 international non-governmental organisations. The Statute of the International Criminal Court was adopted on 17ᵗʰ July 1998, with 120 votes in favour, 7 against (the United States among them) and 21 abstentions. This statute set up the International Criminal Court (ICC) as a permanent institution, authorised to exercise justice over people accused of committing crimes of genocide, crimes against humanity, war crimes, and crimes of aggression. The Statute of Rome also clearly states that State representatives, regardless of their office or position, do not have any immunity for these crimes. Despite its current deficiencies, the ICC, in existence since 1 July 2002, is an important advance in the area of human rights. Its existence will permit future generations to be able to live in a world that is more protected from gross violations of human rights.

such as that of the United States. Thus, they try to resolve their own problems in the same way, whether in Chechnya, Pakistan, China, Palestine, Guatemala or Colombia, to name but a few examples. As a result, it is even more difficult to halt the worrying increase in systematic violations of human rights in any of their forms – from the exploitation of children, violence directed towards women, persecution of political opponents, the existence of the death penalty, or repression directed towards immigrants, refugees or displaced people.

If we take into consideration that the total application of human rights is a battle that cannot be thought of in terms of attaining an absolute victory, the current negative tendencies not only represent an obstacle to the extension of rights, but are also torpedoing the concept of their universality and validity. It is already hard enough to record all the violations by governments that have never had any particular desire to implement what they have signed and ratified in the field of human rights. What is even worse is that now those same governments feel encouraged and supported by those who are attempting to lead, in their own way, the fight against international terrorism. Even more serious is that some of these same governments of developed countries are renouncing symbols of their own identity claiming that international legal safeguards are obstacles in the war against terrorists. As a consequence, they argue, it is advisable to reduce the standards of human rights protection on a national level, cutting back on the rights of their own citizens, and also internationally, limiting the rights of those conceived of as enemies to be defeated. Can we be so sure that renouncing, even for a short period of time, our values and using precisely the methods of those who we criticise that we are going to be able to overcome the challenge and perfect our model of an open society? This certainly does not appear to be the way.

A look at the contents of the Human Development Report elaborated by the United Nations Development Programme (UNDP) about the signing and ratification of international human rights agreements supplies us with significant data. In the area of the ratification of these treaties – and following the report's classification of countries with a high, medium, or low Human Development Index (HDI) – it is interesting to observe that among all the countries with a high HDI, the United States is the only one that has not ratified the signing of the International Convention on Economic, Social, or Cultural Rights, or the Convention on the Elimination of all forms of Discrimination against Women, or the Convention on the Rights of the Child. This situation is comparable to countries with a medium or low HDI such as Nauru, Guinea-Bissau, or Kazakhstan. The case of the United States is not, as it may seem in the context of the current political climate, the result of an opportunistic decision made by the current government. Instead it responds to a decision that has been in effect since the fifties when, abandoning its international profile as a key promoter, among others, of the Universal Declaration of Human Rights, it has become reticent to ratify international agreements on human rights. This tendency could be caused by the fact that the American people have an inclination to believe that their rights have acquired legitimacy as a result of their own consent.

Currently, one of the principal threats to the protection of human rights arises precisely from the behaviour of governments that practice torture, coercion, and abusive techniques against their citizens or against foreigners. This encourages others who have always been less respectful to do likewise. The 2004 annual report of Human Rights Watch indicates, in this regard, that this attitude is granting other governments a greater margin for manoeuvre. To see this, it's enough to remember how the Malaysian authorities justify the frequent administrative detentions that they carry out by citing the situation in Guantanamo, or how the Russians refer to Abu Ghraib in order to justify their treatment of Chechen prisoners.

Despite the fact that these are the dominant features of the current situation, it is necessary to remember that there are very distinct hopeful processes in which common people are progressively acquiring a greater influence. It is also true that there are governments whose policies continue to reflect that respect for human rights and multilateralism are the most efficient ways to build a better world. In this light, what should be pointed out above any other initiative is the creation of the International Court of Justice.

Economic, Social, and Cultural Rights (ESCR)
Economic, social, and cultural rights include, among other things, the right to housing, education, health, food, and water. It was the United Nations that declared back in 1993 the indivisibility and interdependence of human rights, which implies giving all of them the same treatment. To be sure, the attainment of these rights does not only affect developing countries, for there are also deficiencies in developed countries. Indeed, the differences are even more notable, in general, than those stated in constitutional texts with certain groups of people on the fringe of society living a very precarious existence. However, in the first group of countries there exists a series of factors that clearly makes the process of attainment problematic.

It is in the less developed countries where the combined effects of a discriminatory government management of national assets can be seen with the greatest clarity. The measures taken are generally adopted in secret behind the back of the general population. In these cases, the international community has not carried out its responsibility because great population masses in the world are excluded and are left on their own. As if this panorama were not sufficiently bleak, we should not forget the harmful effects of the international business model which is highly unequal and which ignores the exploitation of workers such as children, women, and human beings in general who are condemned to new forms of exploitation that border on slavery. At the same time, in order to complete this brief outline of the problem, it is also necessary to mention the devastating consequences of the austerity programmes, the result of the discipline imposed by the International Monetary Fund on numerous countries which, for various reasons, have suffered crises in their external debt repayments. It is well known that the application of these austerity policies has had a notable social impact, affecting precisely those sectors of society that are most vulnerable, without any compensatory mechanisms being set up which would prevent their falling into an even worse situation. The austerity programmes have not permitted the countries in question, and especially their inhabitants, to either climb out from under the most rampant underdevelopment or, as can be imagined, to enhance their ESCR.

On the other hand, the neo-liberal policies that currently dominate the scene make any attempt to convert into reality what frequently remains fossilised in constitutional or international documents into an uphill battle. This occurs since these policies restrain the activity of the State, the principal provider of these rights and the primary source of pressure to force the multinational economic players, who are very far removed from these concerns, to modify their behaviour.

Referring specifically to the problem of external debt, an authentic dead weight which stops many countries escaping from the quicksand of underdevelopment in which they find themselves floundering, the time has arrived to understand that its pardoning is possible on an economic level, and urgent on an ethical one. The international financial system is sufficiently prepared to take on the unpaid debts on an official basis within the framework of multilateral debt cancelling programmes. There exist, at the same time, very precise analyses to determine which countries should be favoured to take advantage of these types of measures, while others could embark on debt conversion programmes to allow them to invest in their basic social sectors or in the environment. What is needed, once again, is sufficient political will on the part of the creditors in order to renounce the permanent application of pressure on these governments. Here, we are not talking about the promotion of values or principles that benefit the population as a whole and would therefore justify the use of pressure to bring about the necessary reforms to correct unfair national models. Rather, we are referring to pressure used just in the defence of the creditors' own most direct interests.

The United Nations has tried to promote some initiatives in this area. For example, the Sub-Commission on the Promotion and Protection of Human Rights approached the consequences of debt from the viewpoint of human rights, as outlined in its report presented to the

56th Assembly of the UN. The document affirms that debt has become a way of pushing these countries into extreme poverty, as well as in instrument of domination and exploitation. It even argues that debt is a means of private colonisation and a return to slavery, similar to what was experienced in the 19th century.

In this same direction, other innovative initiatives that support the promotion and application of ESCR have been developed. One of these is ESCR-NET, founded in June 2003 in Chiang Mai (Thailand), as the result of an international conference which brought together more than 250 activists from about 50 countries to elaborate joint strategies which promote ESCR all over the world. The Network arises from the conception of human rights, theoretically assumed by the United Nations, that recognises the interdependence and indivisibility of human rights, a principle by which all the people must have their civil and political rights acknowledged as well as their economic and social rights. Starting out from a focus on economic, social, and cultural rights, the following objectives were proposed: the development of decentralised support structures to work together in the promotion of social justice, the empowering of groups on the fringe of society and other social movements, and the strengthening of the use of human rights as a work tool.

Another initiative of interest in this field is the Ethical Globalisation Initiative (EGI) led by Mary Robinson, ex High Commissioner of the UN for Human Rights. Under its mandate, it is proposed to bring key people together in new alliances destined to give a transversal character to human rights, heighten sensitivity to questions of sexual discrimination, and concentrate efforts dedicated to resolving global challenges and problems of governability.

It also depends on you

Although the key to improving the current situation in the practical application of human rights continues to be the role of national governments and international organisations, none of us can ignore an issue that serves as a central element in how we define ourselves as citizens.

This evidently means applying the values enshrined in different agreements and treaties about human rights to our own personal relationships. In the same way, it is essential to internalise the meaning of the increasing cultural diversity of our societies and admit the necessity of modifying many of our behavioural patterns and adapting them to other realities, with the only limitation being our respect for the framework of fundamental rights and liberties of a lawful State. We can not deceive ourselves: the creation of extralegal areas – in which other norms can exist which permit discrimination, violence, or the forced exile of some, whether for reasons of ethnicity, religion, sex, or on any other grounds, will never be the answer.

As in many other fields, education in all senses and the development of sensitivity are vital for achieving both the universalising of human rights and the creation of models of coexistence. The flourishing of diversity has to happen in the context of a common code that can only be based on human rights in all their facets.

Current times oblige us to be vigilant in order to fight against the permanent deterioration of the framework of human rights. It is not risky to affirm that if today we had to debate and approve a Universal Declaration of Human Rights, its contents would be much more restrictive and discouraging. In the short term, we are trying to defend what we already have and we are pushing to achieve that what is written becomes an everyday reality. Looking ahead, we are hopeful that solidarity rights will eventually be recognised, together with all the rest, as universal standards.

A document produced by researchers from the
Institute of Studies on Conflicts and Humanitarian Action (IECAH)
Madrid, January 2005

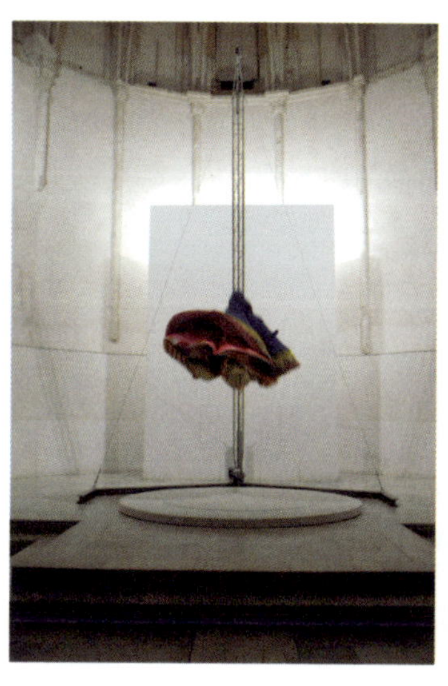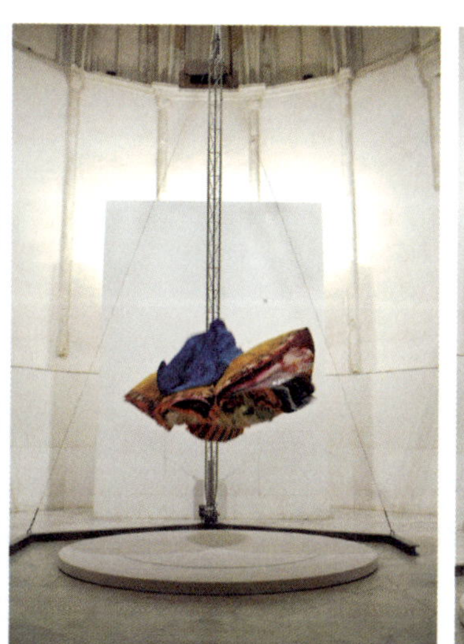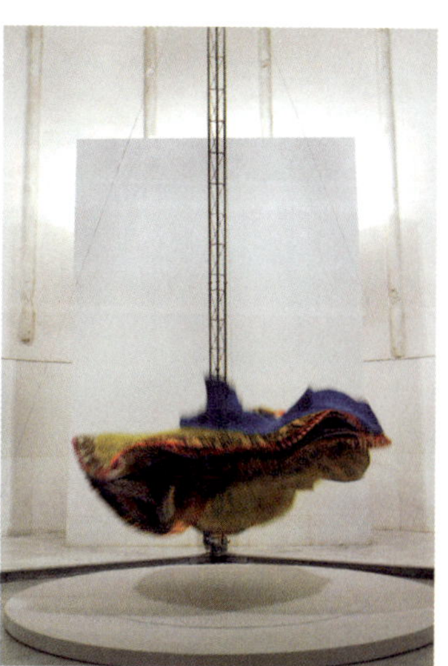

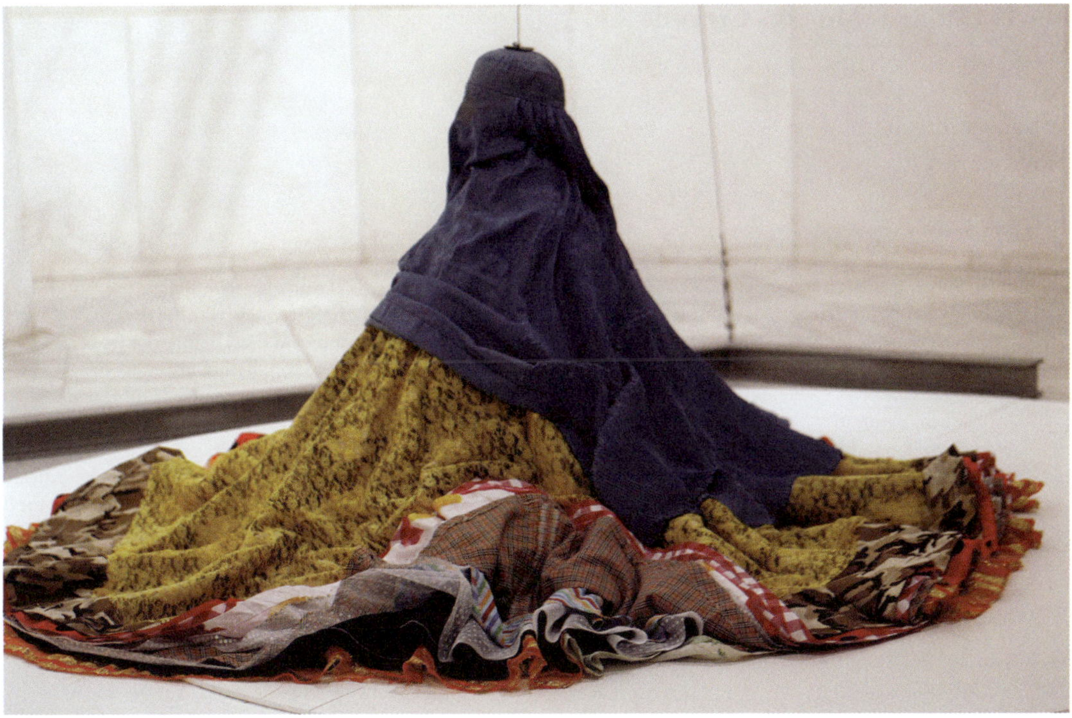

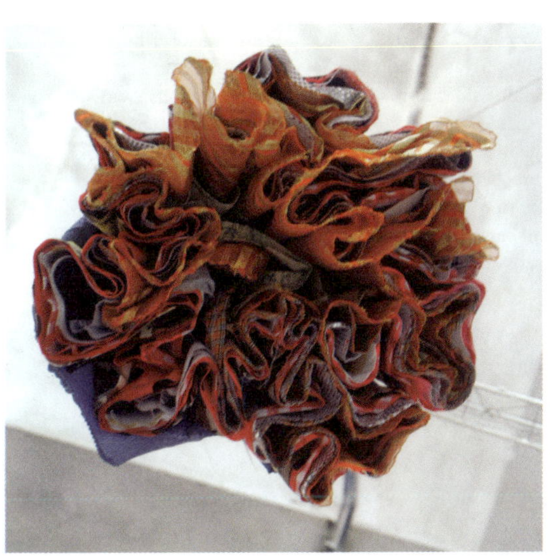

Joana Vasconcelos
Burka, 2002
Installation consisting of iron structure,
electrical system, steel cables, wooden
platform and fabrics
Variable dimensions

251

María Galindo, Mujeres Creando
When?
Now!
When, damn it?
Now, damn it!

The Public Stage:
mates; what do we want?
work!
when?
Now!
When, damn it?
Now, damn it!
shout the whores in Oruro
and the miners in Potosi echo them,
while the peddlers take advantage of
the shout to sell
a drink of boiled peel which evokes
the taste of the fruit

These screechy, shrill and
uninterrupted shouts of tiny,
small, mid-sized or gigantic street
marches are the lullabies from which
we slowly learn to understand life.
It is a repetitive, routine, all-
embracing shout that submerges
you in hopes that circulate viciously
through the streets without fail,
spreading the sole, categorical lesson
of the lucid comprehension that our
time is now!!!
We are part of the marches that do
not seek the revolutions of tomorrow,
because we have understood that our
time is now; that's why it is with it
– with now -, - with now, damn it -,
that we are falling in love, promising
faithfulness and happiness.

We are not seeking immolation,
or heroic redemption, or death;
we don't sabotage life with rumours
of 'Nicaraguan', 'Salvadoran' or
'Bolivian' salvations and revolutions.
We cling to the lucid comprehension
of the now that a chain of interwoven
dreams propose to us. Dreams tied
to old shoes and sweaty feet, dreams
loosened from mouths that are
missing many teeth, dreams tied by
rough, chapped hands that caress
spades, brooms and soot for countless
dozens of hours a week, a month,
a year.
Entire populations in the south
converted into activists of over-
exploitation, forever insolvent and
indebted people who no longer need
a visible patron or a slave trader to
offer themselves up voluntarily for
survival. People who renounce Sunday
because they have sunken it into
their hearts to carry it there within.
Entire populations that celebrate birth
and death with the same festive pomp,
because while life is on one side, rest is
on the other.
**A disturbing challenge of visions
that erase the difference between
emergency and utopia, in order to
convert it into one and the same
thing, which is concrete and is now.**

**It must be now; before the day ends,
before a new war breaks out, before
a friend dies, before the frost ruins
the crop, before my energy runs out,
before by land bleeds to death.**

The Private Stage:
Inside, where the water for the coffee
boils while a girl folds the clothes for
tomorrow, another street circulates.
The luminous, loud, routine and
colourful street of the television.
The street that crosses and invades
all houses, homes, huts and rooms
with its cold, hypnotizing light.
A 24 hour street. A street where a
chef in a luxury hotel in Monaco or
Biarritz prepares exquisite delicacies
for people on diets; a street where
they are not dark-skinned toothless
mouths that smile, but those of the
present-day 'stars'. A street of grossly
gay cheerleaders and girls trained in
profound stupidity. A street of big
sales and fraudulent raffles for a trip
to Miami.
A street that audaciously cuts the
desert, the ocean, the sky, the rain
forest and the mountain down to
'small screen' size. A street that
reduces our history to a 30 second
news flash. A street that imposes
motorway speed on a kiss,

on love, on pleasure, obliging our eyes to refrain from blinking before the domesticating stimulus of our consciences and our bodies.

A street where they habitually anesthetise us against pain, death and war. A street where mutilating 'plastic surgery' operations are performed on human bodies and faces.

Profound anaesthesia, absolute passivity that induces us to consent everything; all the censorship, all the disinformation, all the pollution, all the racism, all the colonialism. To consent all the violence simply sitting in front of the television.

Television that annihilates the notion of utopia and the notion of emergency at one precise instant and with the same effectiveness; in a sort of closed circuit, that blocks your remote control on the same message; channel by channel and hour after hour all around the world and in all languages; 'nothing is in your hands, you can do nothing, you mean nothing'. Annihilation that does nothing but leave us still and silent sitting in the chair for hours, months and years, immobile before our lives and removed from our own desires.

**We Women,
Street Dwellers of History
And Street Dwellers of Television**
Submerged and soaked in one and the other street, strolling along one and the other, we Women Creating have become street agitators of one and the other stage; on the public stage and in the private stage; in the small screen and in the home, and also outside of the home and off-screen.

The relation with the television space was an occupational relation.

Very fearful up against so much annihilating power, intimidated by the eyes of the camera, like someone who gets into a moving war tank, we got into the television with our activism and our street wisdom from marches and more marches.

We got in convinced that it is one more street to occupy, convinced that from that street the voices and shouts are amplified, the body and the skin colour is recovered, and a woman enters her neighbour's house to sit down next to her and drink up a moment of essential encounter.

The first image we launched into the air was us exploding a small television set on the floor. It was hardly more than a gesture, but it was an original, creative, simple, direct, proper,

subversive gesture. A gesture that articulated both streets in one and the same way, an agitating, mobilizing, disturbing, destabilizing, convoking and rebellious way.

To all that graffiti we wrote in the streets, to the hundreds of times we painted 'disobedience, thanks to you I am going to be happy', we later added direct television footage of the very act of painting and the very act of living:

> 'woman, neither submissive
> nor devoted, free,
> lovely and wild',
> 'be careful about the
> present you build,
> it should resemble the future
> you dream',
> 'we don't have a flat stomach,
> we are all curves'.

The eyes of the camera had the power to convert the word into transforming, filmed, televised action delivered to homes still hot, opportune and appetizing. Filming that simplifies the creative gesture because it puts it within reach. Because it demystifies it, deconsecrates it and reduces it to its maximum elementariness. An elementariness that is potent

because it is a common good, an elementariness that is potent because it is in our hands, an elementariness whence, incredibly, it is possible to reinvent the world that has been trapped in the small screen.
In that self-televising context, it is an urgent effort and a fighting strategy that permits us to build a bridge between public and private, between street and home, between the mute, lonely and isolated person and the people that convene this person to utter her words directly, to dance in the streets, to sleep vengefully deep and without debts, to live loves without a husband, to live and to move and to wake from slumber. Having built this bridge, our agitation becomes a circle that adds image to word and concrete action to image and again word to concrete action. **Consuming this composition of creativities has made us effective; it has made us dangerous; it has made us massive and it has converted our ability to disorder social relations, from within and from without, from above and from below, from the north and from the south, into an ability present in the ordinariness of our society. We are here, in the present and in the now disordered social hierarchies; we are in the present and in the now and within reach as concrete reality, not as lyrical promise of tomorrow.**

**Creativity is a fighting instrument
And social change is a creative deed**

This social space opened manually, a social space of which we are neither beneficiaries nor tenants, a social space that is not 'equity quota', a social space that is neither anti-discriminatory concession, nor positive discrimination, a political social space that is neither a morsel for patriarchs, nor parties. This social space over which we are sovereign, everyday actors and builders, contains a basic, elemental comprehension:

    creativity is a fighting instrument,
      social change is a creative deed
    and creative action is a political act.

Comprehension that situates our creativity in the realm of permanent subversion, comprehension that situates our creativity in the centre of social relations as a rebellious force. Comprehension that situates our activity as invented, created and recreated and therefore imperfect, incomplete and convening identity. Identity consisting of rare, prohibited alliances: Indians, whores and lesbians all together, mixed and matched up, disobeying their limits in order to join the dreams and troubles of those who are forbidden to do so. Identity residing in rebellion and not in egocentric self-affirmation. Complex identity that is not the sum of varieties, but the composition of fragments where all the identities composing it are aware they are fragments of identity. Aware they are pieces called upon to be integrated with other pieces, thus completing knowledge, feelings, intuitions and visions.
Fragmentary pieces, builders of a circular identity without avant-gardes. A space of heterogeneity, a space of celebration of the difference and of celebration of the complex unity of differences at the same time. Celebration of unfathomable and inexplicable unity. Celebration of personal stories and existential elections; omen of change and omen of utopia.
Political space of Indians, whores and lesbians all together, mixed and matched up:

Together disobeying cultural
mandates.
Together disobeying privileges and
hierarchies.
Together disobeying familiar
mandates,
Together rewriting our loves to be
sister, friend and lover of whomever
I wish.
Together disobeying religious,
patriotic and military mandates.
Together in assembly of direct voices
that do not admit translations,
mediation, interpretation or
representation.
Together to reinvent ourselves and
also to survive.
Together as omen of utopia and
urgent task at the same time.

Written from a place called bolivia
A place where everything seems impossible
To communicate with us:
mujerescreando@alamo.entelnet.bo
www.mujerescreando.com
Tel: 0059-2-2492151

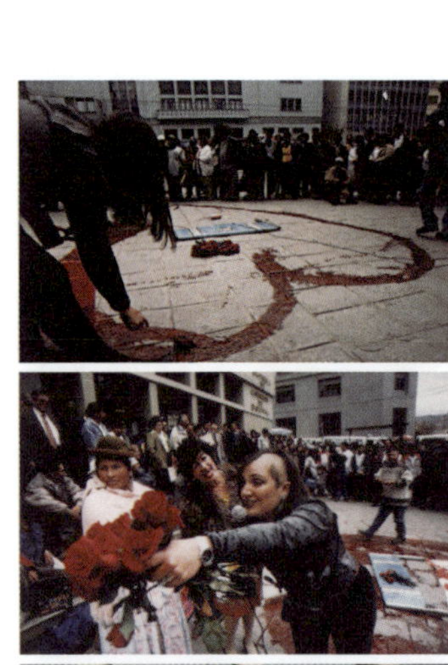
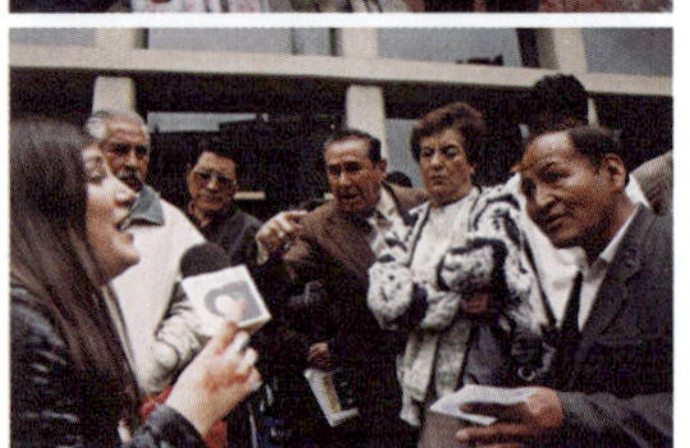
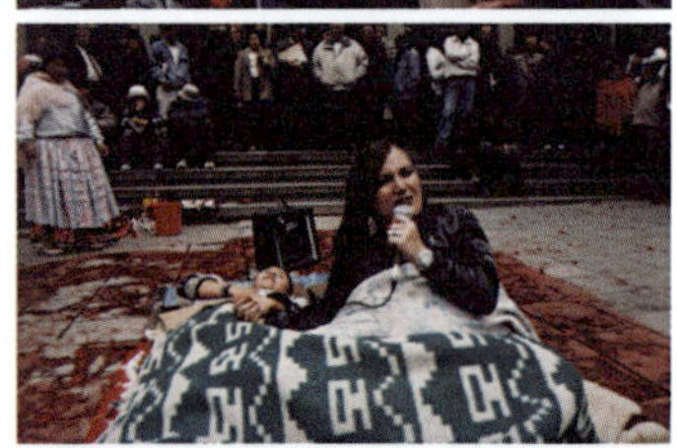
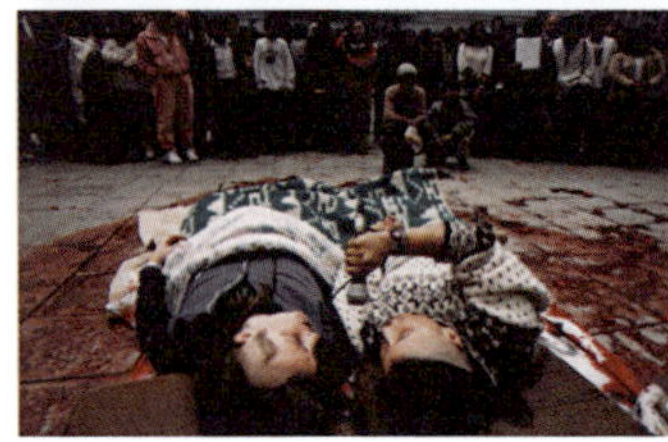
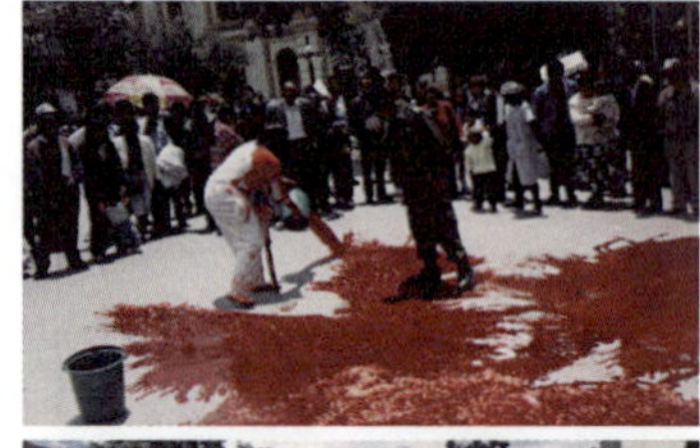

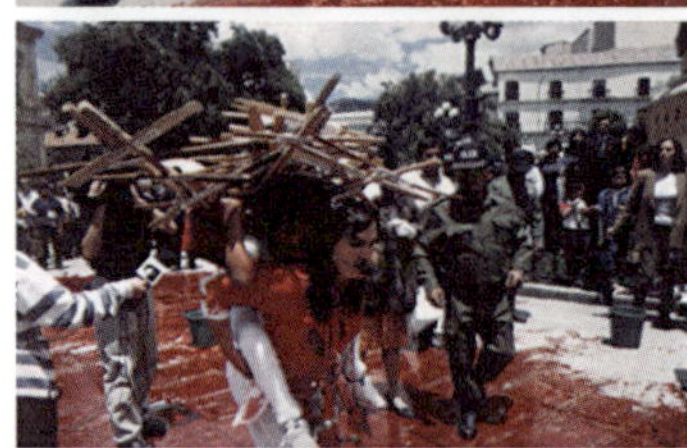
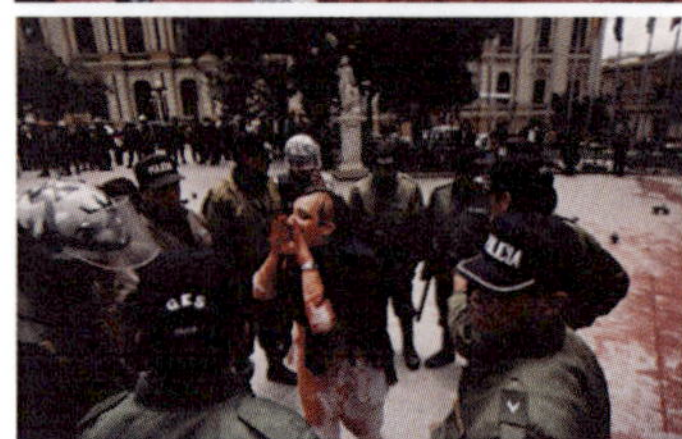
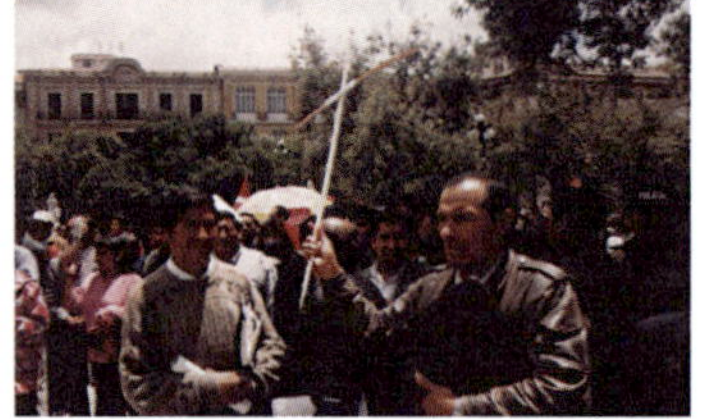
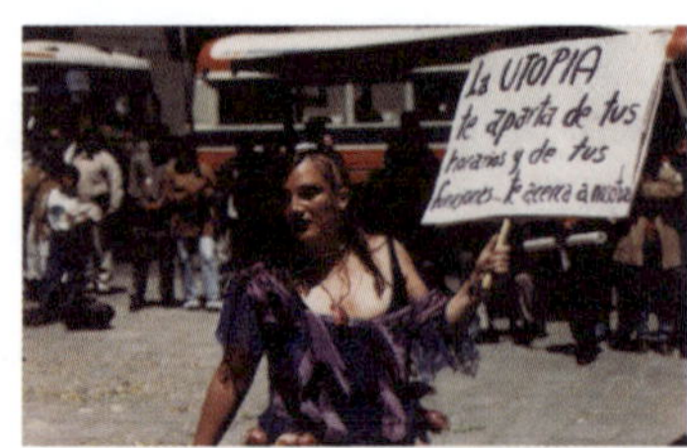
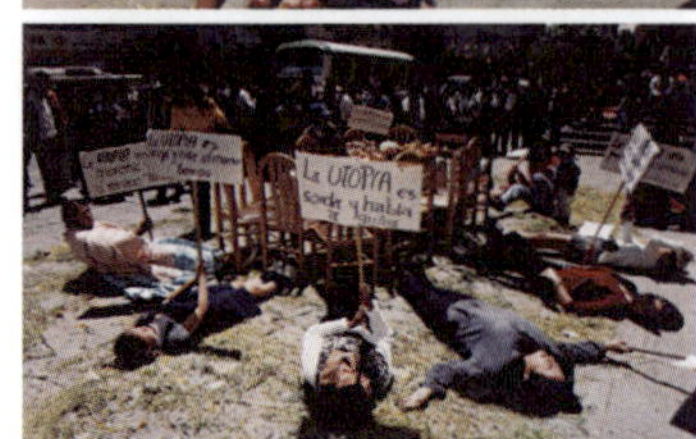
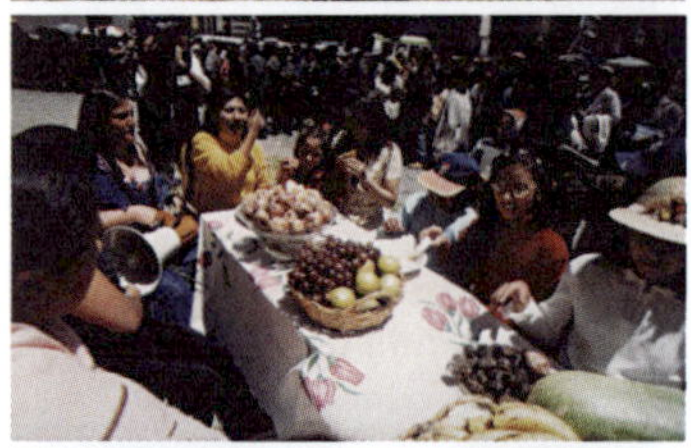
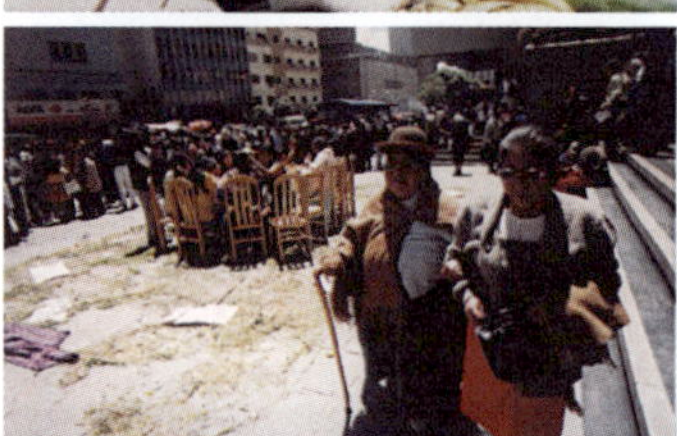

Mujeres Creando
Lesbianismo, 1999
DVD colour video with sound
10'

Dictadura, 1999
DVD colour video with sound
8'

Utopía, 1999
DVD colour video with sound
9'

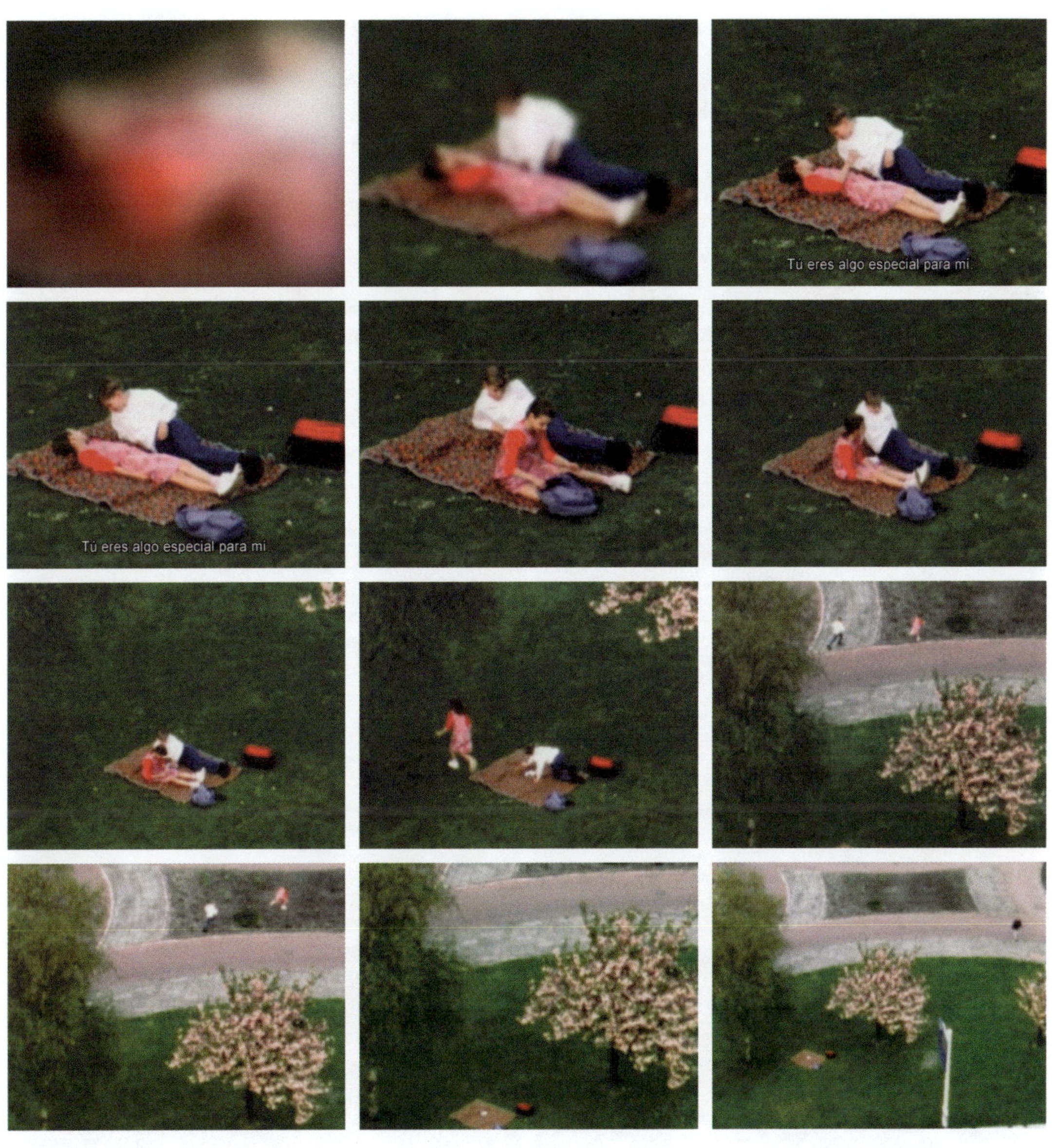

Corinna Schnitt
Das nächste Mal/Next Time, 2003
DVD colour video with sound
5' looped

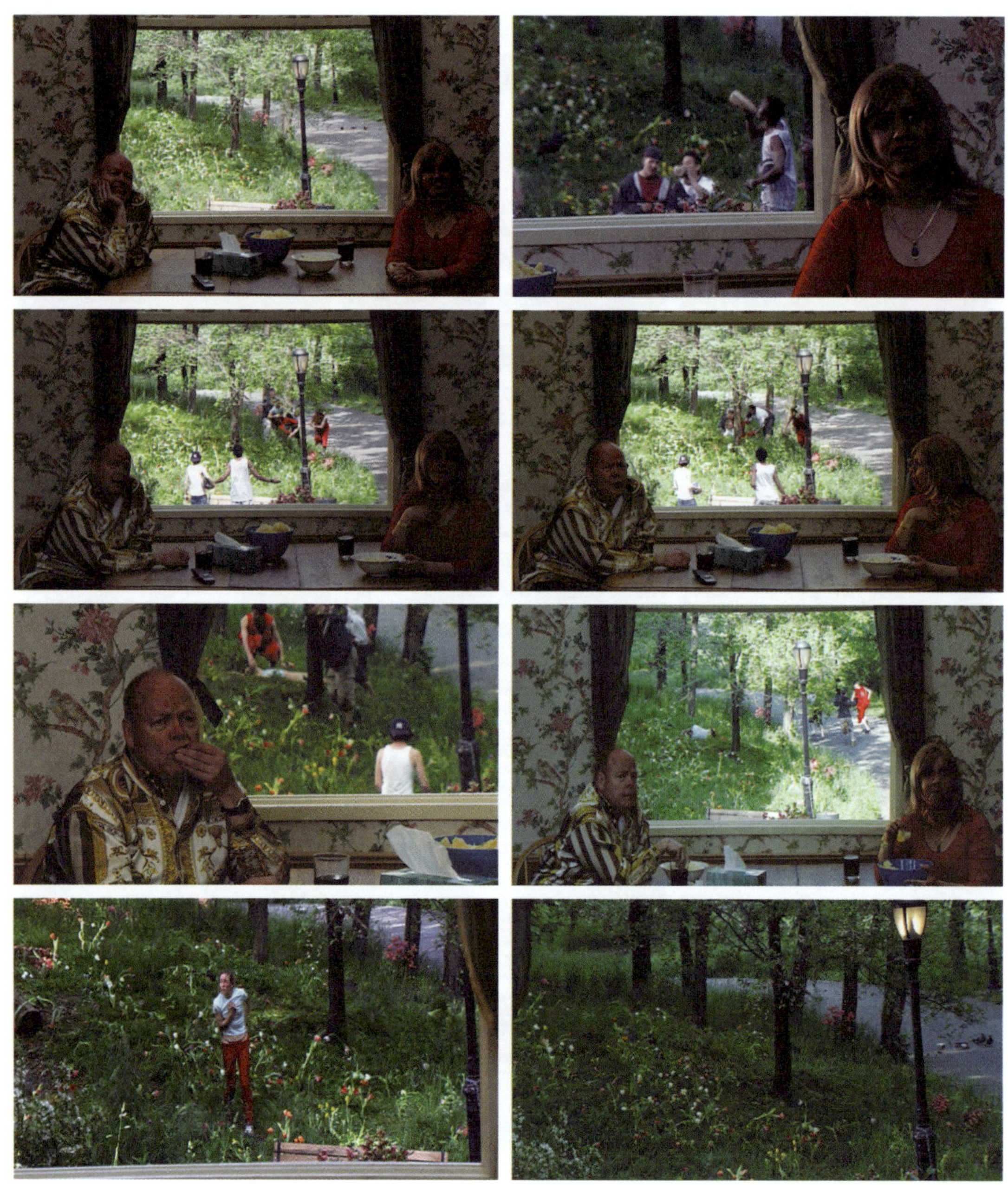

Shoja Azari
A Room with a View, 2004
DVD colour video with sound
8' 20''

258

Paul Graham
"Untitled", from the series *American Night*,
2000-02
Colour photographs
182 x 232 cm

"Untitled", from the series *American Night*,
2000-02
Colour photographs
182 x 232 cm

Further reading

ALSTON, P. (1984): *Conjuring up new human rights: a proposal for quality control*, American Journal of International Law, 8.
CARRILLO SALCEDO, J. A. (2001): *Soberanía de los Estados y Derechos Humanos*, Tecnos, Madrid.
CASSESE, A. (1991): *Los derechos humanos en el mundo contemporáneo*, Ariel, Barcelona.
IGNATIEFF, M. (2001): *Los derechos humanos como política e idolatría*, Paidos, Barcelona.
ORAA, J. and GOMEZ ISA, F. (2002): *La Declaración Universal de Derechos Humanos. Un breve comentario en su 50 Aniversario*, Universidad de Deusto, Bilbao.
POWERS S., GRAHAM A. (2000): *Realizing Human Rights*, St Martin's Press, New York.
ROBERTSON, G. (1999): *Crimes against Humanity: The Struggle for Global Justice*, The New Press.
VIDAL GIL, E. (2001): *Los derechos de solidaridad en el ordenamiento jurídico español*, Tirant lo Blanch, Valencia.

Websites of interest

- Amnesty International: http://www.amnesty.org
- ESCR-NET: http://www.escr-net.org
- Millennium Declaration: http://www.un.org/millennium/declaration/are5552e.pdf
- UNDP Country Reports about Millennium Development Objectives: http://www.undp.org/mdg/countryreports.html
- Human Rights Watch: http://www.hrw.org
- Statute of the International Criminal Court: http://www.un.org/law/icc/statute
- International Coalition for the ICC: http://www.iccnow.org
- Ethical Globalisation Initiative: http://www.eginitiative.org

	Total number of Participatory States	Signatures not ratified
Convention on the Prevention and Punishment of the Crime of Genocide (1948)	135	2
International Convention on the Elimination of all forms of Racial Discrimination (1965)	169	7
International Covenant on Civil and Political Rights (1966)	151	8
International Covenant on Economic, Social and Cultural Rights (1966)	148	7
Convention on the Elimination of all forms of Discrimination against Women (1979)	175	1
Convention on the Rights of the Child (1989)	192	2

Human Development Report, UNDP 2004.

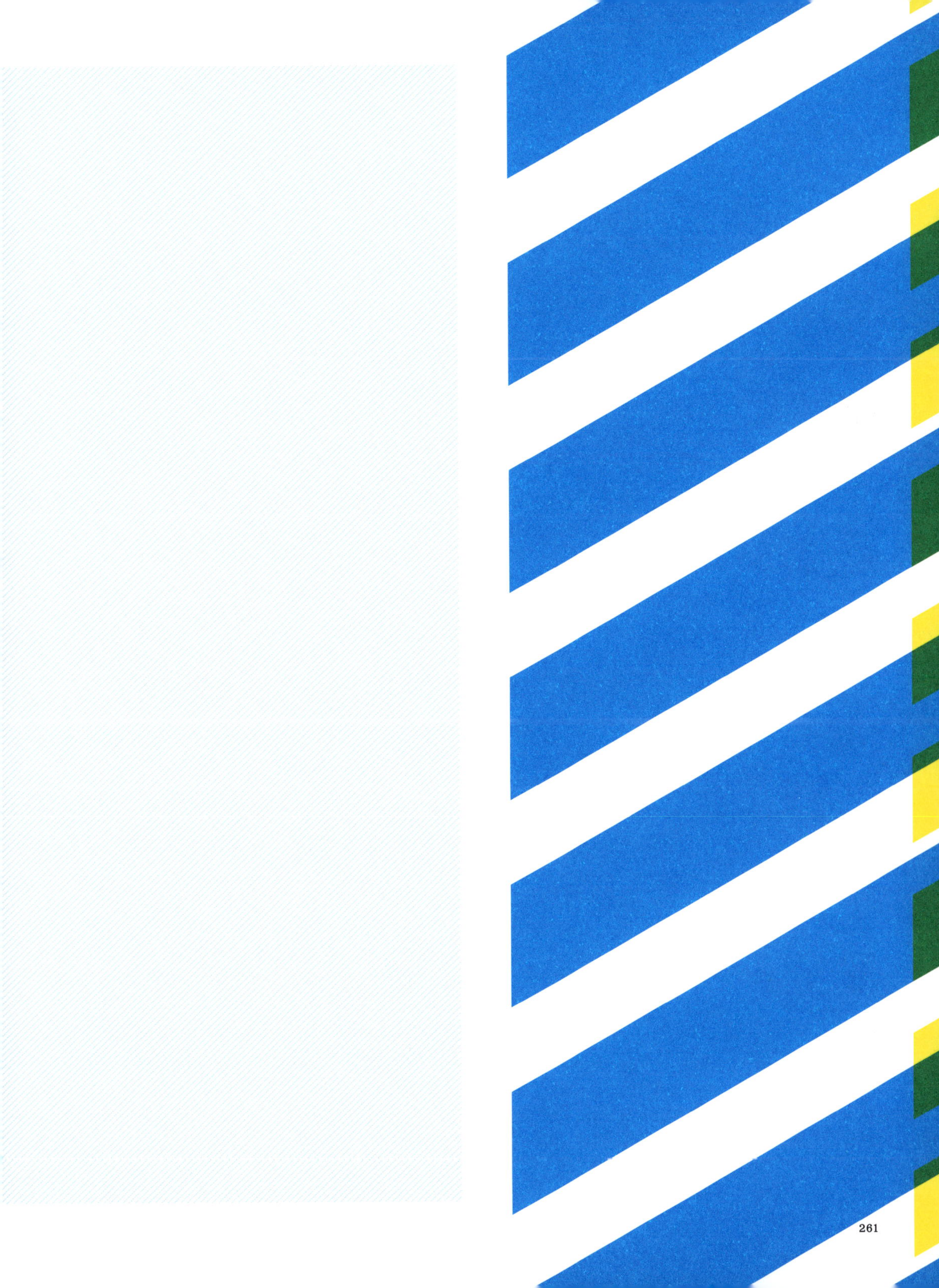

Africa, with its 30.5 million square kilometres (Sudan's 2.5 million at one end of the scale and the Seychelles, with barely 455, at the other) starts out, if you pay any attention to what the vast majority of the media says about it, with a negative and increasingly disturbing diagnosis in which all the bad news that the concept of emergencies implies is concentrated. Without dwelling on its enormous diversity and wealth of natural resources, what immediately stands out is that practically the whole of the continent is off the map, as if the eyes of the rest of the world were selfishly protected by a veil drawn over its very existence, except for those occasions, unfortunately all too frequent, when a catastrophe or a new outbreak of violence takes place.

Its internal development usually goes unnoticed by world-wide public opinion, which always tends to think of it exclusively as a source of raw materials, essential to sustaining the economies of the most developed countries, and as a focal point of disease (the infant mortality rate is 15 times greater than the European average), insecurity, famine, corruption, intolerance, totalitarianism and never-ending violence. In short, a view that attempts to hide, in vain, firstly the historical responsibilities of colonisation and subsequent decolonisation, planned in accordance with the interests of the respective colonial capitals, and then to carry on exploiting its considerable natural resources without scruple.

It is true that, to a great extent, this image corresponds to the truth – it is the only continent where statistics persist in reflecting a level of economic welfare that is lower today than it was twenty years ago, and it is also a fact that the prime responsibility for the current situation falls on the shoulders of the governments of African countries. But it is also true that Africa is on the move, trying to overcome its deficiencies through its own strengths, and that the International Community, or rather, the West, owes a substantial, longstanding and solemn debt to this vast continent, which ought to translate into a far more direct involvement in the search for a way out, in order to ensure a worthwhile and sustainable future for all its inhabitants.

A look back into the past

Even today it is easy to see the deep and disturbing mark inflicted by a colonisation process carried out by several European powers over the greater part of the 19th and 20th centuries, with England and France leading the way, followed at some considerable distance by Belgium, Italy, Spain and even Germany.

When history made decolonisation inevitable, some of these powers still had the reflexive urge to prepare for their departure in such a way as to reduce the impact that the loss of these territories could have on their economies, thus giving birth to the 'French Union' and the 'British Commonwealth'. In any case, most African countries finally set out on the path to independence only after the Bandung Conference of 1955, taking advantage of the window of opportunity presented by the Non-Aligned Movement that emerged from that meeting.

We find ourselves, therefore, facing a continent that is the last to complete its structure as a group of sovereign States, in a birth process that was accompanied on many an occasion by inter-ethnic conflicts – Kenya and the Congo, as typical examples, or by wars against the old powers, Angola and Mozambique against Portugal, or Algeria against France. On the whole, a quick glance at the African political map shows quite clearly the colonisers' total lack of concern for indigenous feelings and realities, which resulted in their drawing up totally artificial borders, condemning groups who had nothing in common to live together within the same nation. And so, right from the beginning, were sown the seeds of a breeding ground for the constant tensions and internal clashes that have come to characterise the recent history of Africa, with their vain attempts to square the circle of clan, ethnic and religious realities totally at odds with the new reality.

As if that were not enough, one cannot avoid mentioning one last example of colonisation/intervention, staged by the South Africa of 'apartheid', which managed to impose internal supremacy over the country's black population through the creation of the sadly infamous 'homelands' (Bantustans), and which tried to dominate new and weak countries like Angola or Namibia through direct military intervention.

In short, a bad start to a process that, ever since and with the usual exceptions, has done nothing other than to exacerbate dismal socio-economic underdevelopment and structural instability imposed forcibly through coups d'état and totalitarian governments, determined to take advantage of their power for their own gain and to the detriment of their people.

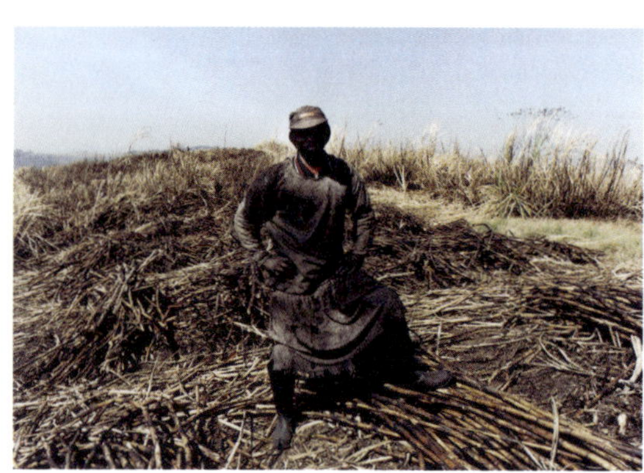 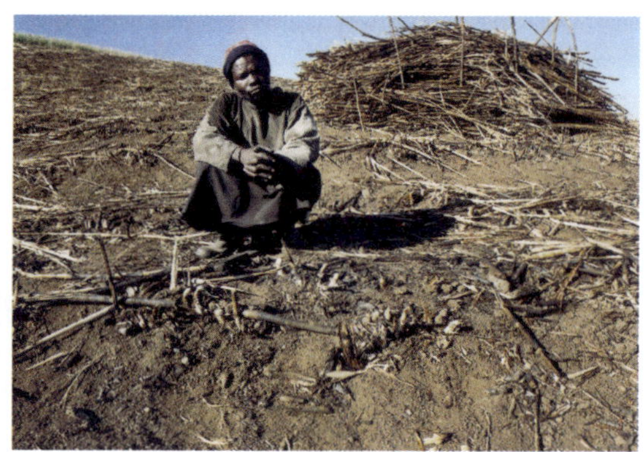

Zwelethu Mthethwa
"Untitled", from the series *Sugarcane*, 2003
Colour photograph
150 x 194 cm

"Untitled", from the series *Sugarcane*, 2003
Colour photograph
150 x 194 cm

"Untitled", from the series *Sugarcane*, 2003
Colour photograph
150 x 194 cm

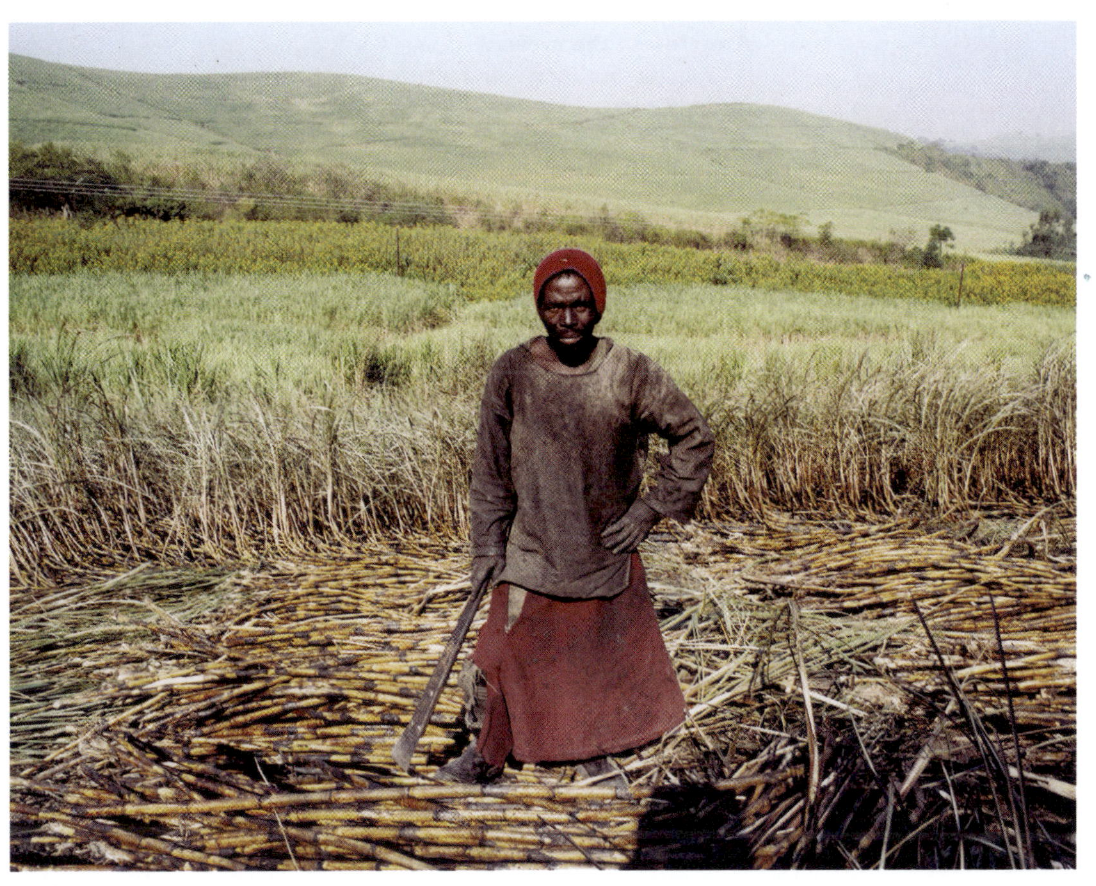

A review of the present

Fault lines are an intrinsic feature of every defining aspect of this oft-ravaged land. They exist internally in every country, bringing confrontation to communities that still are unable to find ways of living together in peace within the framework of a common national territory. These fault lines are also to be found between neighbours, with border claims and permanently unresolved grievances that on many an occasion give rise to armed conflict. And they can also be seen around that immense internal frontier, the Sahara Desert. The feelings towards Africa of those countries that lie to the north of that world of sand are very lukewarm and their aspirations tend to be aimed more towards a greater rapprochement with their neighbours in the European Union, or, somewhat half-heartedly, they play the card of belonging to the great Arab-Muslim family, with its ideal of one day becoming a united political entity. On the other hand, the countries to the south are those that more properly represent the reality of Africa, even though this does not mean, at least up until now, that they share any realistic joint projects.

Broadly speaking, what has come to characterise the continent today is a variety of factors that for the most part are highly problematic, for very different social, economic and political reasons. Essentially, and taking as a point of reference the fact that a total of 32 of the 35 countries in the world with a Human Development Index of lower than 0.50 are African, the following points should be stressed:

• Fortunately, and showing considerable political intelligence, African leaders decided at the time that it was not advisable to reopen the issue of the definition of national borders. It was assumed, despite their undeniable imperfections, that it was better to keep them as they were, while making every effort to foster the processes of integration within the framework of each one of the new states. Doing anything else would have meant fuelling local tensions even more, and as a result, creating a climate of greater instability, which in turn could easily degenerate into violence that would prove disastrous for everyone in the end. Although the process cannot be regarded as having been brought to a conclusion once and for all, there is nothing to indicate that possible future changes – the case of Sudan could come soonest – need necessarily involve a new armed conflict.

Despite that, in the last 50 years, Africa has suffered 35 armed confrontations (quite a number of them still unresolved), which have claimed more than ten million lives, and created a wave of some twenty million refugees and displaced persons.

• Underrepresented on the international scene, and in the expectation that the future reform of the United Nations will allow them to have a permanent member on the Security Council, many of the 51 African states are still going through a phase of internal consolidation, while regional relations have still not overcome the palpable feeling of general distrust. This has prevented them from reaching a joint agreement as to which one should be recognised as the continent's representative. It has also put a stop to the consolidation of regional integration processes, while it is hoped that the newly created African Union will demonstrate greater ability than the now defunct Organisation for African Unity (set up in 1963).

• In general terms, and despite the efforts coming from different directions, not one of the African economies occupies a position of importance on the international scene, and none of their companies, apart from those closely involved in the direct exploitation of their raw materials, with hydrocarbons in first place, is known in international markets. To a great extent, they continue to conform to the model of mono-cultural economies – Senegal with its peanut crop, the Ivory Coast with cocoa, or Libya, Algeria and Nigeria with oil and gas – with a weak private sector and, on the contrary, an omnipresent, inefficient and, all too often, corrupt public sector. And yet the latter has become the leading producer of goods and services within the framework of excessively protected economies, and the leading provider of employment.

• To this day there is a remarkable lack of political progress in the majority of these states – the examples of democracy taking root are still very limited, and only a few have succeeded in joining the select group that includes Botswana, Ghana, Namibia, the Comoro Islands and South Africa. A sense of nationhood is not widespread. As a result, personal identity is mainly defined in terms of belonging

The 'Gacaca'

When thinking back to the terrible genocide in Rwanda (800,000 victims), one cannot overlook the shameful behaviour of an international community that failed to react to the alarm signals being sent out by that country, and even though various actors were fully aware of them, they remained impassive in the face of what was about to happen and what finally did happen. Today, ten years later and without too much support from outside, Rwandans are still working hard to complete the reconciliation process. Many of the countless women who were raped have participated in various group therapy programmes and now say that they want to learn to read and write, while their children are a true reflection of the fact that the bitterness has gradually been subsiding.

For its part, the National Commission for Unity and Reconciliation has set itself as objectives the restoration of human dignity and reconciliation between former rivals. This Commission tries to promote discussion and other activities that facilitate the participation of the population in an endeavour to detect the latent causes of possible conflicts. At the same time, it has been the driving force behind an anti-discrimination law.

One of the best-known ways of achieving success, in terms of both results and the use of a custom that is traditional, and therefore more readily accepted by Rwandans, is the 'Gacaca'. This is the name given to the traditional trials that are held in villages and in which the responsibilities of the guilty and the penalties they must

pay are decided, without further reference to higher authorities and running parallel to the official judicial system. In this way they act as both a means of reconciliation between enemies and a method of bringing justice to the victims. This was what Jean de Dieu Cyiza, among many others, experienced, having admitted that he had taken part in the genocide, killing the children of his Tutsi brother and justifying his actions as the result of pressure by soldiers who made him do it to save his own life. On the day that he was released from jail, and as a preliminary step before starting a new life alongside his erstwhile neighbours, he was judged again by the 'Gacaca' in the preliminary, yet final, step that would confirm his rehabilitation and acknowledgement of blame.

to a clan, a tribe, or an ethnic or religious community, rather than to a state that is considered largely unrepresentative (examples of kingdoms that have already disappeared, such as the 'Ashanti' or 'Yoruba' in present-day Ghana or the 'Merina' in Madagascar are still exceptions to the general rule).

Africa is where the majority of so-called 'fragile states' are to be found. This concept defines those that have not really reached the point of consolidating their authority throughout their territory, including their inability to demonstrate the presence of a monopoly of force, and that have not managed to adequately address the basic needs of a large part of the population. It should therefore come as no surprise that the average life expectancy at birth is barely 46 years in Sub-Saharan Africa (with Zambia at only 32.7), given that the annual per capita income is less than €1500. Indeed, in countries such as Nigeria, Zambia, Burundi, Mali and Niger more than 85% of their inhabitants have less than two dollars a day.

• Furthermore, the state apparatus, rather than existing to serve the citizen, acts as the machinery that serves the interests of the elite who control political power, which usually guarantees that they will also benefit from the exploitation of national resources and wealth. In fact, although officially the democratic process is slowly making progress, there is a long way to go before these values take root in the continent as a whole. Meanwhile, authoritarianism, patronage, and appropriation of the national patrimony by the State for the benefit of the few, not to mention recourse to force to achieve specific ends, continue to define the reality of the situation in many cases.

• The situation is not much better on the social front. A situation of rising instability is the result of a combination of factors: high demographic growth - the population has already reached 860 million, whereas it stood at only 200 million in 1950, and the forecast for 2025 is 1,300 million: a significant rural exodus and an unstoppable urban build-up, against a background of lack of basic necessities in education, health, housing and employment, in a population that is characterised by the extremely high percentage of people below the age of twenty.

• Equally important is the growing pressure of migration which, as much in the North of Africa as in the rest of the continent, speaks for itself regarding the scant expectations that life offers a marginalised and excluded population in their places of origin – inequality and instability are the keywords. Of the continent's population, 43% is concentrated in Nigeria, with its 134 million inhabitants, Egypt, Ethiopia, the Democratic Republic of Congo and South Africa. Although a first reading of this phenomenon might make one think that these export flows of human resources could perhaps shift a heavy burden from these countries, unable as they are to cover their basic requirements, it becomes evident that this is in fact a haemorrhage that weakens to an even greater extent those societies from which the most able flee.

• The processes of literacy teaching and universal education are accelerating, but are still not enough to provide new generations with the basic tools for surviving with dignity in the context of a globalised world in which they have to make their way - the adult literacy level hovers around 63%, although Burkina Faso, Mali and Niger are less than 30%. Similar trends, although incomplete in the majority of cases, can be observed in fields such as health and hygiene. Although the AIDS pandemic, not to mention other scourges like malaria or tuberculosis, continue to cut short the lives of 6,000 people a day across the continent, there have been notable improvements that have given rise to an increase in life expectancy as compared to previous periods. Advances have also been made in the fight against discrimination against women, with policies that run from birth control programmes to the promotion of their integration into public social life, their access to salaried employment, and even their inclusion in political life.

• Shortcomings are evident across the board. To take an example, one only has to remember that, in addition to suffering from a structural problem of food shortages that, to a greater or a lesser extent, affect virtually the whole continent, there is the added problem of famine, occurring with increasing frequency, which adds to the number of deaths – to the everlasting shame of a world that is capable of providing enough food for the entire population of the planet. It is for this reason that it could be said that, properly speaking, hunger is a weapon of mass destruction that attacks too many African countries in a particularly brutal way.

• Finally, the diversity of language and the fragmentation arising from people belonging to different religions (with 33% Christians of whom 16.5% are Catholics, 40% Muslims and the remainder belonging to a multiplicity of traditional faiths), all within the borders of states that tend to be somewhat insensitive to the rights of minorities, are additional factors that go to make up this overall picture of disintegration and constant disagreements. These are certainly the seeds that give rise to tensions, if not to outbreaks of violence of varying intensity.

Is there a future around the corner?
Although everyday life strives to heap tragedy upon tragedy, as if it were necessary once and for all to crush those who refuse to accept that so much misfortune has to be borne by the inhabitants of this oft-forgotten land, Africa still insists on sending out signs of vitality and hope. Is it not ironic to say that Africa has still not lost its smile, despite everything that has been said so far? Not at all. While not having a clear understanding of the reasons – at least from the standpoint of opulent Western societies, for whom it seems that happiness

can only be derived from the incessant accumulation of possessions – the fact is that Africa is still smiling, and showing signs of activity and the desire to get better. It is far from succumbing to misfortune and to the combined effect of so many undesirable rulers and of an international community whose actions fall far short of meeting its potential, or upholding the values and principles that it says it is defending, or its responsibilities.

This is borne out by those who have assumed responsibility for tasks that in theory the State should be taking care of. Such groups would include the indigenous communities who undertake the installation of hydraulic pumps, or the reforestation of the Sahel, or the 'Nana Benz' of Togo, matrons who head up their own companies, driving around in Mercedes and who evoke the image of business women and traders.

At the political level, hope is now focused on the expectations generated by the start-up of the African Union and by the possibilities arising from NEPAD (The New Partnership for Africa's Development). Well aware of their individual weakness and their position of subordination to the great Western powers, the history of intra-African relations is plagued by as many attempts at integration as more or less resounding failures. The list of acronyms of multilateral organisations is bewildering, although they only conceal political conventionality with no real life, not to mention attempts by the former colonial powers to remain in control. From ECA (Economic Commission for Africa) to EAC (Eastern African Community), and on to SACU (the Southern Africa Customs Union), SADCC (Southern African Development Coordination Conference), CEAO (West African Economic Community, within the French sphere of influence), ECOWAS (its British equivalent), UDEAC (Central African Customs and Economic Union) and so many others that represent nothing of the Africa of today.

It is clear that the future of the continent lies in the hands of its peoples, its governments and its economic institutions, but without external support it will not be possible for it to get back on its feet. To start with, this support must involve demonstrating the political will to ease the burden of the load that weighs so heavily on the shoulders of these countries, especially in the case of an unmanageable and, in many cases, unpayable external debt. In some countries it is a question of considering the pure and simple pardoning of accumulated debt, whereas in others a restructuring will be necessary for development, for investment or for increased public expenditure in basic sectors. In short, a more attractive selection of schemes than those devised up until now, including those presented by the G-8 to the highly indebted poor countries, in which Africa is for once over-represented. However, these schemes should not overlook the advisability of including clauses of political conditionality that favour the emergence of societies that are more just, more sustainable and more open.

At the same time, it also involves committing greater and more sustained financial support. Is it necessary to remind ourselves that the group of donor countries, among which are obviously the European Union and the United States, keeps slipping further away from the already mythical target of dedicating 0.7% of their Gross Domestic Product to the underprivileged nations, a figure that is currently hovering around a paltry 0.23%? The commitment to Africa's future, which is also our future, demands a far greater percentage in aid. Only through fair trade rules that do not penalise the agricultural products of these countries and allow them to have free access to the most developed markets, and through a fundamental reform of the current international financial architecture and a transfer of real technology, amongst other things, will it be possible to break the spiral of underdevelopment that, unfortunately, has already become an image of Africa that is not questioned and does nothing to mobilise those who can help to improve it.

It also depends on you
The enormity of the task that Africans face if they are to emerge from the shadows where they have been hidden for so long requires everyone's participation. Whether it be out of altruism and solidarity, or historical shame, or intelligent self-interest – based on an understanding that their development and security are also ours, we are all being summoned to put our shoulders to the wheel.

This summons is not made exclusively to states and international organisations, but rather is also aimed at every individual who is aware of and interested in the emergence of a better world. Africa is the acid test of active multilateralism, of conflict prevention and of the political will to change the basics of an extremely unequal system, which condemns one set of people to be underdeveloped so that others, we others, may be developed.

As citizens of open and democratic societies we have the ability to exercise our rights to elect such representatives as will undertake the mission of contributing to a better world, and to put pressure on them to adopt positive measures towards Africa. At the same time, as consumers, we can bring decisive influence to bear on certain types of corporate behaviour and on some of the inequitable rules of the game that apply to trade at present. We can refuse to consume certain products – whether chocolate that uses cocoa substitutes or those products that do not meet specific criteria to do with working conditions, thus preventing the subhuman exploitation of workers without rights – and we can demand of others that they tighten up the rules of the game in favour of fair and sustainable trade.

Document prepared by researchers from the
Institute of Studies on Conflicts and Humanitarian Action (IECAH)
Madrid, January 2005

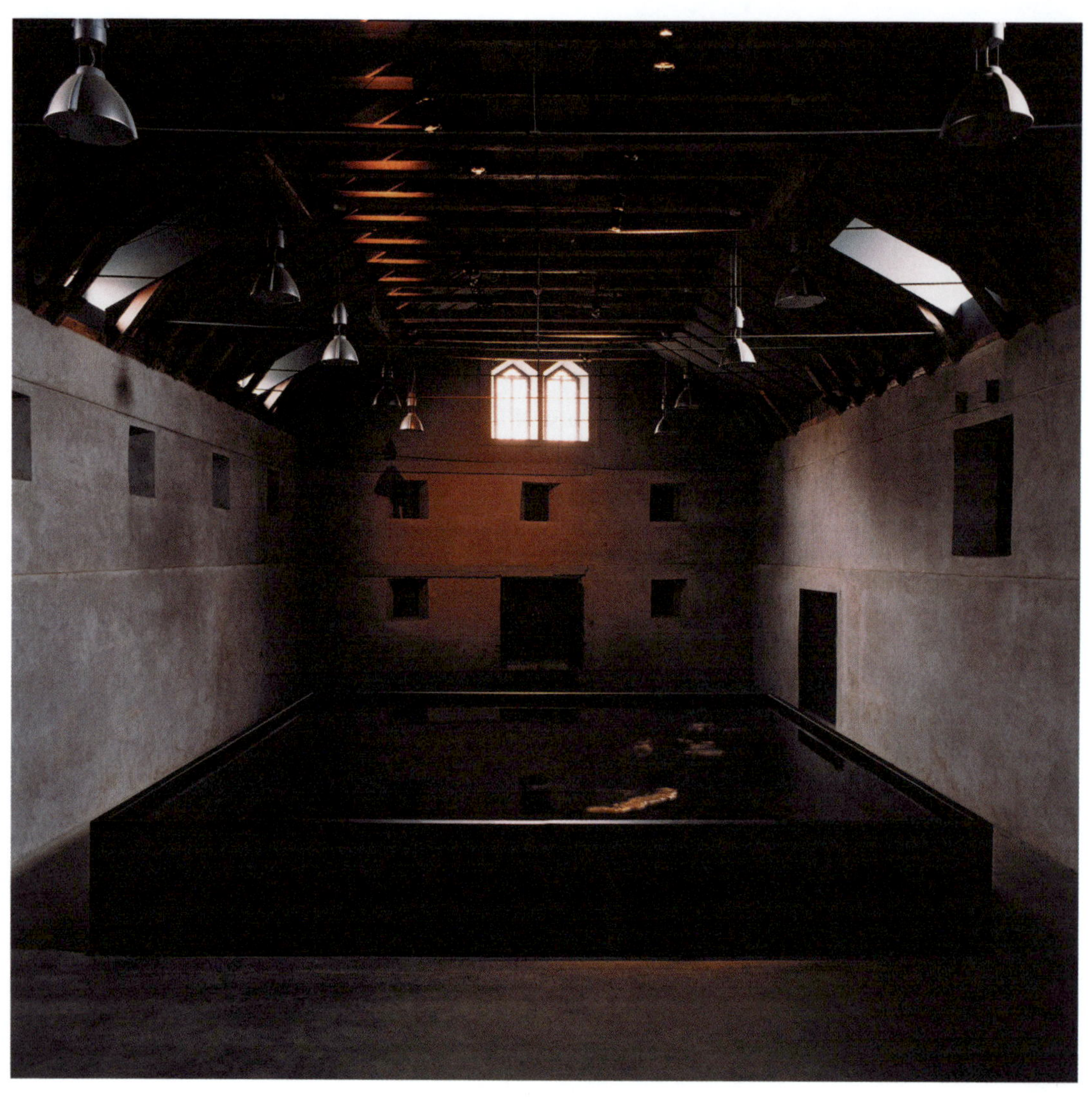

Alfredo Jaar
Emergency, 1998
Installation consisting of a metallic pool
with water and a fibreglass model
750 x 700 x 90 cm

272

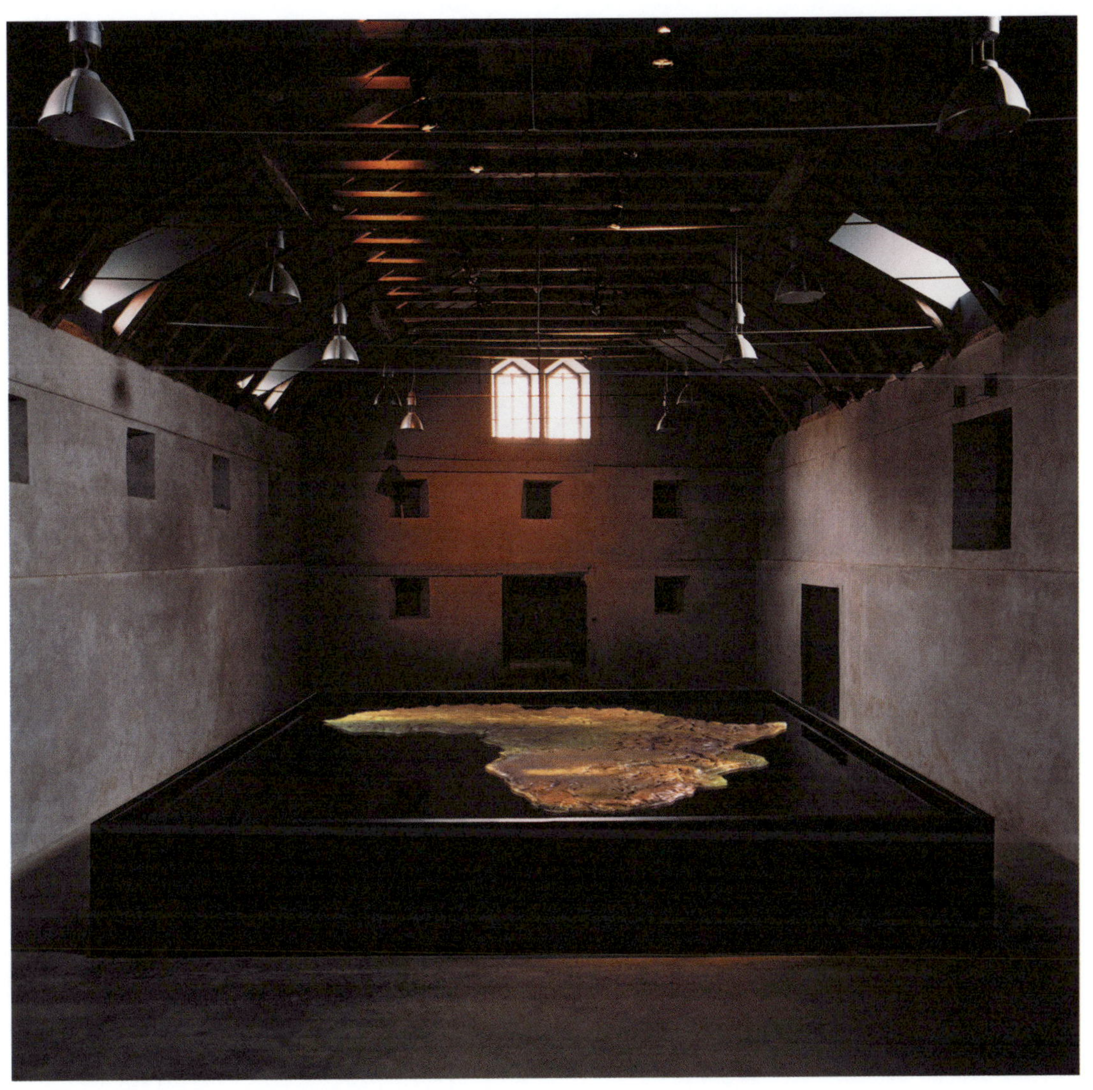

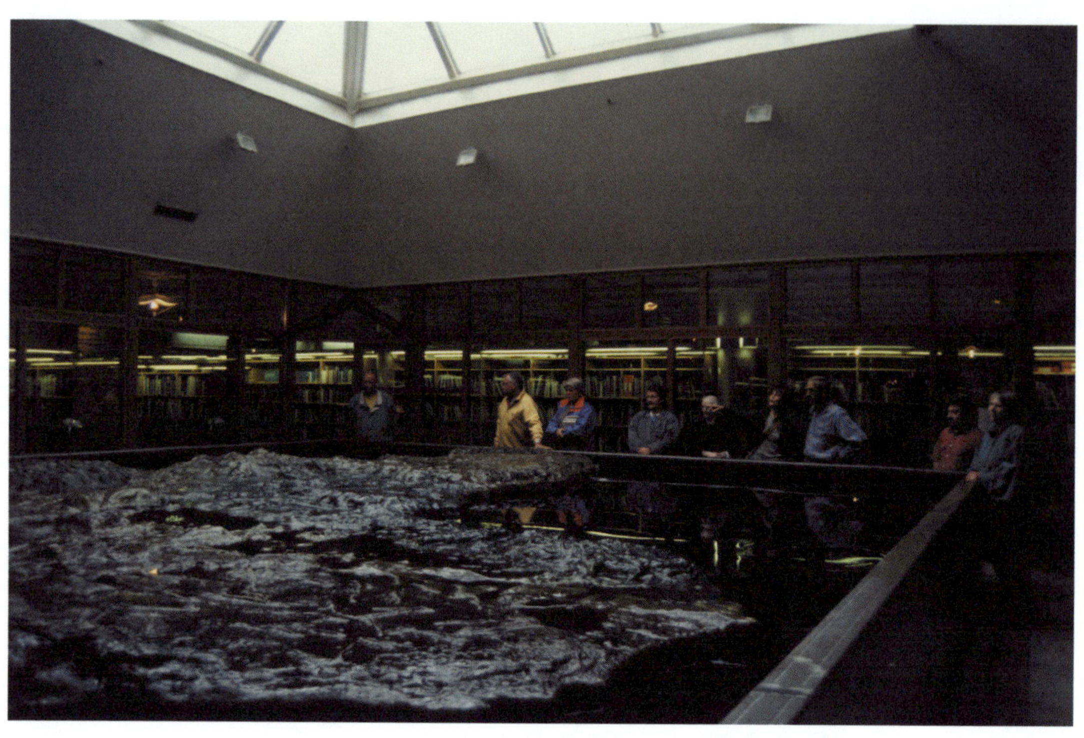

Alfredo Jaar
To Think, to Create, to Resist

Emergency. For an artist, utopia is being alive in today's world. How do you go about making art in a world like the one in which we live? How do you make art based on the information most of us would prefer to ignore? Emergency. For an artist, utopia is having to live in a world like today's. If, as Anatole France thought, utopia is the principle of all progress, how do you progress today in the midst of an unbearable reality? The answer is very simple: you lie, because without lies, as France himself said, humanity would die of despair. And he added: it is essential to rise up on the wings of enthusiasm, for if you were to reason, you would never fly. This reminds me of Gramsci in his cell, who, while writing about the pessimism of intelligence, proposed countering it with the optimism of will. Emergency. How to be an optimist today? Where to get the will to be optimistic? Can one be a utopian optimist? Emergency. The African continent currently suffers from political, economic and cultural abandonment by the rest of the international community; an abandonment that can only be considered criminal. Emergency. How many critical images, how many statistical figures, how many words of analysis, how many reports are needed to spark a reaction of solidarity? Emergency. Utopia is the design of a better future; as Chinua Achebe says, art is the constant effort of the human being to create a different reality from the one he is given. That constant effort is what permits creativity. A living culture is a culture that creates. Emergency. Create to live. Create to resist. Emergency. And yet, is there an aesthetics of resistance? How can you resist culturally? Emergence. Culture is resistance. To think, to create, to resist, said Deleuze. Let us repeat it endlessly: to think, to create, to resist. Emergency. To think, to create, to resist. Emergency. To think, to create, to resist…

Further reading

AMIN, S (1994): *El fracaso del desarrollo en África y en el tercer mundo: un análisis político*, Madrid, IEPALA.
BALTA, P. (1990): *Le grand Maghreb. Des indépendences à l'an 2000*, Paris, La Découverte.
GANIAGE, J. (1994): *Histoire contemporaine du Maghreb du 1830 à nos jours*, Paris, Fayard.
INIESTA, F. (2004): *Kuma, Historia del África negra*, Bellaterra, Barcelona.
LEMARCHAND, P. (2000): *Atlas de África*, Madrid, Acento Editorial.
MIEJE, J.L (1975): *Expansión europea y descolonización de 1870 a nuestros días*, Barcelona.
PALACIOS, R. (2003): *40 días en África un viaje en pos de la magia*, Madrid, Entrelíneas.
PEÑAS, F.J. (2000): *África en el sistema internacional: cinco siglos de frontera*, Madrid, Catarata.
PUJOLLE, T. (1995): *El África Negra*, Madrid, Debate.
RIDAO, J.M. (2000): *La desilusión permanente I "África Violenta y desconocida"*, Madrid.

Websites of interest

- African News Agency: http://www.afrol.com
- Mundo negro: una venta ventana abierta a África: http://www.mundonegro.com
- AlertNet Foundation: http://www.alertnet.org
- African Union: http://www.africa-union.org
- UNICEF: http://www.unicef.org

Basic statistics:
Population density

Peoples

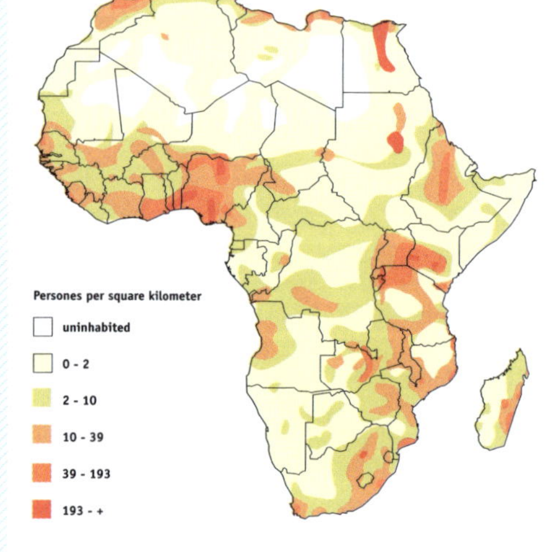

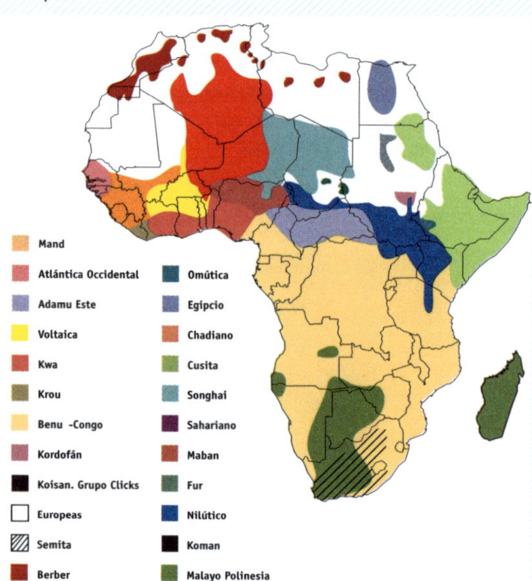

Source: mundonegro.com

Oil	Natural Gas	Diamonds
Tunisia, Gabon, Benin, Angola, Algeria, Libya, Cameroon, Chad, D.R. Congo, Ivory Coast, Egypt, Sudan, Equatorial Guinea, Nigeria	Algeria, Congo, Libya, Nigeria	Angola, Ghana, Central African Republic, Botswana, D.R. Congo, Ivory Coast, Guinea, Liberia, Namibia, Nigeria, Sierra Leone, South Africa, Tanzania

Source: mundonegro.com

Languages

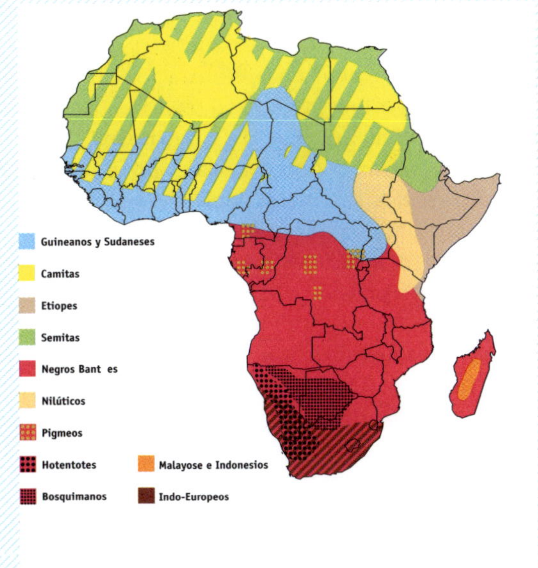

If the Chinese are sincere when, as a sign of good portent, they wish us 'difficult and exciting times' then we who live now are truly fortunate! For the world it has befallen us to live in, suffer and enjoy is anything but easy or insipid. We have been witnesses to the ending of an epoch in all senses and we are now immersed in the emergence of another, as yet unnamed and barely definable. It behoves us, not only as simple observers, but fundamentally as leading players, to collaborate in the emergence of what must be a framework of multiple relations adapted to the global character of our small planet.

There is no way back. Globalisation is a fact that we can not resist, though we can, and should, play our part in making this feature of our present-day reality truly transversal and equitable. At the moment, and to the despair of many, globalisation is acting in a profoundly unequal way and generating new forms of exclusion. Thus far, the advances applied in the transport, telecommunications or computer sectors have allowed some people to reap ever-greater benefits from an international financial and commercial system that has set aside traditional notions of time and space, a system that functions on a round-the-clock basis and on a global scale. For others, however, this same process has meant their definitive marginalistion. It has also become evident that the gulf in terms of inequality between rich and poor, between developed and underdeveloped, or between the included and the excluded, not only continues to grow, but is also opening up in new fields. The yawning digital gap is, perhaps, the most recent sign of the negative effects that this particular type of globalisation is producing.

However, the Chinese, with their visionary capacity, when creating the ideogram for the word 'crisis', included two distinct concepts: danger and opportunity. Danger since every crisis situation contains risks and the possibility of negative effects that lead to suffering. Opportunity in the sense that every crisis brings with it the possibilities of transformation that flow from positive changes. As a consequence, without losing sight of the threats, a situation such as that we are living through now should also be seen as offering a series of opportunities that allow the emergence of new ideas and new ways of responding to the challenges of the present.

A dose of realism, but without desperation

These first notes should not, then, lead us to curse globalisation, nor to yearn for a return to some supposedly natural paradise in which all of us would see all our hopes and desires fulfilled. For the human creatures we are, as social animals, are in fact the most artificial beings on the planet. We are the product of our efforts to improve on the primitive natural state and this process of separation can not be slowed, let alone reversed, in order to recover some idyllic moment in our history that, in fact, never existed. Now, as on so many other occasions in the past, we are living on the crest of a wave that could hurl us against a wall, or carry us forward into some new state of planetary coexistence. The only thing that has changed is the magnitude of the possible crash, or the strength of the forward momentum.

We are, probably, the first generation to have held in our hands the real possibility of destroying all signs of life on the planet – the weapons of mass destruction are still sitting there. But we also have the possibility of meeting the basic needs of every man, woman and child on Earth, allowing human life and dignity to be truly synonymous on a universal scale.

It seems likely that those who lived through the Renaissance, so highly valued now, were not aware of the profound changes that were taking place in front of their very eyes. The everyday problems and that permanent, and positive, sensation of insufficiency that drives us to incessantly improve instead of resting on our laurels, must surely have provoked an unease that found expression in thousands of different ways. The same thing is surely happening to us who happen to be the occupants of the Earth at this time. Occupied, and preoccupied with resolving the problems that confront us on a daily basis, perhaps we still have not come to terms with the repercussions of the collapse of a model that defined much of the last century, shaping every aspect of life. And even less have we had the chance to identify the lines that are currently taking shape and which will, with an equally historic mission, shape the century we are now entering. The quantity and speed of events, and the perception that we have no compass to show us unequivocally which direction to move in, might go some way to explaining both our evident disorientation and the exhausting tendency to follow every new fad – without even realising that many of them are simply rushed rehashes of those of the past.

We need a system of reference – even if only to situate ourselves on its margin, or to oppose it postulates – in order to guide the steps we take, both individually and collectively. While we are searching for this system, or perhaps constructing it, and leaving aside the eternal debate as to whether the glass is half full or half empty, we can at least recognise that never have we been so well off as now – above all if we are looking from the perspective offered by a developed country. Yet it is also true that never have the differences been so marked between the two extremes of the spectrum of human development. Above all, though, we have to face the fact that what has been achieved falls far short of meeting both the necessities and our aspirations, in consonance with our values and principles, for a world that is really fairer, safer, more generous and more sustainable.

If we charge ourselves with the task of creating this better world, and deny ourselves any escapist flights of fantasy, we should begin by demanding of a dose of realism that would force us to face up to what we are, and to the world that, all together, we are constructing. What is evident is that, today, anyone who wants to know what is happening has plenty of ways to find out. We can no longer hide behind the impossibility of our knowing, just as we can no longer claim that what we do – be it art, science or entertainment – is aseptic or non-political. Is it necessary to insist that everything we do, both individually and collectively, is, in essence political? Obviously, we can choose the direction we wish our lives to take, with levels of commitment that, depending on the limitations placed on us in our early lives, will be more dedicated to some fields than to others. But we can not adduce in our defence that we were not aware of what was happening or that we did not think our actions could have this or that consequence. Self-deception, as an attempt to exempt us of responsibility, or as a response to our supposed marginal position with respect to this process, or even when used to blame ourselves excessively, is increasingly out of place.

On the other hand, we have more than enough evidence to enable us to understand that this model of globalisation is not taking us where we want to go. As highlighted in the annual reports of the international agencies of the United Nations and various non-governmental organisations, and without this leading to an outcry in most cases, the turn of the century has not meant a lightening of the outlook nor a positive change in direction. Like quack doctors, the international organisations have become specialists in diagnosing ills but rarely come up with the right treatment. As reflected in greater detail in the preceding chapters, our world is becoming characterised by disparate levels of development. These differences widen and deepen the fractures that separate a small portion of the planet's population, basically identified with the western world, from the immense majority who are sloughed in misery. However, at the same time it is vitally necessary to recognise that within the privileged developed world there are also outstanding cases of exclusion and that, in the opposite sense, in the developing world there are also notorious islands of wealth. The relevance of the visionary phrase "other worlds exist, but this is the one we inhabit" is reinforced constantly.

But our world can also be characterised by an absence, for some a scandalous absence, of adequate reactions. We have an up-to-date diagnosis of the main problems and fractures that beset the planet; therefore, if we do not act, it is not for a lack of information but rather for a lack of will to do so. It is true that we do not always have available to us all the knowledge necessary to deal with the complexity of some questions – be it the connection between marginalisation and violence, the deteriorating environment or a cure for AIDS. But what we do already know should be enough to set off the alarms and make us start to respond with solid, effective measures, drawing on all the enormous resources accumulated over time by individuals, groups, nations and the international community. What the situation requires is that we activate what we have available to us to forestall, as far as possible, a radical, and possibly violent, breakdown of the international system.

The degree of instability and underdevelopment that exists is extremely worrying. On too many occasions we are startled by the outbreak of violence in different parts of the planet, in the form of local, regional or international emergencies. Behind the façade of this unleashed violence we come up, time and time again, against unresolved social, political and economic problems. The conflict breaks out as a consequence of poorly managed coexistence, that has its roots in questions that connect directly with one or other of the multiple varieties of discrimination, with the authoritarian exercising of power, with the monopolising of the use of resources, or with unjust economic, political or social measures imposed at different levels, from the local authorities to the international financial organisations.

In the case that the international community does decide to intervene, something that does not always occur, we confront what international-speak defines euphemistically as a complex emergency, when not faced with a military intervention in response to a situation of low, medium or high intensity armed conflict. Emergencies and conflicts that, with wearying frequency, end up becoming endemic, chronic, since attention is paid exclusively to addressing the more spectacular features, without any effort being made to redress the bases of socio-political and economic management models that are, in themselves, the underlying causes of the violence. Action in this terrain also seems to be directed at resolving short-term problems, ignoring that which since it does not appear on the surface is presumed to be inexistent.

In other words, together with the various local factors that might explain the fact that tensions give way to organised violence, this type of globalisation contributes powerfully to increasing the number of emergencies. Understanding these as the result of a threat or an accident, if we are talking of catastrophes or natural disasters, or of an event caused directly by human action, emergencies have become just one more element on the international agenda. For this to be so, it is necessary to accept them as inevitable, even though their frequency and increasing gravity should convince us that they are not as natural as they appear. It seems we are retreating into a time of mythological interpretations of disasters and emergencies, which were formerly presented as divine punishments or the revenge of nature. And thus it is possible to ignore the connection with other painful realities, the discrimination against women, the exploitation of children, the extreme vulnerability, poverty, hunger, pandemics, as if all these were not linked in any way whatsoever with a model as unequal as that of the existing form of globalisation.

It is shocking to realise, when it proves possible to activate some kind of response to resolve the most flagrant of these situations, that the existing model of globalisation continues to work according to reactive principles. It prefers to act *a posteriori* and only addressing the symptoms. It mobilises great surges of human solidarity or resources that were already available – but without ever losing sight of the fundamental principle that defines the first priority as being the defence of private interests. There is no questioning of the model, which well serves the interests of the most powerful, be they States, ruling parties, social or economic groupings, and the only preoccupation that can be detected is that of keeping up-to-date the means of reacting that safeguard these very same interests. In other words, it is taken for granted that, at some moment or another, there will be a fire. The only thing it is necessary to do is to ensure that our fire brigades are well equipped, while not ruling out disinterested collaboration that might be offered by citizens. But it does not occur to us to ask ourselves if we might not be responsible for the fire and whether it might not be possible to eliminate the causes that lead to it breaking out.

Meanwhile, the pro-active strategies, those that pay attention to the underlying causes that might generate the emergencies, are left very much in the background. Not because they are less effective, for it seems likely that they would be just the opposite, but rather because they do not fit comfortably with the dominant forms of action. In part, because bringing them centre-stage would require the modifying of the tried and tested rules of the game, rules that to date have allowed us, in general terms, to protect our interests. It might even seem comprehensible that there is no wish to change direction so long as the existing system fulfils its function. On the other hand, the reticence to consider the preventative focus can be understood as responding to the fact that visible results would only be achieved in the long term. This flatly contradicts our accelerated way of life, which demands immediate results. It also runs counter to a political agenda that is characterised by the short term and by the search for results that can be 'sold' immediately by those responsible for achieving them as a central element in their strategy for remaining in power.

In this way, we have even taken on a certain complacency convincing ourselves that we, the citizens of the developed North, are the most generous. In fact, we simply react compulsively when the images of horror and emergency exceed the threshold of that which we have come to accept as 'normal'. And yet, our supposed solidarity is not activated to the same extent when it comes to supporting preventative measures, or long term processes; in short, when it comes to preventing the emergencies.

While we continue to ask ourselves whether the existing model of control and domination is valid in order to maintain our interests or whether, in contrast, it would be better to undertake a thorough reform of it, the process of globalisation continues its rapid advance. Yet, its direction is not predetermined by any single factor outside our control. The key, then, is not to set out to slow its progress – something probably impossible to achieve and even counterproductive – but rather to avoid, in the first instance, that it gets out of control and subsequently, to redirect it and extend it to other ambits.

To advance an example in this sense, we might make a brief mention of human rights. At present, and despite the legal instruments that protect them, it is a fact that they are systematically violated in many places and that they are under attack from two different directions. On one hand, there still exist many political regimes for which the Universal Declaration of Human Rights is nothing more than a barely relevant document, and one that can conveniently be denounced as just one more product of western neo-colonialism, in order to better defend themselves against their critics. On the other, these instruments are very often only activated in order to justify a decision that runs counter to the interests of a particular government. This instrumentalising transmits an image of double standards. The appeal to respect human rights does not respond to principles to which no exceptions should be admitted, but rather to the designs of international policies that urge the international community, in some cases, to look away, subordinating human rights to the defence of an ally. It should also be added that, within the dynamics of the 'war against terror', we are seeing a dangerous curtailing of rights and freedoms, even within the so-called developed countries. Security criteria are taking precedence over those of freedom and, in consequence, there is a tendency to reduce even further the level of commitment and demands for respect of human rights, an area that has always been precarious, and one in which no retreat should be admitted.

It would be good indeed, in this field, to bring about an effective globalisation of human rights, attending solely to those values and principles that correspond to this universal aspiration and breaking, in consequence, all cultural resistance and preventing any exceptionality. To do so, it will be necessary to draw on all the enormous potential of globalisation to establish human rights as a fundamental item on the global agenda. It is not a question, then, of less globalisation but rather of more, but of a different kind.

An emerging path that offers a way out

A quick glance at the different themes reflected in the preceding chapters could produce a feeling of discouragement or even of paralysing despair. The global situation is certainly bleak. This same bleakness gives rise to the sense of impotence, frustration, demoralisation or the loss of all hope. 'That's all there is', they tell us and we tell ourselves. And this is a very effective way of paralysing the spirit and aborting any possibility of reacting.

There will always be time for this and there will always be those who prefer to cling on to this vision that offers no way out. However, as is also shown in these same pages, the attempts to forge new paths – in parallel to, or in outright opposition to the existing models – are constant. Perhaps the only, though fundamental, element that all these have in common is their commitment to advancing by peaceful and negotiated means. The use of violence, even when directed at changing clearly unjust situations, would render illegitimate any alternative discourse or strategy. This would also be a step in the wrong direction, returning us to times in which the legitimate use of force would no longer be the prerogative of states, but rather would lie in the hands of the strongest. For this reason, the search for systems of global governance takes on a special importance, systems that must be based on the aspiration to resolve jointly the problems, which are also shared, that truly affect the inhabitants of this planet.

Most of the problems and realities dealt with in these pages are global, in the sense that in one way or another they affect all of us and the scope of the actions required goes beyond national boundaries. Constructing global frameworks to resolve these situations is, then, a fundamental task. However, we must accept that we do not have available a ready-made guide that will tell us how to advance. 'Peace is the way', said Gandhi. 'The path is made by walking' Machado reminded us.

Neither can we suppose that there will be a single player charged with carrying out such a complex job. We know we have a long history of constant advances and setbacks, from which we should learn so as not to repeat those errors that are already known. We also have available to us very many and very powerful social, political and economic instruments, well suited to dealing with problems that, as a whole, are rooted precisely in these very areas. And, finally, we have players of very different types, with the States and the multinational economic actors on the one hand, and the international organisations and the social actors – with the non-governmental organisations and other world movements being the most outstanding examples at present, on the other.

The former, nation states and economic players, have the ability to develop a strategy for dealing directly with the world's problems, since they can act without intermediaries on the variables that shape our world. Depending on their wishes or interests they can have a powerful influence, for good or for ill, modifying trends and producing direct socio-political and economic effects that have enormous repercussions for the population of the whole world. In their case, the key lies not in the availability of resources to respond, given that they have a good number of tools to intervene, too many even. The fundamental question is their willingness to modify the rules of a game that may well benefit their interests in the short term, deciding instead to adopt others that will continue to produce benefits for them – for otherwise we can never imagine that they will decide to try and change the model – though in a different way.

If the formula applied so far has paid almost no attention to 'others', focusing exclusively on guaranteeing private interests at all costs, the time has arrived to understand that personal gain can not be maintained at the expense of the suffering, exclusion and underdevelopment of great portions of the world's population. What the present requires urgently is the breaking of moulds – which are already showing signs of failure that are increasingly difficult to contain – that are based on the most naked selfishness. For it is necessary to understand that only through the global development of the planet as a whole can we think about an improvement in the position of those of us who, thus far, have enjoyed a privileged position.

The latter players, the international organisations and social agents, can only acting effectively within the framework of a strategy of indirect approximation. With their own forces, they can only partially resolve some very specific problems. But their true strength, where they accumulate a really enormous potential, is in their capacity to denounce and criticise the errors and the failures to honour the commitments made by the nation states and the economic players. They have the possibility of raising the consciousness, of sensitising and mobilising the citizens against mistaken policies or actions – whether it be on environmental, economic or, simply, human grounds – and, in this way, put pressure on governments and the multinational economic players in order to bring about a change in direction. Their true work, then, is to act as points of reference in the defence of universal principles and values and, at the same time, to draw up proposals that commit the international community to resolving problems that have been detected, pushing for responses to be made before these situations become unmanageable. If this is true for the international organisations, then it is also true that the social actors have a fundamental role to play in activating the political consciousness, as expressed through the ballot box, and in appealing to us as consumers, so that our actions incorporate criteria of global justice and sustainability that effectively force changes in direction on our governments and the multinational economic players. We are not yet in a condition to directly establish new norms of conduct, but we can exercise a powerful influence in the shaping of the new ground rules, an influence that will be felt to the extent that we are able to make our conviction about the necessity of change felt by those who have the levers of control in their hands.

In no sense is it a question of a battle between one group and another. The challenge exceeds the individual capacity of all of us, and no one is free from error. The key lies in uniting our efforts and our wills, though understanding that the citizens now have the option of playing a role as one more actor in this process. A citizenry that, as was suggested recently in the World Social Forum in Porto Alegre, favours the emergence of a planetary public space. Evidently, the emergence of this citizenry can only take place if it is a phenomenon that is marked by a cosmopolitan character, that transcends frontiers and globalises solidarity and the preoccupation with the 'other'.

This synergy between the most conscious and committed citizens and institutions that are more open to their participation, should be noted at both an international and a local level. Though the local might seem the clearest sphere for this type of expressions – as shown by the examples of the Participative Budgets, the recuperation of open councils or the citizen mobilisations – it is necessary to transcend this setting in order to achieve a planetary sense of citizen involvement, one that aspires to go beyond the ritual aspects of democracy and that is conscious of its ability to influence economic behaviour and regulations.

So far, the channelling of the citizens' thirst to participate in the addressing of public questions has tended to find its most natural form, its most visible form of expression, in the social movements, in that wide-ranging field that covers the voluntary organisations and, more recently, the NGOs. The existence of a 'third sector with a social content, set between the two great poles that are represented by the State and the market, has, in general, been welcomed as a beneficial reality for the working of modern societies.

On many occasions, this third sector demonstrates in its everyday activities and in its strategies a stronger vocation for defending that which is public than the State itself, even if only in its opposition to the existing process of dismantling the so-called 'welfare states'. As someone once suggestively stated, many of the otherwise diverse associations that comprise this third sector are 'privately public'. In many cases, their aims have more to do with achieving objectives that are beneficial for society as a whole than those of some States, which accept and promote the incessant cutting back of their responsibilities, especially in all that has to do with the provision of public services.

Thus the public-private dichotomy is undermined, with the rise of a strong voluntary sector being seen as a magnificent symptom of the excess of goodwill that every society that is healthy, or that wishes to be so, should have. Obviously, the strength of this third sector also brings risks in its train. The clearest of these is that of its manipulation or instrumentalisation on the part of the State or the market. But it is a risk that must be faced, maintaining a constant watch in order to safeguard its independence and establishing complementary relations with the other two sectors, aware that nobody can lay claim to having the exclusive monopoly over wellbeing nor over the search for solutions to the challenges that affect every social entity. Not on a local scale, and even less so on a global one.

Starting from the approximation that could take place between the players mentioned so far, we can raise the possibility of another world in which will emerge new forms of coexistence and new ways to overcome the problems we face today. A basic precondition for putting this process in motion is the necessity of being able to count on free access to information. In order to enable the social movements to carry out their tasks of denouncing and criticising, as well as those of articulating realistic discourses and proposals that meet the needs of our world, it is essential that information, culture and education systems be conceived of in their totality as rights, and not as commercial products that can be submitted to the laws of the market, or to the interests of governments or corporate industry.

It is extremely difficult, if not impossible, that anything will change radically overnight in any of the fields we are analysing in these pages. What normally happens is that, leaping conceptual boundaries, new trends, be they positive or negative, pursue their own course and events defy our desire to classify them. We can not, indeed we do not really know how to, draw a line and start from scratch in order to imagine a better future – for our dreams also draw their sustenance from that which is already known, that which has already been lived. We do not know how to invent from nothing. Thus, we must remember that there already exist, on the margin of the dominant tendencies, other things that allow us to see alternative realities on different scales and hints at what could be a different future. 'And yet it moves', said Galileo before the College of Cardinals and now, in spite of the appearance that only one planned future is possible, many things are shifting to modify the course of history.

The century that has barely got under way must be that in which new forms of economic relations between peoples emerge, relations that will make possible a more dignified life for hundreds of millions of people all round the world. Why be so determined to maintain the external debt of the most impoverished countries when the sums initially lent have been more than repaid and it is impossible for the original repayment terms to be met? Why not establish taxes on financial transactions, such as the so-called '*Tobin Tax*', or on the arms trade or on the profits of the multinationals, that would allow resources to be gathered to finance development? Why wait until a tragedy occurs, such as that which has recently struck southern Asia, before raising the possibility of taking measures that would have saved countless lives had they been adopted before?

In this same direction, and as a continuation of the demands raised in these lines, we should also take on board the ideas contained in the manifesto that has just been made public as part of the latest meeting in Porto Alegre. These include the need to:

— Dismantle progressively all forms of tax, judicial and banking havens which in the end are nothing more than refuges for those involved in organised crime, corruption, and all kinds of trafficking, frauds and tax evasion, criminal operations undertaken by big businesses and even by governments.
— Make viable the exercising of the right to a decent job for all, as well as to social protection and retirement pensions that respect the equality between men and women.
— Promote all forms of fair trade and reject the free-trade rules of the World Trade Organisation (WTO).
— Exclude education, health, social services and culture from the application of the General Agreement on Trade and Services (GATS) of the WTO. The convention concerning cultural diversity, currently being negotiated at UNESCO, should explicitly state that the right to culture prevails over the right to trade.
— Guarantee every country's right to food and security sovereignty through the promotion of peasant agriculture. This must involve the complete suppression of all subsidies on the export of agricultural produce, in the first place by the United States of America and by the European Union.
— Prohibit all patenting of knowledge and of living beings (whether human, animal or plants), in the same way as prohibiting any privatisation of the common assets of humanity, in particular, water.
— Eradicate all forms of discrimination, sexism, xenophobia, anti-semitism and racism, and offer full recognition of the political, cultural and economic rights (including control over natural resources) of indigenous peoples.
— Put an end to the destruction of the environment and to the threat of grave climatic changes brought about by the 'greenhouse effect', and put into practice a different model of development founded upon a restrained use of energy and the democratic control of natural resources.
— Demand the dismantling of foreign military bases and their troops in all countries, except those acting under an express mandate of the United Nations Organisation (UN).

The reform and democratisation of the international organisations, and especially those of the UN, recuperating the idealism of their foundation as reflected in the 'We, the peoples...', must also be an immediate priority for this new century. This involves, at the same time, recuperating the spirit and not only the letter of the Universal Declaration of Human Rights and of the forgotten economic, social and cultural rights. It also must involve incorporating this new world-wide focus we are calling for into the maintenance of global public assets that, like peace or a healthy environment, must form part of the heritage of the whole of humanity.

The struggle against hunger and in favour of achieving food sovereignty of the peoples should also be at the heart of international concern. The eradication of hunger, that weapon of mass destruction as the Brazilian President Lula so aptly referred to it, that is suffered by hundreds of millions of people on our planet, must be one of the most important, and most urgent challenges facing our planet. The Summit Meeting against Hunger organised by under the auspices of Brazil and supported first by Spain, France and Chile and then by more then a hundred other countries and in which many, previously unthinkable measures were proposed, is a hopeful sign in this direction. 2015 might seem very far away, but in that year our leaders will be required to account for the results of all these measures. We must work to ensure that they are positive and not have to continue to accept as 'normal' the fact that reflects shamefully on all of us, the death through hunger of millions of people.

If there is an international ambit to which the adjective 'emerging' could in all truth be applied, it is that of international criminal justice. The long road to the final achievement of a true international justice system has been plagued with ups and downs. Together with those moments in which it seems that the door is open to finally consolidating the aspirations of many jurists and defenders of human rights down the centuries, there have been others in which it has seemed impossible that those responsible for genocide, or dictators, could be made to answer for their crimes before the justice system. And yet, despite these contradictory sensations, today we have the International Criminal Court that will begin to judge its first cases this very year and which, seven years after the approving of its Statute in Rome, is now taking its first, determined steps.

We must have no doubt. The glass will always be half-full, not half-empty. As long as new paths for hope can be opened up, whether it be the creation of the International Criminal Court with all the difficulties this has involved, the signing of the Kyoto protocol, the mobilisations against the war or the approval of the Millennium Objectives, the desires for the creation of another future will continue to grow.

Another world is possible, but first of all we must want it to exist. And then, we must get down to work. And this involves all of us. The reflections of the artists beside these pages form part of this effort. They respond, each in their own way, to a process of the developing of the individual consciousness, to a attempt to heighten the awareness of others and of mobilisation, articulating open paths towards something better than that which we currently have. And that is something we can, and must, aspire to.

Jesús A. Núñez Villaverde/Francisco Rey Marcos
Institute of Studies on Conflicts and Humanitarian Action (IECAH)
Madrid, January 2005

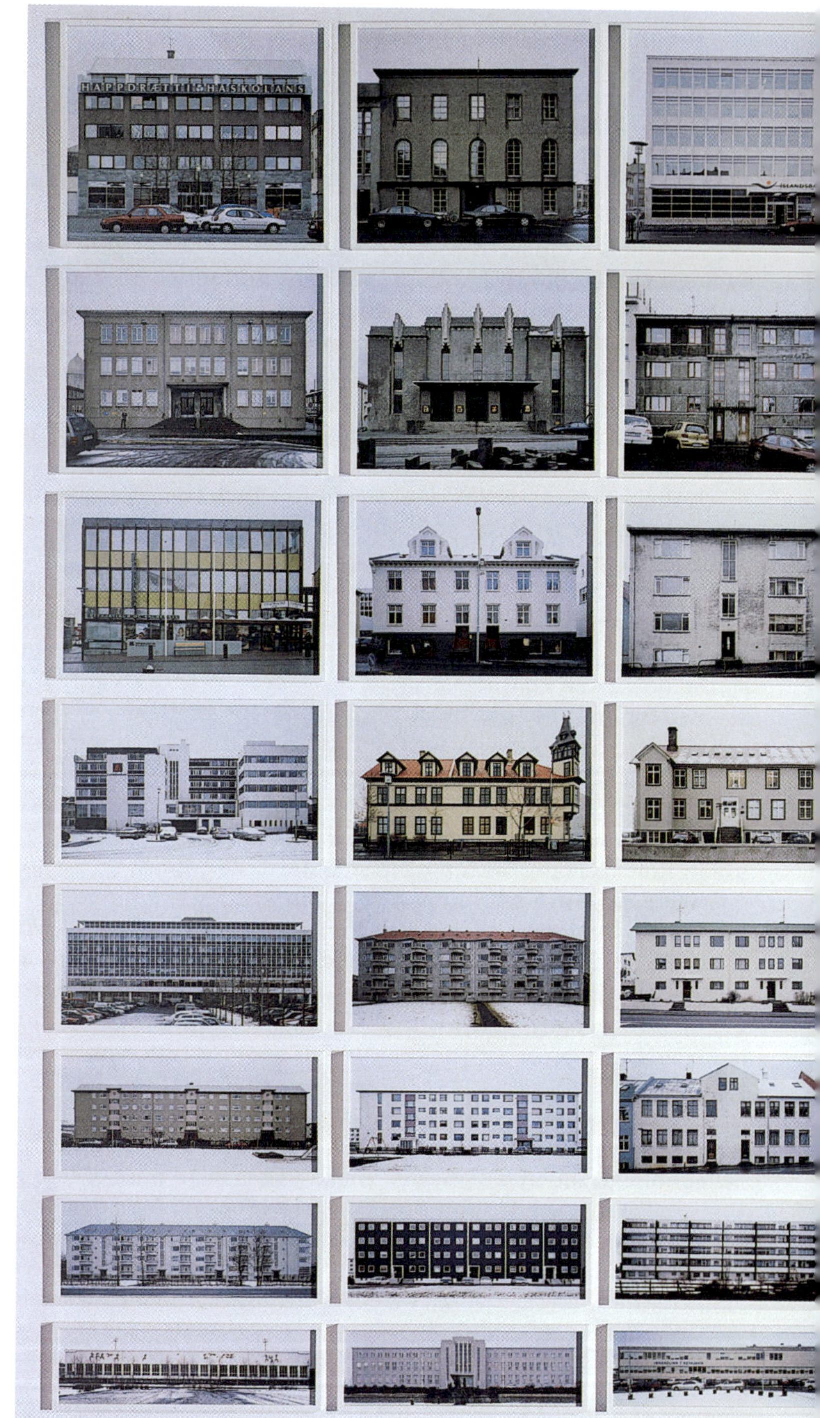

Olafur Eliasson
Reykjavik-Series, 2003
Polyptych of seventy-two colour
photographs
279 x 371 cm

290

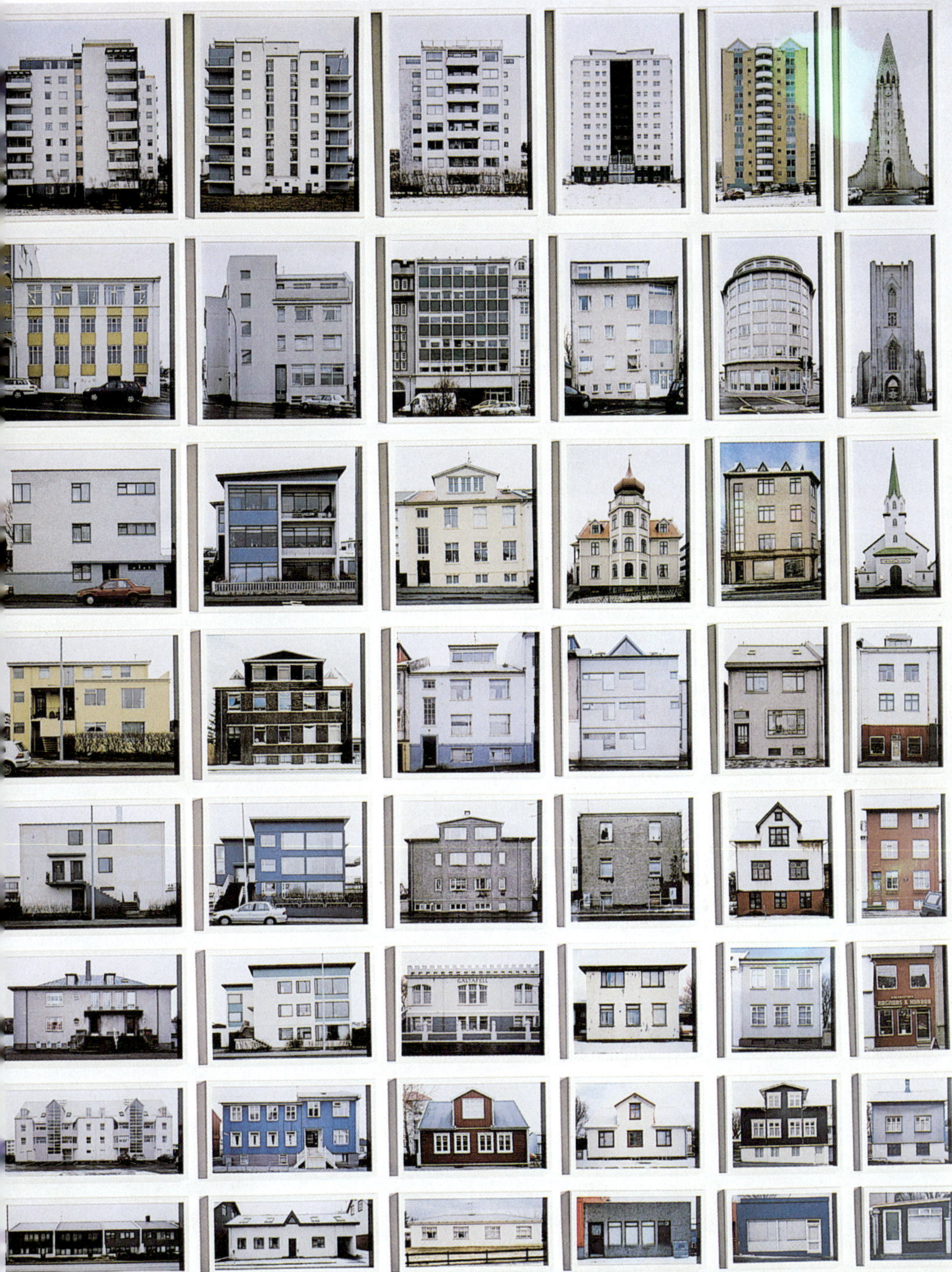

Is it really dangerous to take a taxi in Mexico City?

How many pirate taxi drivers are there in Mexico City?

Why do the media present only the negative side of certain collectives or communities?

Are gypsies dirty?

What does '*payo*' mean?

What internet surfers would visit a website produced by gypsies in Leon?

Can a group of young gypsies from Lleida explain their joys and worries on multi-media cell phones?

Are all messengers from Sao Paulo robbers?

What are the demands of the '*motoboys*' from Sao Paulo?

Does it make sense to organize social communication networks on the Internet through cell phones with built-in cameras?

www.zexe.net
www.zexe.net/TAXI
www.zexe.net/MOTOBOY
www.zexe.net/GITANO

canal*GITANO
Gypsies transmit on the internet through multi-media cell phones

20 young gypsies from Leon move about public and private spaces in the city and its outskirts, carrying cell phones with built-in cameras.

They compile and exchange experiences and opinions, becoming chroniclers of their own reality.

Through audio, video, photo and text messages, they co-ordinate the publication of the previously agreed upon audiovisual channels, in real time and on the Internet. At periodic meetings they analyse the evolution of the existing channels, decide on the creation of new virtual sites and associate with each other through broadcasting stations devoted to each agreed upon channel.

A mobile audiovisual communications project, for collectives without active presence in the preponderant media.

Public digital space

State-of-the-art cell phone technology enables immediate publication on the Internet of multimedia content, from telephones with built-in cameras and through the transmission networks of GPRS and UMTS data. This context makes possible the creation of collective channels of moving and remote broadcasting, without the need for sophisticated and costly recording and broadcasting equipment traditionally used on television.

The receivers of these broadcasts are capable of contributing their own input from stable or mobile terminals, becoming active users of the communication device.

Located at the convergence of the Internet and cell phone networks, the project canal*GITANO proposes a public digital space where broadcasters and users experience a social use of the telematic networks.

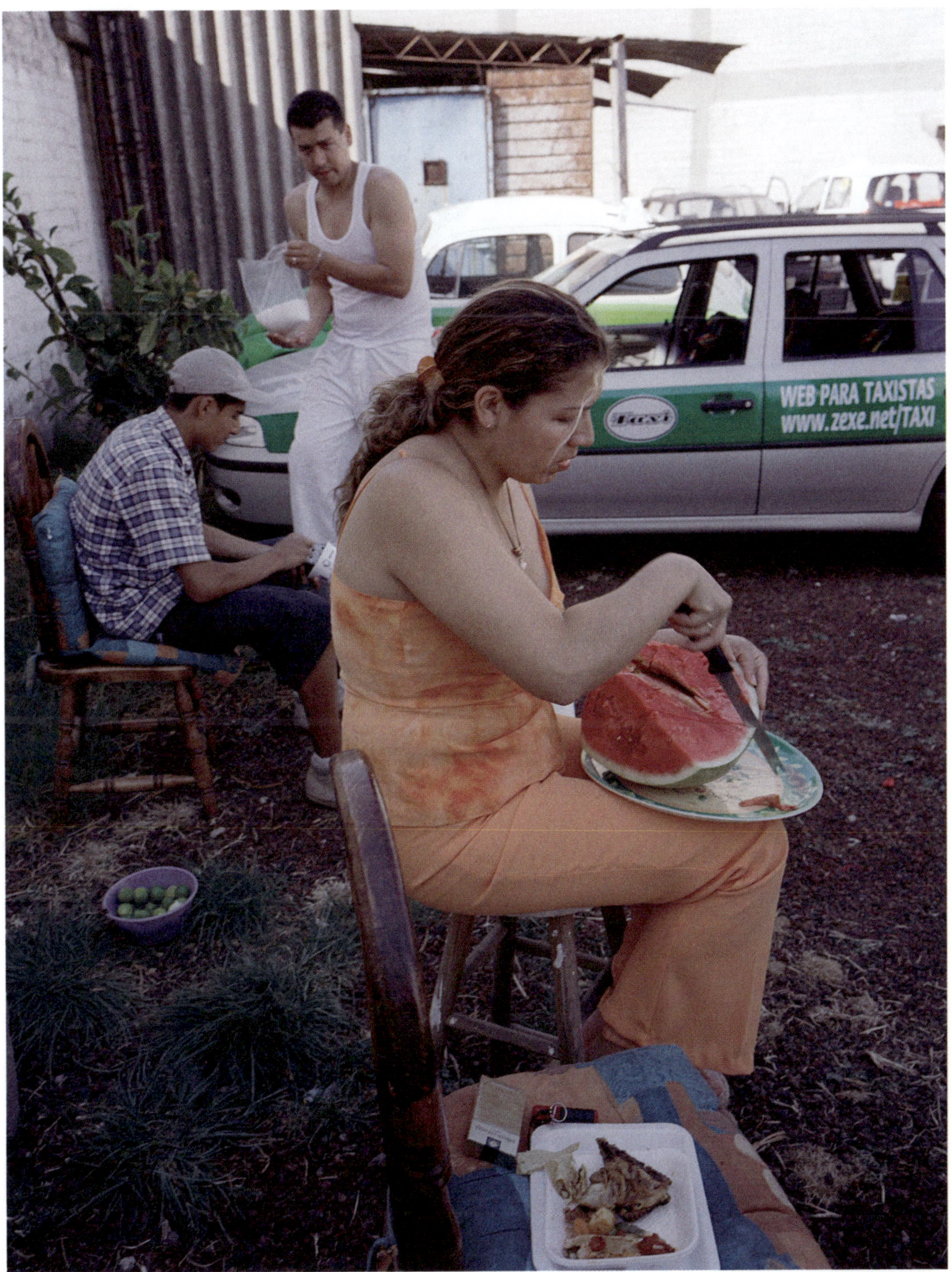

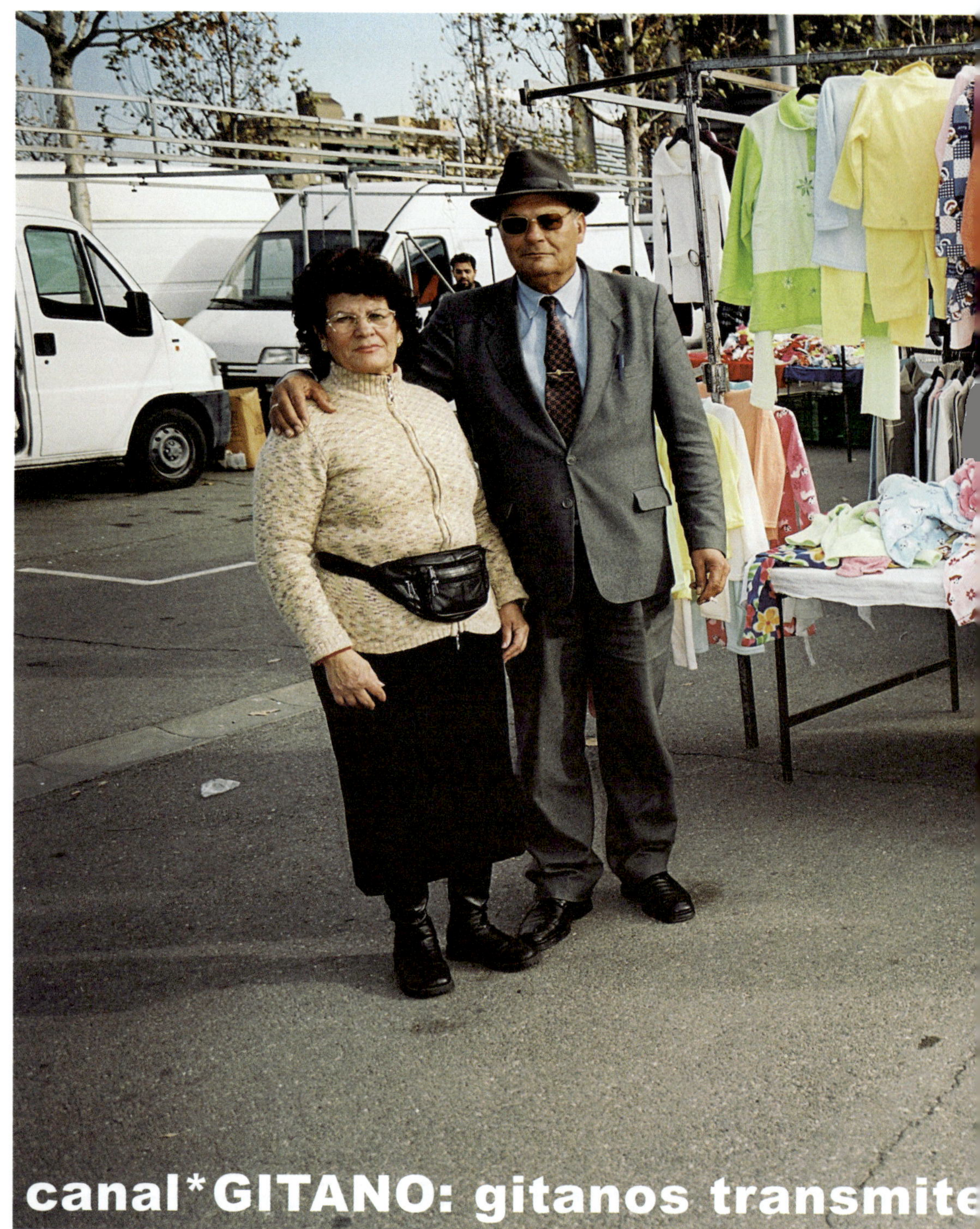

canal*GITANO: gitanos transmite

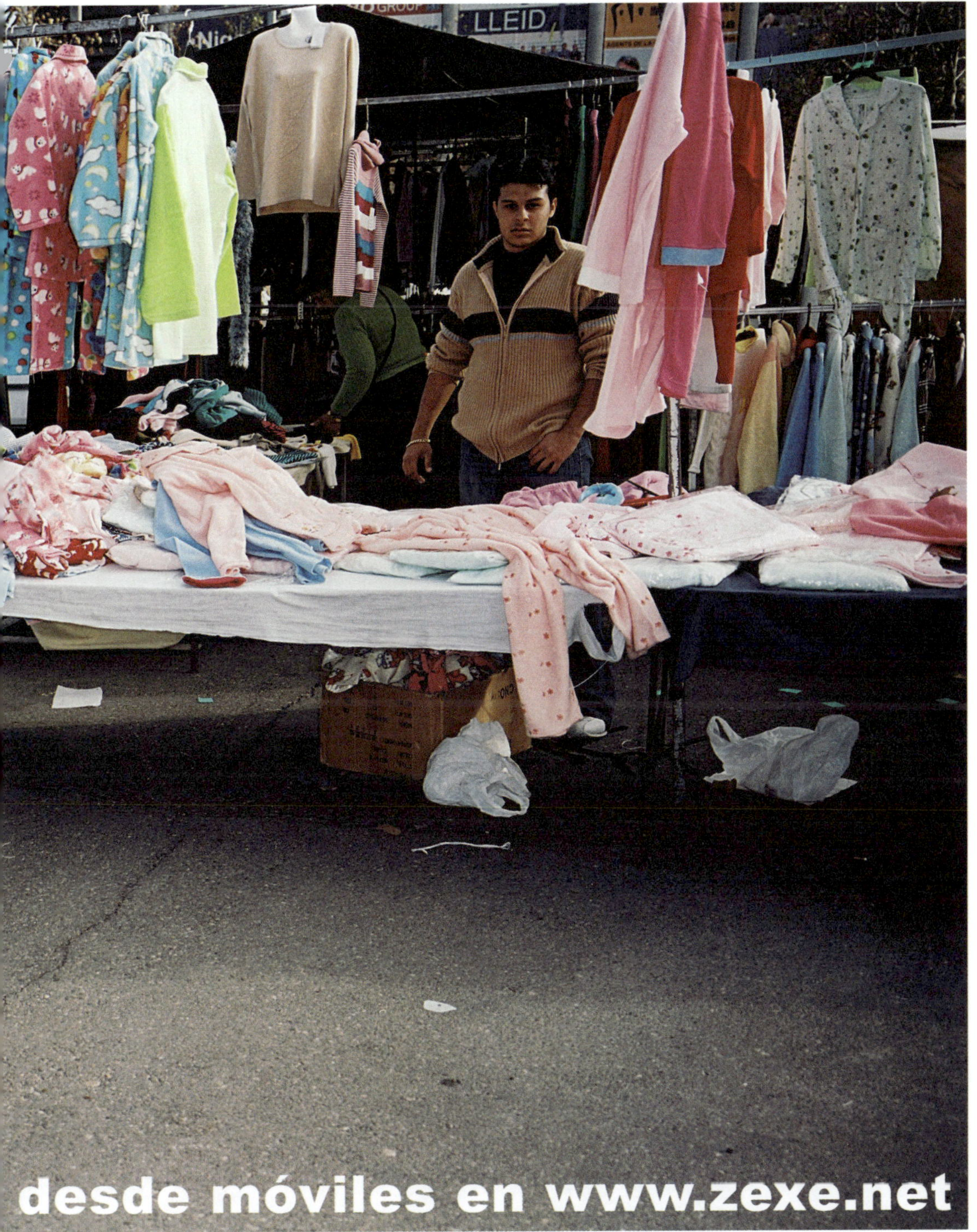

LLEID
desde móviles en www.zexe.net

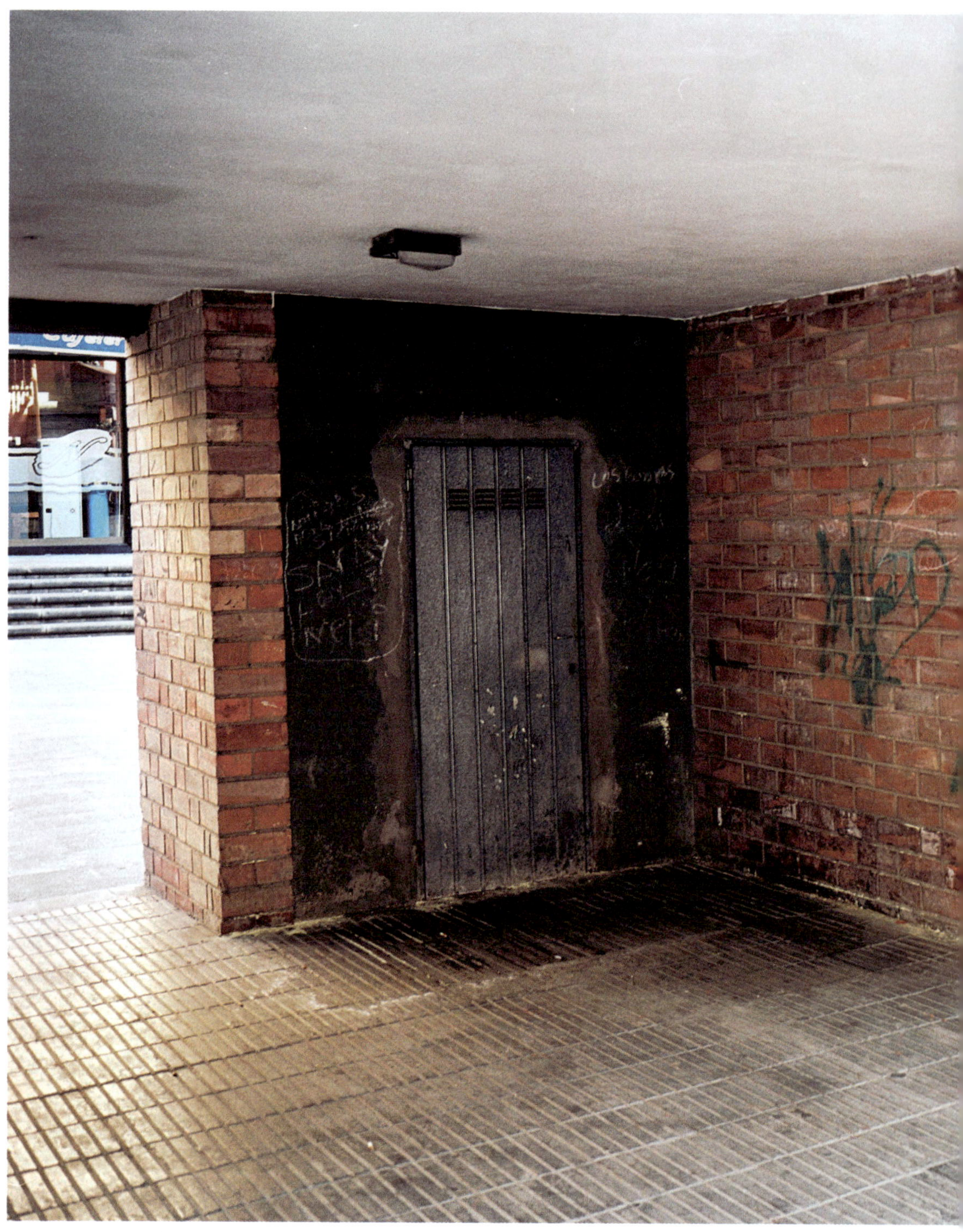

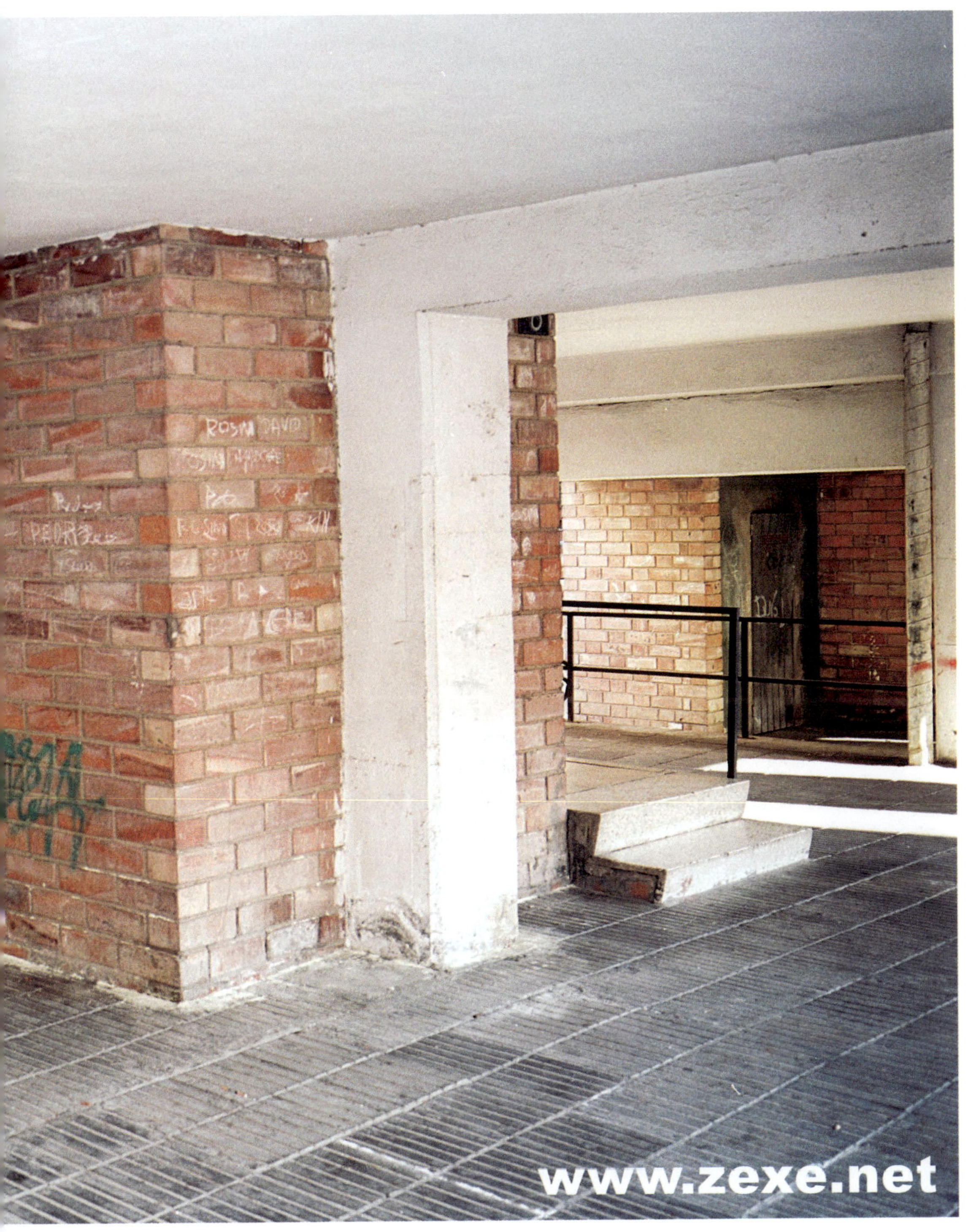

www.zexe.net

List of works in exhibition

Pilar Albarracín
Espejito, 2001
Mirror and interactive
installation with sound
∅ 61 x 11 cm

Eija-Liisa Ahtila
Tänään/Today, 1996-1997
Video installation comprised of
three projections (Film S-16/35 mm
transferred to DVD, 10' looped)
Variable dimensions
Written and directed by Eija-
Liisa Ahtila.
© and produced by Crystal Eye,
Helsinki.
Courtesy of Klemens Gasser &
Tanja Grunert, New York.

Alexander Apóstol
Residente Pulido. Ranchos (serie),
2003
6 colour photographs
195 x 150 cm each

Shoja Azari
A Room with a View, 2004
DVD colour video with sound
8' 20"

Sergio Belinchón
"Untitled", from the series
Suburbia. 2002
Colour photograph
100 x 124 cm

"Untitled", from the series
Suburbia. 2002
Colour photograph
100 x 124 cm

"Untitled", from the series
Suburbia. 2002
Colour photograph
100 x 124 cm

"Untitled", from the series
Suburbia. 2002
Colour photograph
100 x 124 cm

Mira Bernabeu
"En círculo II", from the series
Mise en scène I, 1996
Photographic diptych
120 x 180 cm each

Marc Bijl
Reason to Believe, 2004
Installation consisting of twenty-
two speakers and twenty-two CD
players
Variable dimensions

Daniele Buetti
Joy of My Life, 2001-02
Installation consisting of
photographs, monitor, neon
lights, images and text on PVC
270 x 300 x 50 cm

Luc Delahaye
"Kabul Road", from the series
History, 2001
Colour photograph
111 x 241 cm

"Jenin Refugee Camp", from the
series *History*, 2002
Colour photograph
111 x 241 cm

Olafur Eliasson
Reykjavik-Series, 2003
Polyptych of seventy-two colour
photographs
279 x 371 cm

Sandra Gamarra
*LiMac: Museo de Arte
Contemporáneo de Lima*, 2005
Installation
Variable dimensions

Carmela García
Untitled No2, 2000
DVD colour video with sound
4'

Cristina García Rodero
*Escuela de Modelos. La Habana,
Cuba*, 1997
Black-and-white photograph
76 x 115 cm

Kirsten Geisler
Dream of Beauty 3.1, 2003
DVD colour video with no sound
4' looped

Ruth Gómez
Te sobrealimentas, 2003
Animation. DVD colour video
with sound
23" looped

Pierre Gonnord
"Antonio", from the series
Utópicos, 2004
Colour photograph
165 x 125 cm

Paul Graham
"Untitled", from the series
American Night, 2000-02
Colour photograph
182 x 232 cm

"Untitled", from the series
American Night, 2000-02
Colour photograph
182 x 232 cm

Andreas Gursky
Ohne Titel XIII (Mexico), 2002
Colour photograph
277 x 206 cm

Chus Gutiérrez
El inmóvil viaje, 2003
Video installation (DVD colour
video with sound, 3' looped)
Variable dimensions

Thomas Hirschhorn
United Nations-Miniature, 2000
Installation consisting of
aluminium, wood, models and
other materials
Variable dimensions

Alfredo Jaar
Emergency, 1998
Installation consisting of a
metallic pool with water and a
fibreglass model
777 x 708 x 90 cm

Francesco Jodice
*What We Want-TOKYO-D01AB-
1999,* 1999
Colour photographic diptych
188 x 98 cm / 32 x 24 cm

What We Want-Bangkok-T24-2003,
2003
Colour photograph
190 x 150 cm

Isaac Julien
Paradise Omeros, 2002
16-mm film with sound
transferred to a DVD
18' 51''

Immo Klink
"DKNY", from the series *Mayday
at Mayfair,* 2002
Colour photograph
120 x 180 cm

"YSL", from the series *Mayday at
Mayfair,* 2002

Colour photograph
120 x 180 cm

"Prada", from the series *Mayday
at Mayfair,* 2002
Colour photograph
120 x 180 cm

"Versace", from the series *Mayday
at Mayfair,* 2002
Colour photograph
120 x 180 cm

"Chanel", from the series *Mayday
at Mayfair,* 2002
Colour photograph
120 x 180 cm

"Mc Donald's", from the series
Mayday at Mayfair, 2002
Colour photograph
300 x 200 cm

"Versace", from the series *Mayday
at Mayfair,* 2000
Colour photograph
200 X 300 cm

Valeriano López
Estrecho Adventure, 1996
Animation. DVD colour video
with sound
6' 22''

Rogelio López Cuenca
TEIXH, 2005
Installation consisting of inkjet
print on back-light canvas (300
x 500 cm) and DVD colour video
with sound (6' looped)
Variable dimensions

Jorge Macchi
Un charco de sangre (poema), 1999
Collage on paper
150 x 480 cm

Íñigo Manglano-Ovalle
Climate, 2000
A video installation consisting of
three overhead projectors (DVD colour video with sound, 23' 25'' looped)
and an aluminium structure
1000 x 400 x 230 cm

Gilda Mantilla
"Kelly Kuriyama", from the series
Mujeres peligrosas, 2004
Pencil drawings on squared card
64.5 x 49.5 cm

"Gilda Mantilla", from the series
Mujeres peligrosas, 2004

Pencil drawings on squared card
64.5 x 49.5 cm

"Samantha Marson", from the
series *Mujeres peligrosas,* 2004
Pencil drawings on squared card
64.5 x 49.5 cm

"Lilliam Enid Medina
Hernández", from the series
Mujeres peligrosas, 2004
Pencil drawings on squared card
64.5 x 49.5 cm

Ángel Marcos
Alrededor del sueño 15, 2001
Photographic installation
consisting of thirty light boxes (15
measuring 70 x 50 cm each and 15
measuring 70 x 70 cm each)
Variable dimensions

Enrique Marty
La familia, 1999
Installation consisting of one
hundred oil paintings on board
Variable dimensions

Boris Mikhailov
"Untitled", from the series *Case
History,* 1998-1999
Colour photograph
150 x 100 cm

"Untitled", from the series *Case
History,* 1998-1999
Colour photograph
150 x 100 cm

"Untitled", from the series *Case
History,* 1998-1999
Colour photograph
150 x 100 cm

"Untitled", from the series *Case
History,* 1998-1999
Colour photograph
150 x 100 cm

Tracey Moffatt
"Homemade Hand-knit, 1958",
from the series *Scarred for Life
II,* 1999
Off-set print
80 x 60 cm

"Pantyhose Arrest, 1973", from
the series *Scarred for Life II,* 1999
Off-set print
80 x 60 cm

"Mother's Reply, 1976", from the
series *Scarred for Life II,* 1999

Off-set print
80 x 60 cm

"Piss Bags, 1978", from the series
Scarred for Life II, 1999
Off-set print
80 x 60 cm

"Door Dash, 1979", from the series
Scarred for Life II, 1999
Off-set print
80 x 60 cm

"Scissor Cut, 1980", from the
series *Scarred for Life II*, 1999
Off-set print
80 x 60 cm

"Suicide Threat, 1982", from the
series *Scarred for Life II*, 1999
Off-set print
80 x 60 cm

"Brother was Mother, 1983", from
the series *Scarred for Life II*, 1999
Off-set print
80 x 60 cm

"Responsible but Dreaming,
1984", from the series *Scarred for
Life II*, 1999
Off-set print
80 x 60 cm

"Always the Sheep, 1987", from
the series *Scarred for Life II*, 1999
Off-set print
80 x 60 cm

Julia Montilla(+ Juande Jarillo)
Flame (Capriccio), 2001
DVD colour video with sound
1' 48"

Zwelethu Mthethwa
"Untitled", from the series
Sugarcane, 2003
Colour photograph
150 x 194 cm

"Untitled", from the series
Sugarcane, 2003
Colour photograph
150 x 194 cm

"Untitled", from the series
Sugarcane, 2003
Colour photograph
150 x 194 cm

Mujeres Creando
Barbies, 1999
DVD colour video with sound
11'

Cooperación Internacional, 1999
DVD colour video with sound
11'

Dictadura, 1999
DVD colour video with sound
8'

Justicia, 1999
DVD colour video with sound
9'

Lesbianismo, 1999
DVD colour video with sound
10'

Racismo, 1999
DVD colour video with sound
11'

Utopía, 1999
DVD colour video with sound
9'

Utopía I, 1999
Colour photograph
100 x 140 cm

Multiplicity
The Road Map, 2003
Video installation consisting
of two projections (DVD colour
video with sound, 29' looped) and
four monitors
Variable dimensions

Marina Núñez
"Untitled", from the series *Locura*,
1996
Oil on canvas
155 x 155 cm

Tony Oursler
Boot, 1995
Video projection on a rag doll and
a boot
62 x 31 x 31 cm

Sven Påhlsson
Crash Course, 2000
3D animation. DVD colour video
with sound
10'

Sprawville, 2002
3D animation. DVD colour video
with sound
13'

Consuming Pleasures, 2003
3D animation. DVD colour video
with sound
11'

El Perro
Travelbox (Wayaway), 2000
Installation consisting of a
wooden and polyester cubicle (158
x 156 x 108 cm), a video projection
(DVD colour video with sound, 4')
and a monitor (DVD colour video
with sound, 4')

Jorge Pineda
Santos Inocentes, 2003
Installation consisting of a
sculpture made from plastic,
plaster and white acrylic, and
silicone- coated cloth
Variable dimensions

Marjetica Potrč
*Caracas: House with Extended
Territory*, 2003
Installation consisting of
building materials and
energy and communication
infrastructures
Variable dimensions

Simeón Sáiz Ruiz
*Carretera entre Prizren y
Djakovica cerca de Meja, el 14 de
abril de 1999*, 2003
Oil on canvas
240 x 390 cm

Anri Sala
Dammi i colori, 2003
DVD colour video with sound
15' 24"

Pepo Salazar
Sarabande, 2002
Colour photograph
180 x 360 cm

Fernando Sánchez Castillo
Vivo sin trabajar, 2002
Lit-up sign
1000 x 80 x 15 cm

Martín Sastre
*Videoart: The Iberoamerican
Legend*, 2002
DVD colour video with sound
16'

*Montevideo: The Dark Side of the
Pop*, 2004
DVD colour video with sound
13' 26"

Bolivia 3: Confederation Next,
2004

DVD colour video with sound
10'

Corinna Schnitt
Das nächste Mal/Next Time, 2003
DVD colour video with sound
5' looped

Allan Sekula
"Volunteer Watching, Volunteer
Smiling (Illa de Oms, 12/19/02)",
from the series *Black Tide (Marea
Negra),* 2002-03
Colour photograph diptych
64 x 173 cm

"Volunteer's Soup (Illa de Oms,
12/19/02)", from the series *Black
Tide (Marea Negra),* 2002-03
Colour photograph diptych
203 x 127 cm

"Large and Small Disasters (Illas
Cíes and Bueu, 12/20/02)", from
the series *Black Tide (Marea
Negra),* 2002-03
Colour photograph triptych
127 x 67 cm

"Selfportrait (Lendo, 12/22/02)",
from the series *Black Tide (Marea
Negra),* 2002-03
Colour photograph
51 x 56 cm

"Dripping Black Trapezoid
(Lendo, 12/22/02)", from the series
Black Tide (Marea Negra), 2002-03
Colour photograph
51 x 56 cm

"Percebeiros Working and Army
Preparing (Touriñan, 12/24/02)",
from the series *Black Tide (Marea
Negra),* 2002-03
Colour photograph
56 x 190 cm

"Exhausted Volunteers (En Route
from Illa de Oms, 12/19/02)",
from the series *Black Tide (Marea
Negra),* 2002-03
Colour photograph triptych
185 x 122 cm

"Volunteer on the Edge (Illas
Cíes, 12/20/02)", from the series
Black Tide (Marea Negra), 2002-03
Colour photograph
74 x 102 cm

"Disposal Pit (Lendo, 12/23/02)",
from the series *Black Tide (Marea
Negra),* 2002-03

Colour photograph diptych
48 x 127 cm

"Fishing for Fuel, Surveying the
Damage (Ría de Pontevedra,
12/19/92; Museu do Alemán, Camelle, 12/22/02)", from the series
Black Tide (Marea Negra), 2002-03
Colour photograph diptych
124 x 99 cm

Yinka Shonibare
Dorian Gray, 2001
Installation consisting of eleven
black-and-white photographs
and one colour photograph (122 x
152.5 cm each)
Variable dimensions

Trine Søndergaard
"Untitled", from the series *Now
that You Are Mine,* 1997
Colour photograph
100 x 100 cm

"Untitled", from the series *Now
that You Are Mine,* 1997
Colour photograph
100 x 100 cm

"Untitled", from the series *Now
that You Are Mine,* 1997
Colour photograph
100 x 100 cm

"Untitled", from the series *Now
that You Are Mine,* 1997
Colour photograph
100 x 100 cm

"Untitled", from the series *Now
that You Are Mine,* 1997
Colour photograph
100 x 100 cm

"Untitled", from the series *Now
that You Are Mine,* 1997
Colour photograph
100 x 100 cm

"Untitled", from the series *Now
that You Are Mine,* 1997
Colour photograph
100 x 100 cm

"Untitled", from the series *Now
that You Are Mine,* 1997
Colour photograph
100 x 100 cm

"Untitled", from the series *Now
that You Are Mine,* 1997
Colour photograph
100 x 100 cm

"Untitled", from the series *Now
that You Are Mine,* 1997
Colour photograph
100 x 100 cm

Superflex
*Superflex/Supergas/Massawe
Family, Tanzania, 1997,* 1997
Installation consisting of an
orange balloon (∅ 200 cm),
video projection (DVD colour
video with sound, 6'), photograph
(133.5 x 120 cm) and vinyl
Dimensions variable

Joana Vasconcelos
Burka, 2002
Installation consisting of iron
structure, electrical system,
steel cables, wooden platform
and fabrics
Dimensions variable

JUNTA DE CASTILLA Y LEÓN CONSEJERÍA DE CULTURA Y TURISMO

Councillor
Dña. Silvia Clemente Municio

General Secretary
D. Jesús Ignacio Sesé

Director General of Cultural Promotions and Intitutions
D. Alberto Gutiérrez Alberca

FUNDACIÓN SIGLO PARA LAS ARTES DE CASTILLA Y LEÓN

General Director
D. Jesús Mª Gómez Sanz

Visual Arts Director
D. Rafael Doctor Roncero

MUSAC. MUSEO DE ARTE CONTEMPORÁNEO DE CASTILLA Y LEÓN

Director
Rafael Doctor Roncero

Chief Curator
Agustín Pérez Rubio

General Coordinator
Kristine Guzmán

Coordinators
Carlos Ordás
Tania Pardo
Belén Sola

Internships
Araceli Corbo
Mercedes Díaz
Koré Escobar
Marta Gerveno
Clara Merín
Raúl Ordás
María Soria
Blanca de la Torre

EXHIBITION

Curatorship and General Cordination
MUSAC

Installation Concept
MUSAC

Installation Design
Enguita / Lasso de la Vega. arquitectura

Installation Coordinator
Pedro Gallego

Installation
Exmoarte
Red Producciones
(Thomas Hirschhorn, Marjetica Potrč)

Audiovisual Installation
Salas AV

PUBLICATION

Publisher
MUSAC
ACTAR

Editorial Coordination
MUSAC

Texts
Instituto de Estudios sobre Conflictos y Acción Humanitaria
(Jesús A. Núñez Villaverde, Francisco Rey Marcos, María José Salvador Rubert)

Antoni Abad
Marc Bijl
Rafael Doctor Roncero
Sandra Gamarra
Thomas Hirschhorn
Alfredo Jaar
Isaac Julien
Immo Klink
Rogelio López Cuenca
Boris Mikhailov
Mujeres Creando
Marina Núñez
Marjetica Potrč
Superflex + Will Bradley

Translation
BabelTraductors
Dena Cowan

Graphic Design
Ramon Prat, Max Weber

Printing
Ingoprint S.A.

Paper
Arcoprint 1 E.W, 120 grs
Arcoprint 1 E.W, 225 grs
Distributed by COYDIS
Explanada, 8, 2º A 28040 Madrid
Tel. +34 915 360 688

Distribution
ACTAR
Roca i Batlle 2.
08023 Barcelona, Spain
Telf. +34 93 418 77 59
Fax. +34 93 418 67 07
info@actar-mail.com
www.actar.es

ISBN 84-932325-9-9 (MUSAC)
ISBN 84-95951-88-6 (ACTAR)
D.L. B-13184-05

Printed and bound in the European Union

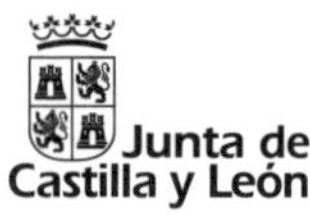

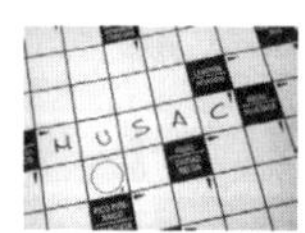